Wooden Images

Wooden Images

Misericords and Medieval England

Juanita Wood

Photographs by Charles A. Curry

Madison • Teaneck
Fairleigh Dickinson University Press
London: Associated University Presses

Associated University Presses
440 Forsgate Drive
Cranbury, NJ 08512

Associated University Presses
16 Barter Street
London WC1A 2AH, England

Associated University Presses
P.O. Box 338, Port Credit
Mississauga, Ontario
Canada L5G 4L8

The paper used in this publication meets the requirements of the American National Standard for Permanence of Paper for Printed Library Materials Z39.48-1984.

Library of Congress Cataloging-in-Publication Data

Wood, Juanita Ballew, 1938–
Wooden images : misericords and medieval England / Juanita Wood ; photographs by Charles A. Curry.
p. cm.
Includes bibliographical references and index.
ISBN 0-8386-3779-5 (alk. paper)
1. Misericords—England. 2. Wood-carving, Medieval—England. 3. Wood-carving—England. I. Curry, Charles A. II. Title.
NK9743.W66 1999
730′.942′0902—dc21 98-36202
CIP

PRINTED IN THE UNITED STATES OF AMERICA

For
Charles A. Curry
"A true, a perfect gentle knight"

Contents

Photographic Acknowledgments

The photographs in the book have been reproduced by the kind permission of the following:

The Vicar and Churchwardens of Beverley Minster

The Vicar and Churchwardens of St. Mary's Church, Beverley

The Vicar and Churchwardens of St. Botolph's Church, Boston

The Dean and Chapter of Bristol Cathedral

The Dean and Chapter of Carlisle Cathedral

The Vicar and Parochical Church Council of Cartmel Priory

The Dean and Chapter of Chester Cathedral

The Dean and Chapter of Chichester Cathedral

The Trustees of St. Mary's Hospital, Chichester

The Vicar and Churchwardens of Christchurch Priory

The Reverend M. S. Wratten, Vicar of St. Nicholas, Great Doddington

The Dean and Chapter of Ely Cathedral

The Vicar and Parish Church Council of the Parish of Fornham All Saints with Fornham St. Martin cum St. Genevieve.

The Rector and Churchwardens of St. Mary the Virgin, Gayton

The Dean and Chapter of Gloucester Cathedral

The Dean and Chapter of Hereford Cathedral

The Dean and Chapter of Lincoln Cathedral

The Trustees of the British Museum, London

The Master Emeritus, Brethren and Sisters of The Royal Foundation of Saint Katharine, London

The Dean and Chapter of Westminster

The Rector and Churchwardens of the Parish Church of St. Laurence, Ludlow

The Vicar of Great Malvern Priory

The Dean and Chapter of Norwich Cathedral

The Warden and Fellows of New College, Oxford

The Dean and Chapter of Ripon Cathedral

The Vicar and Churchwardens of Sherborne Abbey

The Vicar and Churchwardens of Holy Trinity Church, Stratford-upon-Avon

The Dean and Chapter of Wells Cathedral

The Vicar and Churchwardens of St. Mary Church, Whalley

The Dean and Chapter of Winchester Cathedral

The Warden and Fellows of Winchester College

The Deans and Canons of Windsor

The Dean and Chapter of Worcester Cathedral

Acknowledgments

MY FIRST DEBT OF GRATITUDE IS TO THE MEN AND women of the churches and cathedrals of England who have proved to be such good stewards of the structures in their care. Without their vigilance, much of our history would be lost. I also would like to thank the anonymous reviewer who understood the uniqueness of the manuscript, and the copy editor who took such care with my words.

The rest of my acknowledgments are personal and deeply felt. I trust those who are mentioned will know how important they have been to this project, and to my life. My son Ben not only promptly provided me with the "tools of the trade," but continued to be my computer expert and gentle supporter throughout. My daughter Alison provided encouragement, enthusiasm, and faith as she has done throughout her life. It is a gift to have children who care. I must mention one very special little girl, Sophia, who, along with her brothers Ben and Charles, has contributed enormous joy to my life while writing this book.

No one could have provided more loving support for all my endeavors than my wonderful mom, Mattie Cooper. My dad, John Ballew, has been both father and treasured friend. My sister Glinda provided resource materials and biblical knowledge. My brother Michael maintained a gratifying interest in the work. I thank them all, as I do Gary and my Seattle and Berkeley families for their continuing good wishes.

My greatest debt, and the one I am happiest to acknowledge, is to the person who has made my world rich beyond description and proved many times over that the world we live in is still filled with magic and romance, if you have the right companion. After eleven years I still find the old heart skipping beats and the spirits soaring when I'm with him. Relative to the project, however, he literally worked by the "seat of his pants" in serving as project photographer. I can attest that many a choir stall in England is cleaner for his having been there. This book would not be able to stand without his excellent photographs. For that, and so many other happy reasons, this book is for Charles.

Wooden Images

1
Introduction and History

> Art is the manifestation of emotion, and emotion speaks a language that all may understand
> W. Somerset Maugham, *The Moon and Sixpence*

One of the defining characteristics of the Gothic period (approximately 1200 to 1500) was the tendency to embellish and decorate the surrounding environment with a lavishness that can only be described as exuberant. The groundwork laid by previous art forms, particularly the Byzantine and the Romanesque, provided the impetus for the new French Gothic style to emerge, but its adoption and creative spread in England owes much to the long reign and taste of Henry III (1216–72). The active part of his reign from 1227 onward, coincided with what has been characterized as the crucial decades of Gothic expression in France, between 1220 and 1270. While France was preeminent in Gothic architecture during Henry's reign, his active support of the parallel development of a distinctive English Gothic style prepared the way for rapid expansion of the Gothic style in England and, finally, the ascension of English Gothic over French Gothic in the fourteenth century (Kostoff 1985).

Gothic architecture was not introduced into England by Henry III, however. That distinction goes to his grandfather, Henry II, who commissioned the French architect, William of Sens, to rebuild the choir of Canterbury Cathedral after it burned in 1174. William suggested that, rather than try to re-create the choir as it was before it burned, they should begin anew in the French style, which later came to be known as "Gothic." The work was begun by William of Sens in 1175; but when he fell ill, it was taken over by an English builder, William of England, and finally completed in 1185.

Although the design for rebuilding the Canterbury choir was originally French, it took on a distinctively English version of Gothic, which soon spread to the cathedrals at Winchester, Ely, Salisbury, and Exeter, and within fifty years had developed into what is known as the Early English style of Gothic architecture, which differed from the French style (Janson 1971; Beckwith 1985). When high Gothic peaked in France in the mid- to late thirteenth century, England took the lead and maintained it for the next century, producing cathedrals at Wells, Gloucester, Worcester, and York (Kostoff 1985).

It is generally acknowledged that this succession in architectural dominance was due to the influence of Henry III. Not only did Henry endorse the Gothic style he found so charming in France, but his determination to build equally beautiful structures in England resulted in a massive building effort that went on throughout his long reign (1216–72). The king's patronage and initiation of many new churches and palaces during his reign not only initiated the Early English style of architecture, but placed England in the forefront of Gothic architecture. John Harvey (1984, xlii) went so far as to call the contribution made by Henry and his wife, Eleanor, "the greatest single impetus given to art and architecture."

The burst of activity surrounding the building of Gothic cathedrals and palaces generated an unprecedented use of every type of craftsman, especially in decoration. Every piece of church furnishing—including screens, choir stalls, benches, and fonts—was covered with carvings. Stained glass windows told stories in astonishing color. Column capitals were carved with foliage and fabulous beasts, ceilings were painted with biblical references, and statues of saints were on guard everywhere.

The concentration on visual beauty was so pervasive that few surfaces escaped artistic attention. Will and Ariel Durant (1950) delightfully described this feature of medieval times as the "adornment of life," and noted that however intermingled religion was in the lives of the people during the late Middle Ages, the overriding feature of the period was one of men and women working at adorning everything that surrounded them, from cooking utensils to musical instruments to cathedrals. Indeed, Victor Hugo reputedly characterized the age as one in which man had no thought that was not written down in stone—or, one might add, in wood, glass, metal, and so on. It was an unusual celebration of the subjective artistic impulse on all fronts.

Although the beautiful artwork produced was an end in itself, it was also used for other purposes. Not only were the interiors of the churches meant to be beautiful, they were meant to be instructive. The common explanation for such richness in pictorial decoration was that the images served as teaching devices for a largely illiterate population. This assumption has been challenged by those who note, correctly, the difficulty of actually being able to see images on often dark, high capitals, ceilings, and windows. But this does not necessarily exclude their utility as teaching devices. The topical content was rendered in well-known symbolic ways so that an observer would have had no trouble in recognizing the meaning from the symbolism, even if that person could not see the image well. There was a "code of signs" to help the viewer: good people had halos, Christ with an open palm meant "judgment," the single finger pointing meant "condemnation," and so forth (Rouse 1968).

The pictorial images used for instruction were in the public parts of the building. Some sections of the church, however, were reserved for the use of the clergy and were unavailable to the public. In one of these areas, the choir stalls, the artwork differed in subject content from the public areas of the church; and it is here that a unique historical record of medieval life and thought is found. Hidden from "the eye of mischief" (Prior and Gardner 1912), the wood carvings that appear beneath the choir stall seats, now known as "misericords," form an extraordinary social chronicle of life and thought in the late Middle Ages.

Had it not been for the Gothic tendency to decorate every possible space, and the private nature of their location, these carvings would never have been made. Their existence provides us with a most unusual medium for viewing the medieval world.

The History of Misericords

In medieval churches in Europe and England, monks spent long hours throughout the day and night standing while chanting the Divine Office in praise of God. Based on the Rule of St. Benedict, this "Opus Dei" was considered the most important activity in the monk's life. The performance of these offices, however, took place in unheated, drafty buildings that offered little physical comfort to the monks. One of the first pieces of church furniture developed to alleviate part of this discomfort and to offer some protection from the cold, was the choir stall. These were aptly named, for the term *stall* simply means "standing place" in Old English (Jewitt 1875; Glasscoe and Swanton 1978). How much standing took place can be appreciated by recounting the daily routine in a medieval monastery. It began at midnight with Matins followed by

Lauds, the two together lasting about two hours. The monks then slept until daybreak when they gathered to sing the Prime. Breakfast afterwards consisted of beer and bread which, along with the daily offices, they partook of standing. This was followed by Tierce, morning Mass and Chapter, then work, study, or teaching in the cloister. About noon, Sext was sung, then High Mass and Nones before the midday meal. After the meal, the monks continued their work until about 5:00 P.M., when they met for Vespers, after which they had supper and read until about 7:00 P.M., when it was time for Compline. Then they retired (Corry 1965).

It is not surprising that such a rigorous routine would be physically taxing for anyone who was disabled either by the frailty of age or through illness or injury; indeed, such a routine was physically taxing for all monks. Popular tradition suggests that initially the old and infirm were granted the use of a crutch to help support them during the performance of the daily offices, but at least by the thirteenth century, choir stalls were being fitted with seats which tipped up, with a ledge against which one could lean, thus giving the monk the appearance of standing while his buttocks rested on the ledge. These tip-up seats were called *misericords* after the Latin word *misericordia*, meaning mercy or compassion. They were not adopted, however, without criticism by those concerned with modification of the existing rule about standing. St. Benedict, for one, felt that such a relaxation in rules created effeminacy (Jewitt 1875). But his view was in the minority, and misericords quickly became a standard part of church furniture. In the line of choir stall seats shown below, the seat in the center is in position to be sat upon. The seats on either side of the center seat have been tipped up and show the ledge that would have been used to lean against. The section beneath the ledge was adorned with carvings.

It is generally agreed that the stall seats were never used by the monks as seats in the usual sense, most services being conducted while standing; but there were brief periods during some of the services when the monks were allowed to sit (Bond 1910, vol. 2; Clarke 1920). The seats, therefore, usually remained

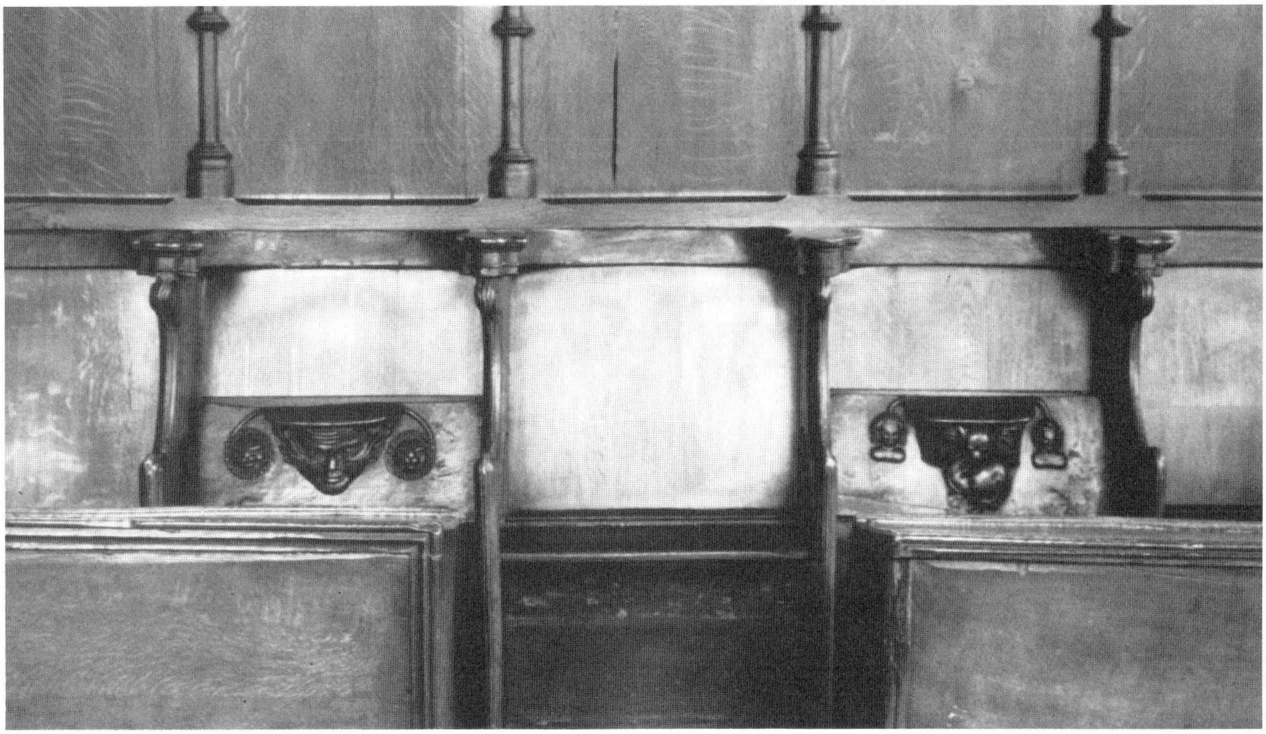

Choir stall seats. Chichester (W. Sussex), St. Mary's Hospital, c.1290.

in the tipped-up position, with the misericord ledge available to be leaned on (Tracy 1987). The tipped-up position also allowed a bit more space in the narrow aisle between rows of seats. It is clear that the use of the tip-up seats soon extended beyond the infirm to the remainder of the order of monks when daily services were performed (Klein 1976; Edminston n.d.). Although written records are scant, there are recorded instructions from Peter of Cluny in the twelfth century, stating that for parts of the daily services, the seats were to be turned up. The presumption made from this is that all monks were making use of the seats at that time (Clarke 1920).

The seats were sometimes derisively referred to as "cheater seats," "indulgence seats," or "nodding stools" in recognition of the monks' tendency to nod off during long hours spent in the choir. The thirteenth-century Cistercian, Caesarius of Heisterbach, wryly describes a fellow monk:

> In the same house is a monk who often sleeps in the choir. . . . more noted for his silence than for his singing. Around this monk hogs are often seen, and the grunting of swine are heard. Methinks they feed on the husks that fall from his mouth
>
> Coulton 1930, 4:244–45

One humorous suggestion was that the misericords were constructed to embarrass monks caught nodding off during services by falling down when the monk became drowsy and bent forward (Edminston n.d.; Jewitt 1875). This is a rather whimsical vision of the drowsy monk who topples from his seat and receives his just reward. Other reports suggest a more formal routine for keeping the monks awake. A designated monk, called a "circation," went round the stalls with a lantern, looking for brothers who had fallen asleep. When he found one, he would wake him and pass the lantern to him to take over the search

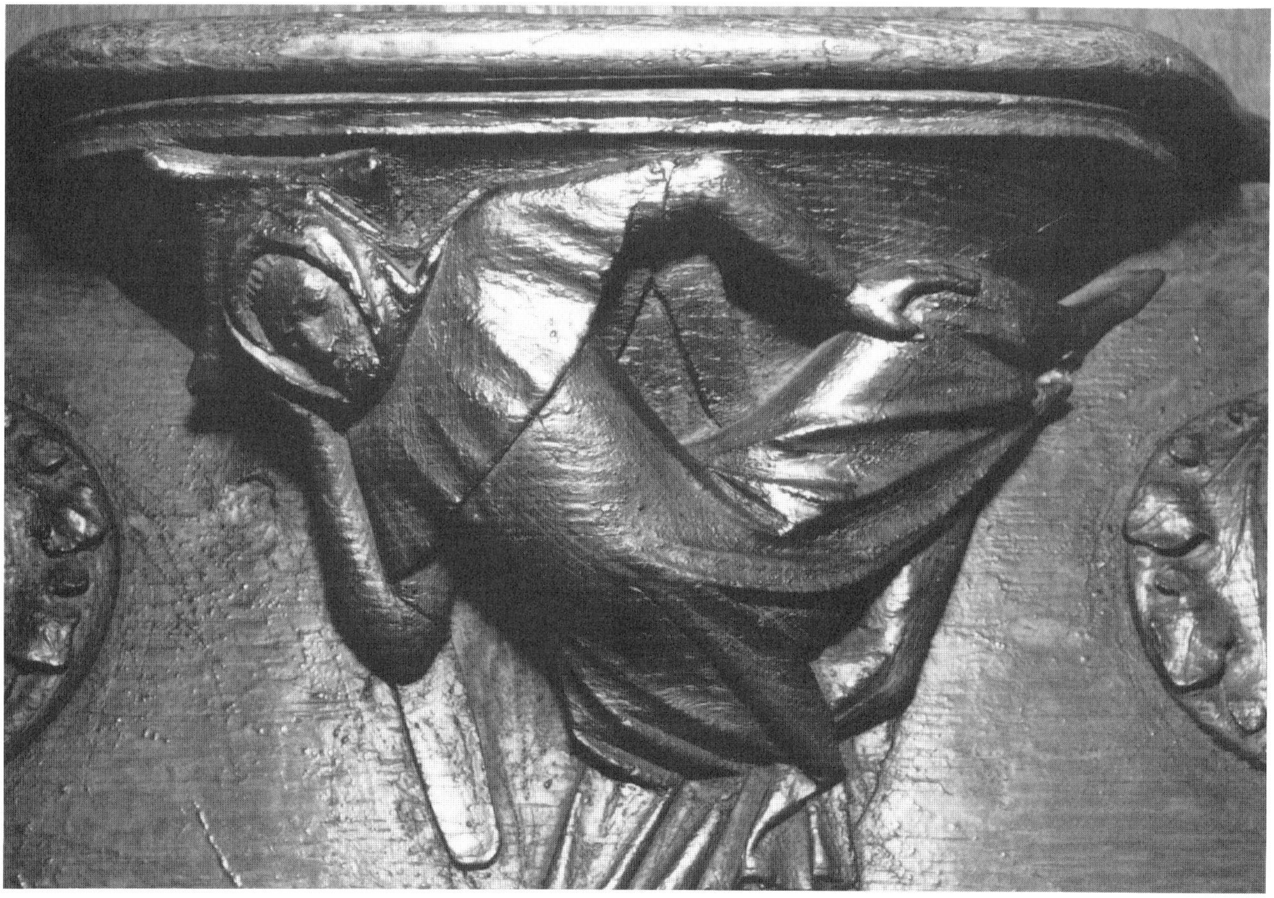

Sleeping monk. Hereford (Herefs & Worcs), The Cathedral, c.1380.

for drowsing brothers (Corry 1965). The carving under the choir stall seat at Hereford shows one such sleepy monk—only this time he is under the seat, not on it.

The amount of time spent by the monks in the stalls meant that they became, in Tracy's (1987) words, "objects of daily personal use." This undoubtedly contributed to the diversity among the elaborate misericord carvings that came to be the customary embellishment for the underside of the ledge.

The misericords were carved from a solid piece of wood, generally oak, to form the seating ledge at the top, with the carving underneath. The carvings under the ledge usually consisted of a larger center carving and, in England, two smaller side carvings, called supporters. In current times, *misericord* has come to refer to the carvings rather than to the seat. Other than illuminated Books of Hours, the misericords are the only detailed record of the life and thought of the ordinary medieval citizen still in existence (Bennett 1979).

It is assumed that the actual misericord carving was done outside the choir, then affixed to the seat, since the space between the rows of stalls is narrow and would make work in place extremely difficult (Agate 1980).

The date when the first misericords appeared in English churches is not known (Hayman 1989) and probably will never be known because of the lack of surviving records. Although written records on the Continent mention misericords at a convent at Hirsaugh, Germany, about the same time (1121) as Peter of Cluny in France used the term to refer to stalls with seats, there is neither written record nor physical evidence of English misericords that early (Bond 1910, vol. 1). The earliest existing examples of misericords in England are from the thirteenth century. Individual examples of this period can be found in Westminster, Christchurch, Hemingborough, and Kidlington (Remnant 1969).

What may have existed before the thirteenth century is difficult to imagine. Losses occurred before the dissolution of the monasteries in the sixteenth century, as well as after, including the loss of many church fabric rolls, the periodic removal of choir stalls from their original sites, and damage to the carvings by the iconoclasts. In many cases, poor care of the woodwork resulted in damage; sometimes the woodwork was removed simply to make way for more modern decoration. Even so, the misericords are almost all that remains of English woodwork before the late Gothic period (Saunders 1932).

Why the misericords were spared when so much other woodwork was destroyed is open to speculation. It may have been because the subject matter in the carvings was predominantly secular. This would have protected them from the iconoclasts perhaps, but not necessarily from Cromwell's men. It may have been that they were hidden when the choir stall seat was down. However, since they were generally tipped up, this seems an inadequate explanation. Perhaps a more utilitarian solution to the question is appropriate: they were left because they provided seating.

Although it is assumed that the earliest misericords were unadorned, those in Europe from the thirteenth century onward contain some form of decorative carving (Kraus and Kraus 1976; Clarke 1920). Initially, the carvings were quite modest, as shown in the thirteenth-century example from Westminster, but they quickly became part of the whole Gothic movement toward embellishment.

The dating of misericords is frequently difficult because medieval craftsmen tended to blend past and present styles and topics, so that, without written records, it is impossible to say with certainty that a particular carving was done at a specific time. Certain characteristics do help, however. The style of the seating ledge varied at different times. The style of foliage was conventional at certain times and natural at others. Heraldic devices often indicate a specific date of a specific stall or the name of the donor. In many cases, because stalls have been moved, there is even uncertainty about the origin of the stalls. Given this ambiguity, it is still possible, using the listing of misericords in Remnant (1969), to say that most of the approximately 3,300 misericords still in existence in about 255 cathedrals and churches in England were carved during the fourteenth (approximately 29 percent), and

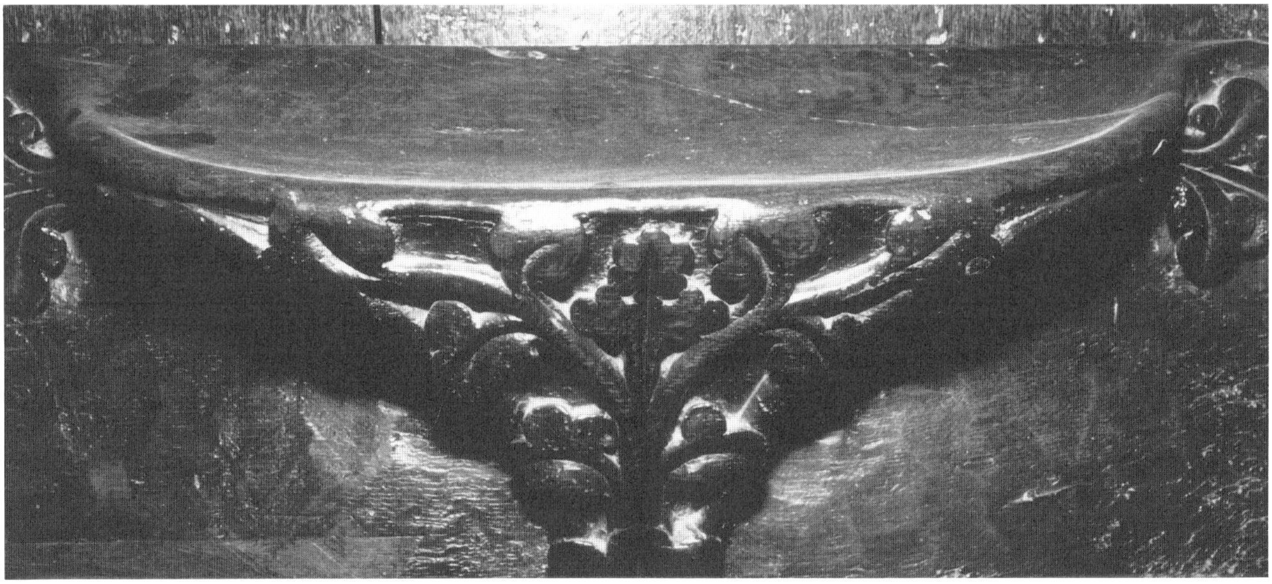

Early misericord. Westminster (London), The Abbey, thirteenth century.

fifteenth centuries (approximately 38 percent).

In terms of the number of misericords present in each church or cathedral, the range is between 1 and 106. Most churches, however, have only a small number, about 86 percent having between 1 and 20 carvings.

Although Bond (1910, vol. 1) gave Exeter the status of having the oldest existing set of misericords in England, dating them between 1255 and 1279, that designation has recently been disputed by Tracy (1987), who maintains that the earliest set of choir stalls are at Salisbury, dated c.1245 (with restoration by Gilbert Scott in 1869). The dispute does not measurably change the date of the first set of English stalls, only the location. All indications seem to confirm that choir stalls were in general use by the thirteenth century, in both England and Europe.

If we cannot be certain when English misericords first appeared, we do know when they ceased to be produced. It is generally agreed that by the seventeenth century, the last set of misericords in the Gothic style were carved by James Clement, at Durham Cathedral, between 1660 and 1672 (Laird 1986). These stalls were to replace those burned, along with all the other woodwork, by the 3,000 Scots incarcerated in the cathedral by Cromwell after the battle of Dunbar in 1650 (Stranks 1987). These were an exception, however; for Gothic misericord production had generally ceased by the end of the sixteenth century in England.

Although a few carvings were done in various churches and cathedrals to replace damaged individual misericords and some building of stalls resumed in the nineteenth century, the period with which misericord carving in England will predominantly be associated is the English Gothic period between the fourteenth and sixteenth centuries.

Uniqueness of English Misericords

While misericords are extant in other parts of Europe—approximately 8,000 in France, 200 in Switzerland, and some in Belgium and Germany—those in England are considered the finest (Kraus and Kraus 1976; Laird 1986). The quality of the English misericord carvings is related to the general development of more sophisticated English Gothic architecture, started under Henry III and enhanced after the reign of Edward I (1272–1307). In fact, there are indications that the Continental Gothic style owes more to England after 1300 than the immense debt England owed France before that time (Harvey 1984). This early fourteenth century independence from French Gothic shows signs of a Middle Eastern influence—the use of the ogee curve, complex geometrical patterns, and the four-centered arch—that were not adopted in other parts of Europe. This influence was the result of contact with Islam through crusades, pilgrimages, and exposure to other travelers (Verey and Welander 1979). Most of the impact of this exchange was felt in architecture, but it also affected the style of interior decoration, including the misericord decorations. The misericord below with its intricately carved geometric pattern, shows the Saracen influence.

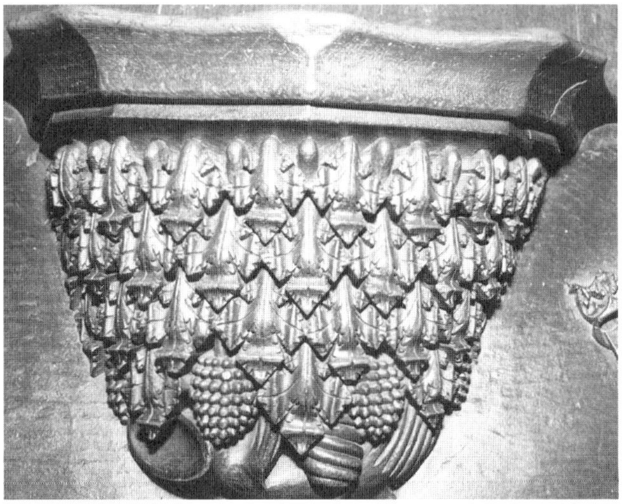

Arabesque design. Cartmel (Cumbria), The Priory, c.1440.

Another reason the English misericords are considered more interesting than the European misericords, particularly the French, is that they exhibit all the characteristics of Gothic art, among them a disregard for harmony, mixture of the grotesque and the ludicrous, and decoration for decoration's sake. It would have been impossible for an English Gothic artist to carve a coordinated set of misericords. The French misericords that remain are of a later period, mostly fifteenth and sixteenth century (Kraus and Kraus 1976), and are more unified in theme, suggesting that they are the work of a school rather than individual workmen.

The major difference between English and European misericords is their use of "supporters." These were made either by extending the molding on the edge of the seat down in curving lines that culminate in a carved design on either side of the central carving, or simply by carving additional scenes on each side of the central carving. Although these supporters can be found on some French misericords, they are believed to have been the original creation of English woodcarvers, appearing on all but a few English misericords. An example of creating supporters by extending the molding is shown below.

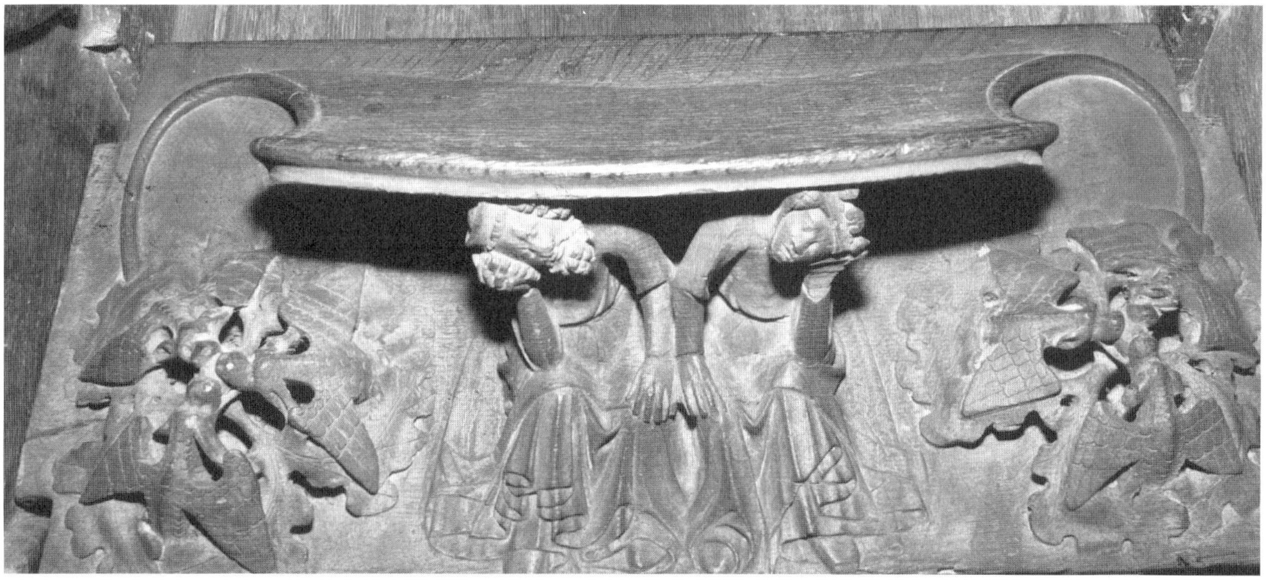

King and queen. Ely (Cambs), The Cathedral, c.1340.

The supporters sometimes complement the subject matter of the central carving, and sometimes they are independent of it; the choice seems to have been left to the individual carver. It is estimated that only about two percent of the supporters are related to the central figure (Laird 1986). This percentage may be low, however, due to varying interpretations given to the meaning of the carvings. Although a respectable amount of work has been done on the iconography of the misericords, much research remains to be done. Meanings that would have been perfectly clear to the medieval citizen are not always clear to the contemporary scholar. Thus, many supporters'now thought to be unrelated may, in fact, complement the central carving.

Finally, English misericords, along with their European counterparts, are unique in their subject matter. The topical content of misericords is outside the usual topic areas chosen for most other church art in the Middle Ages. Stone sculptors, architects, glassworkers, metalworkers, painters, and so forth all chose more heroic or uplifting subjects; the misericord carvers chose everyday life.

Subject Matter of the Misericords

The misericord topics are quite varied, both within and between sets. In addition to the Gothic approach to art previously mentioned, variations are due to several factors: (1) often, particularly in the larger cathedrals, more than one carver worked on a set of misericords; (2) each monk (or later, patron) was individually responsible for the stall decoration; (3) the carvers' topics came from many different sources; and (4) they are in the private area of the church. For all these reasons there are few sets of misericords in England that have a unified theme in the carvings, although certain topics are shown repeatedly across sets.

One of the most commented on characteristics of the misericords is their lack of religious subject matter. Because they are located in religious institutions, it might be expected that they would be concerned primarily with biblical tales or Scripture; but it has been estimated that only about 4.5 percent of the remaining carvings in Great Britain are religious in content, and about 1.5 percent are scriptural (Laird 1986). Most carvings consist of secular subjects that represent the routines of daily life and belief systems of the time, including popular romance tales, travelers' tales, grotesques, fabulous beasts, domestic scenes, and ridicule of elites. It has been suggested that the use to which the misericords were put was of such a "humble" nature that it was inappropriate to carve "lofty" scenes on them (Anderson 1954), or that it would be inappropriate for that part of the body coming in contact with the seat to sit on images of Christ or the Virgin Mary (Kraus and Kraus 1976).

From the fourteenth century on, however, the increasing involvement of the laity in the production of church art must be considered a factor in the choice of subject matter, as must the increasing independence of craftsmen. Although the clergy were crucial to the development and spread of both Romanesque and Gothic art, one difference that distinguishes the two periods is the increasing involvement of the laity in the construction and decoration of the church during the Gothic period. Work that initially had been the domain of monks—ivory, stone and wood carving, painting, metalwork, bell founding, and organ building (Butler and Given-Wilson 1979), was taken over by lay craftsmen. By the fourteenth century, in addition to workshops attached to monasteries, independent shops were being established where work was done on order (Anderson 1935). Naturally, the switch from work controlled by the Church to work controlled by craftsman to some degree, shifted control over subject content.

Because the stalls were for the use of individual occupants in a nonpublic place, and because they were not required for teaching purposes, both the monk and the carver could be more imaginative in the selection of subject. Opinions vary as to who actually selected the subject matter. Some believe the craftsmen were encouraged to "indulge their own whims" in these carvings (Agate 1980; Grössinger 1989; Steer 1973; Camille 1992); others feel that all artistic expression was a result of the taste and desires of the monarchy, nobility, and prelates and not individual craftsmen (Harvey 1984). The latter view was generally true in other aspects of church decoration, but is unlikely to have been true for misericords. Several reasons have been put forward for the unusual independence granted misericord carvers. The carvings themselves were given a lower status in church art due to their private location and to the absence of any intention to use them as teaching devices. This meant that a standardized form of presentation was unnecessary and that the subject content could be more varied. The specialization within crafts also played a role in the enviable measure of artistic control granted the carvers. While master craftsmen were responsible for the overall scheme of the church, most stone masons and woodcarvers were independent craftsmen who worked on small jobs, moving from place to place (Thrupp 1948). The misericord woodcarvers had the additional advantage of working in hidden areas. This made their work a highly individualized product, unlike the rest of the church art.

Because misericord carvings were considered of lesser importance in the decoration of the church, the carver's work was not scrutinized in the same way as the work of other craftsmen. In the area of religious imagery, for example, the artist was allowed to choose neither the subject matter nor the way it was to be presented. Rowling (1987, 157) reports on a German carver in the early fourteenth century who was judged by the Church to have carved incorrectly a crucifix for a London church:

> The bishop ordered that Tideman must surrender the bond . . . which the rector of the church had given him. He also had to carry away the crucifix, secretly and without scandal, before dawn or after dark, into some other diocese.

There is abundant evidence in the carvings that this kind of control was not exercised over the misericord carver. One indication is the extent of political commentary found in the carvings. Camille (1992) argues that the medieval craftsman's art was meant to be subversive, a view supported here. The carver expressed what the ordinary citizen felt about such agents of control as the aristocracy and the clergy, and did it with biting satire. Of course, satire was a favorite medieval tool, and was used not only against the ruling class, but to comment on social life in general. Other social commentary reflected in the misericords mirrored the social concerns of the times. In these carvings one can detect the contradictory feelings men had about women, the preoccupation with male strength, the lusty abandon of a youthful population, the holdover of pagan beliefs, and the mythical and romantic tales of the day.

Another characteristic of the misericords, reflective of medieval life itself, is the dependence on symbolism. The work produced during that period was always couched in layers of meaning. The carvings cannot be "read" without some understanding of the importance of allegory to the medieval mind. The prevalence of meaning within meaning gives an added richness to the world preserved in the carvings.

The contribution of the misericord carver to the artistic embellishment of the period was to take everyday life and thought as his central topic, and thus make everyday human experience art. The lives of the saints and lessons from the Bible might dominate most of the decoration in the churches, but what ordinary people thought and believed dominated this small realm in the choir stalls. This was extremely rare in the middle ages. While at least 75 percent of the people in fourteenth-century England were in the peasant class, they were seldom depicted in artwork (Coulton 1960). The one exception to this was on the borders of illuminated manuscripts, primarily the Books of Hours. However, it is noteworthy that the production of these books was also taken over by the laity (Harthan 1978). The misericord carver, by making everyday life and thought his focus went beyond art to create a unique social chronicle of the time. His contribution to the social history of the medieval time period is inestimable.

The Misericord Carvers

Who They Were

There is an unfortunate lack of information about the identification of the men who actually carved the misericords. It is known that the carvers were trained and that they were not serfs, but craftsmen. Woodcarving, like other trades of the time, was a hereditary art handed down from father to son (Anderson 1955). It is assumed that lesser, or less experienced, carvers were given this task and that it is unlikely the more experienced and sophisticated carvers would have worked on the misericords, unless it was during an apprenticeship (Anderson 1969). According to the practice in the Middle Ages, the names of craftsmen were not generally recorded unless they were master craftsmen (Smith 1886). The church fabric rolls show payments being made to a class of worker (that is, woodcarvers) for carrying out specific tasks, but not individual names. Recognition for individual work was not yet given; the "myth of the great artist" would come after the Renaissance (Martindale 1966).

There is some information on the master carvers. It is known, for example, that William Berkeley was the head carver of the stalls at Windsor (James 1985). It is thought that the master carpenter for both Edward III and Richard II, Hugh Herland, had a hand in selecting the carvers for New College, at Oxford, and Winchester College. Both Hugh and William Herland are thought to have been involved in the Lincoln and Chester carvings as well (Steer 1973). And the names of some of their associates are known, but it is not possible to state that they were the carvers of any particular misericords. There is reason to believe that the chief carver of the choir stalls at Ripon, Beverley, and Bridlington was William Bromflet (Purvis 1924), but not who actually carved the misericords. There is one rare recording of the actual name of a woodcarver, Eatough, at Whalley (Snape 1978), but for the most part these men's names were not recorded.

Even though the individual carver's name

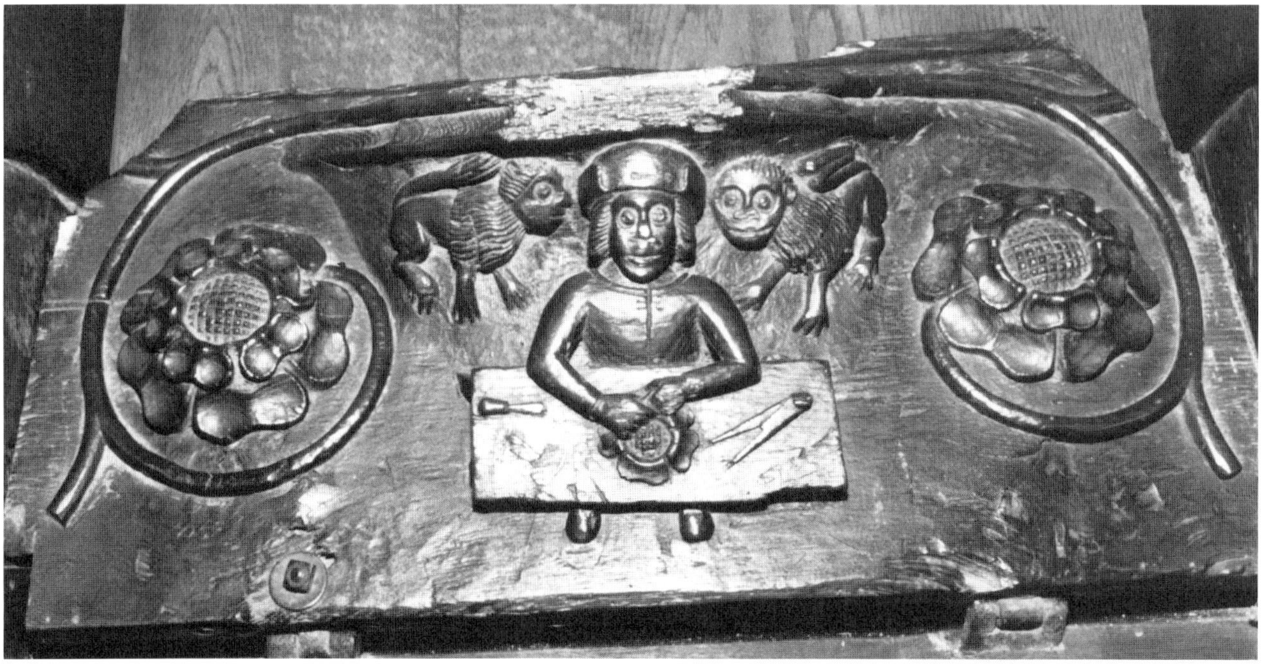

Woodcarver carving a misericord. Great Doddington (Northants), St. Nicholas, late fifteenth century.

did not appear, there are a few cases in which the carver overrode this practice of anonymity by carving his "mark" on the misericord. For example, we have the following:

> Bristol Cathedral: One of the carvers incorporated what looks to be a rabbit into his work frequently as his particular stamp.
> Hayman 1989
>
> Ludlow: Eight of the misericords bear the carver's mark of an uprooted plant.
> Klein 1986
>
> Exeter: There is what could be a carver's mark in the form of concentric circles on a number of misericords.
> Clarke 1920

Medieval stonemasons frequently were required to make their mark on pieces of stone, which enabled inspectors to evaluate their work (Anderson 1935; Lucie-Smith 1981). This may be the reason for these woodcarvers' marks, or it may be an attempt to take credit for the work (an unusual occurrence, if true). Work produced in the Middle Ages was for the glory of God, the king, or the bishop, not for the humble craftsman. When Dante (1265–1321) praised in verse two thirteenth-century illuminators, he was criticized for doing so on the grounds that it was improper to give recognition to men of such low occupation (Bishop 1987). Then there is the story told of William of Wykham (1324–1404), Bishop of Winchester and Lord Chancellor, who had engraved on a wall inside Windsor Castle, "This made Wickham." An envious colleague told the king of this audacious act, commenting that William was trying to usurp the king's glory. William was quick to respond that he meant the statement to indicate that the castle had made him, not he it (Bevan 1992). A questionable explanation, for William of Wykham was one of the most powerful and ambitious men in Edward III's court.

In addition to art being produced for the glory of God, king, or bishop, there was a more generalized feeling that art belonged to everyone, not just the creator. This was certainly true of the literature of the time, which was mostly anonymous (although writers frequently would put well-known names to their work); it was also true of church artists.

Where They Worked

Some scholars have questioned whether the choir stalls were carved on site, either by local carvers or individual carvers who moved from town to town, or whether the stalls were done by carvers in large workshops and then delivered to the church. While it is agreed that the level of workmanship is high enough to support the workshop theory, particularly in smaller parish churches, there is too much individuality in the carvings for this to be taken seriously (Anderson 1954). As Bond (1910, 1:223) observes, "Those of Exeter do not prepare one for those of Ely."

The view that most work was done by craftsmen moving from town to town is a logical assumption, because it is known that many medieval craftsmen did travel in search of work, especially those who worked on cathedrals (Tracy 1990; Wildridge 1879). There are also records of some master carvers being asked to oversee work in different places. The Bishop of Norwich sent his master carver, William Lyngwode, to Winchester in 1308 to build stalls, but it is not known whether he actually worked on the misericords (Smith 1886). Interestingly, the Bishop of Winchester wrote a letter in 1309, requesting that Lyngwode's time be extended until he "shall have finished the said work" (Jervis 1976). There were also schools of carvers, the one at Ripon headed by William Bromflet is known to have been responsible for the misericords at Manchester Cathedral and Beverley Minster (Hayman 1989). Although Bond (1910, vol. 2) disputes the idea of schools or "gangs" of carvers, maintaining instead that the church carvings were done by local men, he does suggest that in the smaller parish churches where the work is of superior quality, it was undoubtedly done by an important center, essentially "shop-made." However, in light of the difficulty of transporting heavy oak stalls overland to various parish churches, this conclusion does not seem reasonable. The debate is likely to go unresolved because the extensive loss of medieval woodwork and records makes it impossible to accurately determine where many of the carvings originated. Tracy (1990, 64) notes that because of this loss, "it is only rarely that the same workshop can be recognized in two or more buildings."

By the fifteenth century, however, when Gothic art was reaching its final peak in Europe, woodcarving as an art had reached such a sophisticated level that the English woodwork being produced was of very high quality. Howard and Crossley (1927) argue that this was the first time woodwork developed as a localized craft. The process was helped along by the growing practice of endowing chantry chapels for a deceased family member. Chantry priests would be paid to say a mass for the departed on a daily basis in perpetuity. The chantry priest also helped the parish priest in other church services; therefore, seating for the chantry priest became a requirement. The endowments of wealthy families frequently resulted in the production of beautifully carved stalls with misericords for additional priests (Anderson 1954). Thus, a friendly rivalry developed between parish churches, each trying to make theirs more impressive than the others.

It is generally agreed that misericord carvers were almost exclusively English, although there are a few records of foreign carvers at work in England. Flemish carvers, for example, participated in the work at royal chapels at Windsor and Westminster (Bond 1910, vol. 2). But, until the latter part of the fifteenth century, there was little influence from outside England (Howard and Crossley 1927). After about 1470, craftsmen, including carvers, began to arrive in England from the Burgundian regions of the greater Netherlands (Harvey 1984) and woodwork from the Continent began to be influential in England.

The Guilds

Whereas the misericord carvers may have had more freedom in the production of their art because of the unusual location of the carvings, craftsmen as a whole were closely regulated during the Middle Ages—first, by the church which wanted to control the religious imagery, and second, by the guilds that controlled the industry. The guilds were more than trade unions protecting workers' rights; they were involved in the life of the guild member in a number of ways. The guild protected the worker when ill or in need. It paid for Masses to be said when a member died, insured that the member's funeral would be well attended (Martindale 1966), and, on occasion, even furnished a dowry for poor girls (Gies and Gies 1978). English guilds precede the introduction of English kings, and they have always been concerned not only with upholding the laws of the community, but also with moral standing (Smith 1924).

As patrons of church art, guilds also supported the Church. Numerous stained glass windows representing the trades were placed in churches and cathedrals and paid for by guilds. In the community, guilds at first participated in, then took over, the production of miracle and mystery plays. The guilds regulated the quality of the work produced, fining or firing members who were not up to standard, and settling quarrels between members. The Beverley carving, right, depicts such a quarrel. The two carvers in the center are threatening each other with the tools of their trade, a mallet and a chisel. On the left supporter, the carver starts the fight by thumbing his nose at the other; on the right, the quarrel seems to have ended with one of the carvers surrendering.

Although the guild's control may at times have been absolute, that control was hard to maintain with stonemasons, carpenters, and carvers because, unlike many other guilds, many of their members were "here today, gone tomorrow," making it difficult to penalize them. This became more pronounced after the Black Death of 1349, when craftsmen could command even greater independence because of their reduced numbers. They began demanding, and receiving, a higher wage. Even though Edward III (r.1327–77) instituted the Statute of Labourers in 1351 to restrict wage increases after the Black Death, the maximum wage for a qualified craftsman rose by about 50 percent after 1350 (Harvey 1984), and the

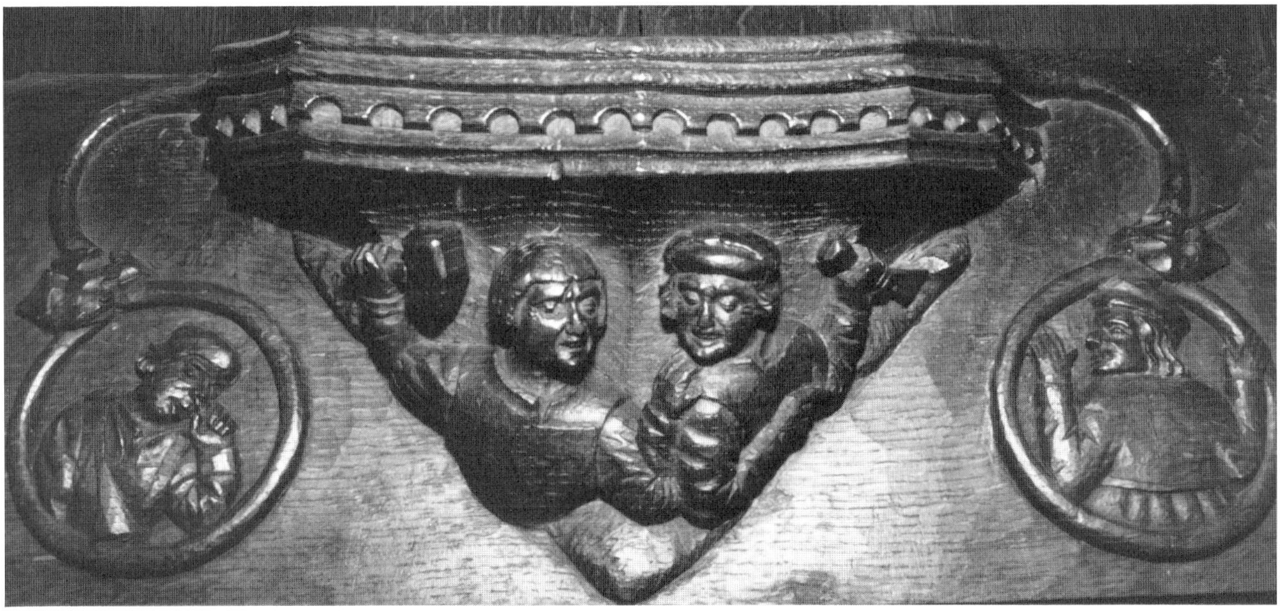

Carvers quarreling. Beverley (Humberside), The Minster, 1520.

usual wage for a carpenter was sometimes double that before the plague (Taylor 1959). The wages of an unskilled laborer also rose as a result of the shortage of labor, and both skilled and unskilled craftsmen continued to realize a steady increase in pay from 1377 until the mid-1390s (Thomson 1983). Not only did Edward violate his own statute when he needed workmen, so too did other landowners who were willing to pay wages above the limit in order to secure labor. It was, in a rare turnabout, a worker's market.

This early action of responding to market demand seems commonplace today, but in the strictly regulated social structure of the fourteenth century, it was a revolutionary act. Even those who would be considered social reformers found the demand for increased wages on the part of the laborers presumptuous. Nonetheless, by this act of rebellion, the workers instituted what was to be a major fissure in the labor structure of the Middle Ages.

Fortunately, these men, about whose individual lives we know so little, have left us with a rich pictorial history of their time. Perhaps they would feel that this was enough and would agree with a modern-day carver who describes carving not only as "an honourable profession where cheating shows and virtue is its own reward," but also one that gives the unknown carver "a little power over the grave" (Barnes 1991).

Although we are limited in our ability to speak of individual misericord carvers, we can speak of the milieu that inspired their work. To understand the Gothic misericord carvings as the carvers intended, it is necessary to place them in their historical context. In the following chapters, the carvings are examined with this thought in mind. It is impossible to cover all the topics present in the carvings; rather, what is presented is, by necessity, merely a series of swaths of English medieval life. Even confining one's work to a seemingly narrow topic like misericords demands the exploration of many related issues. This is both the joy and the curse of the researcher: each bit of knowledge elates even as it brings further awareness of how little we know.

2

Necessary Enticements—from Temptress to Virgin

> Two good days for a man in this life—
> When he weds and when he buries his wife.
> T. F. Thiselton-Dyer, *Folk-Lore of Women*, 1906

> Woman is a man's delight and all his bliss.
> Geoffrey Chaucer, "The Nun's Priest's Tale,"
> trans. by Nevill Coghill, 1966

ONE OF THE MOST ENDURING DEBATES IN THE HISTORY of human interaction has been on the issue of woman's "real" nature and her place relative to man. Is she the natural companion of man or his natural enemy? Does a woman steal a man's soul or enrich his existence? Is she weaker or stronger than man? The dichotomous nature of the debate posing woman as either good or bad has been reinforced for centuries in various ways—through church teachings, art, folklore, myth, music, and literature. Women have been depicted as both the embodiment of good and as totally untrustworthy. In this respect, the late Middle Ages were no different from any other time. The tension between women and men was ongoing and predictable; but, as the misericords show, the battle between the sexes was also revered.

The Church took the view that women were basically evil forces that bore careful watching. For the male lay population, the question was more complex: there were good women and bad women, and sometimes bad women were good and good women bad. The bipolar view of the female population as either good or bad also extended to mythical women. Especially intriguing to the ordinary male was the idea borne from historical legend, that there were tantalizing seductresses trying to steal their souls. Offering some hope in the event temptation overcame one, there was an equally appealing belief in an all-powerful Virgin who could overlook any sin and save one's soul. Between those two ideals, however, were the normal women with whom men came into daily contact. They may have been distrusted, but they were necessary.

Mixed feelings about women are recorded vividly in a number of misericord carvings. On the right are two examples of many displaying the good/bad relations between ordinary men and women; they could be soul mates, or they could be enemies. The first carving is a touching scene as the couple sit companionably, patting each other's face. Things could turn ugly, however, as pats turn into pinches in the second carving.

Questioning the basic nature of woman was part of the lore—and fun—of the time; but the distrust of women was based on beliefs emanating from much earlier. As early as 79 A.D., for example, Pliny the Elder, in writing his *Natural History*, endowed women with frightening, superhuman powers during their menstrual cycle:

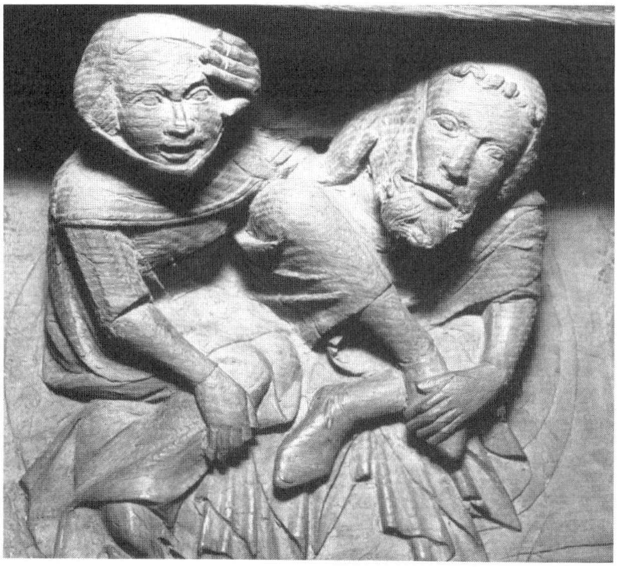

Domestic harmony. Ely (Cambs), The Cathedral, c.1340.

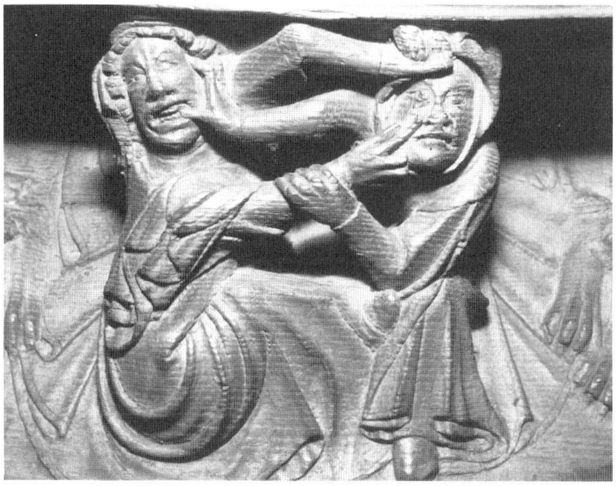

Domestic strife. Ely (Cambs), The Cathedral, c.1340.

> On the approach of a woman in this state, must will become sour, seeds which are touched by her become sterile, grafts wither away, garden plants are parched up, and the fruit will fall from the tree beneath which she sits . . . A swarm of bees, if looked upon by her, will die immediately. . . .
>
> 1855, 2:151

What defense had a mere male to offer in response to such power? And yet, the other feminine qualities were so seductive. Medieval men knew well the role of the enticing seductress.

Legendary Enticers

The perception of women as untrustworthy and duplicitous was based primarily on their presumed sexual allure and alleged ability to entrap a man. Once men were entrapped, the consequences could only be imagined; but it was taken on faith, combined with wonder, that these consequences would be horrific.

Sirens

The concept of women leading men to their doom is pre-Christian. For centuries, creatures with alluring feminine characteristics have been lying in wait for men. Some of the better known were sirens who, according to Greek mythology, were half-bird, half-woman creatures who would captivate sailors with their beautiful song, lull them to sleep, then devour them. Homer used this story in his *Odyssey,* where Odysseus escaped the lure of the sirens by taking the advice of Circe and stuffing the ears of his men with wax, and by tying himself to the mast. In this way, he could not be seduced into altering the course of the boat to go near the rocky coast where the sirens lived.

As the legend of the sirens was passed from person to person over the centuries, a certain amount of confusion developed about their exact form. Homer, for example, ascribed no particular form to the sirens. That he placed them on an island, however, has led to the belief that he did not conceive of them as fish creatures, or mermaids. The *Physiologus* (c. second century B.C.)—ostensibly a work describing the behavior of animals, but attaching to these behaviors judgments about the nature of man, God, and the Devil—placed sirens among the birds (Payne 1990).

In the Middle Ages, "Books of Beasts" (bestiaries) based on the *Physiologus,* but altered to include Christian morals, carried on the myth of the half-bird, half-woman creature with the mesmerizing song. At this time, the siren's sweet voice was said to symbolize worldly temptation that diverted men from spiritual concerns. Houwen (1996) argues that prior to

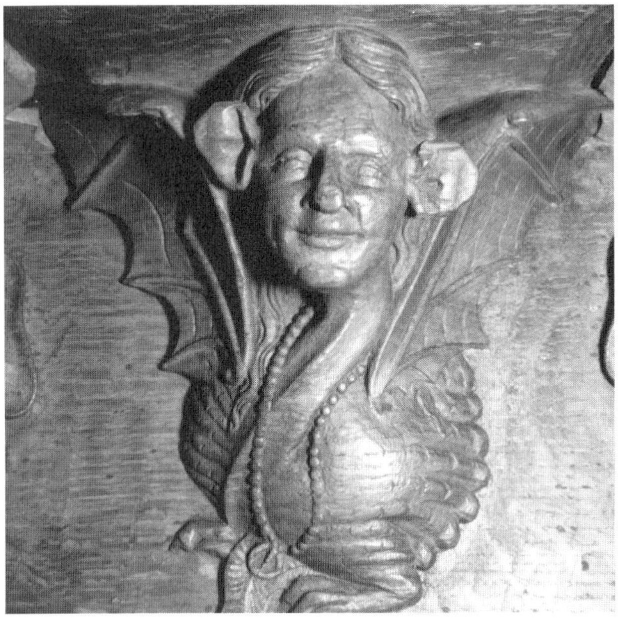

Siren. Oxford (Oxon), New College Chapel, late fourteenth century.

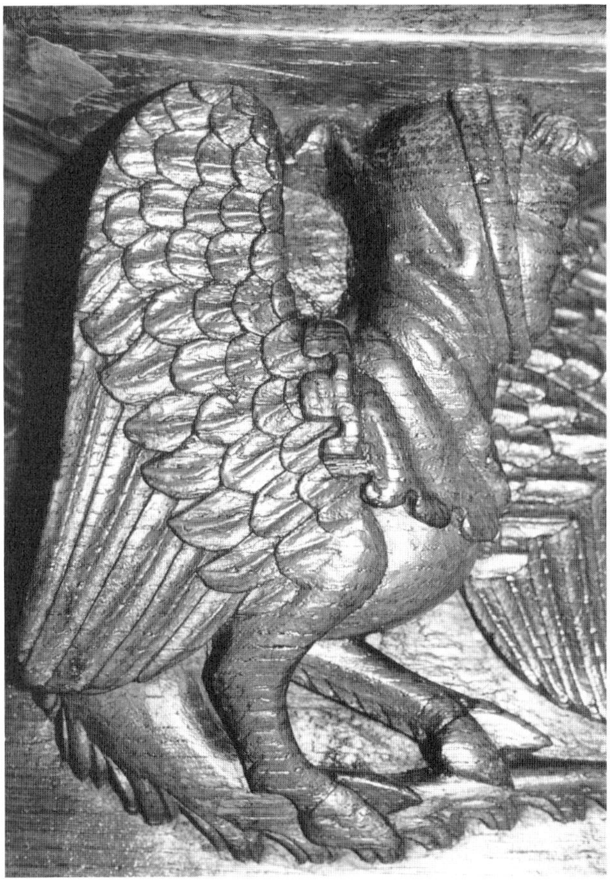

Siren. Worcester (Herefs & Worcs), The Cathedral, late fourteenth century.

the Middle Ages, the siren's song that so tempted Odysseus was appealing because it contained information on world events. During the Middle Ages, however, the siren's temptation was conceived of more singularly as sexual in nature. By the time the characteristics of the siren had been bestowed on the mermaid, any sexual encounter, it was cautioned, inevitably was followed by death.

Perhaps because spiritual concerns were so easily diverted, the misericord carvers recorded the intrigue medieval man had with these creatures in numerous lovely carvings. The carvers endowed the human part of these composite creatures with appealing expressions, but were less sure about how to present the rest of the body. For example, the wings, in the carving, left, are more like bat's wings than bird's wings, and the ears are unflatteringly exaggerated; yet her face is lovely and she is fetchingly adorned with jewelry. The feet on the second carving are not claws but hooves and the carver has added a tail, but, again, there is a charming face. The body may not have been enticing, but the human face was. The variation in body forms can partly be explained by the tendency on the part of the carvers to freely embellish, and partly by the alterations that occur through oral transmission of tales. Descriptions of creatures never seen may take on myriad forms.

Mermaids

Although most bestiaries considered sirens as belonging to the bird family, a French bestiary of the twelfth century described the siren as part woman and part bird or fish (Payne 1990). The Carlisle carving shows the confusion in this transition from siren to mermaid. The torso is a female and the lower body is a fish; the bird association is still present in the form of the feet. Later, the transition was complete, and mermaids assumed the form we know them by today: half-woman, half-fish.

No one is quite sure how the myth of the mermaid took hold, but all the characteristics attributed to the siren were transferred to the mermaid. Depiction of the mermaid as a

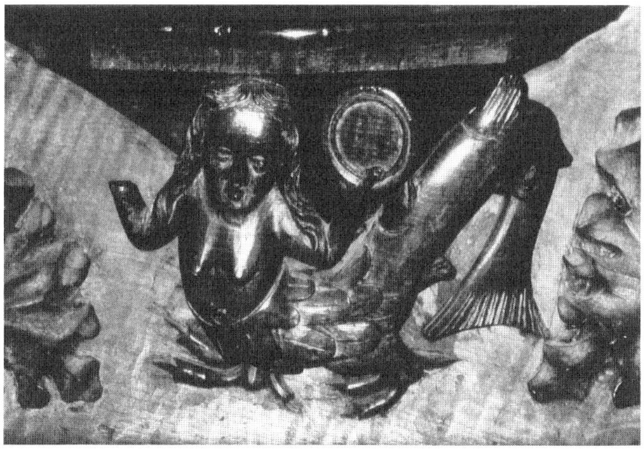

Mermaid/siren. Carlisle (Cumbria), The Cathedral, 1399–1413.

temptress determined to steal men's souls was a popular myth, and one so lovingly depicted by the misericord carvers that one can only surmise that an encounter with these creatures was more to be desired than feared. When shown as temptresses, mermaids would have with them their tools for enticement, the comb and mirror as below.

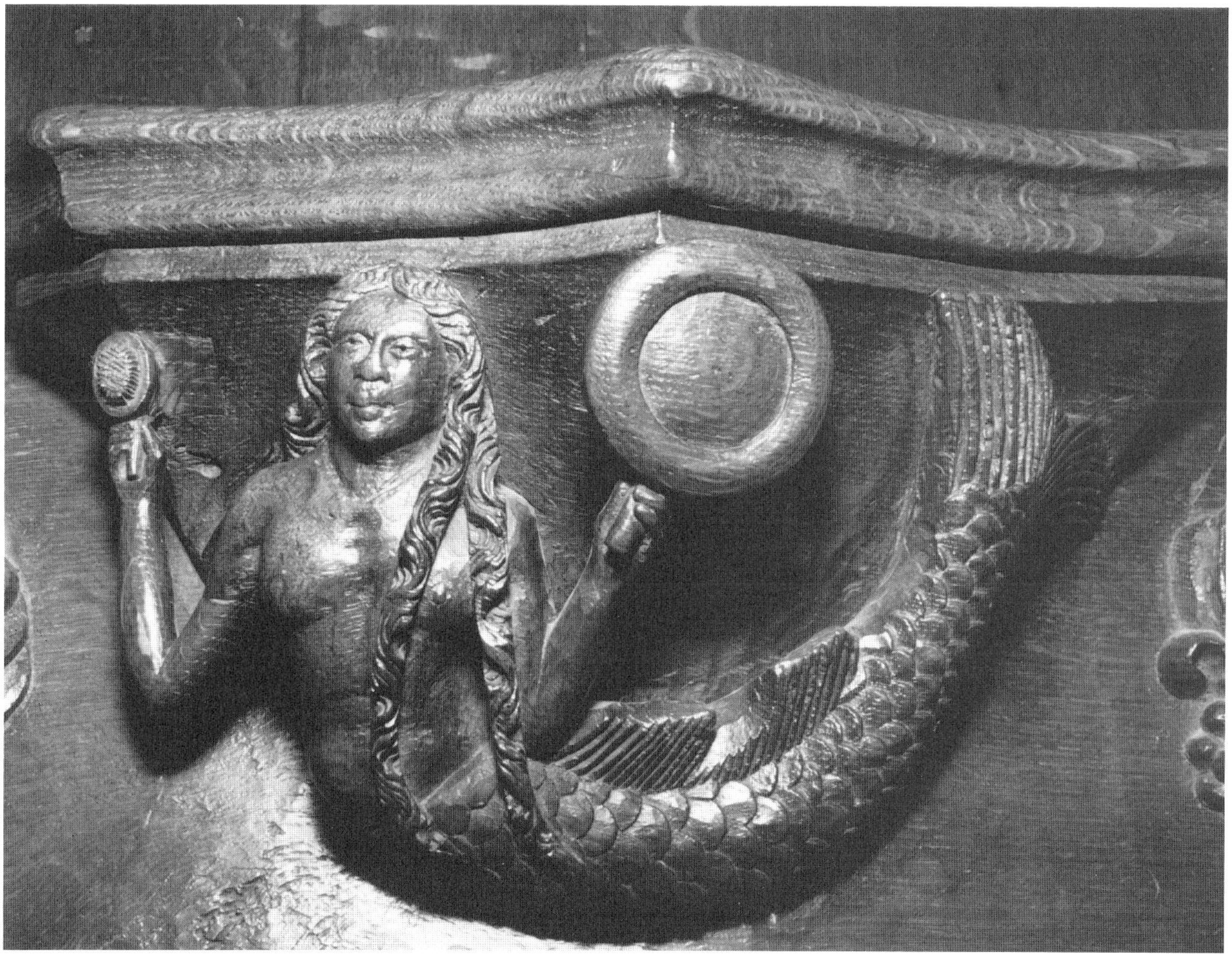

Mermaid with mirror and brush. Ripon (N.Yorks), The Cathedral, 1489–94.

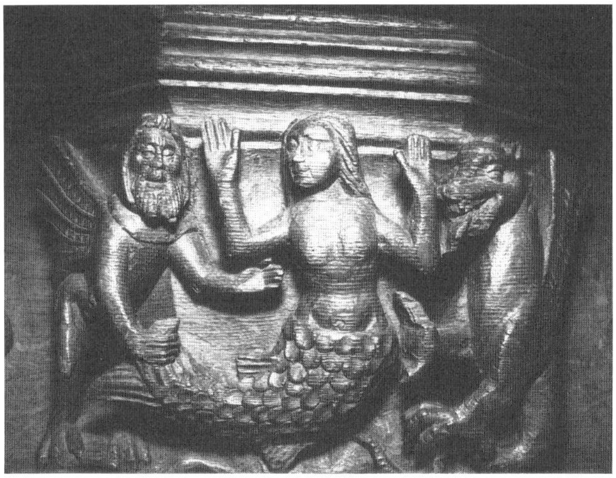

Mermaid with Devil and dragon. Bristol (Avon), The Cathedral, 1520.

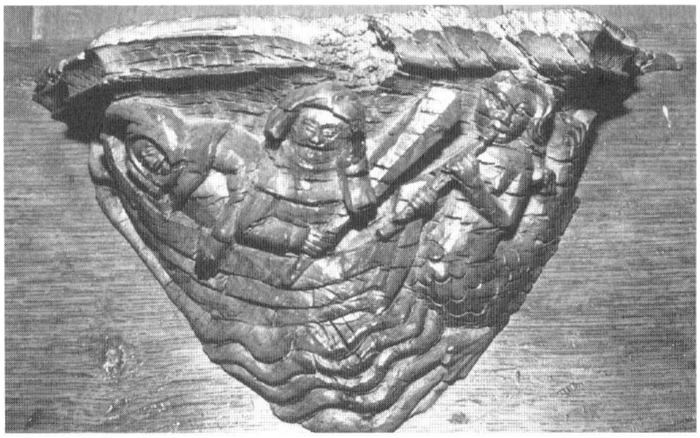

Mermaid piping sailors. Boston (Lincs), St. Botolph, 1390.

The mermaid's devious purpose is made clear in the Bristol carving. She is shown with her associates, the Devil and one of his demons, a dragon. The Devil has her by the tail.

In the Boston carving, the ability of the siren to charm sailors with her sweet music was transferred to the mermaid, with one slight alteration. Here, the mermaid is playing a pipe rather than singing. The only known misericord in which a mermaid plays an instrument, this carving may derive from Isidore's description of mermaids as being partly women, partly birds, "of whom one sang, one played the pipes, and the third on the lyre" (Druce 1915, 174). A modernized version of an Anglo-Saxon verse records the inevitable effect of being tempted by the mermaid:

> Merrily she singeth, this mermaid,
> And hath many voices, many and shrill,
> But they are all ill.
> Shipmen forget their steering
> For her singing.
> They slumber and sleep,
> And awake too late.
> The ships sink through the treachery,
> And never come up again.
>
> Clarke 1920, 23

A more hopeful, secular interpretation of the mermaids' motives comes from early British folklore. Rather than desiring to steal men's souls, mermaids actually wanted to marry men. They would lure men down into the water with the promise of sunken treasure, lull them to sleep with their singing, and entrap them in a cave. If a mermaid married a man, so the story goes, her tail could be exchanged for legs (Whitlock 1979). This interpretation neatly sidesteps the earlier view of the inevitability of death following sexual union, allowing the mermaid to make an "honest man" of the transgressor.

Christian Temptresses

Every era has produced its own temptresses. In the Middle Ages, the Church introduced its own updated version of the seductive woman. Indeed, one of the basic lessons of Christianity was the disaster that befell mankind when Adam bowed to the temptation offered by Eve. The Worcester carving dramatically records the expulsion from Eden.

This act provided clerics with a rationale for the condemnation of women for centuries. Turtullian, who lived between 230 and 160 B.C., was particularly grim in his writings about this "door of the Devil" or this "forfeiter of Paradise," as he preferred to call Eve (Barnes 1971). Because of Eve, he noted, God's sentence of painful childbirth and domination by the husband would hang over the female gender forever—a much flogged sentiment, for Turtullian's curse was still in vogue as late as the seventeenth century. This rationale was the basis on which women were denied participation in the English Parliament in 1632:

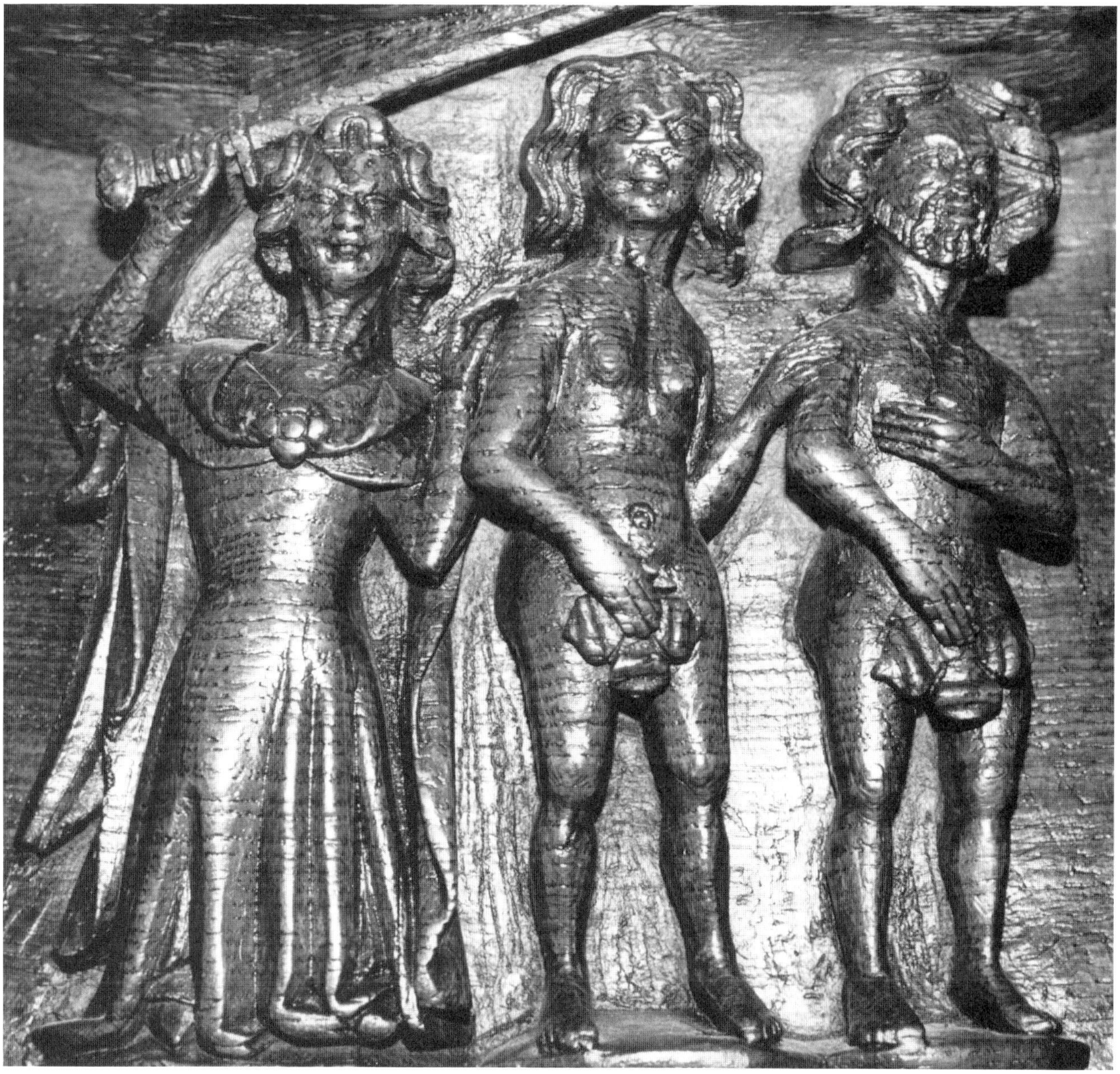

Expulsion from Eden. Worcester (Herefs & Worcs), The Cathedral, late fourteenth century.

> See here the reason of that which I touched before, that women have no voyse in Parliament, they make no lawes, they consent to none, they abrogate none. All of them are understood either married or to bee married and their desires as subject to their husband. . . . The common Law here shaketh hand with Divinitie. . . .
>
> *The Lawes Resolutions of Women's Rights* 1632, 6

Eve occasionally had her male champions, however. In the seventeenth century, at the same time women were being denied a voice in Parliament, an anonymous male author wrote in defense of women by shifting the original guilt from Eve onto Adam:

> . . . but if her Fall's examin'd right,
> We find most Men have banish'd Truth for spight;
> Nor is she quite so guilty as some make;
> For Adam did most of the Guilt partake:
> For he from God's own Mouth had the Command;
> But Woman she had it at second hand:
> The Devil's Strength weak Woman might deceive,
> But Adam tempted only was by Eve
>
> *The Female Advocate* 1686, 2

The Church in the Middle Ages reinforced the perception that the most dangerous temptations were sexual, and Christian mythology created tales about women who reputedly used their sexual charms to the detriment of men. One of the most dramatic of these myths/tales was that of the daughter of Herodias, widely known as Salome. As the story goes, Herodias had an adulterous affair with her brother-in-law, Herod Antipas, and later married him, taking her daughter with her. Scandalized by these events, St. John the Baptist was unwise enough to be heard expressing his feeling that it was unlawful for Herod to have his brother's wife. Naturally, Herodias wanted St. John removed. The opportunity arose on the night of her husband's birthday celebration. On that occasion, Herod asked Salome to dance for the group and was so pleased with her performance that he offered her any reward she cared to name. To please her mother, she asked for the head of John the Baptist. Though regretful, Herod honored his promise, "And immediately the king sent an executioner, and commanded his head to be brought: and he went and beheaded him in the prison. And brought his head in a charger and gave it to the damsel: and the damsel gave it to her mother" (Mark 6:27, 28).

An Ely carver executed the drama in the carving below. On the left supporter, Salome bends backward in her exotic dance. In the central scene, she is presented with her reward, and on the right she dutifully presents the head to her mother—truly proving that one could lose one's head over a woman.

The stylized depiction of Salome, always bending over backwards in her dance and always holding the head of John the Baptist on a tray, was a shorthand way of making the main characters immediately recognizable to the viewer. Also, it was a common artistic device during the Middle Ages to include several high points of a story together in scenes that ran together (Rouse 1968). The twelfth century capital, right, show an early presentation of the story done in the same manner, only in stone, illustrating the link between the stone carvers and the later woodcarvers.

Distrusted Women

Given these treacherous images, it is not surprising that women during the Middle Ages were often treated unfavorably under both Church and civil law. They had few rights and were regarded, at least formally, as people to be controlled. If the woman was beautiful, she was likely to be considered all the more dangerous for, in true medieval fashion, beauty in a woman did not necessarily mean simply that she was beautiful but that, perhaps, the beauty hid "filth beneath the skin" (Tuchman 1978). Similarly, the old proverb, "beware of beautiful women as you would of

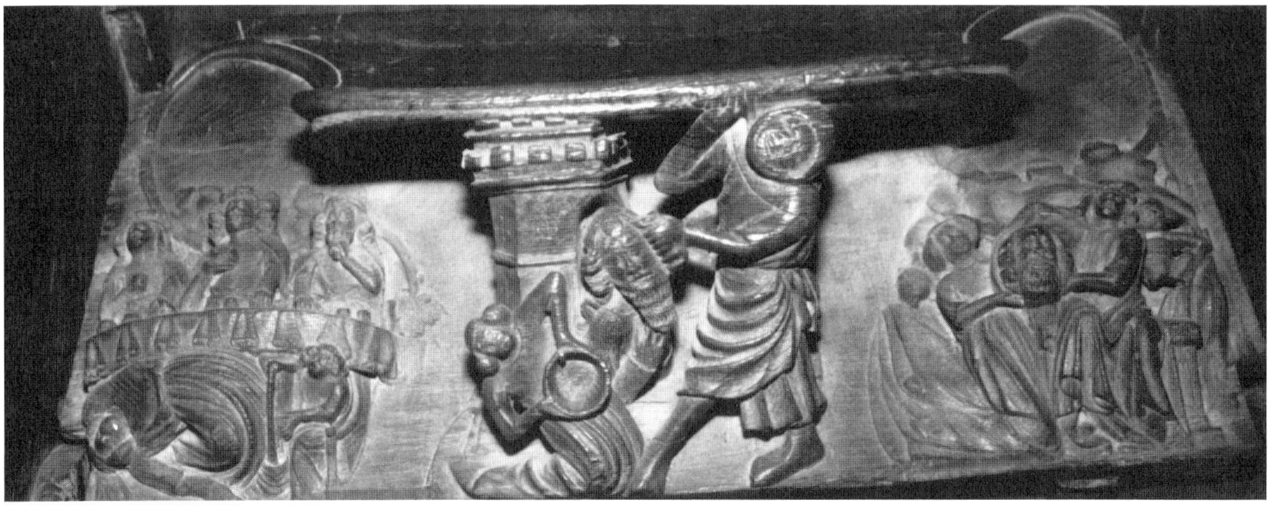

Salome receives the head of St. John the Baptist. Ely (Cambs), The Cathedral, c.1340.

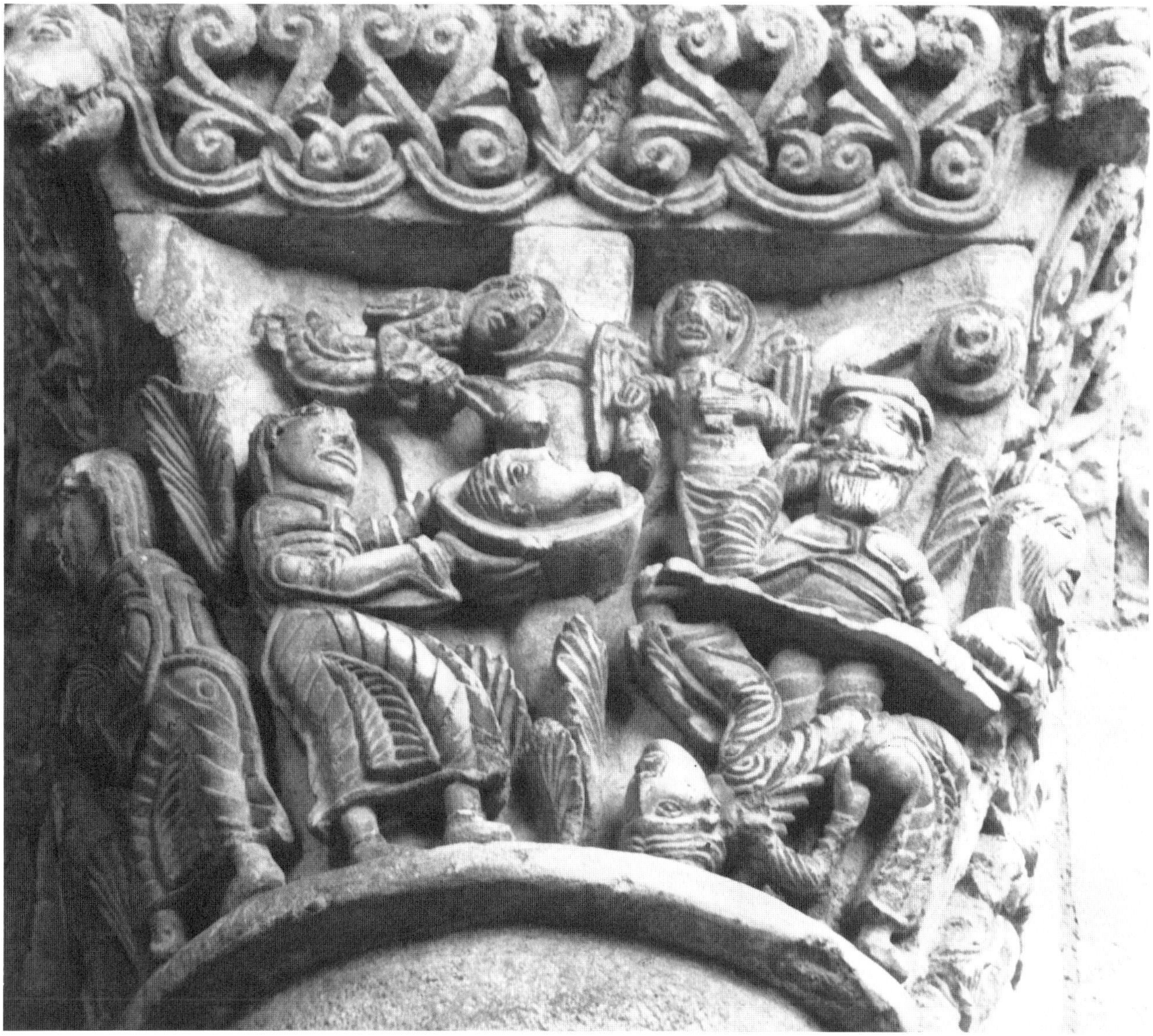

Salome. La Sauve (France), Majeure Abbaye, twelfth century.

red pepper" (Thiselton-Dyer 1906, xii). The carryover of lessons learned about the deception of various types of temptresses retained an important place in medieval men's vision of women.

Desirable Calamities

Although, in general, women may have been viewed as necessary enticements, the view of women as wives was a more skeptical one. If anything, marriage was considered a necessary evil in which romantic love played little part. Once married, the Church warned repeatedly, women who were not checked would disrupt domestic harmony. Indeed, in the fifteenth century, the Dominican inquisitors Jacob Sprenger and Heinrich Kramer were even more vehement, labeling women, among other things, "desirable calamities" and "unescapable punishment" (Sprenger and Kramer 1928). The Church of the Middle Ages was so hostile to the notion of marital happiness that it was said the greatest source of marital disharmony came from interfering priests (Wright 1865). This view was based on the early teachings of St. Jerome, who trumpeted the presumed vices of women as further encouragement for men to practice celibacy (Parry 1941).

Medieval carvers played on the warning about the need to control women in a particular way by showing supposedly uncontrolled women attacking men. Whereas the carving shown earlier of the couple fighting portrays a man and woman engaged in hand-to-hand combat, this was not the typical presentation. Usually, the wife was armed with a cudgel, ladle, or distaff with which to terrorize her husband; beard-pulling was also popular.

In the first example below, the husband has laid down his sword and shield and appears

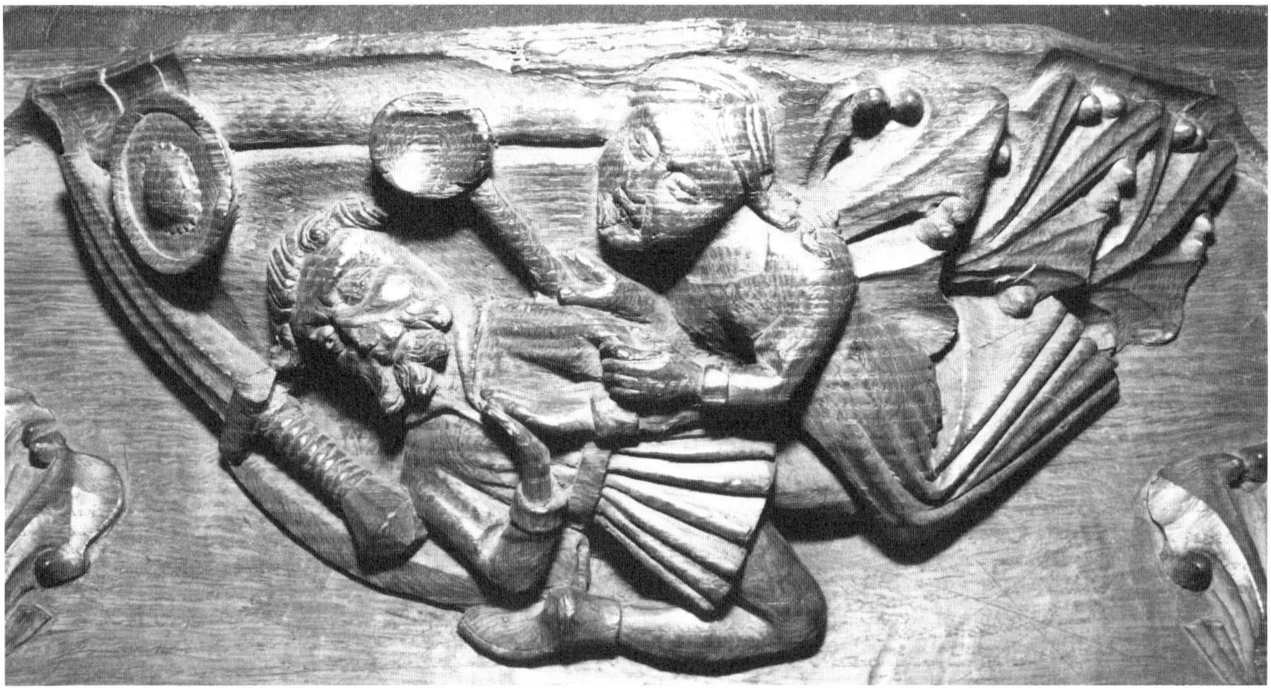

Domestic strife. Whalley (Lancs), St. Mary, c.1430.

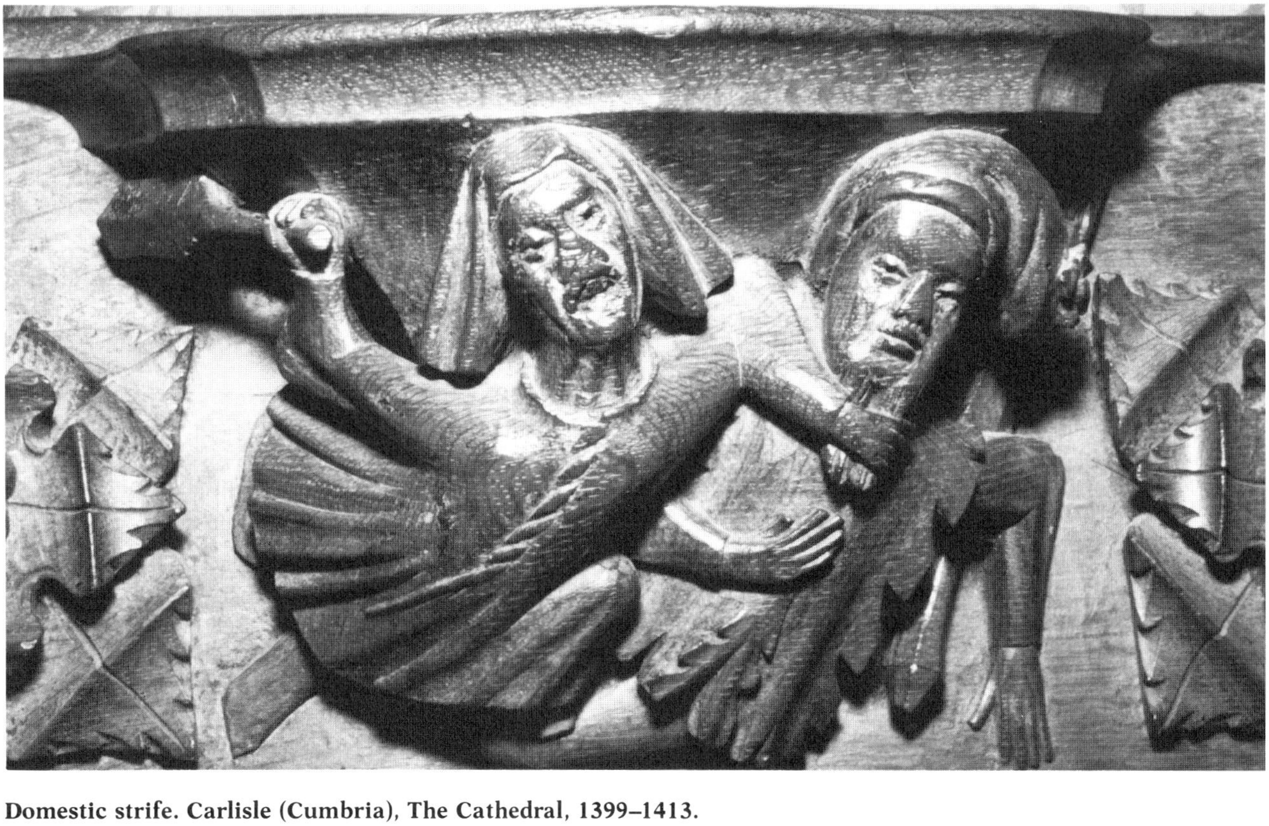

Domestic strife. Carlisle (Cumbria), The Cathedral, 1399–1413.

to be praying for intercession as the wife takes the offensive with her ladle. In the next scene the wife seems determined to keep her husband from retreating by firmly grasping his beard and standing on his leg.

In the final example the husband is learning to stay out of the kitchen when his wife is cooking.

Interestingly, these depictions are the reverse of the accepted practice of the time in which wife-beating was not only legal but expected, at least by the Church. In a theological dictionary compiled during the fourteenth century, advice is given on training a wife:

> Moreover, a man may chastise his wife and beat her for her correction; for she is of his household, and therefore the lord may chastise his own . . .
> Coulton 1928, 3:119

One of the most popular books of the time, The *Book of the Knight of La Tour Landry,* was a series of stories meant to teach young women how to behave like ladies. One tale is of a woman who spoke back to her husband with harsh words in the presence of strangers. At first, the husband simply asked her not to do it again. When his kindness was not rewarded by a change in the wife's behavior, he became so angry, "he smote her with his fist down to earth; and then with his foot he struck her in the visage and brake her nose, and all her life after she had her nose crooked" (Wright 1868, 28). From this story, a young woman was to learn the dangers of arguing with her husband.

This story speaks to the legendary and universal fear of a woman's ability to destroy a man with her sharp tongue, a fear that is the

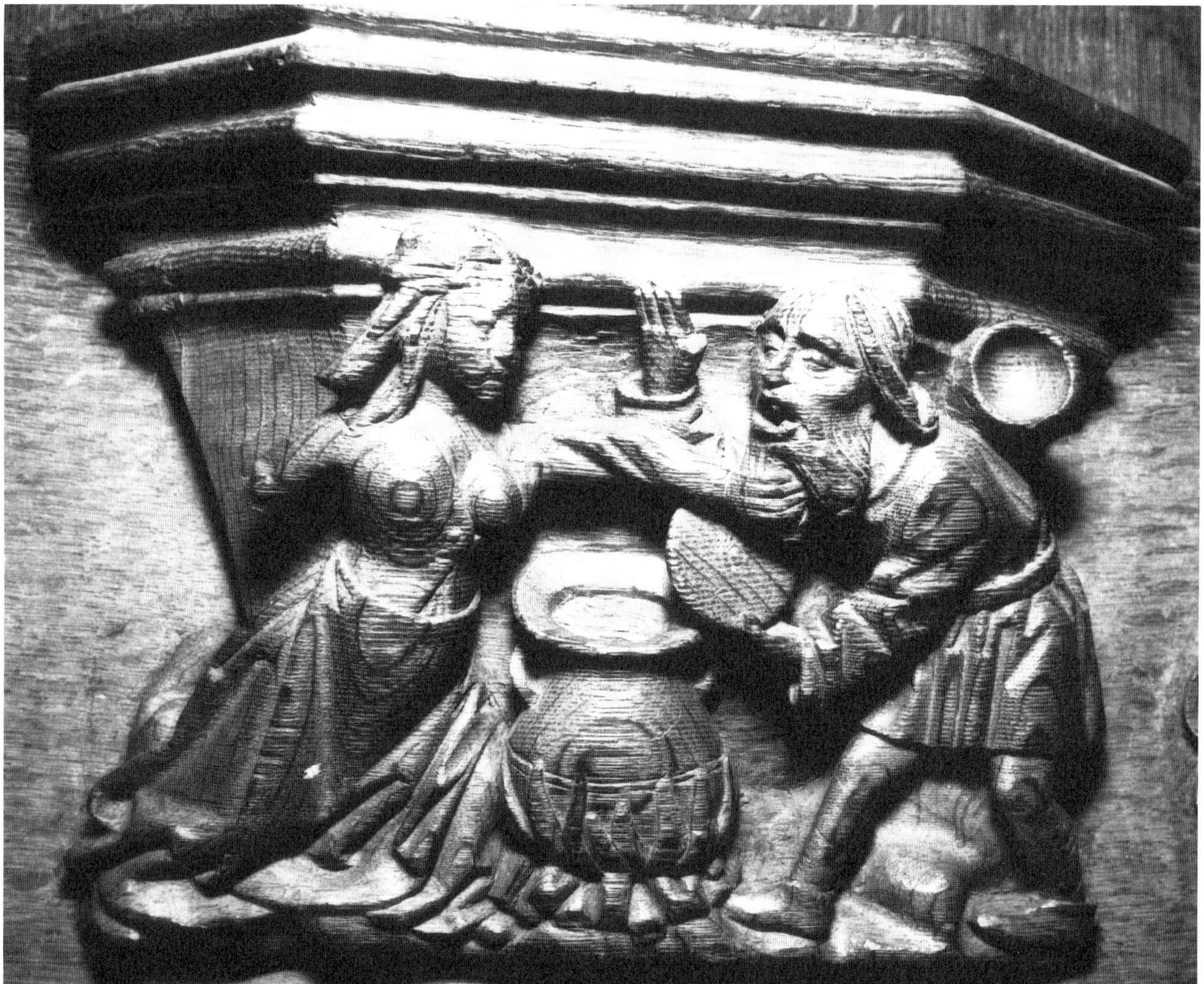

Domestic strife. Bristol (Avon), The Cathedral, 1520.

foundation for an old Japanese proverb: "a woman's tongue three inches long can kill a man six feet high" (Thiselton-Dyer 1906, xii). One can imagine the lecture being given in the Wells carving where the husband seems to be instructing the worried-looking wife.

The notion that men were the more important figures in their families was reinforced in a number of ways. One of the more amusing was in the confusing area of reproduction. Even though the process of procreation was not understood, it had been suggested for centuries that the woman's role was of lesser importance than the man's. Aristotle, for example, reasoned that the man's role was the more important because he contributed the life or soul to the child, while the woman contributed something lesser, called "matter." The enhanced status of the male fetus was even said to produce a more comfortable pregnancy:

> Those that are pregnant with a male foetus usually pass through the time more easily, and retain a better colour throughout. If a female is conceived, the contrary is the case; for they are generally more discoloured and suffer more during the period of gestation
>
> 1862, 181

Alburtus Magnus, the teacher of Thomas Aquinas, carried on with this notion but in a different vein. For Alburtus, the male's contribution was stronger because of the female's sex drive. Women, he opined, enjoyed sex more than men and, since women were imperfect beings, they were ever desirous of sexual union with men, who were perfect beings (Gies and Gies 1978). Thomas Aquinas reinforced earlier teachings by suggesting that fathers should be more revered than mothers since their role in procreation was active, while the mother's was passive (Tuchman 1978), and that the active force produced the more desirable male child. When a female child was born, it was a result of some defect in the active force. Of course, it was such views as this that elicited a number of rejoinders by

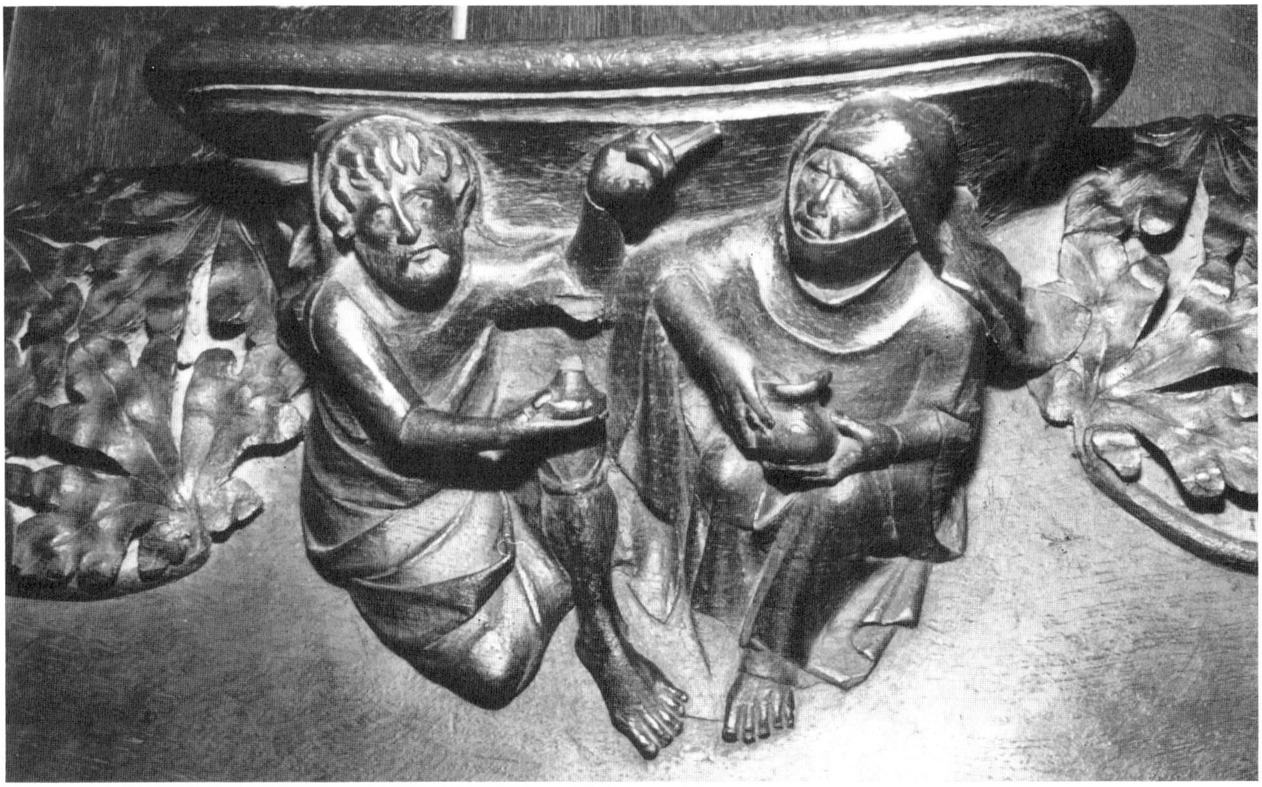

Man and woman talking. Wells (Somerset), The Cathedral, c.1330–40.

detractors of Thomas Aquinas. Erasmus, for example, proclaimed: "Thomas scarcely knew Latin, and that was his only tongue . . ." (Allen 1914, 12).

It is clear that, from the moment of conception on, women were considered to be trouble, and a husband had best not forget it. One option a husband had when his wife was disobedient was to publicly humiliate her. This was usually done by taking the recalcitrant wife to the ducking pond. Ducking (or cucking) stools, which seem to have been peculiar to the British Isles, were present from Anglo-Saxon times. Probably, the custom of ducking originally had to do with pagan agricultural rituals in which water was sprinkled on the field, or people were immersed in water in the belief that this would make them more fruitful (Chambers 1945). Over time, however, human immersion became more a form of ridicule and punishment. In medieval times there is at least one reference to a city, Chester, in the Domesday book as having used this method of punishment. These "stools" were used in the Middle Ages to chastise "shrews" and others publicly. It is uncertain whether the offender was always ducked in the water or whether, initially, they were simply made to sit in the chair exposed to public ridicule (Wright 1845). Nevertheless, the practice proved such a popular mechanism of behavior control that stools were still being used in England until at least the early part of the nineteenth century—not just for errant wives, but for others as well, such as tradespeople who gave "short measure."

An example of a ducking stool is one on display at the Church of St. Peter and St. Paul in Leominster. It was last used in 1809, when one Jenny Pipes, alias Jane Curran, was ducked in the local stream.

A tablet on the wall of the church records an anonymous verse describing the experience of being ducked:

> Down in the deep the stool descends
> But here at first we miss our ends;
> She mounts again and rages more
> Than ever vixen did before
> So throwing water on the fire
> Will make it burn up but the higher
> If so, my friends, pray let her take
> A second turn into the lake;
> And rather than your patience lose,
> Thrice, and again repeat the dose,
> No brawling wives no furious wenches
> No fire so hot but water quenches
> Scolds, butchers, bakers, brewers
> Apothecaries, and all who gave
> Short measure or adulterated food.

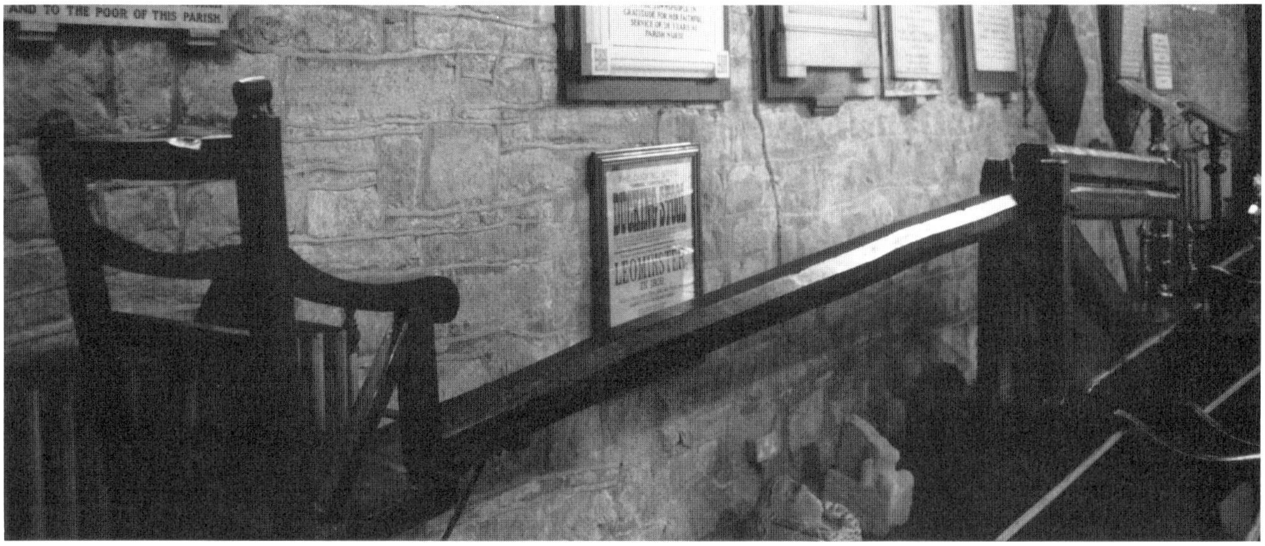

Ducking stool. Leominster (Herefs & Worcs), St. Peter & St. Paul, n.d.

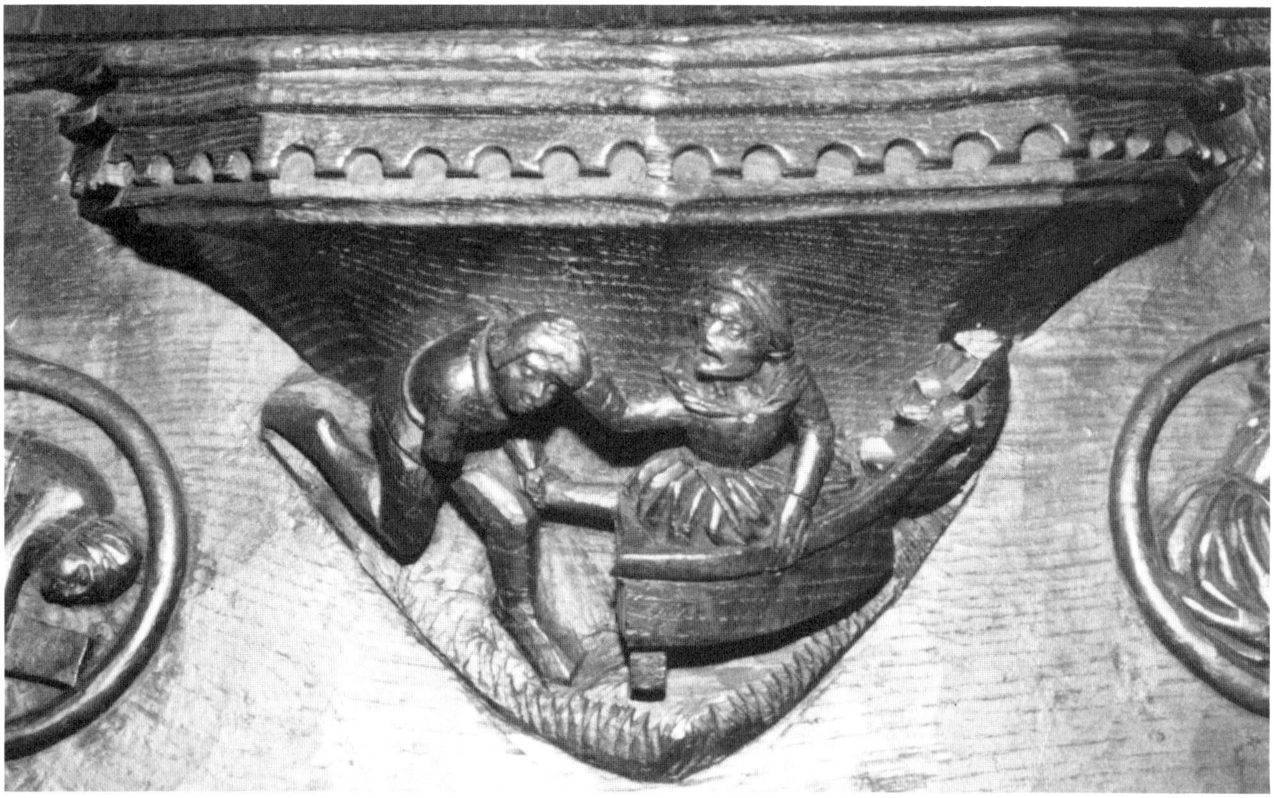

Being wheeled to ducking pond. Beverley (Humberside), The Minster, 1520.

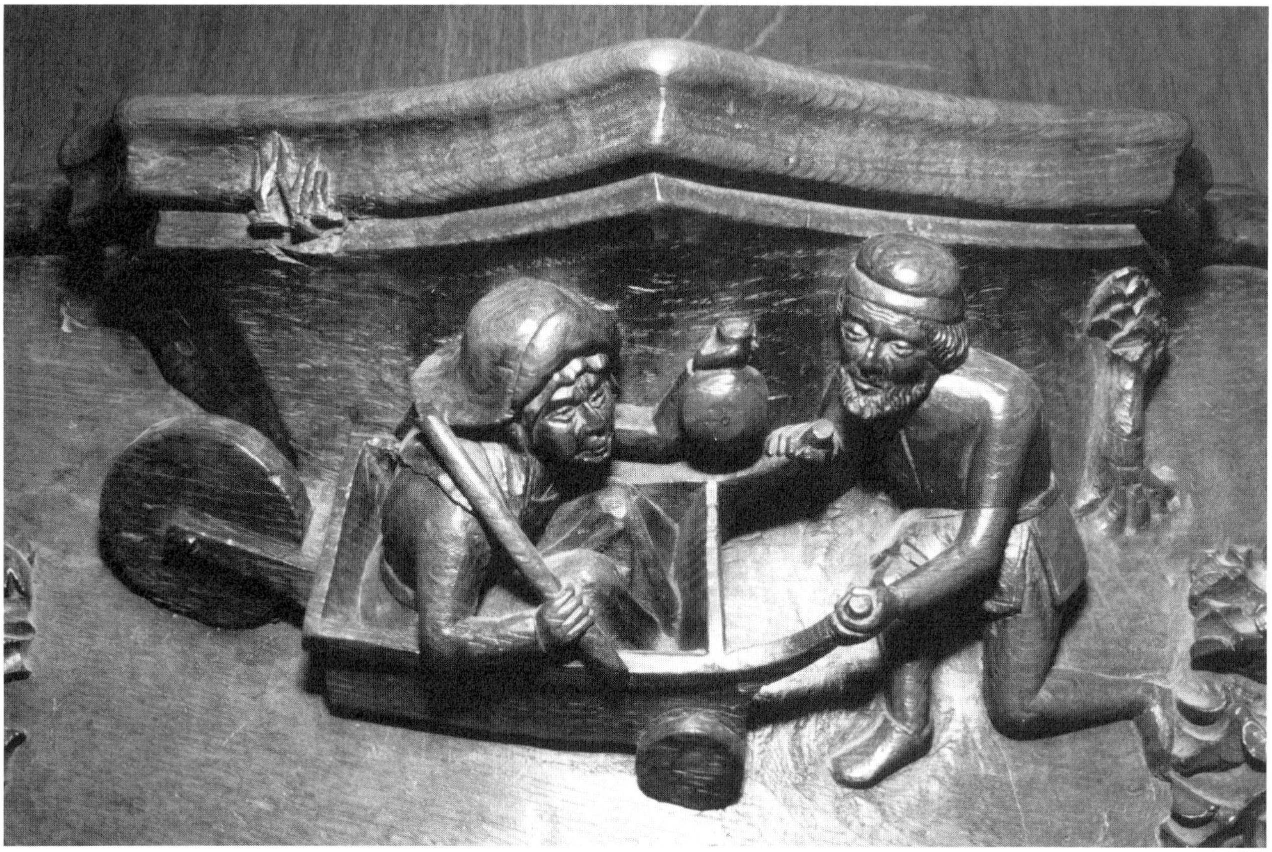

Being wheeled to ducking pond. Ripon (N.Yorks), The Cathedral, 1489–94.

A misericord from Beverley shows the wife being wheeled to the ducking pond, fighting against her husband all the way.

In the Ripon carving, copied from a fifteenth-century German engraving (Ottley 1826), the wife appears to offer little resistance.

Though much rarer in application, a man could also be publicly punished for beating his wife; more common was for a man to be punished if his wife was seen beating him. In Scotland and northern England, the punishment meted out was to make the husband "ride the stang." This consisted of the guilty husband being made to straddle a pitchfork which was then lifted up onto the shoulders of two other men who carried him through the town "in his most uncomfortable and unenviable wooden saddle" (Wright 1845, 55). The husband would either be carried to the river and dunked, or he would be forced to ride the stang until he agreed to pay a fine in the form of money or alcohol.

Riding the stang was used for other offenses as well and was a popular form of public chastisement in both England and France. In addition to the pitchfork, the punishment could include being made to ride on a pole, on a hobbyhorse, or on an ass or horse facing the tail (Chambers 1945; O'Faolain and Martines 1973). The man could also be required to ride naked, as shown below.

Marriage Rejecters

With all the promotion, serious and humorous, of the idea that marriage was insufferable, it was still the preferred state for both men and women—the old adage that marriage was an evil, but a necessary one, was accepted. Nor was one to be too fussy about whom one married. It was said that women who were rebellious enough to reject all suitors and die unmarried were destined to lead a pack of apes in hell. The apes represented the souls of unmarried men:

> Pity that you, who've served so long and well,
> Should die a virgin, and lead apes in hell
>
> Thiselton-Dyer 1906, 178

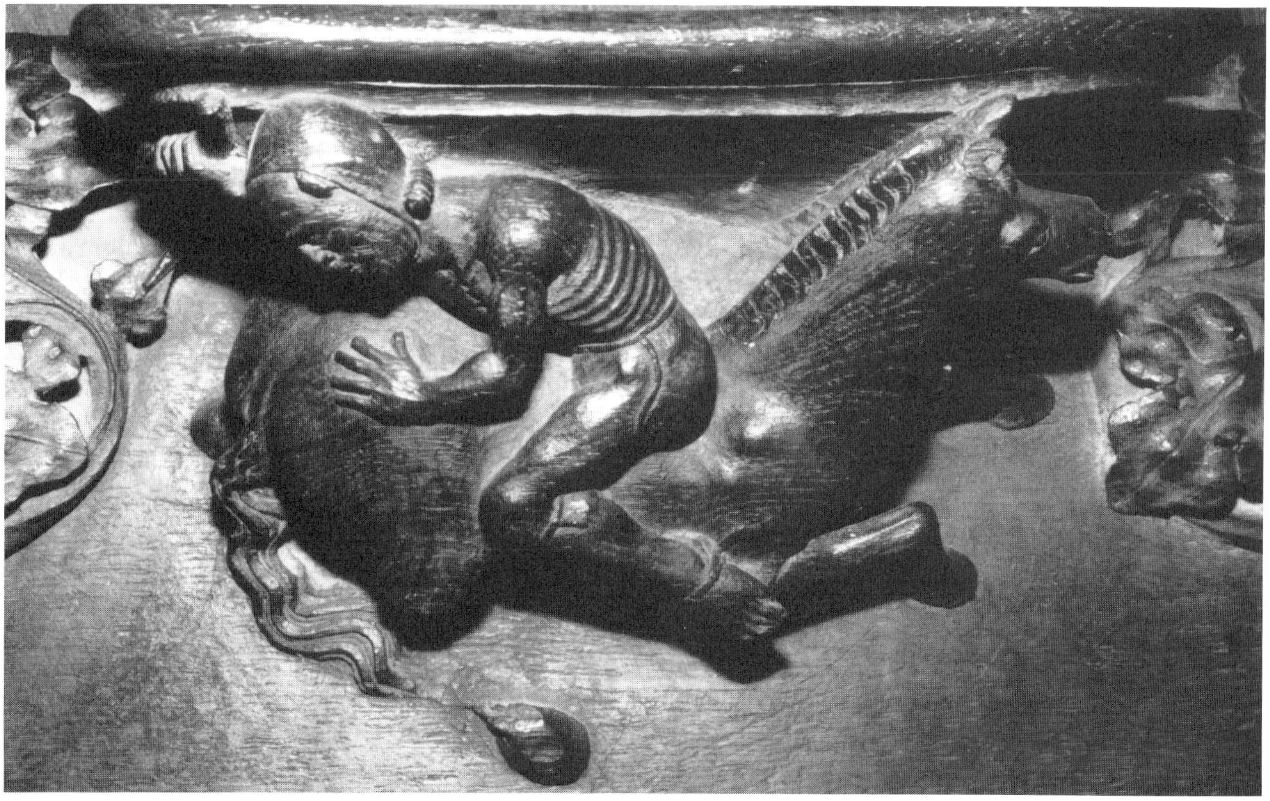

Nude man riding the stang. Wells (Somerset), The Cathedral, c.1330–40.

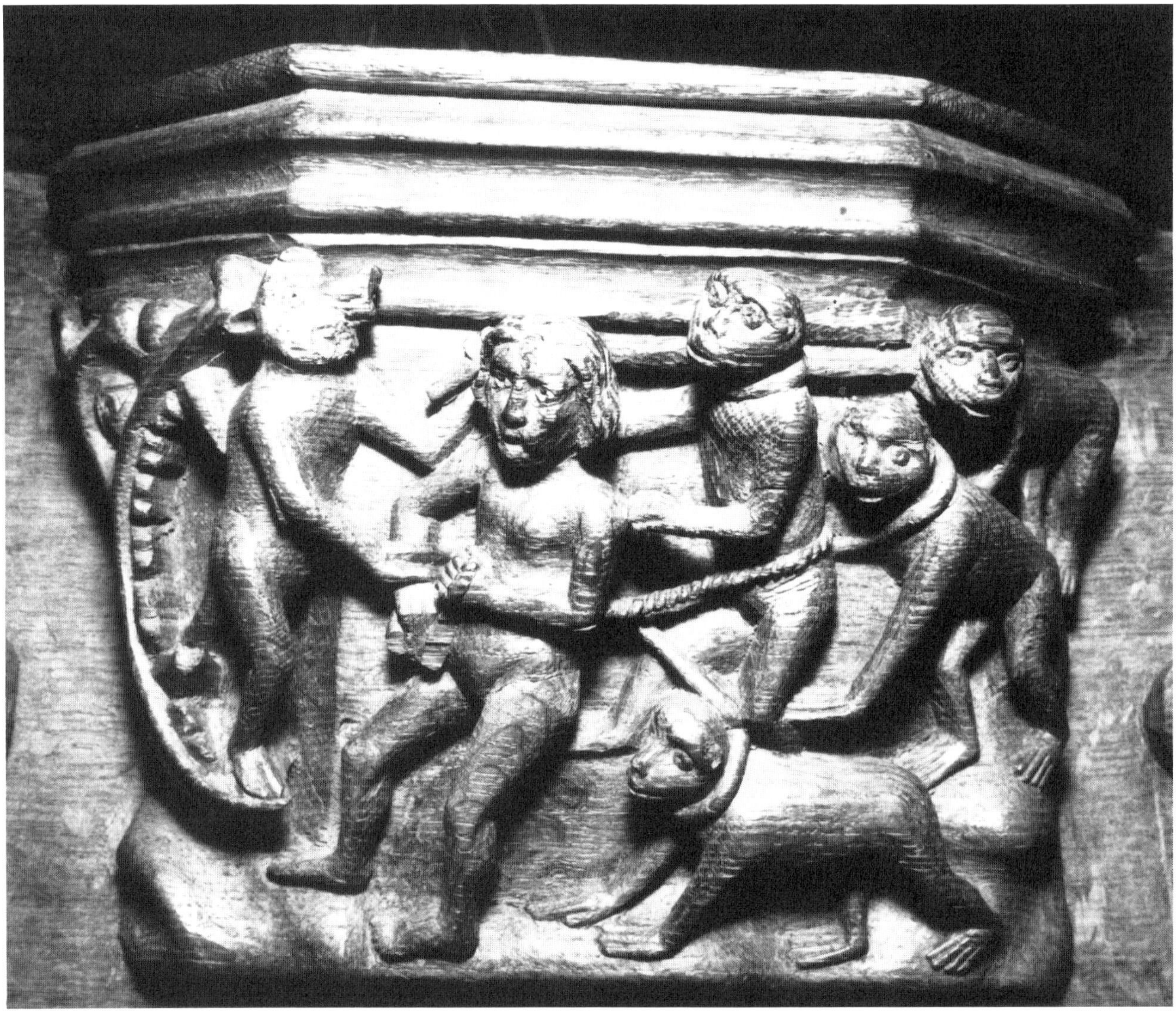

Fate of unmarried women. Bristol (Avon), The Cathedral, 1520.

This proverb is illustrated in a Bristol carving in which a maid has been severely punished by having to lead not one, but four, apes toward the "Jaws of Hell." An eager demon grabs at them to pull them in.

So popular was this myth that it was still being alluded to by Shakespeare in the sixteenth century when he has the older daughter, Katherine, speaking to her father of his partiality to her sister, Bianca:

> She is your treasure, she must have a husband.
> I must dance bare-foot on her wedding day. And
> for your love to her lead apes in hell
> *The Taming of the Shrew* 1982, 2.1.32–34

The reference to dancing barefoot is to an old custom whereby, if a younger sister marries first, the elder sister must dance barefoot at the wedding to avoid becoming an old maid.

Grim Reality or Tongue-in-Cheek?

Were the relations between men and women really so grim? Or was that assumption based on formal rules encoded by the Church and the legal system, which granted most power to men? That was the formal structure, but medieval history records any number of women who were able to get around men informally by doing just what the Church feared: using their charms. For, as wicked and treacherous as women might be, their appeal was such that, "the whisper of a beautiful woman can be heard further than the loudest call of duty" (Thiselton-Dyer 1906, 76). In the domestic-dispute carvings, is the carver depicting the worst fears realized by showing women disrupting domestic harmony, as the Church warned, or is he playfully indulging in a tongue-in-cheek representation of the ongoing battle between the sexes? Given the tenor of the period, the latter is more logical.

Domestic harmony was one of the most heavily satirized topics of the Middle Ages—with comic episodes abounding in plays, carvings, and literature. A popular literary work of the fourteenth century, Chaucer's *The Canterbury Tales*, for example, has many delightful passages on domestic satire. In "The Wife of Bath's Prologue," we find the humorous depiction of a husband who has just been assaulted by his wife:

> Xantippe poured a piss-pot on his head.
> The silly man sat still as he was dead,
> Wiping his head, but dared no more complain
> Than say, "Ere thunder stops, down comes the rain."
>
> Chaucer 1966, 294

It is quite likely that, on a daily basis, and away from the Church, interactions between men and women were frequently amicable. There are many indications that at least for common citizens, the give and take between the sexes was much more relaxed and less proscribed than it was for the nobility. Many avenues were open for equality in play that were enthusiastically embraced. The customs of "Hock-tide" (probably the Monday and Tuesday following Easter Sunday), for example, allowed for equal merriment. On Hock-Monday, the women "hocked" the men, which involved women wandering the streets with ropes used to catch and bind unwary men. The men were released when they paid some sort of fine—perhaps a kiss, perhaps money. On Hock-Tuesday, the tables were turned, and the women were hocked.

There were other similar customs, such as "heaving," where men were captured and tossed into the air by a group of women until they agreed to pay the fine requested. On the following day, it was the women's turn to be heaved. Then there was the practice of wives whipping husbands on Easter Monday and husbands whipping wives on Easter Tuesday.

These customs of capture and payment are assumed to derive from pagan customs involving capture and sacrifice (Chambers 1903). Transformation of customs in medieval times from those of religious significance to those of amusement meant that the sacrifice exacted was less than one's life. Not only did the Church allow these games, it profited from them as well, since the fines frequently were a source of revenue for the local church.

Aside from beguiling men with their charms, women of the lower and middle classes garnered a measure of independence because they participated in village life on a more equal basis than might be supposed. Here, men and women worked together, in the same enterprises and frequently with the same status. Women were members of guilds, albeit often because they were the daughter or wife of a member, and were sometimes businesswomen in their own right. If there was a shortage of marriageable men (those with land holdings), a woman could take her dowry and strike out on her own, hiring herself out and doing the same work as a man. Although wages for the labor of men was generally higher than those for women, by the late Middle Ages, this disparity was beginning to disappear (Gies and Gies 1978).

Under feudalism, peasant women could also hold and own property. So important was the concept of inheritance through bloodlines that a man marrying a woman with land would take her name to make sure the land remained in the family. This, of course, meant that the new husband frequently acquired the name of the deceased husband. The holding would not pass to the husband on the wife's death, but would remain in her bloodline (Gies and Gies 1978). In 1319, independent women householders comprised four percent of all London taxpayers (Thrupp 1948). Not a large percentage, yet a significant one, if the general view of medieval women as oppressed is to be examined.

Certain industries became the province of women, such as wool spinning and silkmaking, and in certain instances women were able to control their commercial fate. For example, in the mid-fourteenth century, the "silkwomen" of London protested to the mayor about unfair competition from Lombardy, and in 1455 their descendants lobbied for a prohibition on imported silk (which resulted in passage of a restrictive tariff act [O'Faolain and Martines 1973]). Although the life of medieval women was never as independent as that of men, neither was it always a life of domination. The "grit" of women was recognized and commented on in various ways. One lighthearted verse notes:

> Where is the man who has the power and skill
> To stem the torrent of a woman's will?
> For if she will, she will, you may depend on't,
> And if she won't, she won't, so there's an end on't
> Thiselton-Dyer 1903, 139

Aside from the textile industry, the other major area in which women played a commercial role was the food industry. In cities and villages alike, women often were the brewers of ale, and sometimes the "ale conner," or taster, as well. Given the vast quantities of ale drunk, this was an important position; but, as will be seen, it was also one in which the issue of woman's trustworthiness is raised once again.

The Dishonest Alewife

In England, as well as Europe during the Middle Ages, drinking was an important part of life, and ale was both plentiful and cheap. In England, it was the job of the alewife to brew each tavern's ale. When she had prepared a fresh batch, she would put out an alestake as a signal for the ale conner to come and test the brew. If it was up to standard, the tavern opened; if it wasn't, the tavern was closed and the drink confiscated (Bishop 1987). In medieval Scotland, the "Burrow Laws" declared that if an alewife served substandard ale, "contrair to the use and consuetude of the burgh, and is convict thereof, shee sall pay ane unlaw of aucht shillings, or sal suffer the justice of the burgh, that is, shee sall be put upon the cock stool" (Wright 1845, 50). The prevalence of lore on dishonest alewives suggests that giving short measures or concocting foul brew was commonplace; but more important was the opportunity this body of lore provided for satirical expression.

It was assumed that publicans were dishonest and merciless, as many a client found who could not pay for his or her drink. The publican would often seize the patron's clothes to hold until payment was made (Wright 1865). The notion was pervasive that one had to be wary of being cheated in the amount of ale, along with the belief that such behavior deserved public chastisement. A dramatic scene of an alewife being punished for giving short measure is depicted graphically in the Ludlow misericord, right, (damaged). Here however, the woman's fate was more dire than simply being wheeled to the ducking pond.

The alewife is shown wearing the type of peaked headdress condemned by the Church and clutching the false measure in her hand. She is being carried to the "Jaws of Hell" by two feathered demons, one playing bagpipes. The figure with the scroll on the left represents the demon, Tutivillus, reading out a list of her sins, while the scene on the right supporter shows her being thrust into the Jaws of Hell.

In the Ludlow carving appear several indications that the alewife is considered a base person. First, the headdress is of the type the Church considered a "devil's snare" (Coulton 1928, vol. 3)—thought to encourage an unhealthy interest in vanity at the expense of concern for the soul. Second, the bagpipes being played by one of the feathered demons were considered undesirable instruments in the Middle Ages because they were believed to bring out animal passions in people (Grössinger 1989). Finally, the alewife is naked, implying that she is guilty of a sexual sin, for which one punishment was public whipping while naked (White 1974). As Hindley (1979) notes, the local alehouse sometimes doubled as the whorehouse and, unless otherwise in-

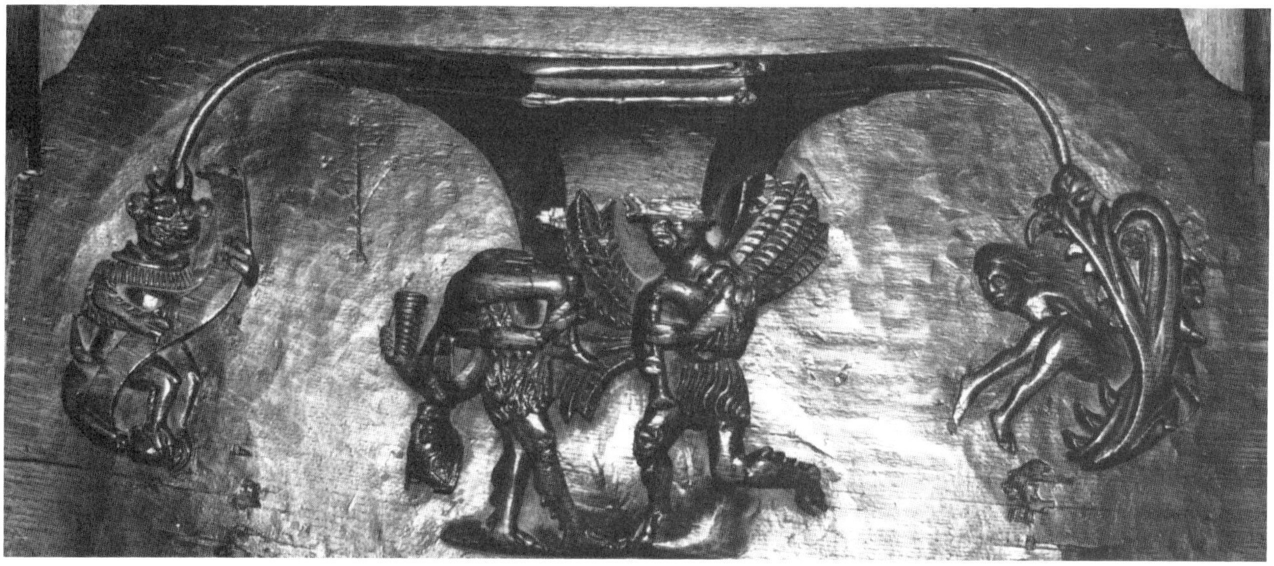

Fate of dishonest alewife. Ludlow (Salop), St. Laurence, c.1425.

formed, one could assume the alewife was approachable. The carver has presented a mean picture, indeed.

Portraying the cheating alewife in the worst light has to do with the importance given food and drink in medieval Europe. It was generally acknowledged that the provision of food and drink was a serious business, one not to be tampered with. Berthold von Regensburg, a thirteenth-century Franciscan monk instructed on the importance of being "true and honest" in the selling of meat and drink:

> for other deceit dealeth only with earthly goods, but this deceit with a man's body, which many would not give for all the goods in the world . . .
> Coulton 1928, 3:59

Admonitions to the contrary, fraud and deceit were commonplace in the Middle Ages, perhaps even more so than at any other period of history. Wright (1865) suggests that, while deception was carried out on a shameless scale and was frequently mentioned in the work of medieval writers, it was difficult to characterize pictorially; thus, it was seldom depicted in other media. This makes the Ludlow carving a rare acknowledgment of a deceptive practice and its consequences.

As in many other areas of medieval thought, one detects an infusion of humor into even this most serious of offenses. The scene of the alewife's punishment in the carving is so elaborate that it must be interpreted as parody through exaggeration. This is supported by other evidence of humor surrounding the figure of the dishonest alewife. For example, the medieval Pageant of the Harrowing of Hell performed by the Cooks and Innkeepers Guild of Chester included a humorous segment at the end of the play in which Christ frees all the tormented souls save one—the alewife. In the end, she makes a detailed confession of her shortcomings and receives an offer of marriage—not from a handsome suitor, but from a demon, to the immense delight of the audience (Hindley 1979; Anderson 1963).

Romanticized Women

The image of women as creatures to be distrusted and controlled had its opposite view in the perception that in certain areas women were good, not only to be revered but sought after. There is an amusing story told of Richard II's wife, Queen Anne, and Geoffrey Chaucer. Queen Anne felt Chaucer's first great work, *Troilus and Griseyde,* judged women too harshly when he suggested that they were less faithful than men. As atonement for his offense, Queen Anne commanded Chaucer to write a retraction (Bevan 1990). He did so the following year (1386), when he produced an installment of what came to be known as *The Legend of the Gode Women*. The work was never completed, however, because, as his disciple, Lydgate, noted, it "encumbered his wits too much to think of so many good women" (Coghill 1966, 11).

Courtly Ladies

The ideal of the sought-after woman reached its height during the fourteenth century, when noble ladies had a specific role to play in the ritual of the vaunted "courtly love" of chivalry. The idea of love for love's sake fired the imagination not only of noble ladies and their knights, but of writers, troubadours, and storytellers everywhere. These romantic tales of the love affairs of noble ladies were avidly listened to by noble and peasant alike.

While it was understood that in the higher social classes, marriage was based on political considerations, it was equally understood that courtly love was based on grand passion that had nothing to do with marriage. In fact, the lady in question was already married. Courtly love was by nature clandestine love, with all the drama of tragic romance. Unlike adultery in the lower classes (which was treated as satire), among the upper classes it was treated as romantic love (Gies and Gies 1978).

Courtly love as it was practiced in the fourteenth century was based on the "art of love" concept that emerged in twelfth-century France, primarily under the patronage of Eleanor of Aquitaine. An avid supporter of troubadours, she brought them to her court in northern France when she married Prince Louis of France, and to England when she married Prince Henry (later Henry II). Like knights, male troubadours also courted their unattainable patronesses. One of the best-known troubadours at Eleanor's French court, Bernart de Ventadorn, arrived after being banished by a noble husband for falling in love with the man's wife (Nichols 1962). Irrepressible until his reputed retirement into a monastery, Bernart went on to woo Eleanor with verses such as the following:

> Lady, love another in public, and me in secret, so that I may have all the benefits and he the fine talk
>
> Bernart 1962, 58

The romantic verse of the troubadours, combined with the ancient writings of Ovid (1959) on the topic of the "art of love," prompted Andreas Capellanus, the chaplain of Eleanor's daughter, to set down formal rules for this game of love. In his *The Art of Courtly Love* (1941), he, like Ovid, championed illicit unions and offered advice on love; but his approach was slightly different from that of Ovid. In this new concept, one followed the rules of the "Court of Love" and knights become soldiers in the army of Cupid. The ladies they chose were recognized to be of a higher station than they and therefore their masters in this court. Whereas Ovid meant his rules as a satire on the learned writings on the topic of love in his day, Andreas took his rules (and himself) quite seriously, often boasting of his success with nuns (Parry 1941).

In Ovid's writings, the instructions have a practical stamp. They range from winning a woman to being cured from losing one. Ovid believed, for example, that only men with moderate amounts of money needed to be coached in the art of love; men with large amounts of money could have any woman they desired. He also had advice for women on winning and retaining a man's affection:

> Dress well, but do not over-dress, smell sweet; attend to your teeth; see that your legs are not hairy . . . above all, if you want to keep your good looks, keep your temper . . .
>
> xx

Once the affair was winding down, Ovid had many suggestions for falling *out* of love, among them:

> So far as you can, depreciate the qualities of your mistress and warp your own judgment. . . . If she's plump, say she's stodgy. . . . If she's slim, say she's a skeleton. . . . If she has no voice, urge her to sing. . . . If she can't play a note, beg her to play. . . .
>
> 201–202

Available in both Latin and the vernacular (Parry 1941), Ovid's work was very popular in both France and England in the twelfth and thirteenth centuries. While it is certain that his work was the foundation for the courtly love of the Middle Ages, one major divergence occurred. For Ovid, love was illicit and sensual; for Andreas and others in the Middle Ages, love was illicit and romantic. This is shown in the contrast between the instructions proffered by Ovid above and those by Andreas below:

> When she was convinced of the complete faithfulness of this knight and understood how boldly he had striven, she rewarded him with her love. Then she called together a court of a great many ladies and knights and laid before them these rules of Love, and bade every lover keep them faithfully under threat of punishment by the King of Love.
>
> 1941, 186

In practice, some knights were less eager to enter into a lifetime of adoring one unobtainable woman and chose instead to promise fealty to several ladies in order to extract favors from them through lovely words of undying love and devotion (Tuchman 1978), something of which Ovid would have heartily approved.

The theme of courtly love was replayed several times, fittingly, in the misericords using the popular romance story that, if not written for her, was certainly inspired by Eleanor of Aquitaine—the story of Tristan and Iseult. The story was thought to have been written by Thomas of Britain for Eleanor of Aquitaine in the late twelfth century (Parry 1941). The story was so popular and so well circulated that eventually it became part of the Arthurian legend (Bellingham 1990).

Although the story has several versions, the main theme is that Tristan falls in love with Isuelt as he escorts her to Cornwall to marry

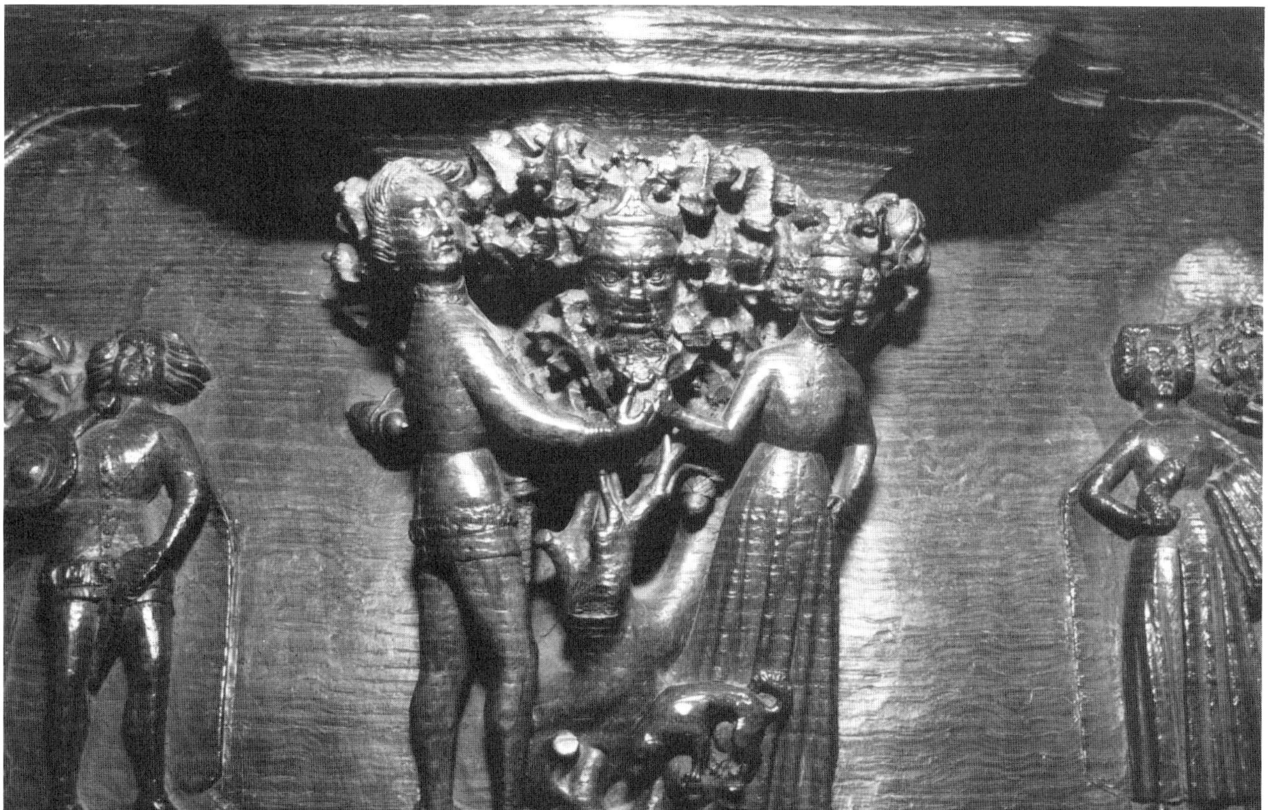

Tristan & Iseult. Chester (Cheshire), The Cathedral, c.1380.

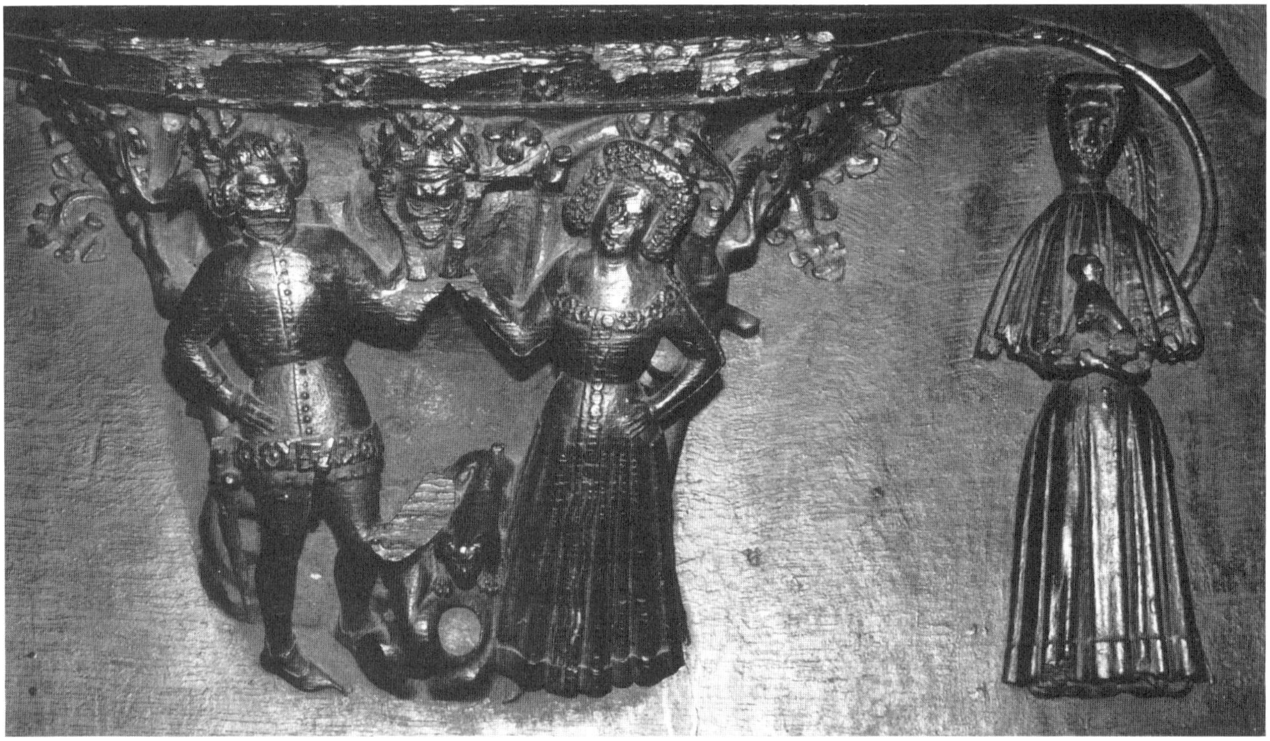

Tristan & Iseult. Lincoln (Lincs), The Minster, 1370.

King Mark. To keep King Mark from knowing that Iseult is no longer a virgin, Tristan persuades the lady-in-waiting to slip into the marital bed on the first night. Thereafter, there are a series of adventures—arranged meetings and a decision to part; in the end, Isuelt impales herself on Tristan's sword as he lies dying so that they can be united in death.[1]

The segment of the story that the misericord carvers and other artists most often chose to illustrate is the point at which King Mark, who has been informed by Tristan's enemies at court, finds the lovers at their usual meeting place and has them seized. The scene always includes trees and a pond because Tristan would hide in a tree while waiting for Isuelt. When she arrived he would throw twigs or leaves into the pond as a signal that he was there. For the denouement, King Mark's men, hid him behind another tree to observe the lovers. In the carvings King Mark has been placed in Tristan's hiding place in the tree and is always shown as a head among the tree branches. In the Chester misericord the left supporter represents one of King Mark's men and the right, Iseult's lady-in-waiting standing guard. In the Lincoln carving, King Mark's head can be seen, but the tree has been damaged. A lady-in-waiting is on the right supporter.

The sympathy generated for such lovers was displayed in various works. Dante (1954), for example, expressed his commiseration for ill-fated lovers by assigning them a relatively mild punishment in his *Inferno*. Here, the lovers are whirled about and buffeted by winds, much as they were tossed about by passion in life. In one passage, the poet expresses his pity for them to Virgil.

The widespread popularity of these romantic visions of courtly love was fueled by the increasing number of women in an affluent leisure class that formed an audience eager for this new type of literature (Gies and Gies 1978). That this class of women would find these stories intriguing is not surprising; that they were enjoyed by the working class as well is more interesting, given the impression that the ruling and working classes had little in common. However, good tales were a staple of medieval culture, on all levels. In addition, these particular tales of courtly love provided a welcome, "wacky" view of the ruling class to bemuse ordinary citizens.

Righteous Virgins

Virginity in the Middle Ages was regarded as an unnatural state calling for special treatment. In true either-or fashion, if a woman chose to remain a virgin, she tended to be viewed as either in need of punishment or worthy of veneration. Real-life women, such as those who died unmarried, were doomed for all eternity. Other women who chose chastity, either as daughters of the Church or for other reasons, were granted not only respect but frequently, superhuman powers which destined them for sainthood. While there are many legends of female saints, only two examples are given here, St. Margaret of Antioch and St. Werburge of Chester.

The legend of St. Margaret of Antioch tells of her great beauty, which captured the heart of the pagan governor of Antioch. When he met her in a field one day and fell in love with her, he felt he was bestowing the greatest honor upon her by proposing marriage—if she would renounce her Christian faith. Her prompt rejection so enraged him that he had her seized and thrown into a dungeon. Here, she was repeatedly tortured but still she refused the governor's offer. After a while, a devil in the form of a dragon appeared before her to scare her into renouncing her virtuous decision. In one version of the story, she simply holds up her crucifix and the dragon is vanquished; in another, she resists temptation and the dragon swallows her. Margaret, however, has the might of righteousness on her side. When she makes the sign of the cross the dragon bursts open and she is free (Hogarth 1979). Or, as one fourteenth-century chronicler described it, the cross swelled:

> And whan hyr cros in his mouth dede encrees,
> He brast on two, and she scapyd harmless.
>
> Bokenham 1938, 20

Not only did her action gain her sainthood, but appropriately, she became the patron saint of women in childbirth. According to *The Golden Legend* (Jacobus 1948), Margaret asked that whenever a woman in childbirth called her name, her child be delivered without harm. When a voice from Heaven told her that her prayer would be granted, she called on the executioner to draw his sword so that she might receive the "crown of martyrdom."

The tale of Margaret's valor was present from early times in England. There are written versions of it from the eleventh to fourteenth centuries, in both English and Latin (Lucie-Smith 1981). Another measure of her

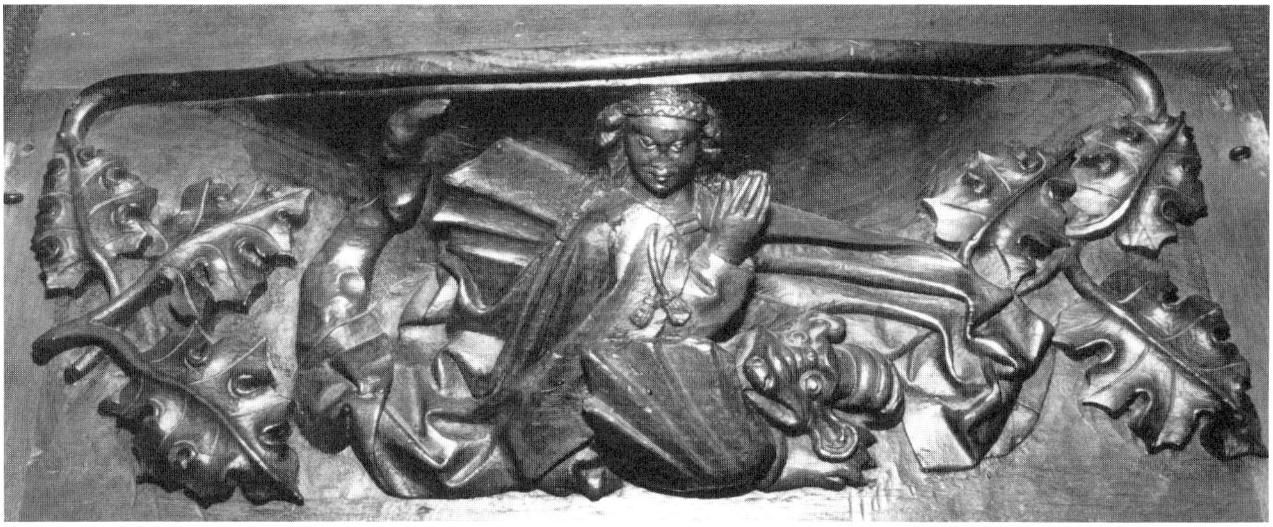

St. Margaret. Sherborne (Dorset), The Abbey, 1436.

popularity is evident in the 261 English churches dedicated to her (Laird 1986). The Sherborne carver shows Margaret kneeling in prayer at the moment when the dragon bursts open and she is freed. The dragon's wings are on either side of her and a somewhat flattened dragon head lies before her.

Another woman destined for sainthood for her righteous stand against sin was the compassionate St. Werburge of Chester. The theme of the story is the sin involved in the theft and killing of a goose, and St. Werburge's miraculous response. As the story goes, Werburge, an abbess in Chester in the seventh century, was asked to remove some hungry wild geese from the surrounding fields. She rounded them up and put them in an enclosure to be released later. When Werburge returned to the pen, she found that one was missing. The other geese told her that one of her servants had stolen the goose and killed it for his dinner:

> . . . The goose that was taken/and stollen afore away,
> Was rosted and eten/the same nyght, doubtless;
> So whan it was asked/for upon the other day,
> The bare bones were brough(t)/afor this lady, veray;
> And there by the vertue/of her benedyccon
> The byrde was restaured/and flewe away full soone
>
> Bradshaw 1887, 99

The other geese flew away as well, leaving the crops unmolested. The servant learned a moral lesson, and Werburge went on to become a saint.

This story was reenacted in the carving below. On the left supporter St. Werburge and her servant are gathering the troublesome geese into a pen. On the right, the penitent servant begs forgiveness, and in the center the servant has brought the dead goose to St. Werburge where she restores it to life. It rises to join the rest of the flock which is circling overhead.

The saints were acknowledged for their goodness and compassion, and patron saints, both male and female, were appealed to for help in their specific areas. If one were in childbirth, one appealed to St. Margaret; if one's crops were endangered, one appealed to St. Werburge, and so on. But it was not until the late Middle Ages that the people con-

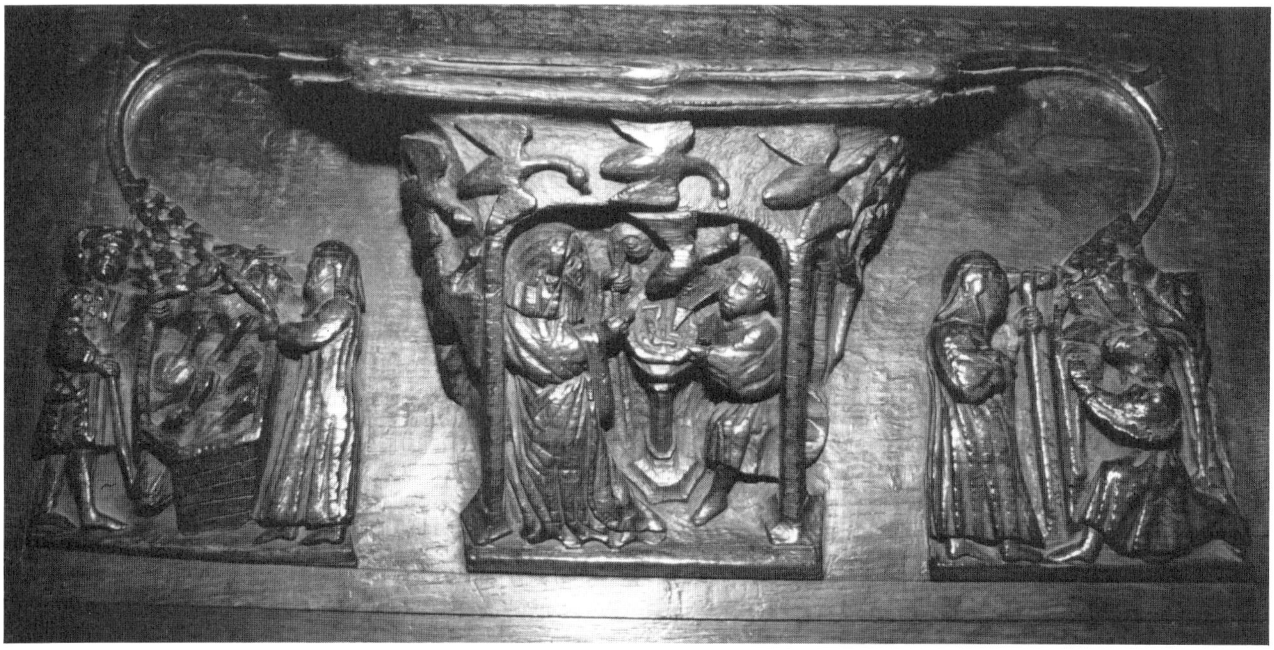

St. Werburge. Chester (Cheshire), The Cathedral, c.1380.

structed one figure who could be appealed to for anything and everything. It was for this figure that feelings of deep veneration were reserved. That figure was female, and it was the Virgin Mary.

The Greatest Enticer: Our Lady

By far the most important female figure during the Middle Ages was the Virgin Mary. So universal was her appeal that her many followers have been described as a cult (Harthan 1978; Tuchman 1978; Penn 1933). Although the Church in general had lost the confidence of the people during the late Middle Ages, confidence in the Virgin grew. In particular, there was a growing belief that the Virgin could, and would, intercede on anyone's behalf regardless of his or her station or the particular sin involved. It was firmly believed that, while Mary would be kind to all, the ones she loved most were the poor, the disreputable, and the humble—in other words, those most in need of protection.

The most interesting thing about the cult of the Virgin was its ability to wrest the sanctified, passive image of Mary from the Church to create a Mary of unlimited power and, most important, a woman with a mission: the protection of her people. The image created by her following was not the placid, tranquil otherworldly figure of the Church but one of a woman whose traits encompassed the more human characteristics of compassion, pettiness, vindictiveness, jealousy, and humor. She was, in essence, created in response to the needs of the people, by the people.

It is not clear exactly why the cult of the Virgin became, and remains, so immensely popular. The foundation for special recognition may have been laid as early as the tenth century when a short service in her honor was made part of the Breviary (text of the Divine Office; Harthan 1978). In the thirteenth century, this section of the Breviary, the "Little Office of Our Lady" became detached and was often used as the basic text in Books of Hours, personal prayerbooks produced for the laity. A major factor in the growth of the cult of the Virgin was the acceleration in the production of these Books of Hours. This enterprise was transferred from the Church to the lay community, changing both the nature and the speed of production. The demand for this type of devotional material increased from the thirteenth to the fifteenth century, primarily because it was written in the vernacular rather than Latin, thus greatly increasing its appeal. This change in the language of the Books of Hours owes almost everything to the efforts of noble medieval laywomen who commissioned such books to be written in the vernacular.

Restricted by the Church from learning Latin, many noblewomen in the Middle Ages still had a desire to be educated as well as an obligation to educate their children. One way to satisfy the desire for self-education and fulfill their teaching obligation was to commission books to be translated into the vernacular for their use. There are accounts of laywomen book owners starting in the twelfth century and increasing especially in the fourteenth and fifteenth centuries (Bell 1989). The women commissioned devotional works and popular works alike. The Books of Hours represented an avenue to devotional literature denied to laypeople by the Church's adherence to works in Latin, a language not understood by most people outside the Church. In their insistence on access to devotional and literary works, laywomen not only helped increase literacy but, in the case of the Virgin, aided in the creation of a new image of Our Lady as an accessible figure.

The Books of Hours were more than books of piety—they were produced to the individual's specifications, with choices made about both the text and the artwork in the margins. In the text, for example, the owner could choose between the Hours of the Cross, the Hours of Saint Louis, the Hours of the Virgin, and so on. Many laywomen chose the Hours of the Virgin and, in doing so, contributed to her growing cult status.

The decorated margins of these manuscripts were influential in depicting women in new ways, especially as appreciators of books. In many margins, the owner was shown reading; and in others, the Virgin Mary was shown reading a book. There were, for example, manuscripts that included books in the Annunciation scene; scenes where the Virgin Mary is shown reading as midwives prepare her for childbirth; scenes where the Virgin is relaxing with a book after childbirth. In one of the most charming scenes, the Virgin is shown sitting on a donkey reading while Joseph carries the baby during their flight into Egypt (Bell 1989).

The image of women as readers is the topic of the Worcester carving below. The source of

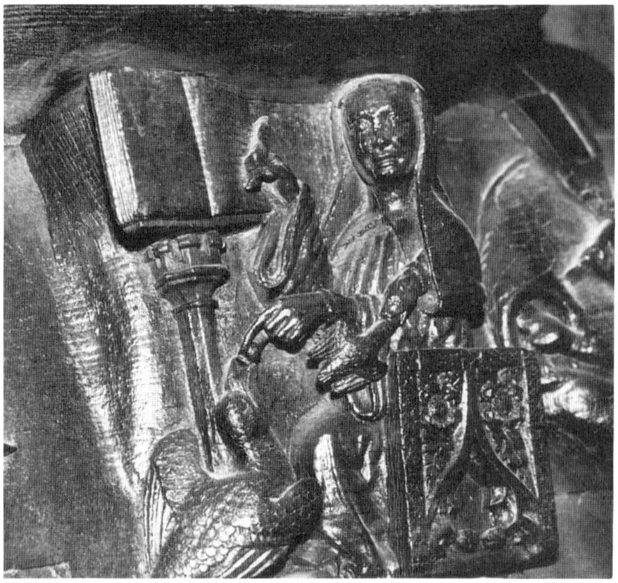

Woman reading. Worcester (Herefs & Worcs), The Cathedral, late fourteenth century.

the carving is unknown but is assumed to be based on a Book of Hours (Anderson 1969). Undoubtedly, it was meant to represent the female owner.

Books of Hours were so widespread that they constitute the single, largest remaining type of illuminated manuscript (Harthan 1978). Though not solely the property of women, they were being commisioned by both men and women by the fourteenth and fifteenth centuries, and every noble and member of the upper class owned one. These books were so prized that they were not only used to teach young girls how to read, but became a standard gift to brides (Bell 1989).

In the misericords, the popularity of the Books of Hours based on the life of the Virgin is recorded in the numerous carvings depicting scenes from the "Little Office of Our Lady," the most popular being the Coronation. In the Chester carving below she is shown

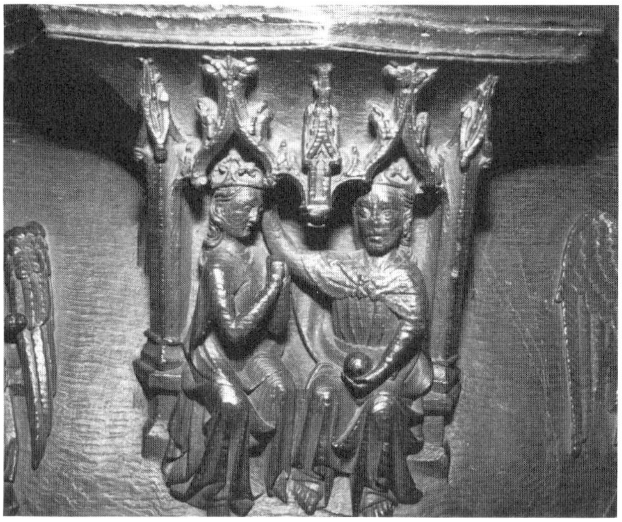

Coronation of Virgin. Chester (Cheshire), The Cathedral, c.1380.

with Christ placing the crown on her head; in the Carlisle misericord the angels crown her. The crown confers on her the status of Queen of Heaven in both carvings, but an additional feature is added in the Carlisle carving. Difficult to see, the angels also hold a branch of mistletoe in front of the crown, which confers on her the status of Empress of Hell. In combination, the two symbols make her Lady of All the World (Grundy 1991); it is this vision that

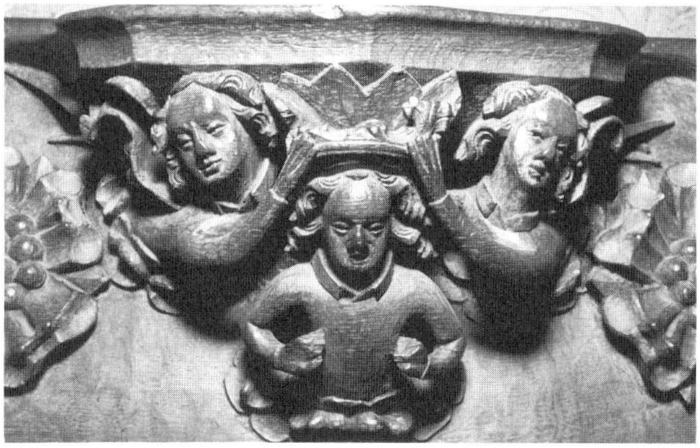

Coronation of Virgin. Carlisle (Cumbria), The Cathedral, 1399–1413.

was constructed by, and preferred by, the citizenry of the late Middle Ages.

It has been suggested that these Books of Hours contributed to the growing cult of the Virgin in the thirteenth century because this mystical, idealized version of womanhood fit so well with chivalric ideology (Warner 1976). This, however, does not give due credit to the persistence and influence of medieval laywomen in the production of Books of Hours based on the life of the Virgin. Nor does it explain the growth of the cult among the nontitled citizens who, overall, derided the ideals of chivalry. Anderson (1955) makes the distinction between the theological community that exalted the transcendent Virgin and the "simple folk" who were more interested in her earthly life—an explanation that is both too dismissive and too simple. Ordinary people needed an intercessor, and they undertook the audacious act of constructing one.

Although no miracles were attributed to the Virgin during her lifetime, by the eleventh century, word of the Virgin's miracles was being passed around, in both theological and lay communities. By the fourteenth century, the cult of the Virgin had reached mythic proportions, fueled by the retelling of her miracles. The Mary legends include several miracles associated with the clergy and the nobility, but it was ordinary people who created most of the legends and kept them alive. As Coulton (1923) points out, monks recorded the Mary legends made up by people, but only after the stories had "made their mark"—in other words, after they had passed into the realm of folklore. This reinforcement of the tales by the clergy further legitimized and expanded Mary's cult status. Shrines devoted to the Virgin each developed their own set of miracles (Powers 1928); in the process, a number of legends that had been attached to other saints were transferred retroactively to Mary after she had achieved cult status.

In France during the fourteenth century, an illuminated manuscript, *Miracles de Nostre Dame par Personnages,* appeared which contained forty miracles supposedly performed by the Virgin. Neither the author of the miracles nor the illuminator is known, but the manuscript was the property of a guild somewhere in northern France. It is thought likely that, between about 1345 and 1380, the guild performed plays based on the miracles in the manuscript once or twice a year and that this collection of miracles formed the basis for a number of scenes in miracle plays, in France and elsewhere, from that point on (Penn 1933).

Unlike the increasingly bawdy and sensational mystery plays that were also popular, miracle plays strove for greater realism and more romantic visions. The underlying theme, however, was that the Virgin would respond to a plea for help, either by suggesting a solution or by consoling the stricken supplicant.

In conjunction with the popularity and spread of Books of Hours based on the Virgin's life, the increasing reliance on the Virgin's presumed power also had to do with superstition and with events that led to a perception of dire need. It was felt that a benevolent force was required to counteract conditions that appeared to be uncontrollable. These conditions became especially apparent in the fourteenth century. Even before that time, people had been prone to view anything different as an ill omen—for example, the birth of deformed animals or a comet in the sky. Because they were unexplainable, these events were assumed to be warnings from some mystical being (Evans 1896). Events occurring in the fourteenth century, however, eclipsed the standard worries and brought forth large-scale panic about the wrath of God.

In the early fourteenth century, several situations created difficult times for the people of England: overpopulation, overcultivation of the land, famine, flooding which ruined crops, and a loss of jobs due to a decrease in industrial production (Gillingham 1992; Bishop 1987; Tuchman 1978). Recovery began in the 1320s, but it was barely underway before the population was again felled by disaster. The plague (later to referred to as the "Black Death"), which began in England in 1348 and recurred three more times between then and 1377, was devastating. The first outbreak (1348–49) was by far the most destructive of human life, with estimates of the loss of human life placed between 40 and 50 percent of the total population (Hatcher 1977). Although accounts vary as to the exact number killed, by any calculation it was significant. In a country still predominantly agrarian, the loss of laborers to harvest the crops was overwhelming—as was the loss of trained craftsmen, holy men, and citizens from every segment of the social order. It simply was not possible to carry on with life as before; the gaps in the social fabric were too great.

Not knowing what caused the plague led to various explanations, such as the belief that Jews had poisoned the water, thus setting off a period of persecution of the Jews (Tuchman 1978). The most prevalent belief about the plague, however, was that it was caused by the wrath of God. People felt they were being punished—for what, they did not know—and they struggled with how to reverse the scorn of God in a growing spirit of pessimism:

> God is deaf now-a-days and deigneth not to hear us, And prayers have no power the Plague to stay
> Briggs 1983, 86

Hostility toward the clergy became even more pronounced after the Black Death. Even though people were afraid not to believe in the teachings of the Church, they found it increasingly difficult to support the clergy. In Worcester in 1349, citizens broke down the gates of the Priory of St. Mary and chased the Prior with bows and arrows. In Yeovil that same year, the Bishop of Bath and Wells was besieged as he held a thanksgiving service for the cessation of the plague. He and the congregation were trapped in the church until help came the next day (Tuchman 1978). This growing hostility would prove fatal in the sixteenth century, when Henry VIII decided to dissolve the monasteries. As Butler and Given-Wilson (1979, 119) note, the most surprising thing about the Dissolution was that "it met so little hostility or obstruction."

After the Black Death, the increasing popularity of the Virgin was expressed in a number of paintings showing her with her cloak open, protecting her chosen people. It was said that the clerics and laymen who worked with the bodies during the pestilence prayed to her. Frequently during this time, the paintings of the Virgin with her cloak outspread included figures wearing the cloaks and hoods that were the costume of the people who worked with the bodies (Warner 1976).

This tendency to see a preference on the part of the Virgin for certain classes of people was common, as was the theme of the spreading cloak under which to gather those she held most dear. This symbolism pervaded European art; the fresco from Parma and the misericord from Gayton are two lovely examples.

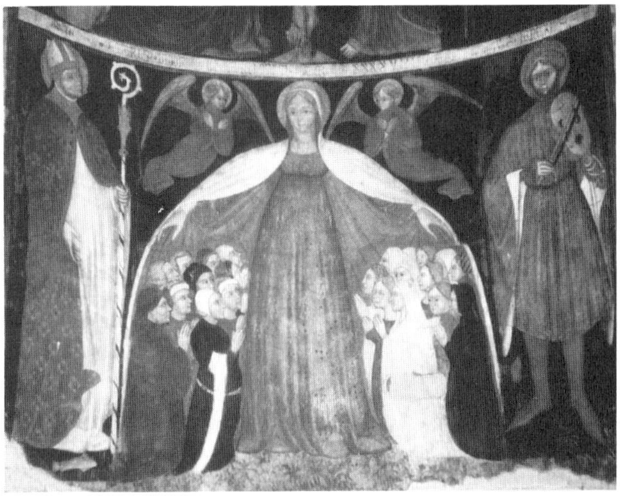

Virgin protecting souls. Parma (Italy), Baptistry, thirteenth century.

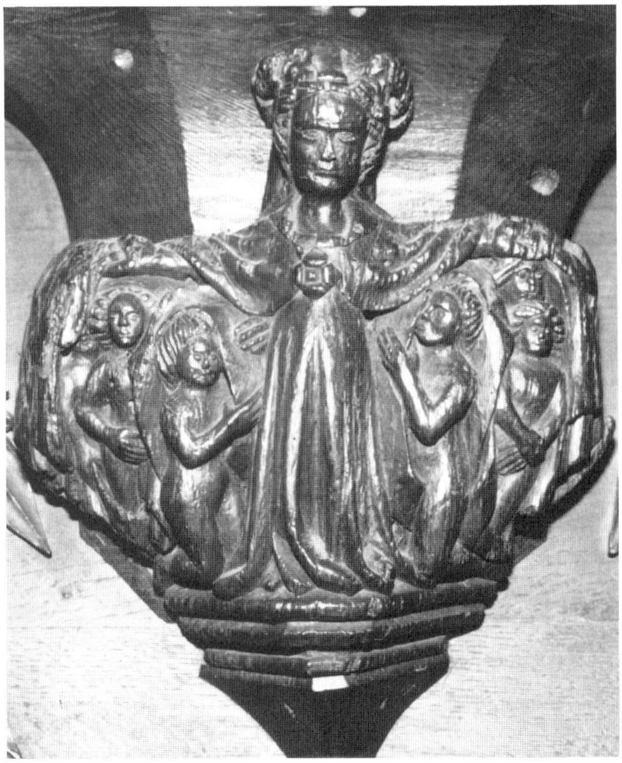

Virgin protecting souls. Gayton (Northants), St. Mary, fifteenth century.

The extreme veneration of the Virgin not only gave the people hope, but constituted a populist revolt on the part of the people against the Church. By their actions, the citizens challenged one of the most basic Christian beliefs of the time—that one's salvation depended solely on one's "good works."

The turning away from the clergy to the Virgin denied the principle of good works, substituting instead the belief that faith was more powerful; this sentiment would become the cornerstone of the Protestant Reformation. The foundation of the Mary cult was that if one simply had faith in the Virgin and never wavered, she would ensure the salvation of one's soul. This belief, and the stories that grew up to verify it, made it possible for an ordinary person to sidestep both the clergy and the need for good works. Even if one were a scoundrel, as many reported miracles attest, Our Lady would help—as long as the scoundrel never forgot to give the Virgin her due. Above all else, she demanded loyalty.

A repetitive theme in the Mary miracles, both written and transferred by word of mouth, was the idea that the Devil can be cheated and that Mary took great delight in snatching "her sinners'" souls from him—sometimes to the chagrin of the living. In one fifteenth-century collection of miracles (Herolt 1928), a tale is told of an immoral clerk who died and was buried in a ditch outside the church. Because during his lifetime he never forgot to kneel and weep before her image, the Virgin threatened awful vengeance on the clergy if they did not immediately dig him up and put him in the choicest part of the cemetery. He may have been a sinner, she is reputed to have said, but he was *her* sinner.

In another miracle, a thief never forgot to say an Ave to Mary before embarking on his thievery. When he was caught and sentenced to the gallows, it was not possible to execute him because the Virgin stood beneath the gallows for three nights, holding his feet up with her white hands (Power 1928).

In some legends, Mary played the coquette, as she did when a knight had had his amorous entreaties to his master's wife rebuffed and prayed to the Virgin for help. When he left the church, she was holding his horse and appeared to him as an exceedingly beautiful woman. Mary asked if her appearance pleased him and if he would like to have her for a bride. When he responded enthusiastically, she said that she would be his wife and beckoned him to kiss her, saying, "Now are our nuptials begun, and on such and such a day they shall be completed in the presence of my Son." The knight, realizing at last who she was, was forever after relieved of the longing for his master's wife (Caesarius 1929, 1:500). Or she would be sympathetic to acts of passion. There is a famous story of Beatrice the Sacristan in which the nun, Beatrice, ran away with her lover. When she finally returned to the convent, she was surprised to find that the Virgin had filled in for her as Sacristan for the 15 years of her absence (1:503). On the other hand, a disapproving Mary could be ruthless. She is reported to have "smote" a woman on the jaw for agreeing to meet a clerk after church. The blow is said to have cured the woman of her desire (1:500).

At other times, Mary became the great Earth Mother figure. Medieval mothers were said to approach her not just with pleas, but as mother-to-mother with demands that she make things right. Sometimes they would remove her child until she made sure their own lost sons and daughters were returned (Power 1928).

One of the more amusing stories about the Virgin's love of soldiers and a good battle is told by a chronicler of the life of St. Louis. The chronicler speaks of a soldier in Syria who was possessed by the Devil and subsequently taken to one of the shrines to Our Lady to be cured. Upon reaching the shrine and asking for help, the Devil responded: "Our Lady is not here, she is in Egypt, helping the king of France and the Christians who will come to land this day. . . ." (Power 1928, xxi). Our Lady was present on every battlefield.

The threat presented by the cult of the Virgin was that Mary would replace Christ as the most revered figure in Christendom, a situation the Church was not willing to tolerate. It was not until the last session of the Council of Trent (1562–63), however, that the "Madonna of Mercy" was officially proclaimed contrary to Church doctrine and all imagery of the Virgin as a protector or intercessor banned (Warner 1976). Church doctrine and private beliefs, however, don't always coincide; so the Virgin has held her niche as the people's intercessor far beyond the sixteenth century. The lure of a figure who could not only forgive anything but was willing to exchange the saving of one's soul for loyalty, made her dear to the hearts of the people as the greatest female enticer of all.

The carvers recorded all the feelings medieval men had about women. Some were accurate, some were defamatory, and some were plain wishful thinking. They left us a record of the past that confirms: whatever else might be said of him, the medieval man spent a great deal of time thinking about women.

3
Men and Challenges—Up to the Test

They have Hercules of monsters conquering;
  Huge great giants, in a forest, fighting
With lions, bears, wolves, apes, foxes, and grayes,
  —Oh, these be wondrous frayes!
Joseph Strutt, *Sports and Pastimes of the People of England*, 1810)

THE IMAGES GENERATED IN ANCIENT TIMES ABOUT the character and nature of women were complemented by an equally compelling view of men. As with the female gender, this view was brought forward to medieval times in somewhat altered form to accommodate the contemporary milieu. Whereas the underlying question in evaluating women was, "Is she trustworthy?" the basic question in assessing men was, "Is he strong?"

The need for strength was based on the perception that the physical world was always unsafe—not just physically unsafe but spiritually unsafe. Women were one problem for medieval man in the quest to retain control of his sanity and his soul, but other treacherous forces also had to be dealt with on a daily basis. In an era when Christian dogma had given corporeal form to the Devil and his demons, men were acutely aware that they were surrounded by temptations and threats. Just as there was an unquestioning belief in the ability of Christ, the Virgin, and the saints to perform miracles, so too was there an unhesitating faith in the ability of the Devil to destroy.

The medieval Church was not always successful in replacing pagan beliefs with Christian doctrine; but, in the case of the Devil, the Church was able to blend old superstitions into a new embodiment of evil that found ready acceptance. There was a long-standing reception to the idea that humans existed in one world, but were influenced by coexisting spirits in worlds above and below.[1] Thus, the Church's warnings about spiritual danger everywhere reinforced old notions and were accepted with the proper alarm. Men braced themselves for the tests at hand.

The model for the idealized medieval strong man emerged very early, but the first written record comes from the Sumerian epic, *Gilgamesh*. Although it had an earlier oral tradition, the epic was written about 3000 B.C. in cuneiform on stone tablets and for the next two thousand years was incorporated into subsequent civilizations with very little alteration (Temple 1991; *Gilgamesh* 1984). This epic contained two of the most important elements woven into medieval man's image of the ideal male: (1) heroes, in this instance, Gilgamesh the King and his friend, Enkidu, who possess supernatural strength; and (2) evil, as represented by supernaturally strong beasts. Both elements were given enormous weight in subsequent centuries.

Gilgamesh became the model for the Greek Hercules, the Christian Samson, and the medieval hero, St. George. Enkidu, whose strength was said to derive from his being part man/part animal, was the original "wild man" character and was the model for the Hebrew Ishmael and the British Celtic figures of Myrddin and Merlin. In the Middle Ages, the wild man remained a tantalizing, sometimes curious, sometimes romanticized figure who eventually became institutionalized as a stock character in medieval celebrations. Ferocious beasts of various types continued to represent evil in the ongoing battle between good and evil throughout the medieval era.

Most importantly, however, the *Gilgamesh* epic set the standard from ancient times on for one of the most admired ways to measure male strength. The ultimate test was to be a battle between an individual man and a beast of overwhelming strength. The admiration for this type of contest and its enduring acceptance as the standard for male strength is evident in the nineteenth-century quotation given at the beginning of this chapter. The measure of male mettle was not just in being victorious in battle, but in being victorious in a particular kind of battle, against a beast deemed so ferocious that to be victorious would transform it into a battle between giants. In the epic of *Gilgamesh*, a lesson about the finiteness of life is learned, but in the late Middle Ages this lesson was far less important than the image of man as equal to the tests of strength to which he was put.

In the late Middle Ages, there was a related development of another type of battle. In this struggle, the figure of the warrior-knight emerges and is transformed over time into the performing knight. It could be said that the battles with ferocious beasts descend from the ancient, pagan tradition and the battles of the knight from the Christian tradition; in both, the strength of the individual man is tested. The purpose of the test changes, however. In one, the person fights for his soul, in the other for honor—although it could be said that in both, the real struggle is for personal glory.

The perceived necessity for men to do battle with the Devil in his beastly disguises allowed an opportunity for exaggeration to be elevated to an art form as the medieval carver captured the dreams, and the embellishments, of every man in his carved versions of the heroic battles with the beasts. The carver was aided in this endeavor, perhaps unwittingly, by the Church when it gave the Devil new guises with which to threaten men, making heroic battles necessary. Both the Church and the carvers made important contributions to keeping the tradition of the ancient contest between man and beast alive.

Fabulous Battles

In *Gilgamesh*, the evil beasts are gods and are described in appropriately terrifying ways. Two gods were killed by Gilgamesh and Enkidu. The power of the first god, Huwawa, is described:

> Huwawa—his roaring is the Great Flood,
> His mouth is fire, his breath is death!
> Temple 1991, 30

And the second:

> With the snort of the Bull of Heaven, pits were opened,
> And a hundred young men of Uruk fell into them.
> With his second snort, pits were opened,
> And two hundred young men of Uruk fell into them.
> 65

In Gilgamesh's time, the beasts' strength came from the fact that they were gods. In medieval times, Christianity changed beastly gods to beastly demons, and their strength derived from the supernatural power of the netherworld. The Church's part in preserving and adapting the need to test men against beasts occurred when it took the ancient bestiaries[2] and assigned allegorical moral meanings to what originally were descriptions of the existing natural world. Suddenly, beasts were not simply beasts, but were cast, in Christian terms, as symbols of good or evil. The bestiaries included both mythical and real beasts, although that distinction was not made at the time, and the characteristics of many of the animals were linked to the attributes of the Devil. In this intellectual framework, the Devil was perceived of as a corporeal, ubiquitous being who took on numerous disguises, thus providing many encounters to test both the spiritual and physical strength of men.

A slight alteration in purpose, one promoted by the Church in the late Middle Ages, was the idea that the battle between good and evil was a struggle to save one's soul. This is a shift in focus from the purpose of the battle in the *Gilgamesh* epic. Gilgamesh and Enkidu also fought against evil, but it was to increase their own stature. Here we have another area where it is difficult to judge how successful the Church was in gaining acceptance of its interpretation. Although men in the Middle Ages may have, in theory, believed that they were engaged in soul-saving contests, indications are that they also shared a desire for personal glory. Despite the intent of the Church, the misericords indicate that the image of physical superiority was just as important to medieval men as it had been to their ancient counterparts.

Popular travelers' tales reinforced Church warnings about the existence of dangerous beasts, along with the notion that men could win contests with these beasts. There were numerous, widespread accounts of men being confronted by, and doing battle with, all types of exotic animals. Dragons, for example, were a staple of medieval lore, and battles with them were legendary.

Yet it was the medieval carver who contributed the most intriguing aspect of the legacy of the ancient battle. Building on ancient lore, Church teachings, and current beliefs, the carver provided a tantalizing visual image of the battle, particularly in his renderings of the fabulous beasts. In addition, carvers contributed an alteration of their own to the ancient tradition. A process of democratization took place in the misericord carvings as the carvers introduced a new element. They suggested that while the most exciting battles might take place between heroic men and beasts, it was not only heroes who fought these battles; ordinary men were subject to the same tests. It is in this area, and in the visual construction of fabulous beasts, that the finest examples of exaggeration in carving occur.

The following examples are typical of the genre. The first shows a monstrous beast atop a man armed only with a small ax with which

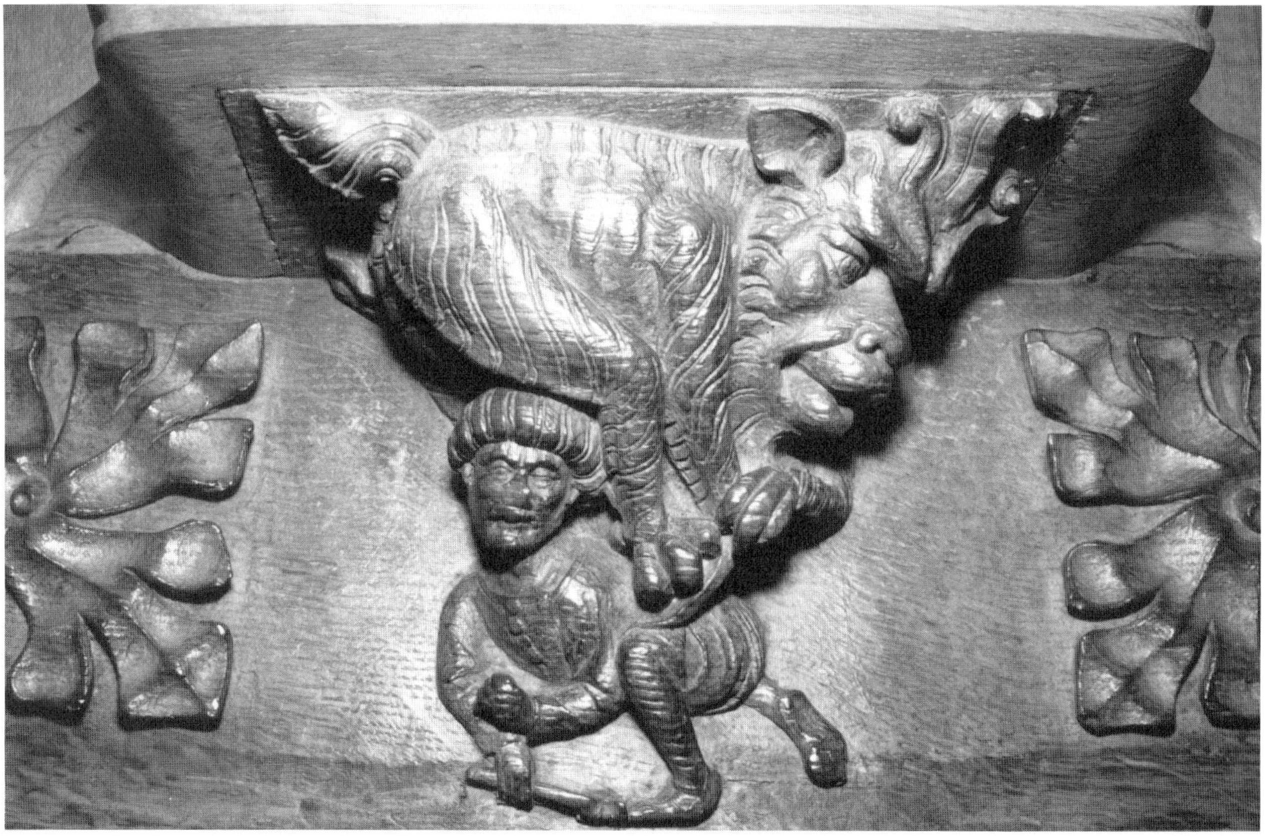

Monster seizing man. Oxford (Oxon), New College Chapel, late fourteenth century.

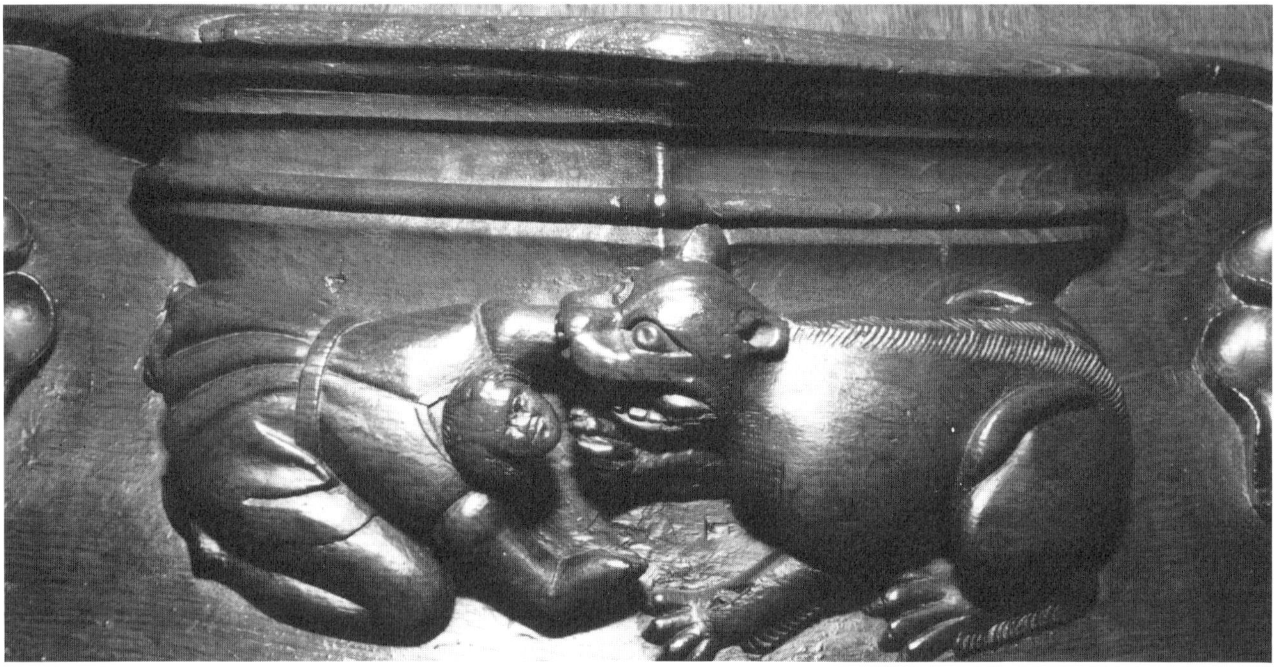

Man fighting beast. Windsor (Berks), St. George's Chapel, 1477–83.

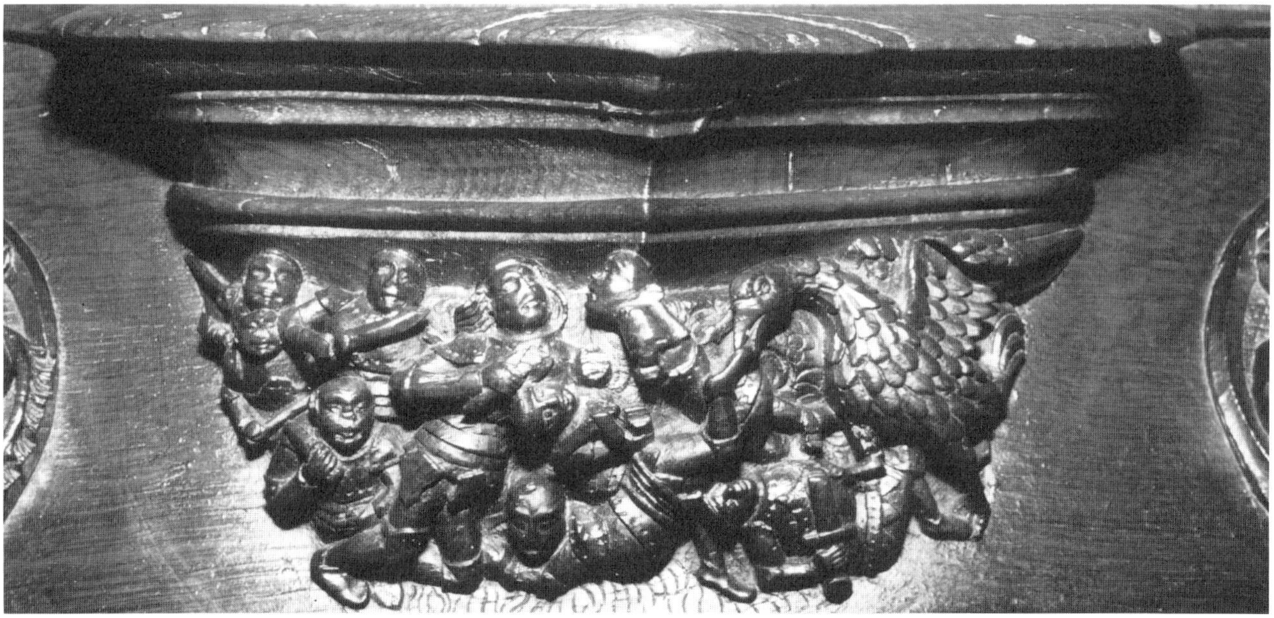

Men fighting bird. Windsor (Berks), St. George's Chapel, 1477–83.

to defend himself. In the second, the man is unarmed (or about to be, literally) and facing a much larger beast. In these battles of overwhelming odds, the carver presents the medieval equivalent of the "fish story."

In the third example, the story expands to include eight men fighting against an enormous bird. The warriors apparently have been unable to subdue the bird and are in disarray. The bird holds one warrior down with his claw while grasping the foot of another in its beak. The outcome presents a far more comic image than the one-on-one scenes, but it stays true to exaggerating the size of the beast and, hence, the threat. In this carving, however, satire was given the upper hand as a band of seemingly clumsy men wrestle with the monstrous bird. In the previous two carvings where the outcome is not shown, it is possible to believe that the men were victorious against the odds. In the last carving, it is doubtful that any of these men will have a flattering tale of victory to tell. The bird in the carving was merely one of several mythical bird-beasts medieval man was likely to encounter. Far more terrifying was the notorious griffin.

Griffins

Presumably due to its surly nature, the griffin was one of the few animals in the bestiaries to have escaped assignment of a Christian moralization to its characteristics. Griffins were believed to possess enormous strength because they were said to be the offspring of a lion and an eagle, two of the strongest creatures known. Sometimes a predatory beast and sometimes a protective figure, the griffin was known long before medieval times; by the late Middle Ages, however, griffins were characterized by two major traits: their reputed hostility toward men, accompanied by a desire to dismember them; and their practice of carrying off live creatures to their nests (Payne 1990). The griffin showed no mercy, finding an animal, infant or man equally appetizing. In the carving below, the griffin has just snared a swaddled baby.

One of the finest examples of the bravery of

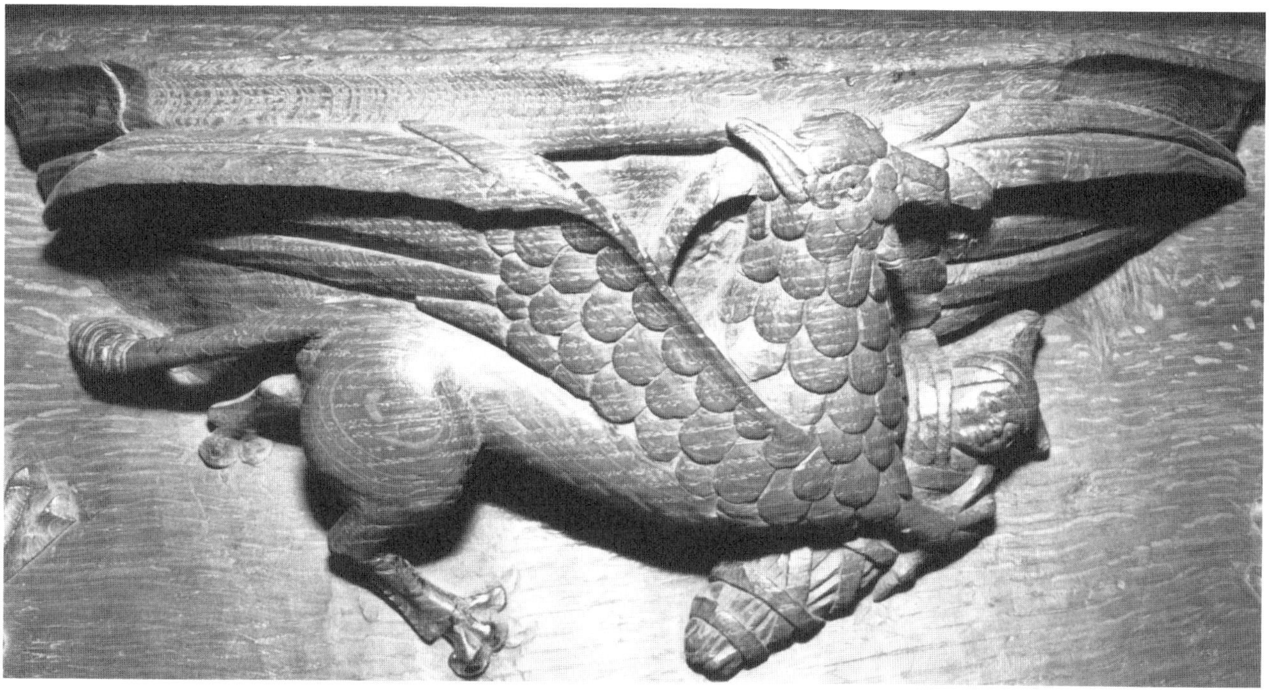

Griffin with infant. Whalley (Lancs), St. Mary, c.1430.

men in this bitter struggle with the griffin is shown in the Norwich carving below. Here, the greedy griffin has already snatched an animal with one claw and is trying to grab a man with the other. The man's shield is barely adequate protection against the griffin's claw, but he does not recoil from the assault.

The carving, right, is a rare depiction of the outcome in one of these encounters. The man has lost the battle and is being transported to the griffin's nest; yet the carver remains faithful to the myth by stressing the disparity between the size of the man and that of the griffin.

Griffins were not unconquerable. Although ordinary men might find the outcome of their battles with the griffin uncertain, there was one hero who did not: Alexander the Great. Alexander knew how to subdue a griffin, as his flight to the sky established. This legend had appeal on two levels—as a foil to the griffin's power and as an adventure to an unknown world.

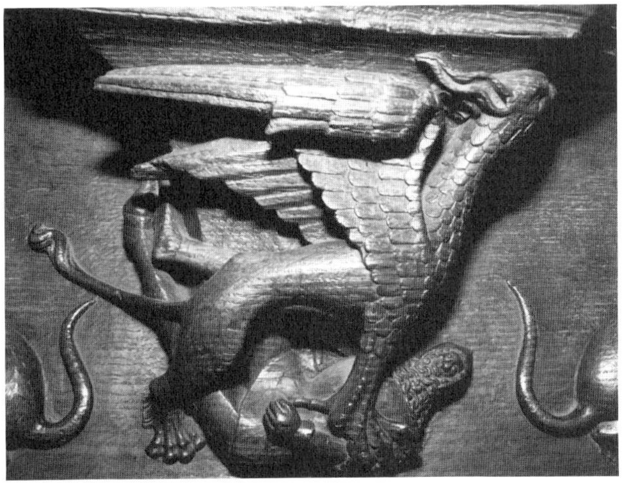

Griffin and man. Chester (Cheshire), The Cathedral, c.1380.

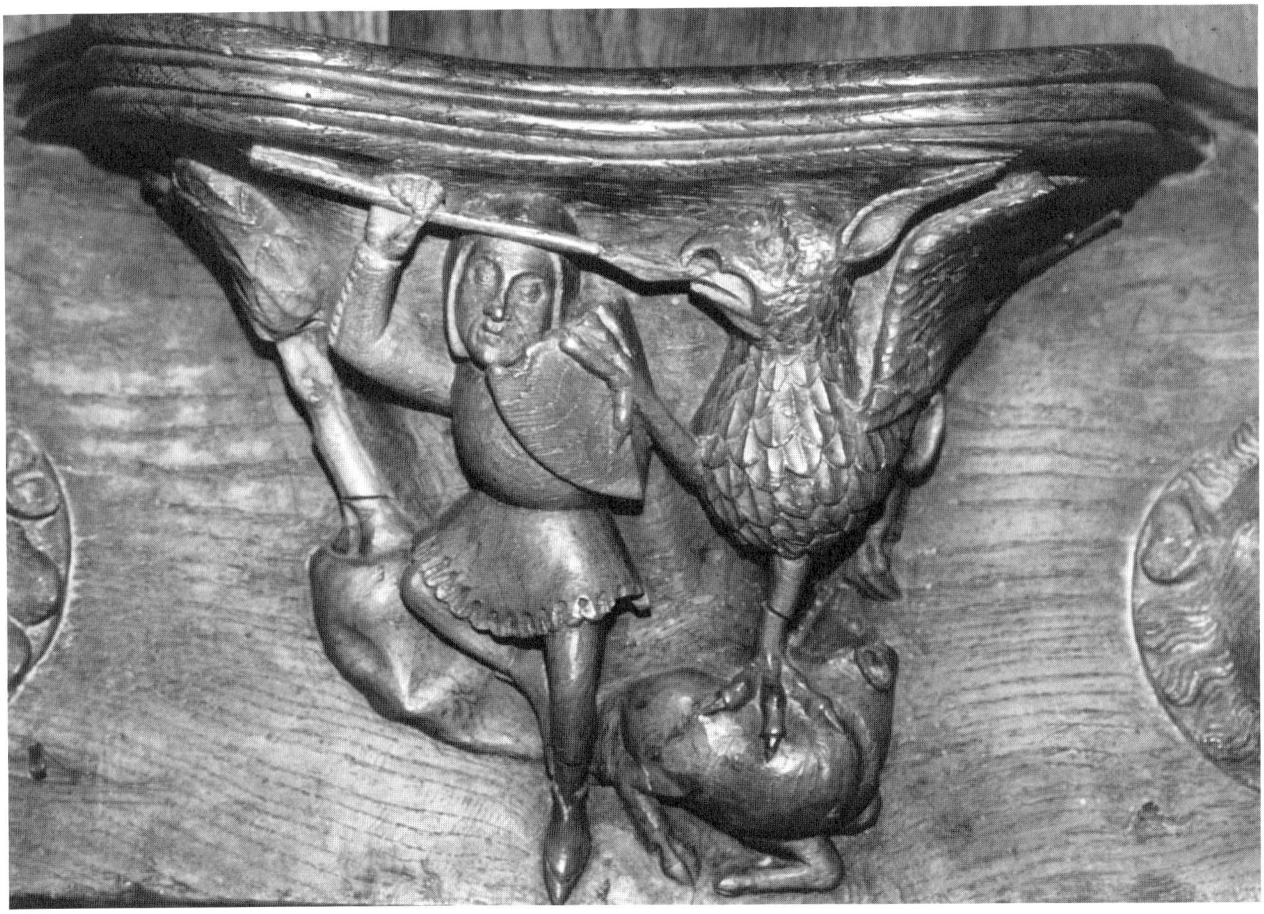

Man with griffin. Norwich (Norfolk), The Cathedral, 1480.

Alexander

Through popular works such as *The Travels of Sir John Mandeville* and *The Golden Legend,* people were exposed to different experiences in different countries. Nevertheless, the tale of Alexander's flight to the sky entered a realm where few could claim to have been. Alexander, it was presumed, was entering the invisible world above, making the legend all the more tantalizing.

The basic story is said to have originated in Alexandria about 200 A.D. in a romance written by a man called Pseudo-Callisthenes. This work did not include Alexander's journey to the sky, however (Dodgson 1905); that part of the legend appeared in a tenth-century Latin version written by Archpriest Leo of Naples (Anderson 1935) and subsequently became the best-known of Alexander's legendary exploits. These legends, which grew up after Alexander's death, placed more emphasis on "records of a journey rather than a man" (Lamb 1946, 371).

The story takes the form of a letter written by Alexander to his mother, Olympias. He describes his desire to know the truth about whether the world really ends where it meets the sky, and how he proposed to find out. He tells her that, first, he had his soldiers catch two very strong birds. He knew they were strong, for, when his soldiers went to catch them, they flew up carrying the soldiers. Most versions of the story name the birds as griffins, but this time they were carrying a man to the sky rather than to the griffin's nest, which was the fabled fate of ordinary men. Eventually the griffins were subdued by starving them for three days. Then Alexander wrote:

> I ordered a piece of wood to be constructed, in shape like a yoke, and a basket to be fastened in the midst thereof, with two spears set up therein . . . having horse's liver at the top . . .
>
> Dodgson 1905

The scheme was that, in their hunger, the birds would fly up, attempting to reach the meat and thereby lift Alexander, who was sitting in the basket, up to the sky. When he was finished surveying, he would lower the spears and descend to earth.

In both the Lincoln and Worcester carving, the carver has thought about how the "basket" on which Alexander would have sat would

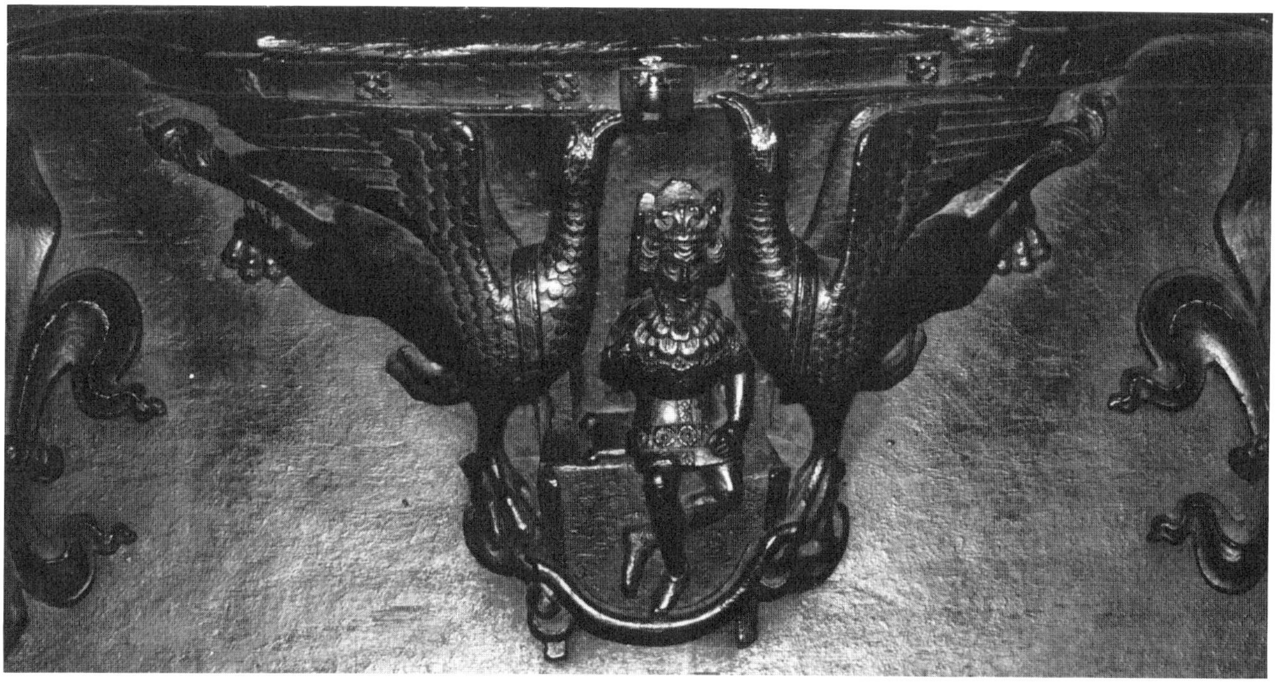

Flight of Alexander. Lincoln (Lincs), The Minster, 1370.

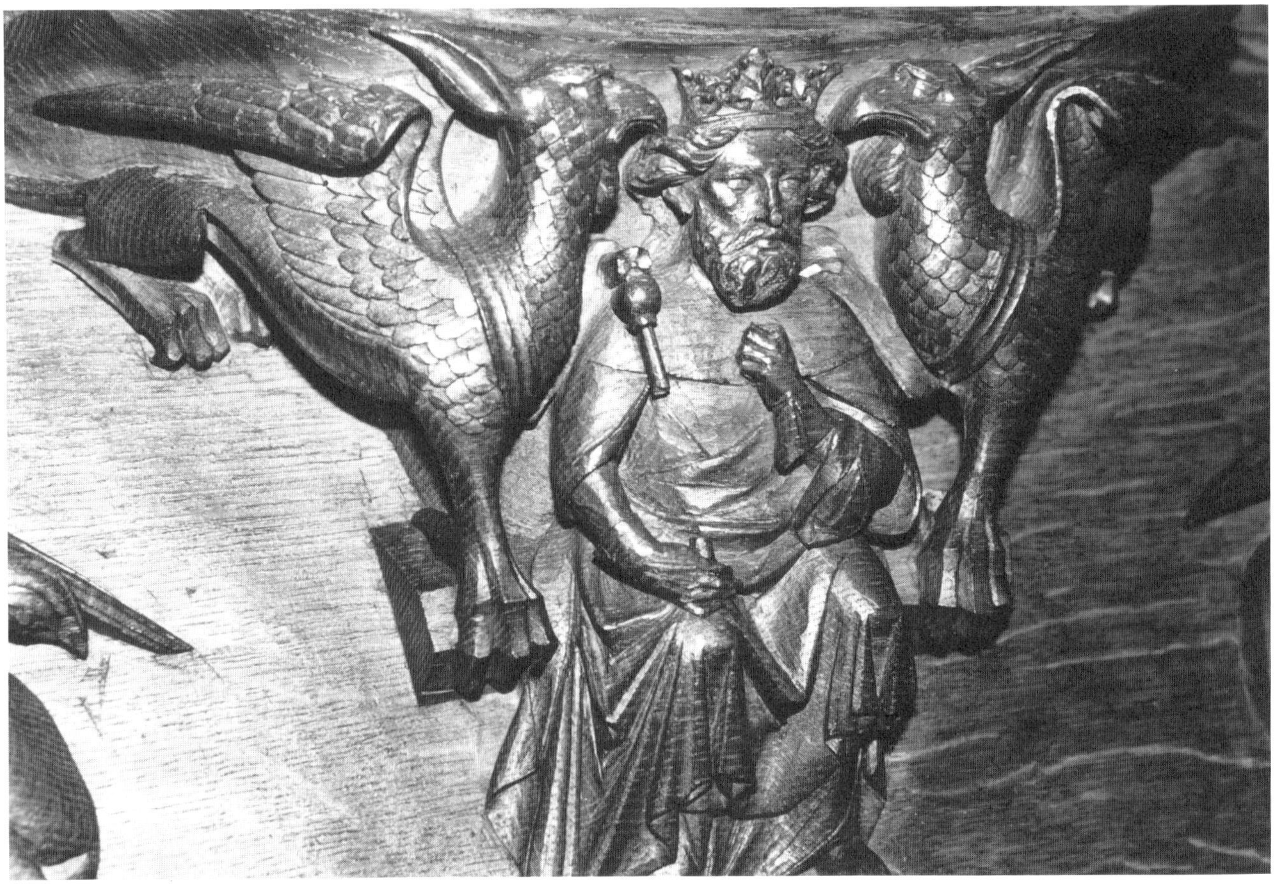

Flight of Alexander. Worcester (Herefs & Worcs), The Cathedral, late fourteenth century.

have looked. The Lincoln carver devised a substantial looking wooden seat with bars underneath for the griffins to grasp. In the Worcester carving, the griffins are carrying Alexander on what looks to be a plank. In both carvings, the griffins have harnesses around their necks.

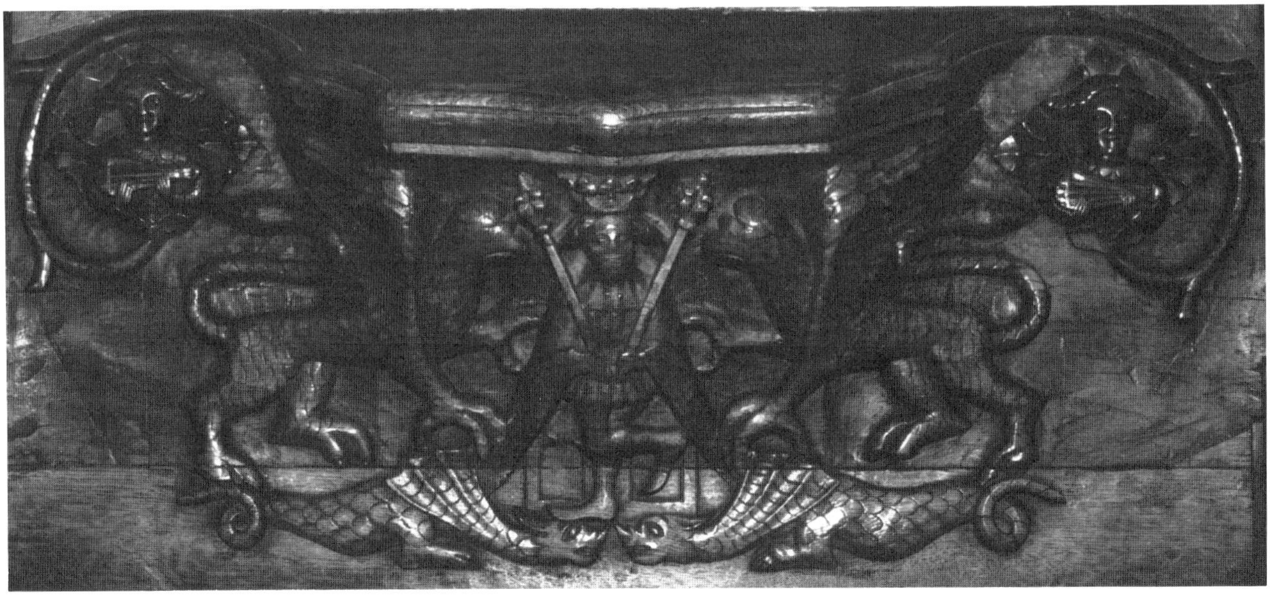

Flight of Alexander. Beverley (Humberside), St. Mary, c.1445.

Moralists, always eager to make a point, proffered another version of the tale. It was said that Alexander, because of his exploits in life, had no chance of entering heaven upon his death in 329 B.C. Therefore, he had devised the idea of harnessing two hungry griffins to carry him there (Colchester 1978). The moral given this version was that a person should always hunger for heaven.

Apparently, Alexander was successful in this endeavor as recorded on the rather jaunty carving at Beverley. Here, he strikes a relaxed pose, with legs crossed, one resting on a dragon's head. This is meant to indicate that he has triumphed over evil and is on his way to heaven. Angels are waiting on the supporters.

Even heroes were not always protected from the wicked humor of the carver. As much as the legendary Alexander might have been revered, he too fell victim to the carver's pervasive desire to satirize. This is displayed in the Cartmel carving. Examination of the "griffins" on either side of "Alexander" shows that they are not griffins at all. Rather, the carver has substituted two disreputable-looking composite beasts for the powerful griffins. On the left, the animal combines some characteristics of the dragon and bat but has cloven feet. On the right, the ridged back of a hyena and bat-like wings can be discerned. In the parody, the carver has made use of the ape, this time to represent the figure of the great Alexander. In one further ironic twist, the carver has shown "Alexander" with his ribs sticking out, suggesting that it is he who has been starved for three days. Or perhaps the carver meant to say that it should have been Alexander who was starved, rather than the animals.[3]

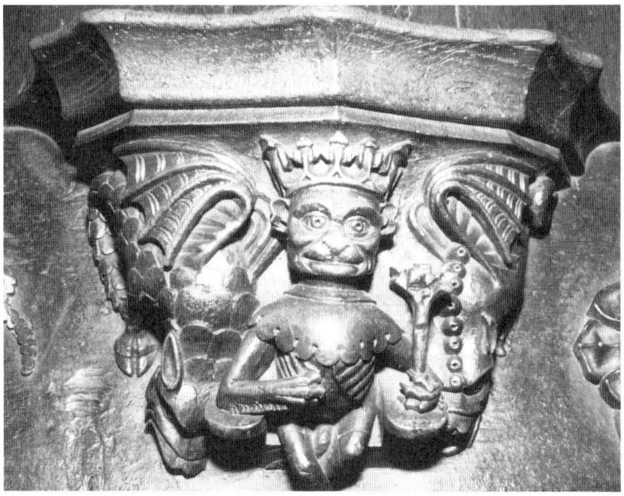

Parody on Flight of Alexander. Cartmel (Cumbria), The Priory, c. 1440.

The misericord carvers were steadfast in their portrayal of fabulous beasts, always maintaining the vision of supernatural strength. The challenges ordinary men faced in the medieval world were made as awesome as those faced by kings and gods of yore. The carvers did not neglect to pay homage to tradition, however. They kept the heroic image of Gilgamesh alive in such figures as Samson and St. George, and the half-man/half-animal image of Enkidu in the generic figure of the wild man (discussed below).

Samson

Although the figure of Samson descended from earlier heroes such as Gilgamesh and Hercules, in the Middle Ages the legend was altered to reflect contemporary Christian beliefs. The strength of ancient heroes' derived from their status as gods. The strength of medieval heroes was conferred by their God. Implicit in this conferral was the assumption of righteousness:

> a young lion roared against him, and he and the Spirit of the Lord came mightily upon him, and he rent him as he would have rent a kid, and he had nothing in his hand . . .
>
> Judges 14:5–6

Numerous misericords depict this event, all of them showing the same method of "renting" the lion. Samson straddles the lion, pulling his mouth apart with his bare hands. The carvings suggest no great struggle; indeed, the lions seem almost docile, as if acknowledging the inevitability of their defeat.

Samson's reputed strength was not only recorded in the Bible, it became a source for storytellers everywhere as tales of his strength expanded beyond his chastisement of the roaring lion. One of the more popular episodes was the tale of the "Gates of Gaza." It was included with other "true" adventures in the popular

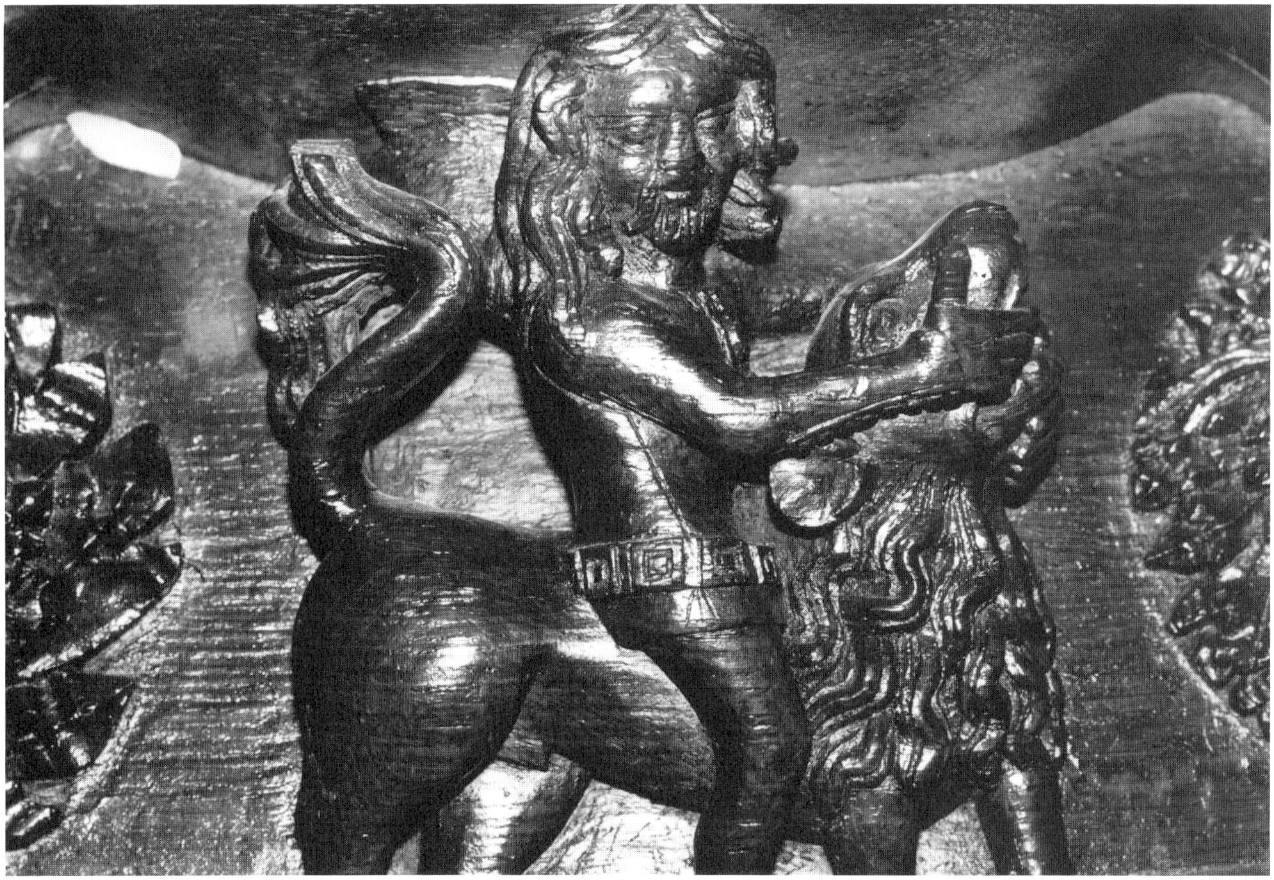

Samson and lion. Worcester (Herefs & Worcs), The Cathedral, late fourteenth century.

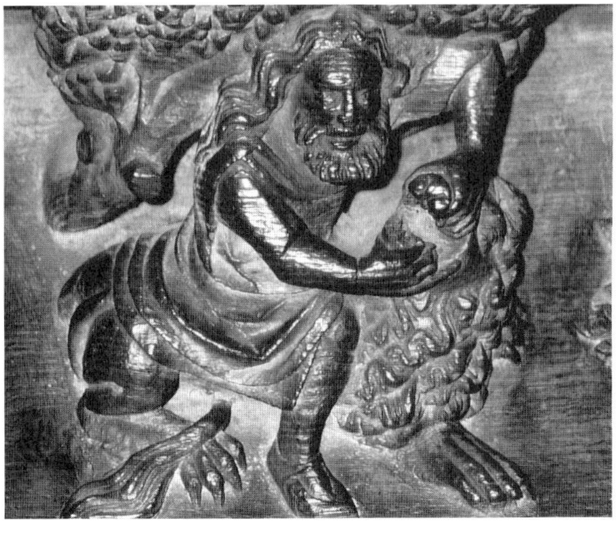

Samson and lion. Ely (Cambs), The Cathedral, c. 1340.

The Travels of Sir John Mandeville (Krása 1983). Although these particular travels, written by an anonymous author who attached Mandeville's name to them, were later proven fictitious, they were avidly received as real accounts throughout the late Middle Ages.

The story recounts the ongoing animosity between Samson and the Philistines and the Philistines' plan to ambush Samson. He was to be killed as he passed through the gates of Gaza in the morning. Samson, however, rose at midnight, dismantled the city gates, and simply carried them off.

Even heroes have their weaknesses, however. It is not surprising to find that the downfall of Samson, a Christian hero, came at the hands of a woman. In the Gloucester carving, the carver has given an intriguing representation of the famous cutting of Samson's hair. In this carving, Samson is gigantic in proportion to Delilah, leading one to wonder whether the carver was extolling the larger-than-life image of Samson or ridiculing his downfall at the hands of such a tiny woman.

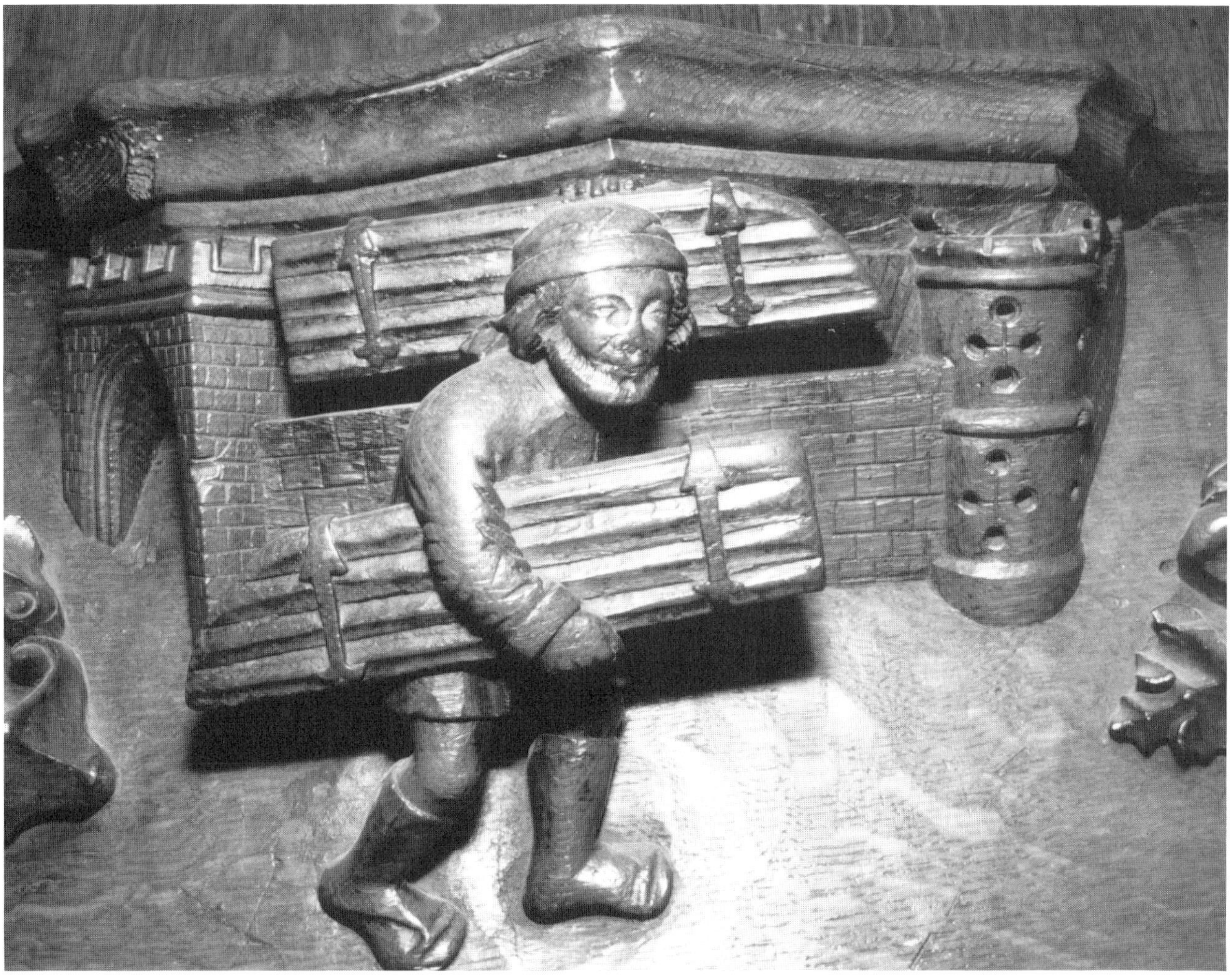

Samson at Gaza. Ripon (N.Yorks), The Cathedral, 1488–94.

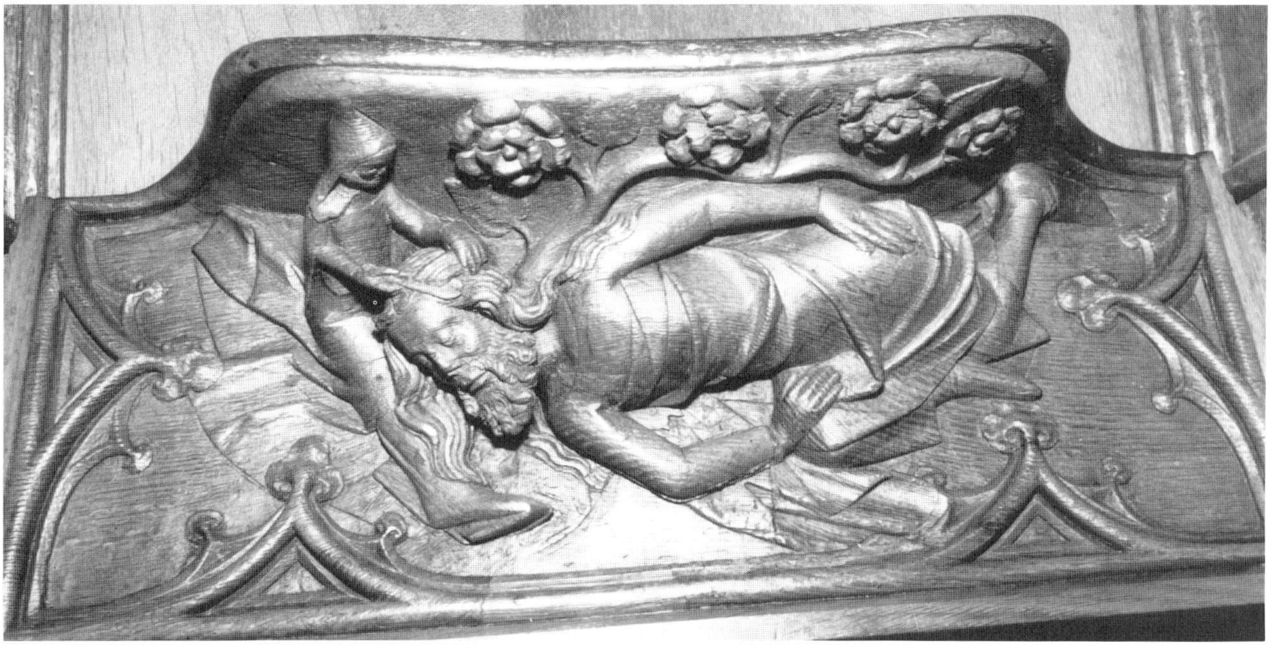

Samson and Delilah. Gloucester (Glos), The Cathedral, c. 1350.

Samson and other heroes received a respectable amount of attention, but real adulation was reserved for one of the most celebrated heroes of Christendom, St. George. His and other stories of saints were preserved in a thirteenth-century work by Jacobus de Voragine, archbishop of Genoa. Jacobus set down in writing legends that had been constructed by others, making Christianity seem an exciting quest filled with adventure and reward. Although he called his work *Legend of the Saints*, the work was so admired that it came to be known as *The Golden Legend*. When William Caxton published it in England in 1483, his respectful foreword read, "For in lyke wyse as gold is moste noble above al other metalles, in lyke wyse is thys legendes holden moost noble above al other werkys" (Ryan and Ripperger 1948, vii). Mâle (1949) credits this work as one of the most important documents of the Middle Ages, "For the reader . . . these lives were the richest treasury of wisdom, and in this book every man could find a model for himself" (83).

Whether every man was looking for a model or simply an adventurous tale, there is no disputing the widespread popularity of the legends, most particularly that of St. George.

St. George

It is uncertain on whom the figure of St. George is actually based, or even if he existed. Certainly he is a variation on all strong men fighting evil, starting with Gilgamesh; but there are other theories as well. There have been male figures in most ancient religions who have slain dragons, so he could be a composite taken from earlier myths. One theory suggests the legend of St. George evolved from ancient Egyptian religion, where the god Horus, appearing as a warrior, slew the demon Seth-Typhon with a spear (Pritchard n.d.; Evans 1896). Seth-Typhon appeared as a crocodile. Another suggestion is that St. George was an early Christian in Asia Minor martyred for tearing down the emperor's decree against Christians. It was thought that his name was "George," that he had once served in the Roman army, and that he had lived in the Cappadocia region of Turkey (Jacobus 1948; Hogarth 1979). The assumption is that the two legends merged in Asia Minor and were brought back to Europe by the Crusaders.

It was during this period that the image of St. George as a warrior was recast as the virtuous warrior-knight who attacked and killed the reviled dragon, thus symbolizing the triumph of good over evil. This transfer took place on the pages of *The Golden Legend* in the thirteenth century, and created what has become the most enduring image of St. George. In this legend, a dragon lived in a lake in Libya. He had such poisonous breath that the countryside was threatened. The residents began first by sacrificing two sheep per day to appease the monster; but when they ran out of sheep, they drew lots to see which children should be sacrificed. In one lot, the daughter of the king was selected. As she was being led out to be sacrificed, St. George appeared. The princess unselfishly entreated him to flee and save himself, but he valiantly refused. When the dragon rose from the lake, St. George attacked with his spear and the dragon was wounded. The dragon was so subdued by the experience that the princess led it docilely back to the village where St. George baptized the entire village and beheaded the dragon. As a reward, he was given the hand of the princess.

This favorite scene is re-created in the carving, right. St. George is engaged in battle with the dragon, while the princess kneels outside the castle. The king and queen view the struggle from within the castle walls.

While numerous events in the life of St. George could have been used to identify him, only his battle with the dragon came to prominence. St. George's strength was defined by these battles with what were believed to be the largest serpents in the world and the fiercest beasts alive. There could be no greater test of male strength.

The fear and awe surrounding the mythical dragon was the culmination of an extensive history of dragon lore going as far back as the Babylonian Creation Epic c.1750 B.C., in which the figure of the dragon was female. By the

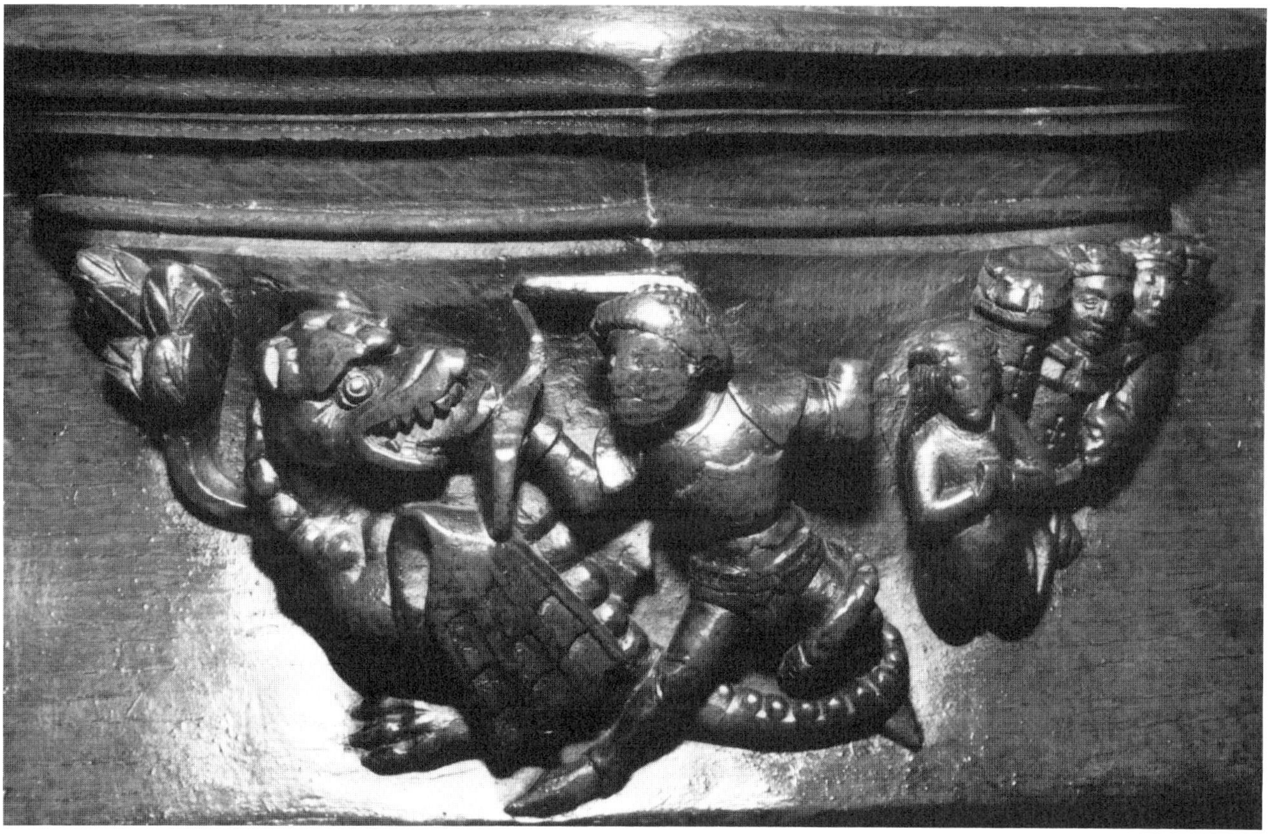

St. George. Windsor (Berks), St. George's Chapel, 1477–83.

Middle Ages, however, the dragon had undergone many alterations, coming finally to be perceived as an entity with masculine characteristics. The creature on which the myth of the dragon was based was probably a crocodile, with the subsequent descriptions becoming more fabulous. For instance, in the thirteenth century, Roger Bacon thought dragons were flying creatures. Marco Polo, in the same century, described them as ten paces in length, with a mouth large enough to swallow a man in one gulp (Hogarth 1979). Clearly, the carver from Worcester had no trouble imagining such a beast.

Whatever the description, in the retelling of the stories, many embellishments were added until the beast had been transformed into a monster of epic proportions. Carvers and other artists vied to create a dragon fierce enough to match St. George.

St. George was rumored to be so nearly invincible that even death could not defeat him:

> . . . he is described variously as having been crushed to death, made to run in red-hot boots, scourged, cast into a well with a heavy stone tied round his neck, beaten with sledgehammers, roasted, poisoned, and buried alive in quicklime. Yet after every episode, he was restored miraculously to life and health
>
> Hogarth 1979, 141

Ironically, his martyrdom, when it finally occurred, was the result of his legendary success in saving souls. When he saved the soul of the Empress of Persia, the Emperor became so enraged that he had St. George beheaded on April 23, the day still celebrated in England as St. George's Day (Johnsgard and Johnsgard 1982).

The legend of St. George was so pervasive that he became a prominent member of society in a number of areas—as a beloved character in mystery plays, as the patron saint of England, as a protector of those engaged in

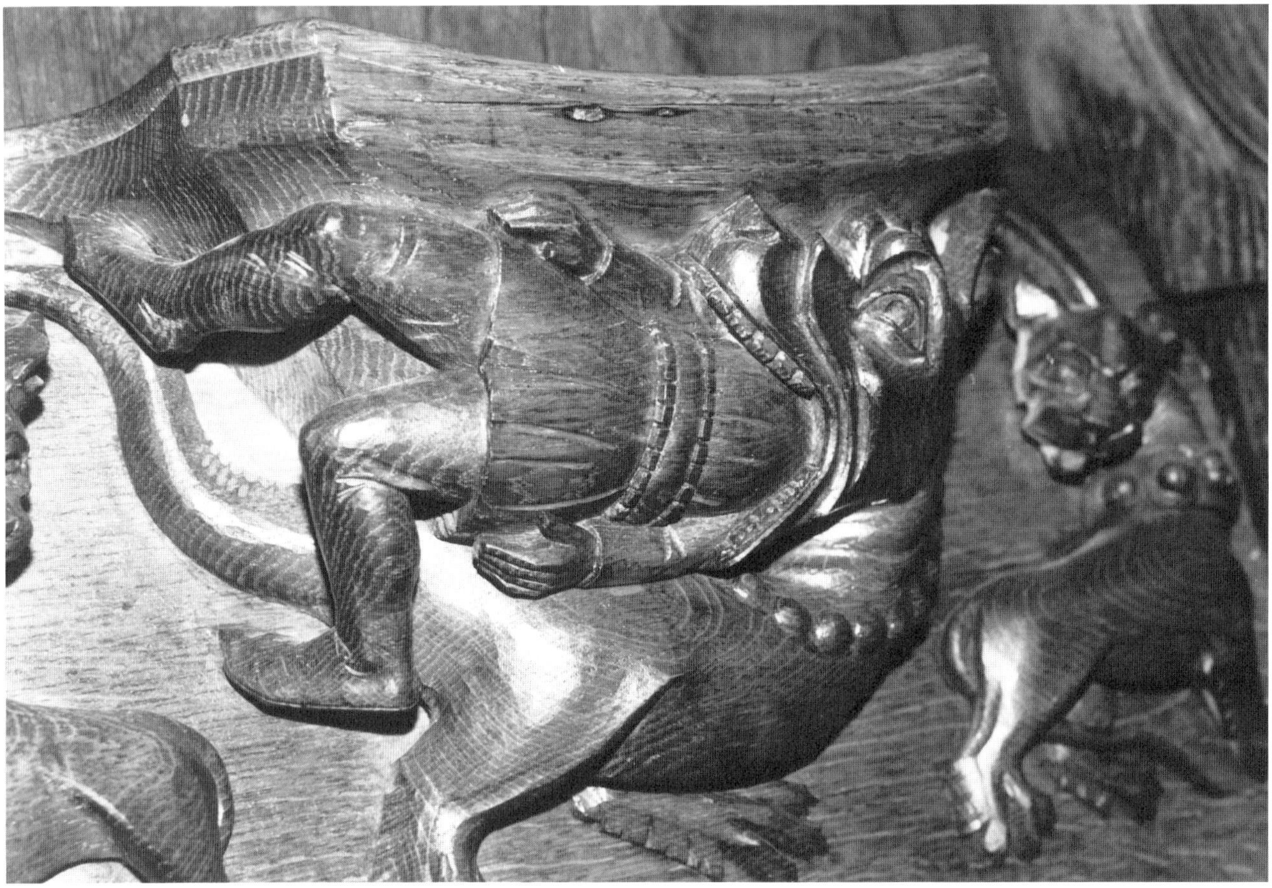

Dragon eating man. Worcester (Herefs & Worcs), The Cathedral, late fourteenth century.

battle, and in the literary and artistic expressions of the time. Many misericords were carved of St. George; most often, the other participants in the legend were excluded, leaving the focus on his strength as he battled the dragon. St. George would be shown either attacking on foot or on horseback, but in the fashion of all truly strong men, he always fought the battle singlehandedly.

The legend of St. George fit well with the ideals of knighthood. He was regarded as the patron saint of all Christian knights, and leaders of the Crusades asked for his special protection during every crusade. In 1222, during the reign of Henry III, St. George was made the patron saint of England and the banner of St. George was carried in every battle on land and sea (Pritchard n.d.).

However, it was Edward III, in the fourteenth century, who made St. George an especially English symbol. Edward was known not only as a great military leader but as the greatest champion of chivalry of his time—characteristics also attributed to St. George. Edward was the first English monarch to incorporate the concept of the civilized warrior as part of the royal court (Johnson 1973). He did this by establishing the Knights of the Garter and naming St. George as the order's patron saint. The order was convened on St. George's Day in a new hall at Windsor Castle, where it was said King Arthur had founded his castle with its Round Table (Briggs 1983).

Whereas St. George was adored by the general population, they were not necessarily pleased to have the aristocracy adopt him as a symbol of their own. St. George, after all, had been a legendary champion of the people before he became the epitome of medieval knighthood. In response, some carvings were made that, on the surface, seem to ridicule him. These were not really aimed at the char-

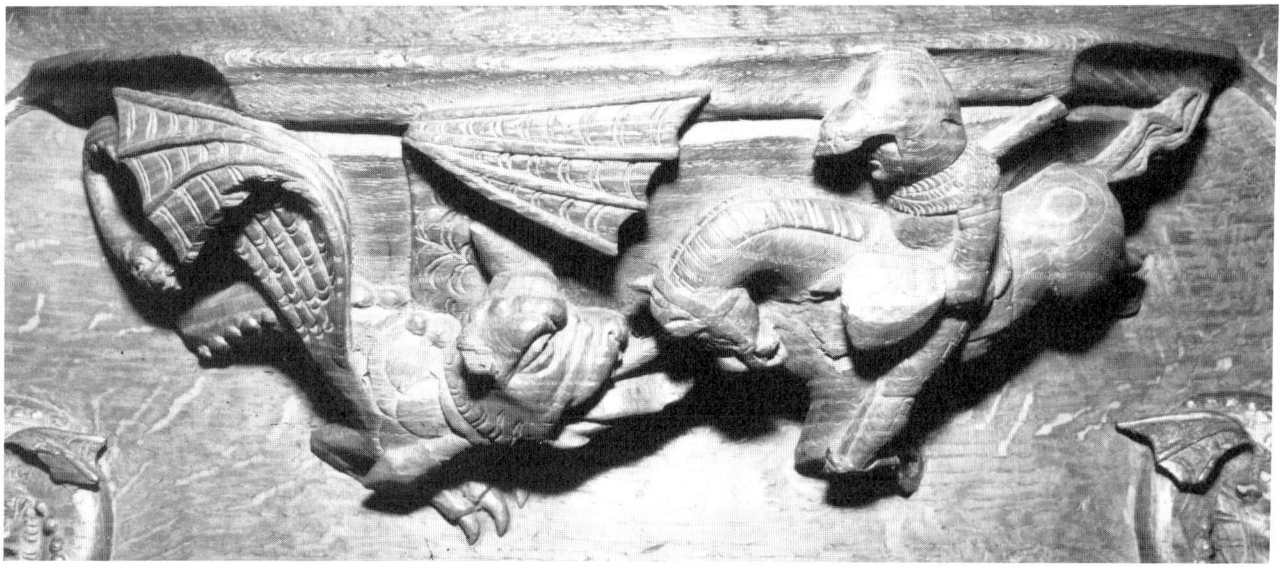

St. George. Whalley (Lancs), St. Mary, c. 1430.

acter of St. George, but rather at the airs of the brotherhood of knights who appeared to equate their prowess with that of the revered St. George.

The Beverley carving is one such delightful parody, and might be overlooked as such if one did not include the supporters in the interpretation. The central carving shows a man encircled by the tails of the two dragons. This could be taken to represent valor in the face of overwhelming odds; but when the left supporter is examined the joke becomes clear. Here, the sloppily dressed knight is spearing a snail. On the right, he fearfully hides his head in a sack. Upon reexamining the central carving, we see that the more likely interpretation of what is going on is that someone trying to emulate St. George has clumsily gotten himself entangled in a very difficult situation, something that would never have happened to St. George.

Satire aside, the real fear (or desire) of every man was that he might be called on to prove his strength in the manner of St. George. This situation is realized, at least in the carved record, in a number of misericords where ordinary men wrestle with dragons. The Wells

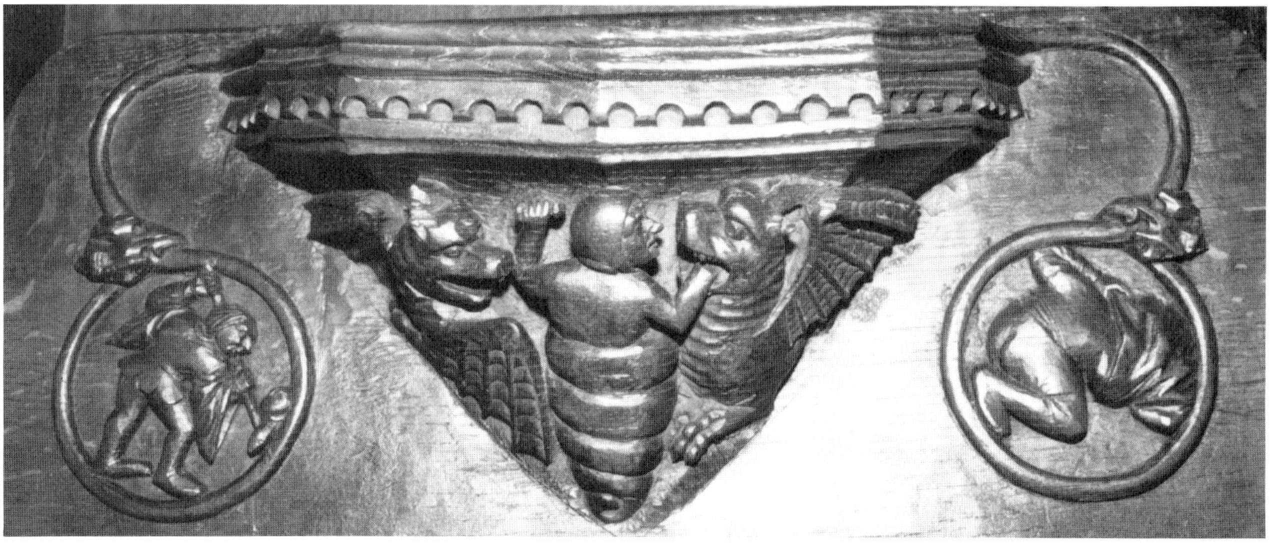

St. George parody. Beverley (Humberside), The Minster, 1520.

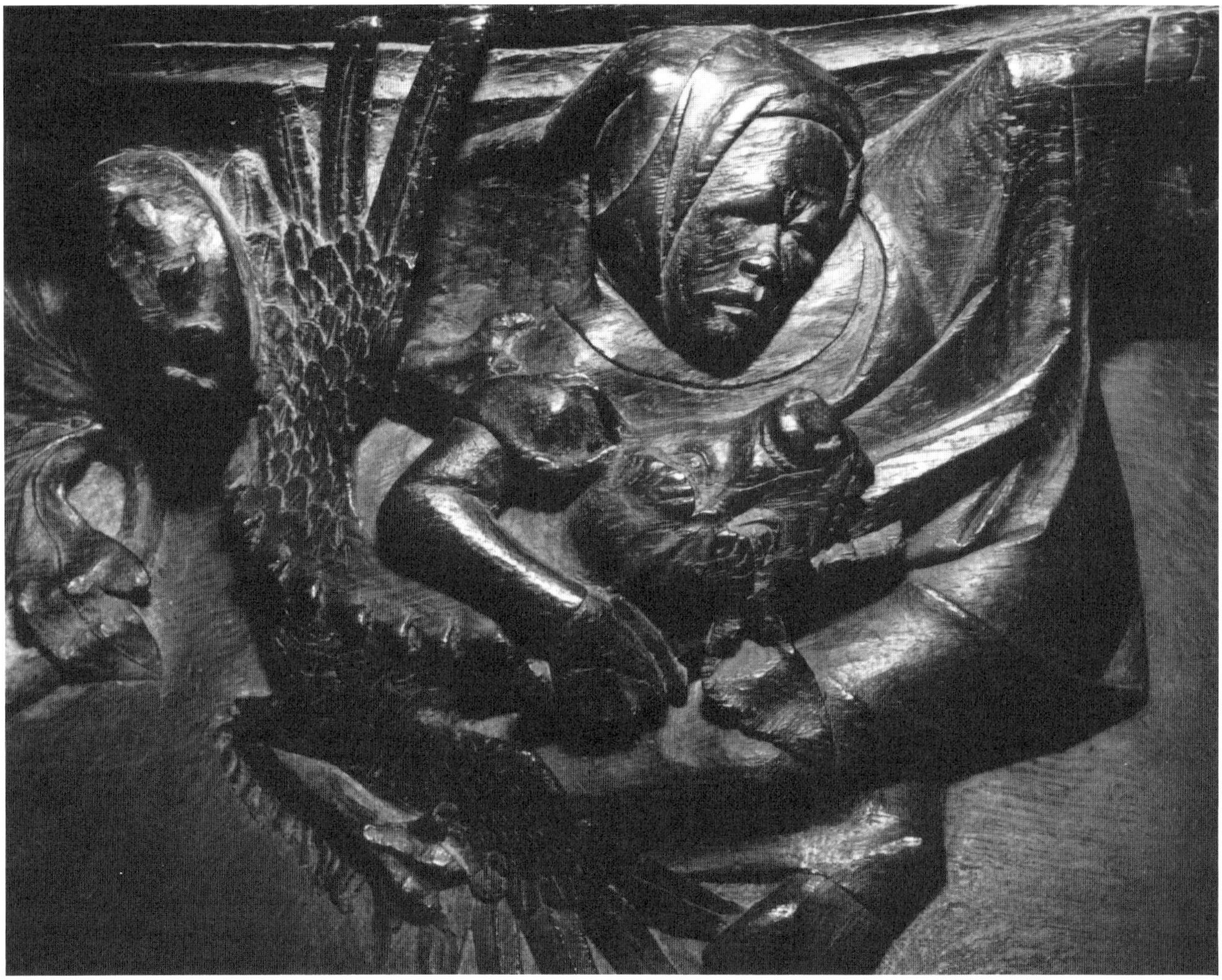

Man spearing dragon. Wells (Somerset), The Cathedral, c. 1330–40.

carver has his man gamely grasping the dragon around the neck with one hand while spearing him with the other (the spear is missing from the damaged carving).

It is even suggested that ordinary men might do better than St. George, perhaps conquering not one, but two, dragons with their bare hands.

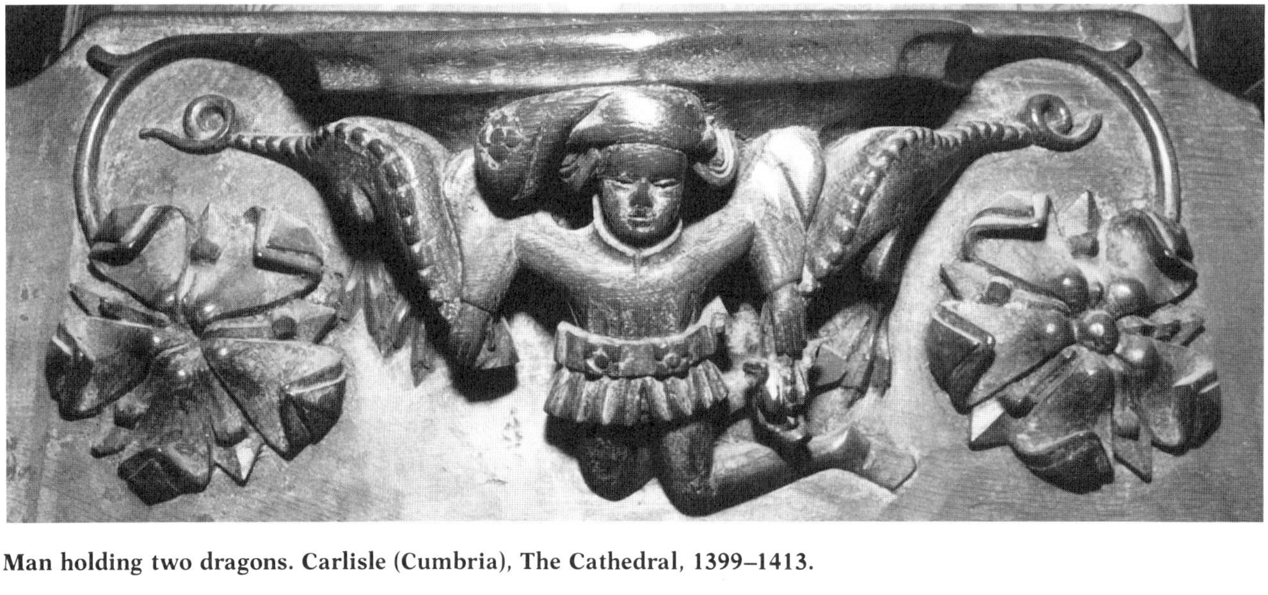

Man holding two dragons. Carlisle (Cumbria), The Cathedral, 1399–1413.

The obsession with slaying dragons came to an end during the sixteenth century, when they were scientifically proven not to exist. The news prompted the Pope to have all accounts of the dragon removed from the official Church version of St. George's life. Erasing the image from the people's minds was not as easy. As late as the seventeenth century, we find Spenser, in *The Faerie Queen,* describing how George became a saint. Spenser tells of George's treacherous journey, which includes battles with Saracens, being deceived by a woman, fights with dragons and giants, until finally George reaches the point of suicidal despair. It is then that he is led into the house of Holiness and told his fate:

> Where is for thee ordaind a blessed end:
> For thou emongst those Saints, whom thou doost see,
> Shalt be a Saint, and thine owne nations friend
> And Patrone: thou Saint George shalt called bee,
> Saint George of mery England, the signe of victory.
>
> 1611, 48

The imagery of St. George fighting the dragon has endured into the present century, despite the Church's wish to dissociate St. George from the fabulous beast. One example in the misericords comes from Chester. It was carved in 1919, to replace a plain seat after a restoration of the choir stalls (Bennett 1979). The carver has incorporated a contemporary political sentiment by equating the League of Nations with St. George. The righteous League of Nations is going to save the world, as the banner proclaims, "League of Nations to the Rescue."

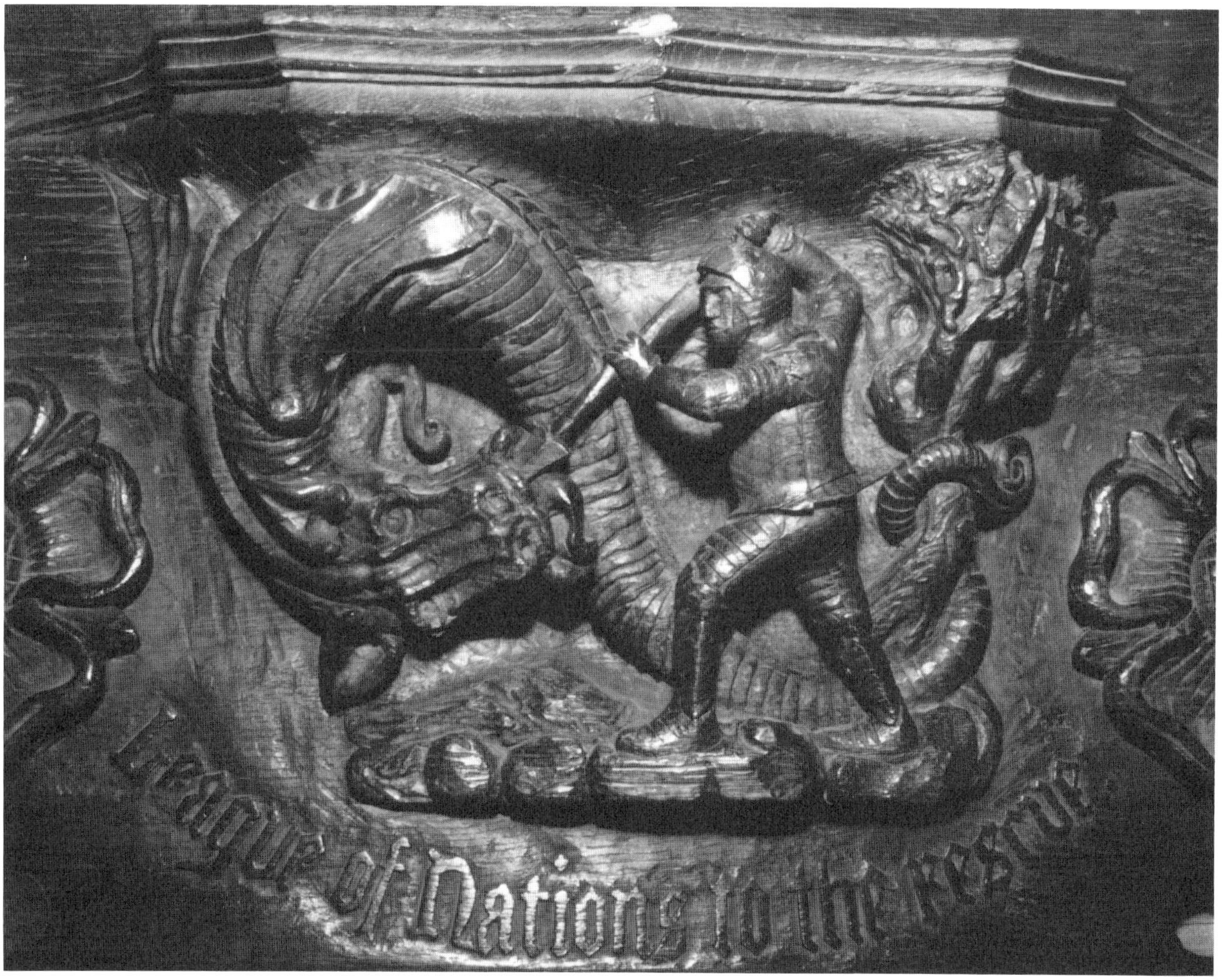

St. George and dragon. Chester (Cheshire), The Cathedral, 1919.

With the rise in chivalry, another means of measuring male strength occurred that did not require one-on-one male-beast contests. The men of chivalry defined their strength through regulated contests with other men that included a set of rules by which to be judged. The battleground was the tourney field, but the struggle was still for moral and physical superiority.

Knights Noble

As we have seen, the concept of a civilized warrior-knight at court was introduced by Edward III at the height of chivalry in fourteenth-century England. Warrior-knights, however, had been in existence for more than 200 hundred years prior to Edward. They originated with the First Crusade in 1099, when the Christians took Jerusalem. Christian control of Jerusalem initiated waves of pilgrims making their way to visit the holy city, creating, in turn, the need for protection as they traveled, and knighthood was born (Zarnecki 1966). The Knights of the Order of the Hospital of St. John of Jerusalem, known as Knights Hospitallers, were the first military order established to protect Christian pilgrims from Muslims as they made their way to Jerusalem. This order was soon followed by another, the Knights Templars.

The Church recognized the contradictory nature of the concept of warrior-knight: under Church doctrine, killing was immoral. To justify having warrior-knights, the Church prepared a rationale: since Christians were engaged in a holy war against those who denied their beliefs, knights had a "moral right" to protect the Church, the oppressed, and any others in need of help. This was solemnized by having each warrior-knight go through a purification ceremony in which he took an oath to uphold the code of chivalry before being received in the name of the Trinity (Tuchman 1978). Thus, from its inception, knighthood was imbued with an aura of righteousness and strength conferred by God, as illustrated by the magnificent kneeling knight.

At first, knighthood was a military rank that could be conferred on any deserving soldier by another knight, a military officer, a member of the nobility, or a member of the royal family (Zarnecki 1966). The privilege of conferring knighthood soon became the prerogative only of the king, however, and by the fourteenth century, knighthood was reserved for the upper classes. It was expected, if not required, that all young men of a certain station would train for the knighthood. Knighthood went hand in hand with feudalism, for the duty of the knight was to fight in the service of his feudal lord (Bishop 1987). Many young men of noble families embarked on an apprenticeship in chivalry that could last months or years and be very costly. For example, France in the twelfth and thirteenth centuries was preeminent in the area of tourneying, and many young English knights spent at least two years on the French tournament circuit (Barber and Barker 1989).

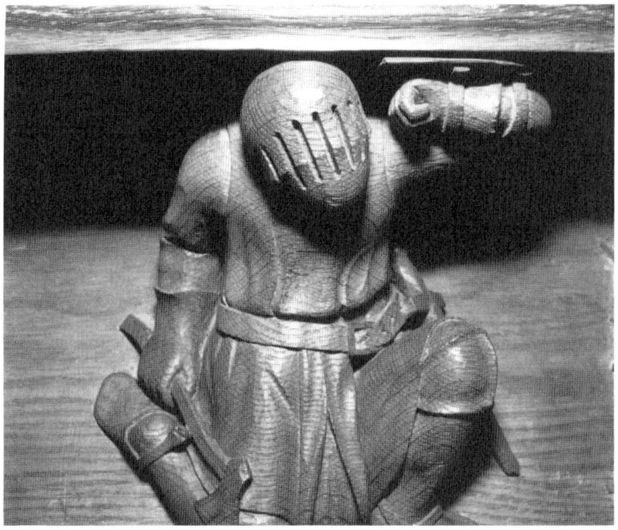

Warrior-knight. Ely (Cambs), The Cathedral, c.1340.

To be an accomplished knight was demanding and dangerous. In the chronicle of the Spanish knight, Don Pero Niño, his biographer describes the dangers of battle, especially from crossbows. The biographer is so eager to present his master as the perfect knight, however, that the account must be read with a certain amount of skepticism. Don Niño is wounded at the beginning of the battle when an arrow "knit together his gorget and his neck," but he is only momentarily hindered by this event and presses on, clearing a bridge into the city of Pontevedra:

> the people of the city,. . . . fired many crossbows at him. . . . He went forward with his face uncovered and a great bolt there found its mark, piercing his nostrils through most painfully, whereat he was dazed, but his daze lasted but a little time.
>
> de Gamez 1928, 37

The danger of crossbows in battle is captured beautifully by the carver of the "Falling Knight of Lincoln" below.

The social status of knights changed over the years as events altered their function. By the thirteenth century, knighthood had become less exclusively military in function, and in the fourteenth century this function was further diminished. It was during this time that Edward III's concept of the "civilized" warrior-knight at court evolved. The royal emphasis on chivalry and pageantry moved knights away from a focus on training for war exclusively, and toward the achievement of individual expertise in arranged competitions. At the same time, this shift transformed the essence of knighthood. The tenets of the chivalric code—honor, loyalty, and courtesy—were still observed, but individual prowess became *the* essential element of knighthood (Tuchman 1978; Bishop 1987; Briggs 1983).

The emphasis on individual strength and skill was aided by the growing popularity of tournaments. Tournaments took the place of war as the arena where knights demonstrated their martial skills before an appreciative audience. The Church frowned on these contests; but, despite bans and dire warnings, their popularity grew—as did the possibility of great material gain for the knight.

When tournaments were established in England in the twelfth century, they were melee style with few rules. Knights simply leapt into the fray. Later tournaments became more structured, and sides were evenly matched

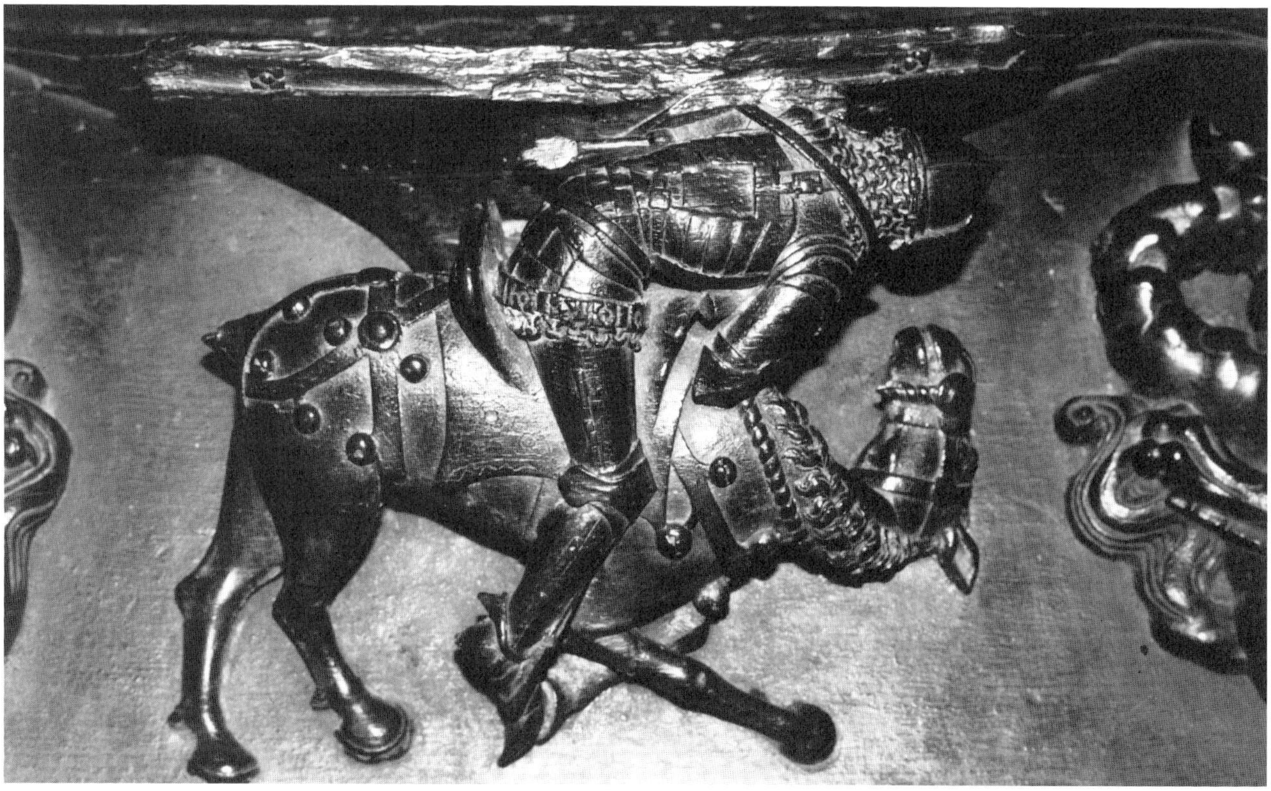

Falling knight. Lincoln (Lincs), The Minster, 1370.

with precise goals—generally doing battle for a specified period of time. These tournaments were complex events, often lasting several days, with knights coming from distant places to participate. In addition to prizes, the victors gained rewards through taking fallen knights, their armor, and their horses and holding them for ransom. Because of the splendid accoutrements and elaborate preparations for tournaments, they were expensive and soon became almost exclusively productions of the Court. They also became primarily ceremonial and were used to mark great occasions of state such as marriages, births, and martial victories.

Attendance at these events was not restricted to members of the Court, however. Considered a combination sporting event and festival, tournaments drew vast numbers of spectators. Along with mystery plays, they contributed greatly to the emergence of the English secular theater through their use of disguises. It was rumored, for example, that the women of Queen Philippa's court disguised themselves as knights and took part in the tournaments (Johnson 1973). On other occasions, nobles would take part wearing various disguises to enter the contest—at one event, for example, seven knights presented themselves as the Seven Deadly Sins against all comers (Barber and Barker 1989).

Tournaments were also the arena for another form of drama. It was here that some of the rituals of courtly love were enacted. The knight would display his personal skill and courage before an audience which included his chosen mistress, who, in turn, would award him the prize if he won his match.

The showpiece of the tournament became the joust between two knights and was the ideal forum for the exhibition of individual prowess. In the melee style group tournaments, the emphasis was on actual combat or training for combat, whereas jousting was between two men and required a great deal more training. The point in jousting was not to kill your opponent, but to unseat him from his horse.

A chronicler of the time, Chrétien de Troyes, recorded the feel of a joust:

> The ranks shudder on both sides, and from the clash there rises a loud din, with a great cracking of lances. Lances break and shields are holed,

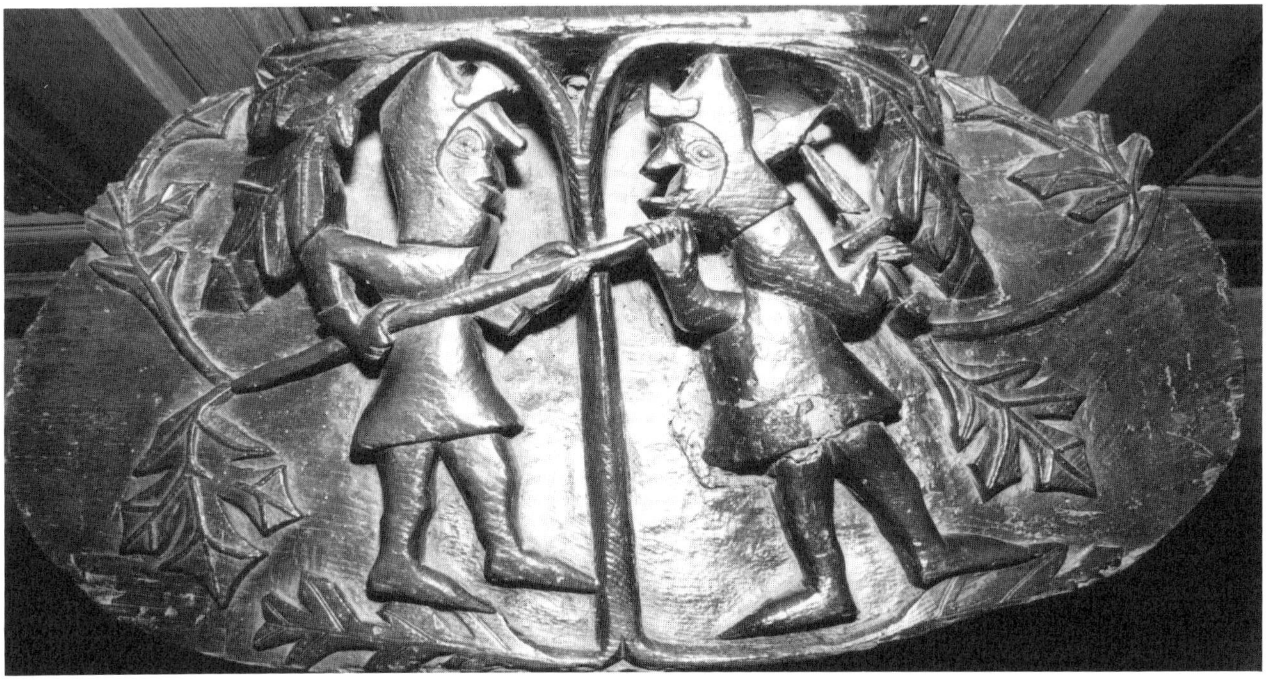

Knights fighting. Ripon (N.Yorks), The Cathedral, c. late thirteenth century.

and hauberks are torn and rent, saddles are emptied and riders tumble, the horses sweat and lather. All draw their swords on those who clatter to the ground.

1987, 29

The scene de Troyes describes is captured in the Ripon misericord at the moment when the knights may have "clattered" from their horses to the ground but continued to fight.

The Worcester carving below, thought to have come from an illustrated manuscript (Anderson 1969), shows the unlucky knight just as he and his horse are falling.

Bond (1910, vol. 1) has suggested that this carving is a satire because the man with the drums, on the left supporter, supposedly is looking on with horror, fearing that he might be crushed in the fall. This interpretation is unlikely. Not only is the action in the carving believable, but when the carvers wanted to satirize, they usually replaced humans with ridiculous animals. What the side carvings illustrate is the common practice, on the part of the nobility and monarchy, of having their musicians in attendance during jousts and battles. At the battle of Hastings, in 1066, for example, Taillefer the Jougleur marched at the head of the Norman army, twirling his sword in the air and singing the Song of Roland (Chesterton 1959). Later, the issue of musicians carrying weapons was reconsidered, at least for tournaments. Fearing that the musicians might come to the aid of their masters, they, along with other attendants at these affairs, were forbidden from carrying weapons at tournaments by laws passed during the reign of Henry V (1413–22) (Strutt 1810).

Knights Absurd

There is ample evidence, however, that the common man thought the ritual of knightly jousting both ostentatious and ridiculous, and understandably felt little love for the combating knights. For one thing, the ordinary citizen's circumstances were rarely taken into account when sites were chosen for tournaments. It was not unusual for the combatants in a tourney to destroy crops and take over farm buildings and village streets as they fought, generating costs for damages that were not borne by the knights (Barber and Barker 1989). In addition, if the king and his court required supplies, food, or lodging, the suppli-

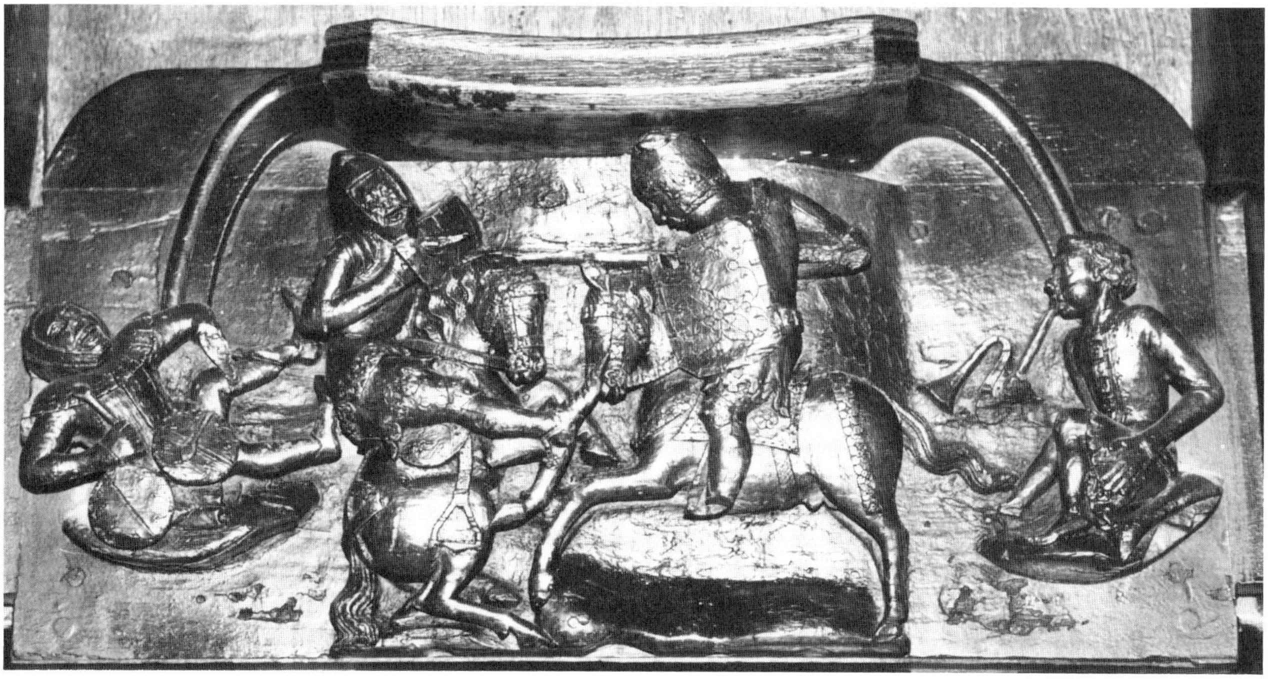

Knights jousting. Worcester (Herefs & Worcs), The Cathedral, late fourteenth century.

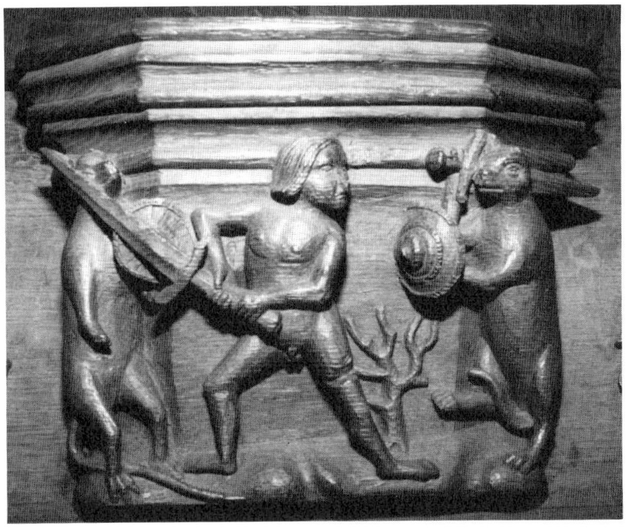

Tournament parody. Bristol (Avon), The Cathedral, 1520.

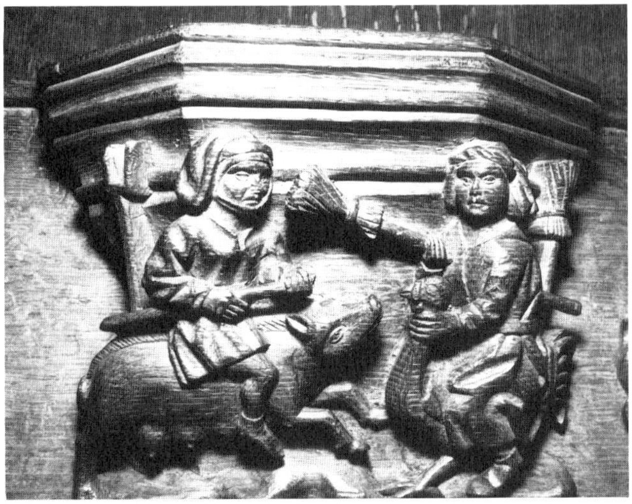

Jousting parody. Bristol (Avon), The Cathedral, 1520.

ers were seldom paid in cash for the items; rather, they would be issued a "tally" to be paid at a later date. How well this system worked is illustrated by the case of Henry III. At the time of his death, he owed one community four hundred pounds for supplies his purveyors had taken from the community over the past twenty years (Harris 1898). Not surprisingly, the carvers found in the joust and tournament fertile ground for mocking the nobility.

The carver at Bristol produced some of the most cleverly drawn parodies. In the first carving, the combatants have again clattered to the ground, and the "knight," without his fine armor, is doing combat with what looks like very large rats.

In the next carving two common men are jousting, but they are making the joust a ludicrous experience. Rather than use the fine equipment and steeds of real knights, these men engage each other riding one on a sow and the other on a turkey. Their weapons are brooms (the one on the left is broken).

In the last example, from Beverley, a knight approaches his opponent, a boar, with his

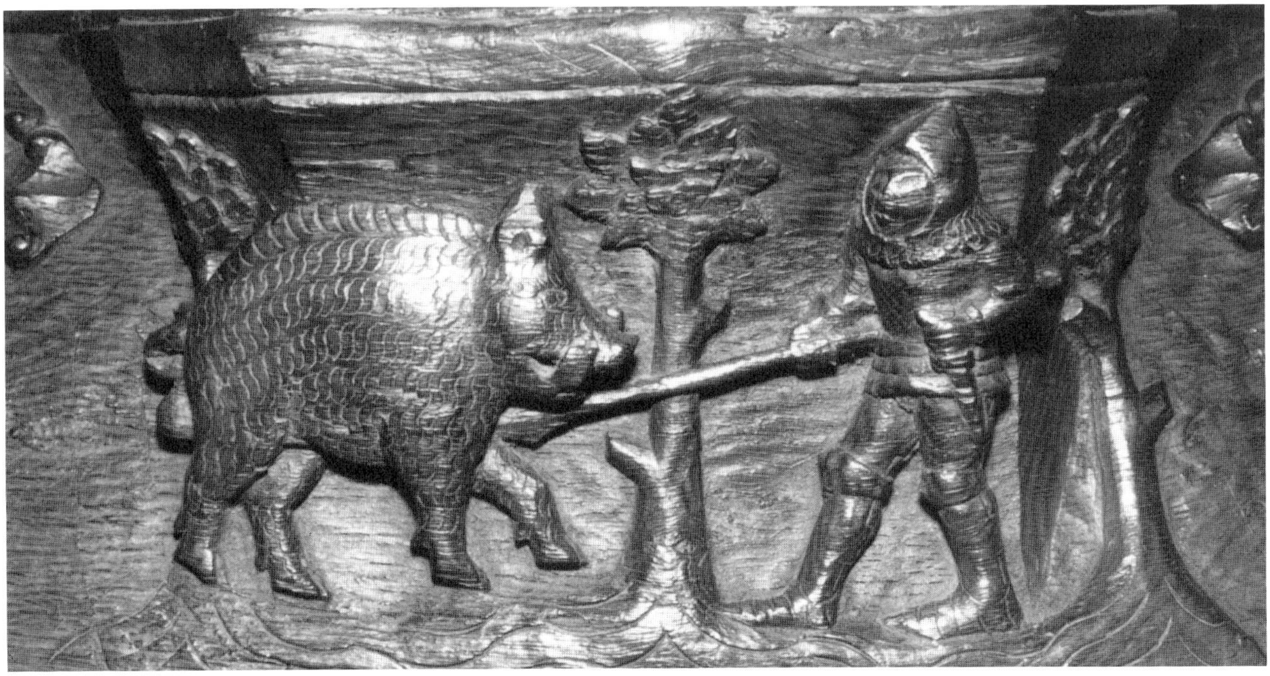

Knight and boar. Beverley (Humberside), St. Mary, c.1445.

lance at the ready and his hand on his knife. Boars in the bestiaries were symbolic of boorish, rustic behavior (Payne 1990) and were generally regarded as being extremely stupid (Wynne 1779). Whereas the image of ordinary men approaching a wild, fierce beast would have been a flattering one, here the carver questions which of the two combatants is the more ignorant one. It would seem to be the knight, because he uses the specialized weapons of the joust against a stupid animal in the field.

Tilting

Although jousts and tourneys were the province of the nobility, similar contests were available to ordinary men. One was tilting at the quintain. This required simple materials, no special dress, and no formal pageantry. Originally a military game from antiquity that preceded tournaments and jousts, it was carried forward primarily as an exercise for youth (Strutt 1810; Plot 1677; Stow 1633).

Tilting at its most basic level required only a pole with a shield stuck in the ground for the practice of combatants. As in jousting, men raced their horses toward the object with lance in hand, intent on hitting the shield. If they had no horse, they would run on foot. The pole and shield could be as elaborate or as simple as desired, but most had some sort of pivot so that the shield, or its equivalent, would be on one side of the pole and a weight on the other. When the shield was hit, it would be pushed out of the way of the rider—if all went well. Robert Plot, in his seventeenth century history of Oxford-Shire describes a tilting contest he had seen:

> . . . against this board they anciently rod with spears; now as I saw it at Deddington in this County, only with strong staves, which violently bring about the bag of sand, if they make not good speed away it strikes them in the neck or shoulders, and sometimes perhaps knocks them from their horses.
>
> 1677, 200

The rider taking a fall, of course, elicited a great deal of laughter and ridicule from the audience. In the Bristol carving below, the carver presents some comic elements of tilting to poke fun at his fellow man: the use of anything at hand to create a quintain, in this case a dog holding a bag of sand in his teeth; riding an ill-suited slow animal (here, a bear); and, to increase the odds of actually hitting the quintain, the attachment of a broad wooden disk to the tip of the lance.

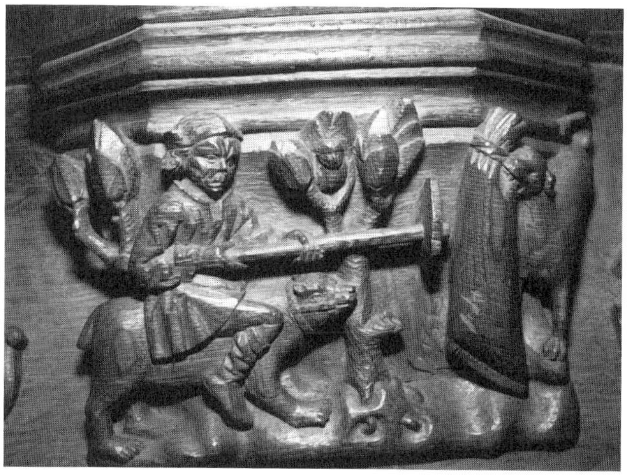

Tilting parody. Bristol (Avon), The Cathedral, 1520.

As good-humored as tilting events could be, there were occasions when the competitive aspects created animosity. In his chronicle, Matthew Paris recorded one such episode in 1253, involving a contest in London between some local young men and Henry III's servants from Westminster. The king had offered a peacock for the best performer, but in typical regal fashion assumed that his servants would be the better performers. The king's men, however, made the error of calling the Londoners names and verbally abusing them:

> . . . the said Londoners being wrongfully abused, fell upon the King's servants, and beat them shrewdly, so that upon complaint made to the King, he fined the Citie to pay a thousand Marks
>
> Stow 1633, 77

Thus demonstrating that one may win a moral victory, but at a price.

By the seventeenth century, tilting had become mainly a ritual performed at marriages. The groom would run at the quintain while carrying home the bride (Plot 1677), no doubt creating a feeling of unease on the part of the bride.

The Demise of Knighthood

Changes in military requirements finally eliminated the need for the civilized warrior-knight. This occurred as a result of two major events. One was the introduction of artillery in the fourteenth century and the subsequent training of specialists in its use. These specialists were not drawn from the ranks of the civilized warrior-knights, but from the middle and lower classes (Gies 1984). The elite status of the knight was further eroded with the second major event—a change of recruiting practices throughout Europe, including England. The indentured system in place during the Hundred Years War (1337–1453) was replaced by a private contract system. The new system placed knights at the same level as other recruits. They received the same pay, wore the same uniforms, and rode the same kind of horses (Gies 1984). War, with the help of new weaponry and a new type of professional soldier, was thus modernized. The new military profession had moved beyond the scope of the warrior-knight.

Knighthood did not disappear though; instead, it was retained primarily for ceremonial purposes. Throughout the fifteenth and sixteenth centuries, chivalric customs, especially tournaments, continued on for state occasions. Recognition that knighthood had finally become passé was perhaps most pointedly expressed in a book published in 1605 by a former Spanish soldier, Miguel de Cervantes Saavedra. His *Don Quixote* was meant to be a stinging commentary on the practice of chivalry through the character of Cervantes' foolish knight. Cervantes was successful in a way he perhaps never intended; for, while the plight of his unfortunate knight may have been perceived as comic in the seventeenth century, Don Quixote has endured as a poignant figure who, sadly, had outlived his function. Acknowledging this, Don Quixote, on his deathbed, turns to his friend, Sancho Panza:

> Forgive me, my friend, for having caused you to appear as mad as I by leading you to fall into the same error, that of believing that there are still knights-errant in the world
>
> Cervantes 1958, 698

Although knighthood and fabulous beasts would be phased out with the closing of the Middle Ages, the other figure of strength brought from ancient lore was much more enduring. The fate of Enkidu, carried on in the guise of the medieval wild man, was incorporated as part of the ritual of village festivals.

The Wild Man

Although the subsequent versions of the wild man[4] vary from the original epic, there is generally agreement that the wild man had tremendous strength and originally lived in the animal, rather than the human, world. In the *Gilgamesh* epic, the description of Enkidu provides the prototype:

> Matted hair was all over his body . . .
> This Enkidu was innocent of mankind . . .
> Enkidu was in the hills
> With the gazelles—
> He too ate grass.
> He was at the water-holes.
> With the wild beasts—
> They jostled each other
>
> Temple 1991, 6–7

The ancient writings of Herodotus and Pliny refer to wild men as creatures who roam with animals; Pliny's description, however, makes the wild man figure seem more fully animal than human. Later writings returned to the romantic picture of a "noble savage" who combined the characteristics of humans and animals but was more akin to man than to beast (Moore 1992; Bernheimer 1952).

In different versions of the wild man legend, his description and traits vary, but the attribute of superhuman strength remains. There were no beasts, real or imagined, who could not be conquered by the wild man. In the Carlisle carving, right, the wild man copies Samson's method of using his bare hands to rip apart a beast's jaws. The beast the wild man

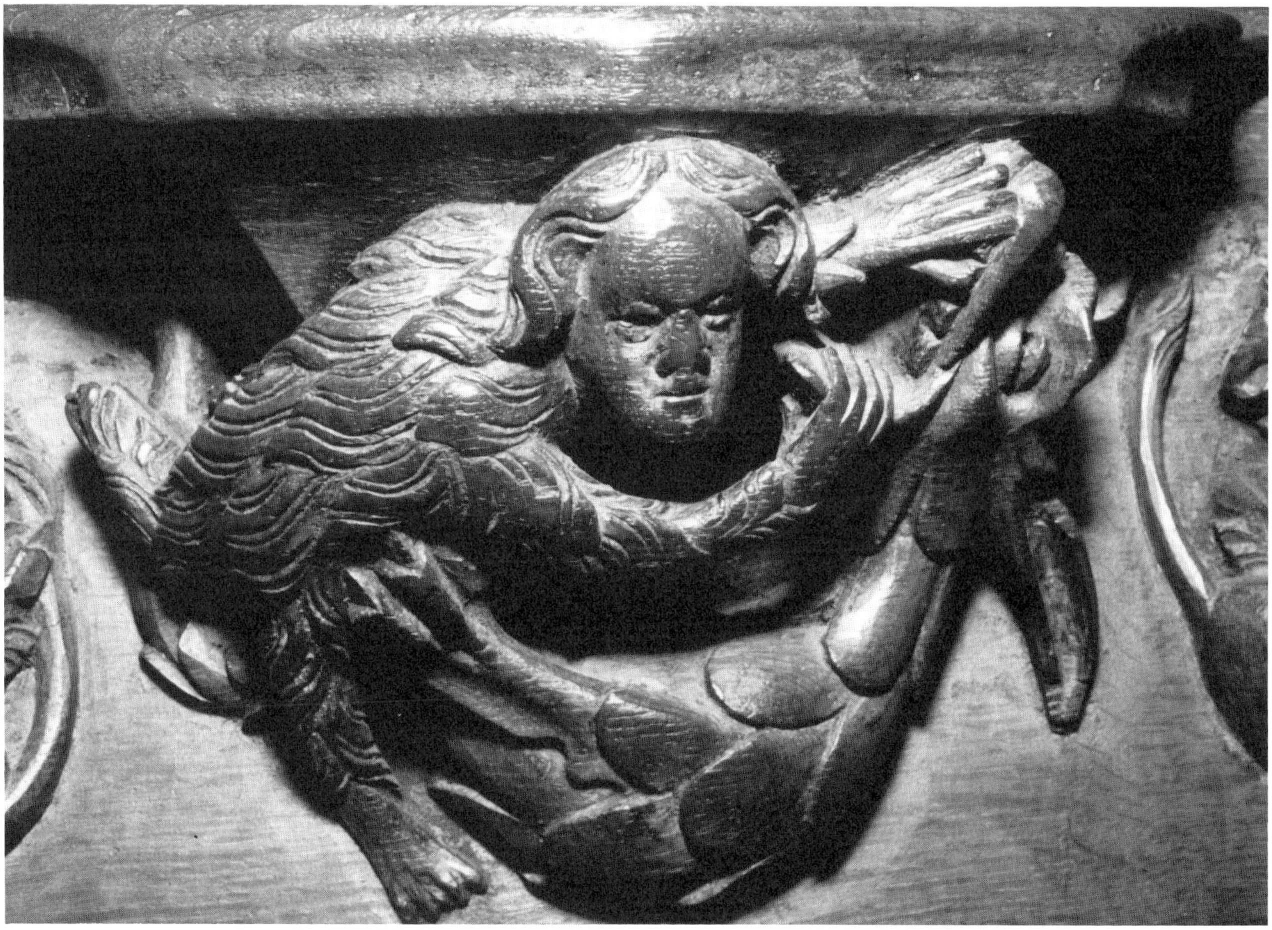

Wild man and dragon. Carlisle (Cumbria), The Cathedral, 1399–1413.

attacks, however, is far more dangerous than a mere lion. His prey is the most dangerous creature in the medieval world: a dragon.

Although most accounts continued to describe the wild man as covered with hair, like an animal, in one early fourteenth-century French bestiary he is described as a naked savage who kills a lion in order to clothe himself (Druce 1915). The Hereford carver combined these images as on the next page. The wild man is covered with hair but pulling at the lion's skin in an apparent attempt to obtain the fur, perhaps to supplement his wardrobe.

The battles the wild man engaged in were always fierce, but he was never beaten. As a result of his victories, so the medieval myth goes, defeated animals recognized the wild man's superiority by becoming his servants, usually by serving as his steeds (Bernheimer 1952). In the Chester carving, the hairy wild man rides a subdued lion.

In a more stylized version, the Beverley carving shows the wild man trampling on dragons while standing between two docile lions.

In the Middle Ages, the figure of the wild man was admired by nobility and commoner alike and was a favorite at court, especially in the fourteenth century, when "masques" were in vogue. There are records showing, for example, a figure called the "woodwose" in a court masque in England in 1348. Lists also show costumes issued for the Christmas and Epiphany celebrations in England in 1347 and 1348, which include those for "wildmen" (Withington 1918). The wild man also appeared at public festivals, one of his function being to carry large clubs of "fireworks" to clear the

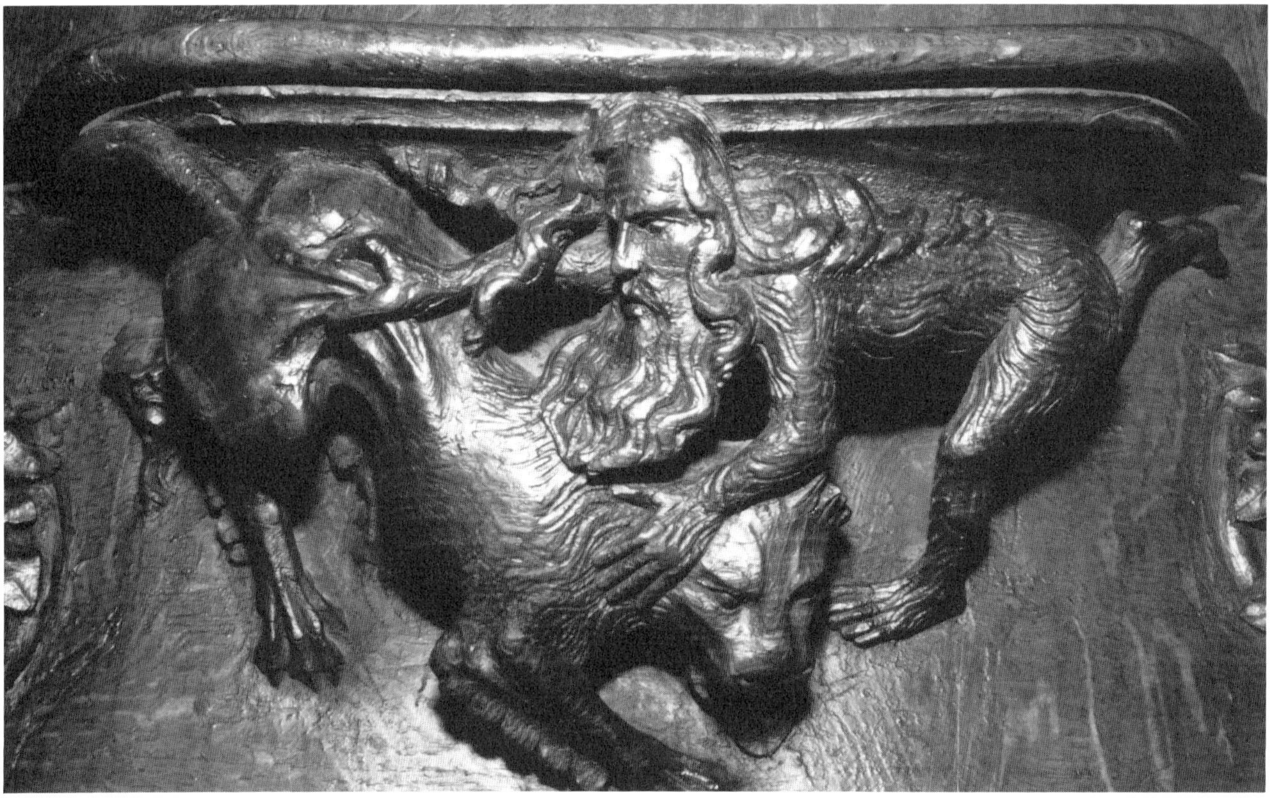

Wild man and beast. Hereford (Herefs & Worcs), The Cathedral, c.1380.

way for the procession (Strutt 1810). This ritual had connections to older views of the wild man with his club going into battle; but here, he was transformed into a symbolic, rather than actual, figure of fierceness.

Part of the routine of the wild man disguises included the wild man dances in which men assuming the role of wild men would join hands, become part of the "Wilde Horde," and dance in a circle. There is a widely reported story of a masque in France in 1392, when Charles VI and five of his nobles dressed as wild men in suits of "pitch and flax." Unfortunately, the nobles were dancing chained together when a torch brought too close to them ignited their costumes and they burned to death. The king was unharmed because he was not dancing with the group (Barber and Riches 1971).

The fascination with the wild man image during the Middle Ages, has been explained in various ways, one of which involves the medieval concept of wildness as a rather romantic version of madness. In the chivalric tales, grief could produce a kind of madness in which the afflicted would, as far as possible, retire from human society. Thus, in some segments of the Arthurian legend, Lancelot spends years wandering in the woods as a grief-stricken wild man before he comes to his senses (Bernheimer 1952). This is reminiscent of Gilgamesh's anguish upon the death of Enkidu, which sends him off on a long, fruitless journey before eventually returning to his senses:

> "I touched his heart. It does not beat."
> He covered the friend's face like a bride's.
> "Like an eagle I circled over him."
> Like a lioness whose whelps are lost,
> he paces back and forth.
> He tears and messes his rolls of hair.
> He tears off and throws down his fine
> clothes like things unclean.
>
> *Gilgamesh* 1984, 187–88

On other occasions, madness and wildness were labels assigned to behavior considered incomprehensible. St. Francis and his followers, for instance, were compared by some to

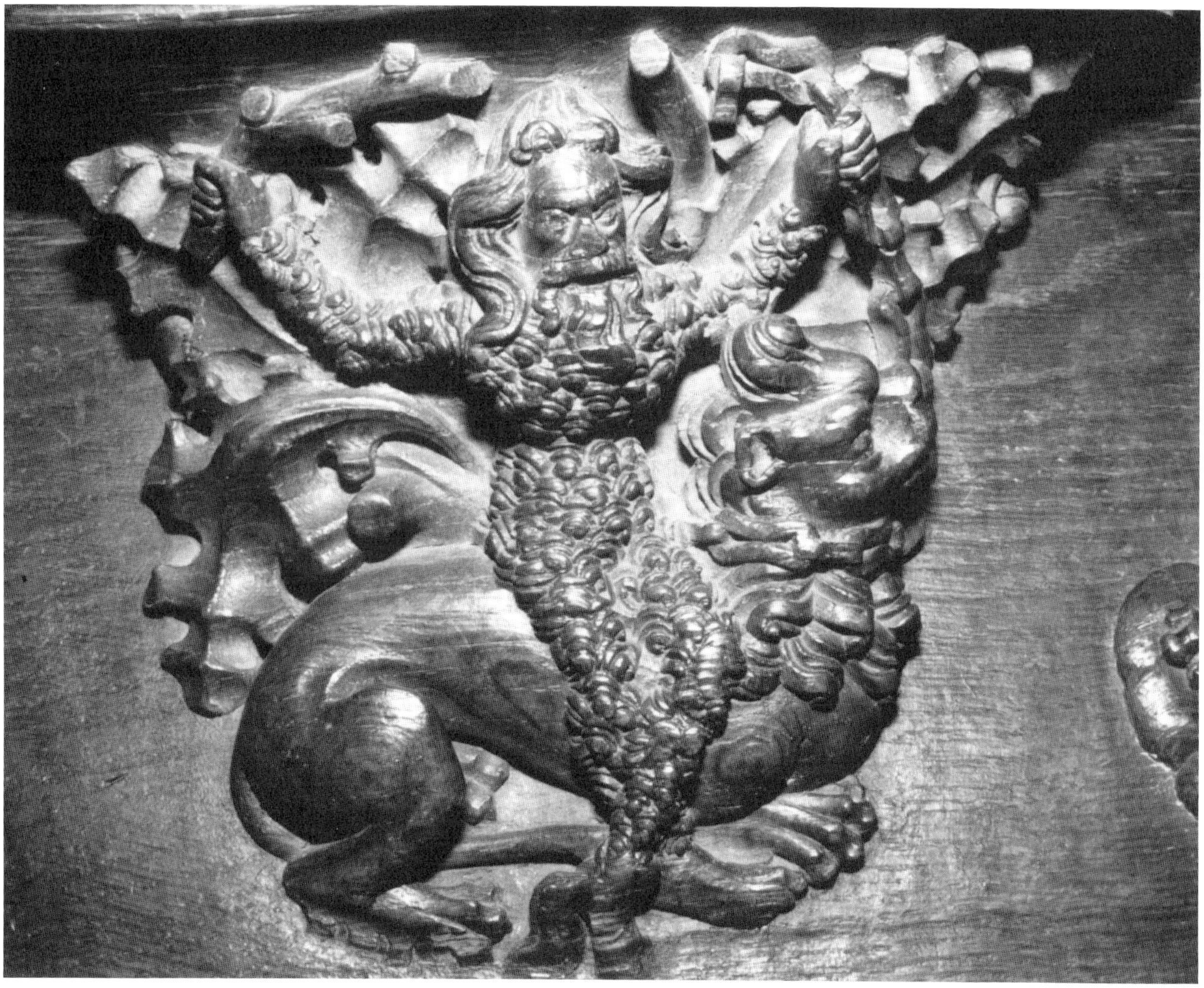

Wild man on lion. Chester (Cheshire), The Cathedral, c.1380.

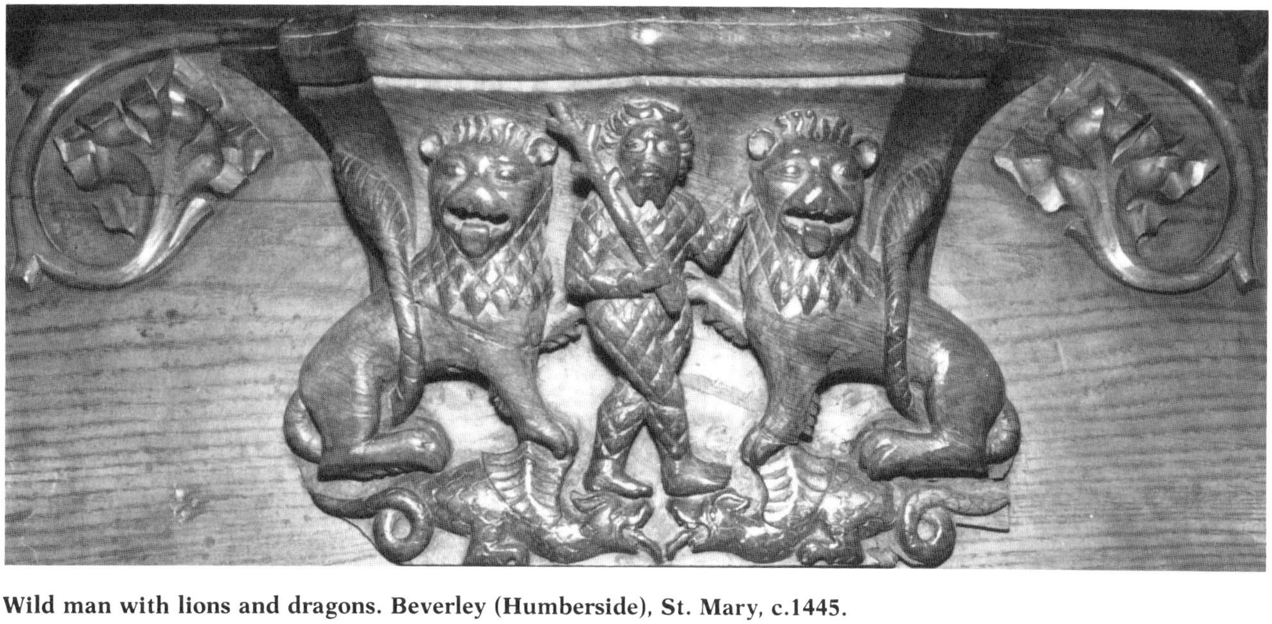

Wild man with lions and dragons. Beverley (Humberside), St. Mary, c.1445.

wild men because they renounced all worldly goods and slept in the wilderness. It was noted that "those who visited the friars described their sleeping places as like the lairs of wild beasts" (Armstrong 1973, 24).

The most prevalent image of the medieval wild man, like other medieval heroes, however, was as a figure admired for his ability to triumph over equally strong adversaries—the dragon, the lion, and so forth. For a time in the fourteenth and fifteenth centuries, in a uniquely medieval twist, the wild man was used as a proxy for every man when he was pitted against the aristocratic knight with all his affectations. In particular, the common man, with the aid of carvers, matched wits against the more refined, chivalrous knight for the favors of women. This was based on an extension of the wild man legend to include a purportedly insatiable appetite for women (Barber and Riches 1971). No doubt, this characteristic played a part in the popularity of joining in the "Wilde Horde" dances; but it also placed the wild man at odds with the more gentlemanly knight. The wild man's approach to women was closely akin to that of many ordinary men, but derided as crude and untenable by medieval knights. Thus, for a period during the height of chivalry, knights were said to challenge the unassailable wild men. Bernheimer (1952) suggests that in all the various artistic renderings of the conflict between the wild man and the knight, the knight is shown winning—until the demise of knighthood itself late in the fourteenth century. In the ivory carving from a French casket, the knight still enjoys the advantage as he vanquishes the lusty wild man. We are made to understand that the knight's deed is moral by the scene on the right, showing the knight being welcomed by St. Peter, presumably at a later time.

By the fifteenth century, however, the situation had been reversed and the wild man eclipsed the knight in the contest for the affections of women. In the carving on the right, the wild man gazes adoringly at a maiden holding a banner inscribed with a French phrase which translates as: "think much and speak little," apparently indicating a preference for another of the wild man's peculiarities—lack of human speech.

In a final victory, the romantic image of knighthood faded, but the admired traits associated with the wild man ensured his inclusion in pageants and processions well into the seventeenth century (Briggs 1976).

There were many other, less dramatic tests of strength for medieval man—football, wrestling, foot races and board games—but none quite satisfied the epic image of battles with the beasts. As dragons and other beasts became unavailable for slaying, as the skills of knighthood became outmoded, and hand-to-hand combat was replaced, the professional athlete has increasingly shouldered the burden for proving the physical strength of every man, no doubt a safer enterprise but a far less adventurous one.

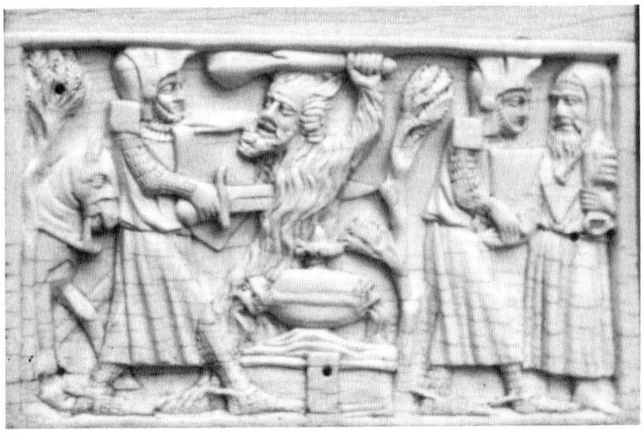

Knight slaying wild man. Paris, fourteenth century. Courtesy of the Trustees of the British Museum, BM Ivories 36–9.

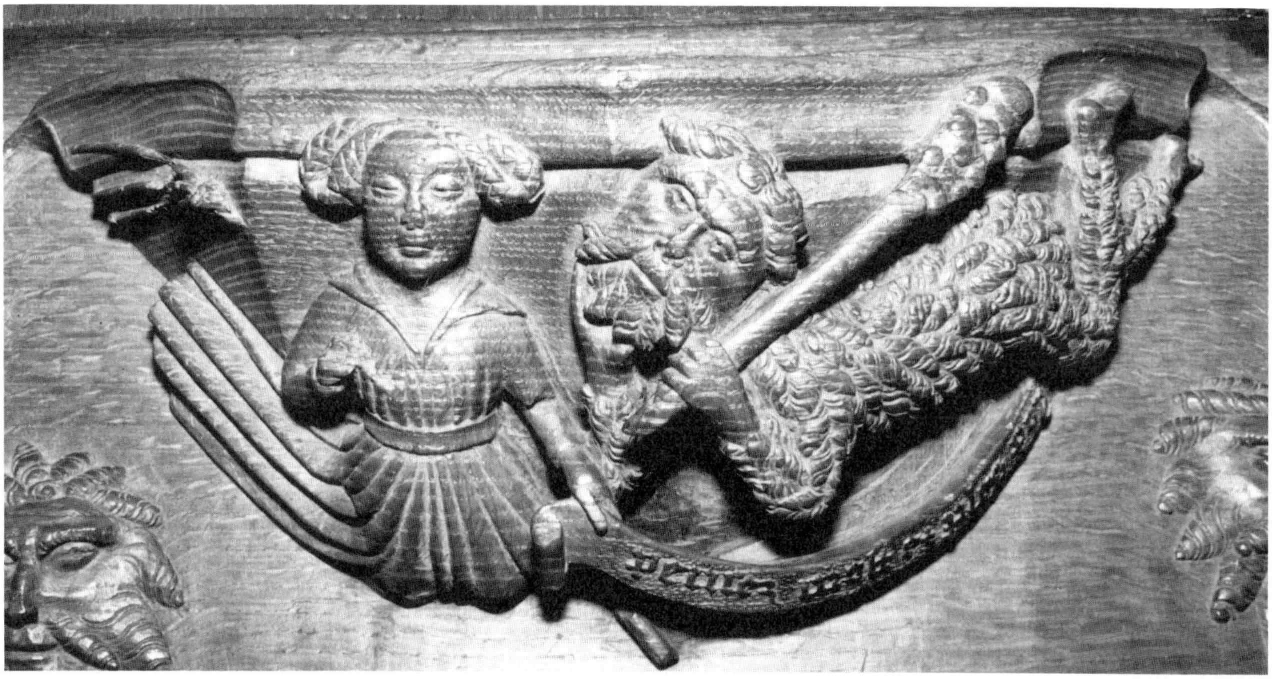

Wild man and maiden. Whalley (Lancs), St. Mary, c.1430.

4
Mayhem and Merriment—Medieval Entertainment

And every instrument of minstrelsy
He well knew how to play, while melody,
Poured from his throat, clear joy to hear him sing.
Geoffrey Chaucer, "The Manciple's Tale," fourteenth century

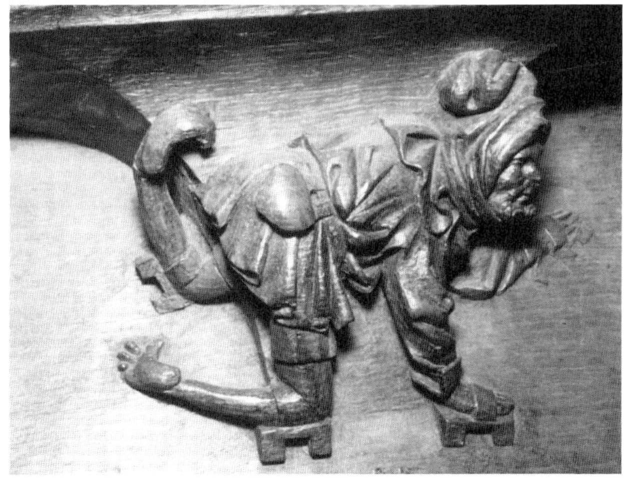

Deformed beggar. Winchester (Hants), Winchester College Chapel, late fourteenth century.

WE KNOW THAT THE LIFE OF THE MEDIEVAL CITIZEN was not easy. There was disease, hunger, unrelenting hard work, and uncertain heavenly rewards. People were frequently unfairly taxed, abused by their landlords, and denied comfort by the legal system. If illness struck, one hoped that home remedies would work. If one were born deformed, or became so through misfortune, so one remained. The plight of many of these unfortunates is poignantly expressed in the carving of the deformed beggar from Winchester College.

Even though medieval life was difficult and the work hard, there were still occasions when life was not only enjoyed, but celebrated. The medieval citizen was openly sensual, a lover of pranks and jokes, a happy participant in celebrations involving drinking, gambling, dancing, sexual play, and a willing spectator at public punishments and executions; yet, he or she also believed in God and the importance of following the teachings of the Church. These characteristics seem contradictory in current times but were not viewed as such in the Middle Ages, by either the citizenry or the clergy.

The celebrations enjoyed were a curious blend of Christian and pagan elements. There were festivals honoring various saints, for example, as well as traditional pagan rites such as Rogationtide or May Day. The Church itself fostered a blending of the sacred and the profane as it strove to replace pagan beliefs with Christian dogma. Being a part of the historical moment themselves, many of the clergy engaged in nonreligious play alongside the laity. Indeed, the clergy enjoyed ribaldry as much as the next person, and monks and nuns produced their share of risqué tales (Durant and Durant 1950).

The robustness of medieval life is accounted for partially by the norms of the time, but also by the fact that the population was young. For example, Tuchman (1978) estimates that in the fourteenth century about half the population of France was under 21 years of age and about a third under the age of 14. It is not possible to derive accurate estimates for the English population for the same period, English records being inferior at the time to those of the French. It was not until 1538 in England that parish registries were kept on a regular basis and not until 1841 that vital statistics were first collected (Wrigley 1966). The earliest recorded list that includes the age of inhabitants (for which statistics are available) was for 1599, in the town of Ealing in Middlesex. In that listing, the figures mirror Tuchman's estimates for France: 45.4 percent under the age of 20 and 34.6 percent under the age of 15. The median age in that community at that time was 20.3 years for men and 23.2 years for women (Laslett 1966). Hurd-Mead (1938) reports that in the sixteenth century, the average life span was 18 years throughout Europe. These figures offer some confirmation that the population in England in the late Middle Ages was indeed young—and one with youthful interests. In other words, a population that coveted lust and laughter.

Merriment

The medieval world was an intensely interactive society, perhaps most acutely displayed in its hands-on forms of entertainment. The human body was used as the primary instrument of entertainment, whether through song, dance, sport, or acting—with frequent, and eager, participation of the spectators.

One of the most elaborate and thoroughly enjoyed forms of celebration during the medieval period was the formal theatrical presentation. Two types predominated, the miracle play and the mystery play. According to some scholars, the mystery play was based on the Holy Scriptures and was meant to have both a "hidden mysterious significance" and an obvious meaning. As the term implies, miracle plays were based on the miraculous acts of saints.

The distinction between mystery and miracle plays has been challenged by some, who suggest that the term *mystery play* itself was not used in England before 1744 and that *miracle play* was a generic term that included all plays performed outdoors (Chambers 1903). In this view, miracle plays were simply an extension, or outgrowth, of the mystery plays that came earlier. It is perhaps more useful to think of both types as religious drama that was taken over by the laity in the Middle Ages and converted into secular, staged drama.

Staged Drama

The earliest known English mystery plays still in existence are those collected under the name of the "Towneley Mysteries," named for the owner of the manuscript. Probably written in the fourteenth century, they comprise 32 plays that begin with the Creation and end with the Last Judgment (Wright 1865; Anderson 1963). Originally, plays were performed inside the Church and probably initially involved only pantomime or simple chanting. Over time, Latin dialogue was introduced, but it was still chanted rather than spoken, at least at first. The more conservative members of the Church were skeptical about the appropriateness of the plays. As they continued to grow in popularity, however, performances became too large to contain within a church. By the end of the fourteenth century, this growth, combined with active Church criticism in some quarters, resulted in the production of the plays being taken over by the laity, primarily the guilds. The plays were then performed in the open street, becoming a major part of community life, which they remained throughout the Middle Ages.

The shift in sponsorship from Church to the citizenry changed the tone of the plays. Under the guidance of the Church, they were solemn affairs meant to underscore the human condition, redemption and resurrection; but under the sponsorship of the guilds they were far different, becoming increasingly more secularized and irreverent. Although emphasis on the biblical story was retained, the guilds extended the content to include dialogue intended to amuse the audience, mainly through the use of vulgarity and coarse, scatological language (Wright 1865). This was not as defiant as it sounds, for, in the Catholic Church of the Middle Ages, vulgarity was not considered offensive. In fact, Ciardi (1954, 188) makes the distinction between Protestant and Catholic cultures around this issue by noting that "the offensive language of Protestantism is obscenity; the offensive language of Catholicism is profanity or blasphemy." It was perfectly acceptable to speak of bodily functions using coarse language and vulgar behavior, as long as one did not dispute the tenets of the Church.

Each guild had its own pageant, its own set of actors, and its own series of plays in which the guild took great pride. The guilds paid actors for their performances, although these actors were guild members who performed as amateurs. In addition, although amateurs, the actors were expected to meet certain standards. A public proclamation at York, for example, required that actors be "good players, well arrayed, and openly spekying" (Smith 1963, xxxvii).

Many towns had their mystery plays. In England, the most famous were those at Chester, York, and Coventry. By the fifteenth century, mystery plays had become such lavish community productions that some of them lasted forty days (Bishop 1987). Most, however, seem to have lasted four to seven days and covered, in increasingly elaborate presentation, the period from the Creation to the Last Judgment. These plays took place in some forty English locations, mostly in the north and east (Chambers 1945).

The guilds would first organize a procession, or "riding," on their patron saint's day. These ridings paralleled the development of the "royal entry" as a pageant. Like the royal entries, they drew their audience from every segment of society, from peasant to king (Withington 1918). For instance, some accounts indicate that, while still Duke of Gloucester, Richard III and his duchess took part in the procession of the annual York mystery play. This play, like others around the country, was considered the main event of the community's year. It involved as many as 600 players in 50 or more scenes (Seward 1983). Referred to as a "cycle" of plays, each cycle presented a specific segment of the story; each segment, or scene, was associated with a specific guild. At York, for example, the carpenter's guild, including carvers, was responsible for the resurrection scene (Smith 1963), the plasterer's guild for the creation of the earth, the shipwright's guild for the building of Noah's Ark, and so forth (Bates 1893).

The ordinances of most guilds required member contributions to support the productions. Because the plays were so revered, it is likely that these contributions were willingly given. The pageants[1] were taken so seriously that the guilds appointed "pageant-masters" to collect the contributions, allocate disbursements, and oversee the actors' conduct (Smith 1963).

The usual method of presenting sequential scenes was to place each scene on a separate wagon. But stationary platforms could also be erected, thus requiring the audience to move from platform to platform. In York, when wagons were used, the stages would be drawn to designated stopping places, and there the scene would be enacted before moving on to the next stopping point. The first wagon at York started at 4:30 A.M. on Corpus Christie day in early June. These stopping places became status symbols as individuals paid to have the pageant stop before their house. In 1417, the city formalized this practice by passing an ordinance decreeing that people willing to pay the highest fee were privileged to have the play stop before their house (Purvis 1951).

Accounts differ as to how the wagons were constructed. Sometimes they are described as carts with platforms on two levels, with the lower level curtained off to serve as a dressing room from which actors emerged on cue (Taylor 1959). Anderson (1963) disagrees with this description, arguing, instead, that medieval actors did not change their costumes in the course of the play, so the lower level could not have been a dressing room. She suggests that it was used for stage machinery and as a place for actors to disappear when not needed on stage. Other accounts describe the wagons as tri-level affairs, with the upper level representing heaven, the middle level earth, and the lower level hell (Wright 1865). The tri-level wagons may have been used more often for staging miracle plays than mystery plays; but there is disagreement as to whether they were prevalent only in England or only in France (Penn 1933; Bates 1893). Whatever the form, stage construction was a complicated and costly endeavor and care was taken to preserve the sets for use from year to year.

Preparation for the plays became increasingly elaborate as they became more sophisticated, taking months to construct stage sets and costumes, not to mention the rehearsing of an enormous company of actors. The cost of production rose with the lavishness of the presentation as companies vied with each other to present the most spectacular production. The quest for realism became dazzling. Tuchman reports on one such production in the fourteenth century:

> A system of weights and pulleys resurrected Jesus from the tomb and lifted him to a ceiling of clouds. Angels and devils were to appear magically through trapdoors. Hell opened and closed its monstrous mouth, and Noah's flood inundated the stage from casks of water overturned backstage while stone-filled barrels turned by cranks resounded with thunder.
>
> 1978, 311

The focus of the plays shifted as well, from solemn reminder to farce, as they progressed under the supervision of the guilds. They were designed, above all, to entertain.

The number of comic characters increased in the plays as contemporary stagers adapted and altered the presentation and dialogue to amuse medieval audiences. Satirical pokes were taken at particular characters who became stock butts of jokes. The previously mentioned alewife's fate of being paired with a demon in marriage rather than being released from hell was one such standard scene that never failed to elicit a laugh. The difficult wife, another stock character, was used by the guilds to infuse the plays with more commentary on contemporary life—commentary, in this instance, on the view of women as disrupters of domestic harmony.

THE DIFFICULT WIFE

The concept of the difficult wife was joyously played out from the time of the Towneley plays in one standard scene where Noah is pitted against his reluctant, shrill wife. Noah, though successful in building the ark and gathering the animals two-by-two, has little success in persuading his wife to come aboard. Not only does she ridicule his building of the ark, she refuses to set foot on board until finally, when the water reaches her feet, she rushes aboard. Noah greets her with a masterly flogging, but she refuses to beg for mercy. Instead, she turns to the audience and, to the delight of the female spectators particularly, wishes all the husbands in the audience dead. Finally, a beaten Noah offers up his own advice to husbands:

> Ye men that has wifes, whyles they are yong,
> If ye luff your lives, chastice thar tong
>
> Bates 1893, 66

In the Ely carving below, we can see Noah

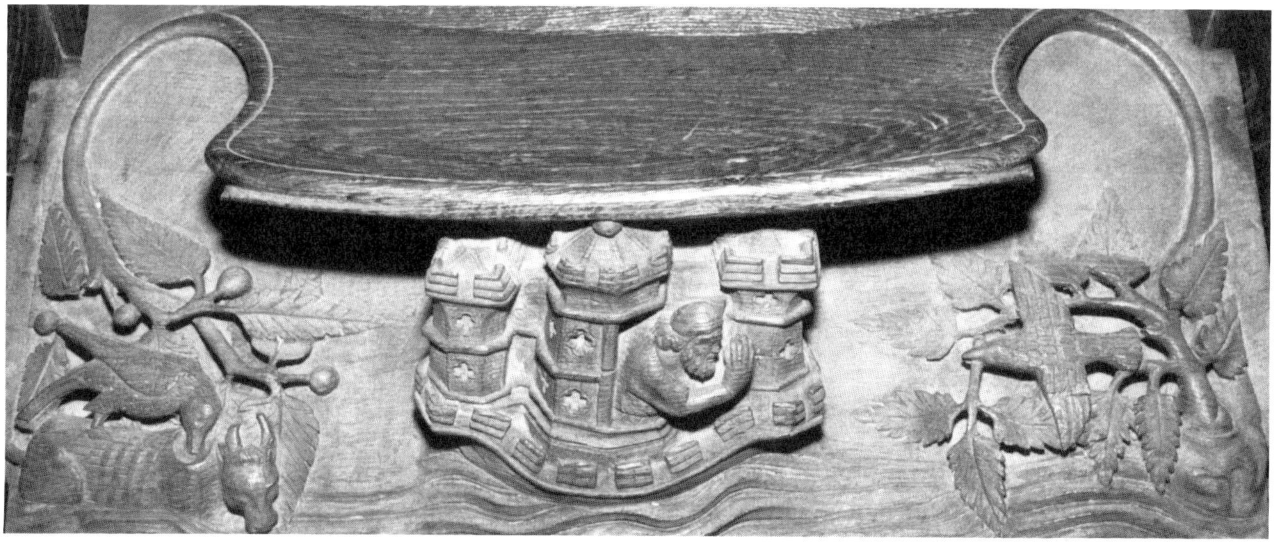

Noah in Ark. Ely (Cambs), The Cathedral, c.1340.

beckoning, perhaps to his wife, to come aboard.

Clearly, the creation of Noah's wife as a reluctant, shrewish person is an alteration made by the guild to entertain the audience and make the play more lively. The wife in the biblical passage is far less troublesome:

> Noah went in, and his sons and his wife and his sons' wives with him, into the ark, because of the waters of the flood
>
> Genesis 7:7

TUTIVILLUS

The most comical characters of mystery plays were the Devil and his underlings, whose antics were guaranteed to amuse. Impersonations of the various demons ranged from the relatively mild to the obscene:

> The most striking costume was that of the devil, who was as shaggy and beast-like as possible, black, horned, clawed, with cloven feet and a forked tail, and, sometimes with pipes of burning gunpowder in his ears
>
> Bates 1893, 42

One well-known demon from the Towneley Mysteries is "Tutivillus." His origin is uncertain, but Tutivillus is charged with keeping accounts of different sins committed. All of these recorded sins were to be kept in his safekeeping for use on Judgment Day. This figure was especially popular in the plays because he was used symbolically to settle scores against those who had in some way offended the ordinary person, for example, dishonest traders and the nobility. The audience would respond with raucous approval as the miscreants were hauled off to hell. This theme was popular throughout Europe during the Middle Ages, with Tutivillus appearing on guard in many art forms. The stone carving, right, from the facade of San Pietro in Spoleto, is a very humorous interpretation of the Last Judgment.

In the top panel, St. Peter is shown at the far right and far left holding the key to heaven, waiting to see whether the man lying dead will be granted admission to heaven or be sent to hell. St. Michael stands over the body, his scales ready to weigh sins against good deeds. Both listen as Tutivillus reads from his list. The outcome is shown in the bottom panel, where the scales have tipped against the man as Tutivillus sits atop him reading out his sins. On the right, St. Michael turns to walk away, leaving the man to his fate; on the left, we see a demon shoving him into a boiling cauldron.

The favorite depiction of Tutivillus was as a recorder of idle chatter or mumbled devotions in church—comic because almost everyone was guilty of this sin—especially, it was said, women. Sometimes the sins committed were so abundant that Tutivillus had trouble finding enough space on his scroll to record them all. When this happened, his solution was described in a fourteenth-century manuscript where one saint asks the other why he was laughing during mass:

> . . . he answered, that he saw the fende write alle the laughinges that were between the women at masse, and it happed that the parchemyn that he wrote in was shorte, and he plucked harde to have made it lenggen with his teeth, and it scaped oute of hys mouthe, and hys hede had a gret stroke agenst the walle, "and that made me to laughe"
>
> Wright 1868, 42

The Ely carving re-creates this scene with a friendly-looking devil hugging two women chatterers. Tutivillus is seated in the left supporter, trying to lengthen his scroll by tugging at it with his teeth. On the right supporter, he is shown sitting at ease, having been successful.

In the carving from the Royal Foundation of St. Katherine a far more fierce-looking demon hovers behind the women while Tutivillus waits at his desk on the left to begin recording their sins.

In the Towneley plays, Tutivillus carries the idle words and other sins of the offenders in a sack and speaks dog-Latin as he travels with other demons on the road to the Last Judgment. In these plays the dialogue between the demons is meant to be tongue-in-cheek, to satirize the vices and vanities of most church-

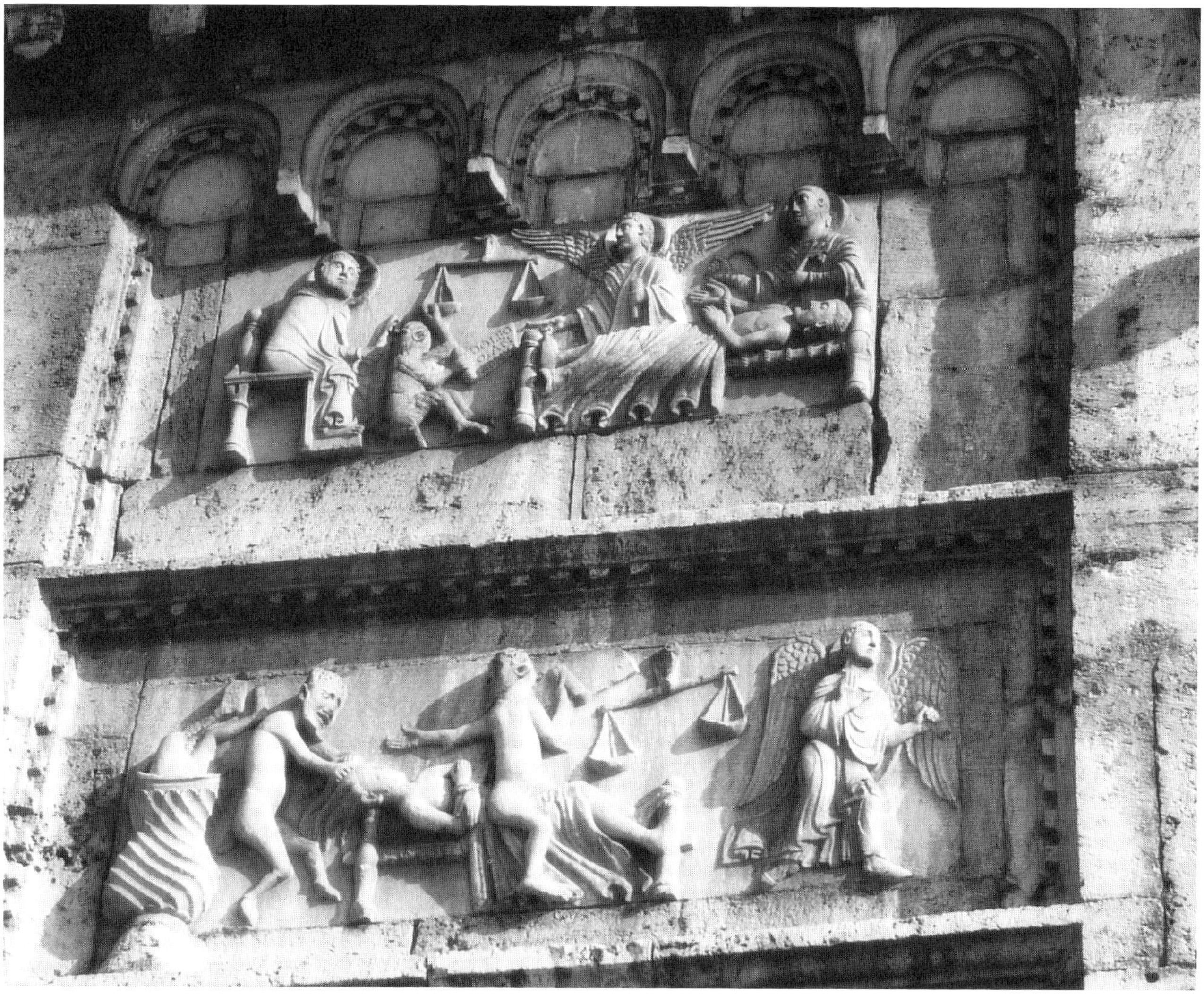

Last Judgment. Spoleto (Italy), Church of San Pietro, twelfth-thirteenth century.

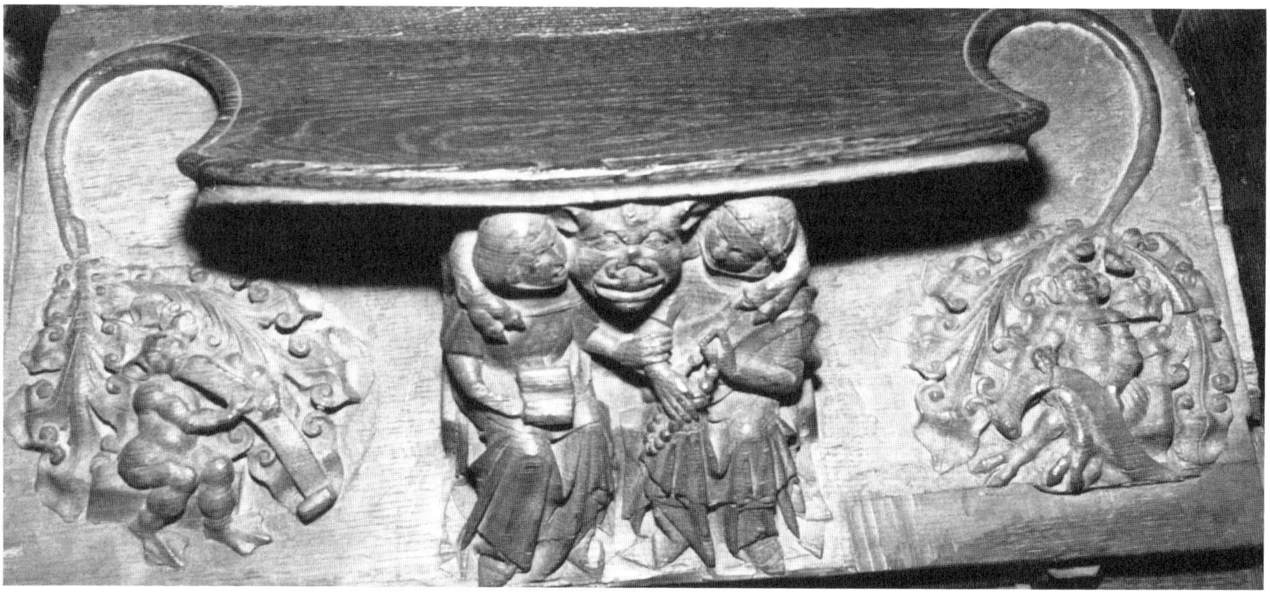

Tutivillus. Ely (Cambs), The Cathedral, c.1340.

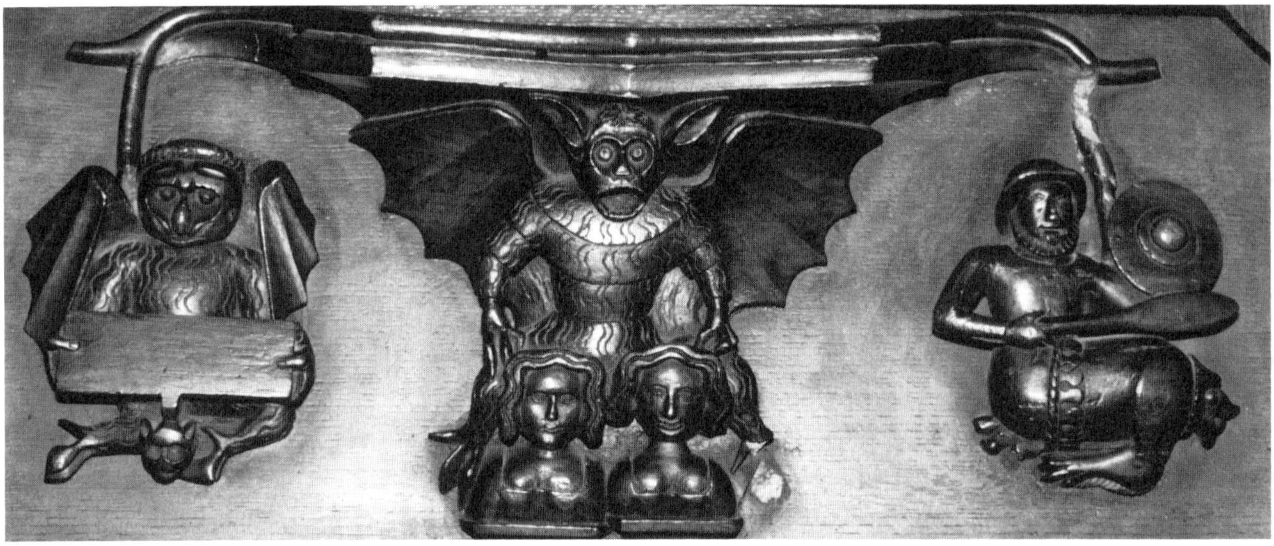

Tutivillus. London, The Royal Foundation of St. Katharine, 1377.

goers. In a doomsday scene in the Towneley series, Tutivillus appears carrying his bag of sins. He and another demon gleefully discuss the various exploits that have been collected in the bag to be used against the sinners. They are congratulating themselves for such good work:

> Souls come so thick now of late to hell,
> that our porter at hell gate is ever held
> so close at work, up early and down late,
> that he never rests
>
> Wright 1865, 72

JAWS OF HELL

Invariably, the Last Judgment scene in the mystery plays included the use of the dragon's mouth as the "Jaws of Hell." This was a dramatic entry into hell for those judged unworthy of heaven. The lost souls would be pushed into the dragon's gaping jaws by demons. The stage productions would have flames issuing from the mouth, accompanied by the sound of thunder (Saunders 1932; Taylor 1959) while actors portraying demons would go among the audience, prodding selected individuals (Bishop 1987).

As we have seen, demons in the plays were considered comic rather than terrifying characters. This was also true for the Hell Mouth constructions. Meant to be farcical, they were also meant to awe with their dramatic presentations. Richard Carew, in his 1602 history of Cornwall, notes the drawing power of the demons and other "devices":

> The country people flock from all sides, many miles off, to heare and see it: for they have therein, devils and devices, to delight as well the eyes as the eares.
>
> 1723, 71

The Hell Mouth was a vivid factor in Romanesque art, appearing frequently on tympana outside churches and on capitals inside. Though perhaps meant to alarm in Romanesque times, the symbolism became a source of hilarity in Gothic times. However, it could be argued that hilarious elements also entered into the dour view of Romanesque art. One of the best examples is from the tympanum of Ste. Foy de Conques in France, where a comic demon makes sure each sinner enters the mouth of the dragon to receive his or her just reward.

The capital from Chauvigny shows the next step in the poor sinner's progression as his head enters the dragon's mouth.

And, finally, a Gothic carver brought this idea forward, by showing the sinner one step closer to being devoured.

Sometimes sinners were pushed into the Jaws of Hell by demons, sometimes they were

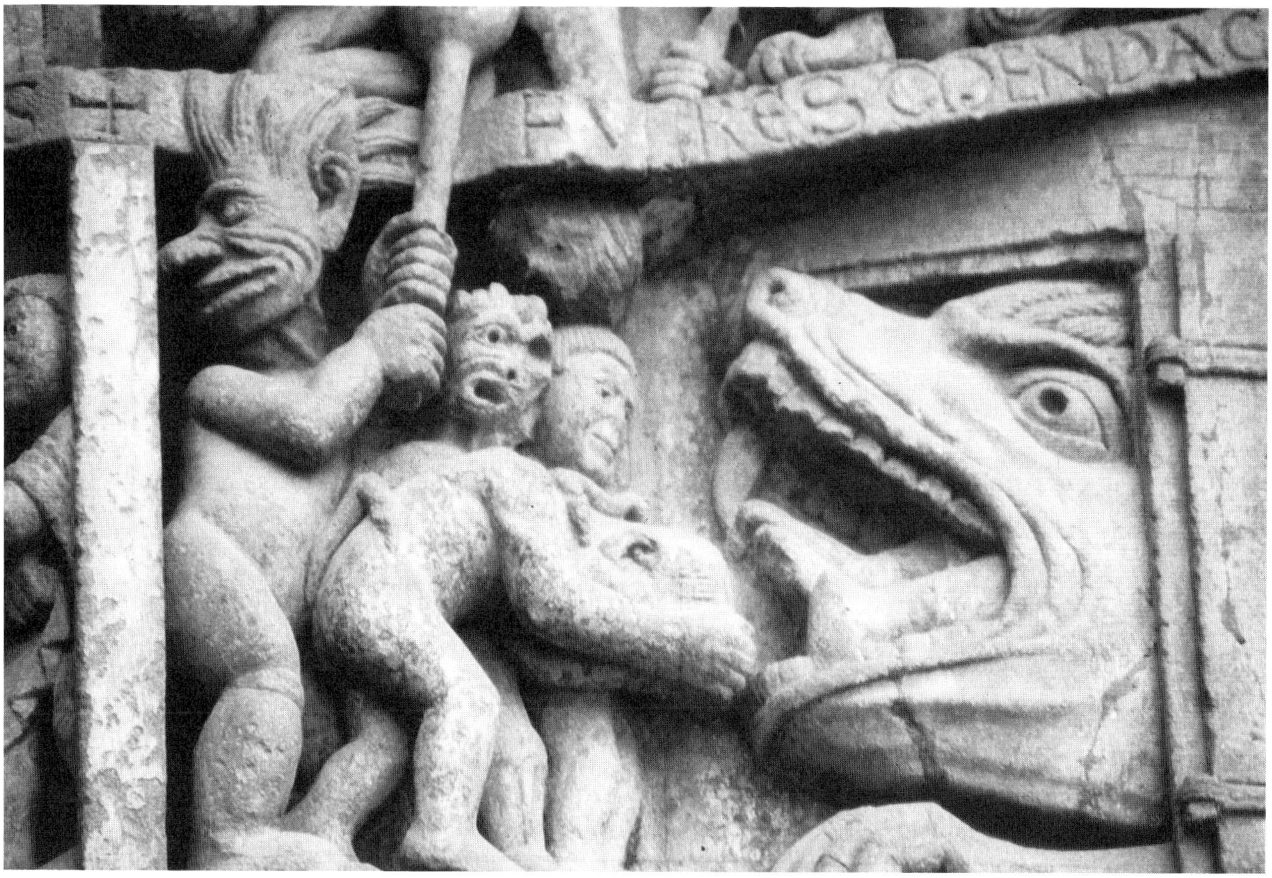

Hell Mouth. Conques (France), Ste. Foy de Conques, eleventh century.

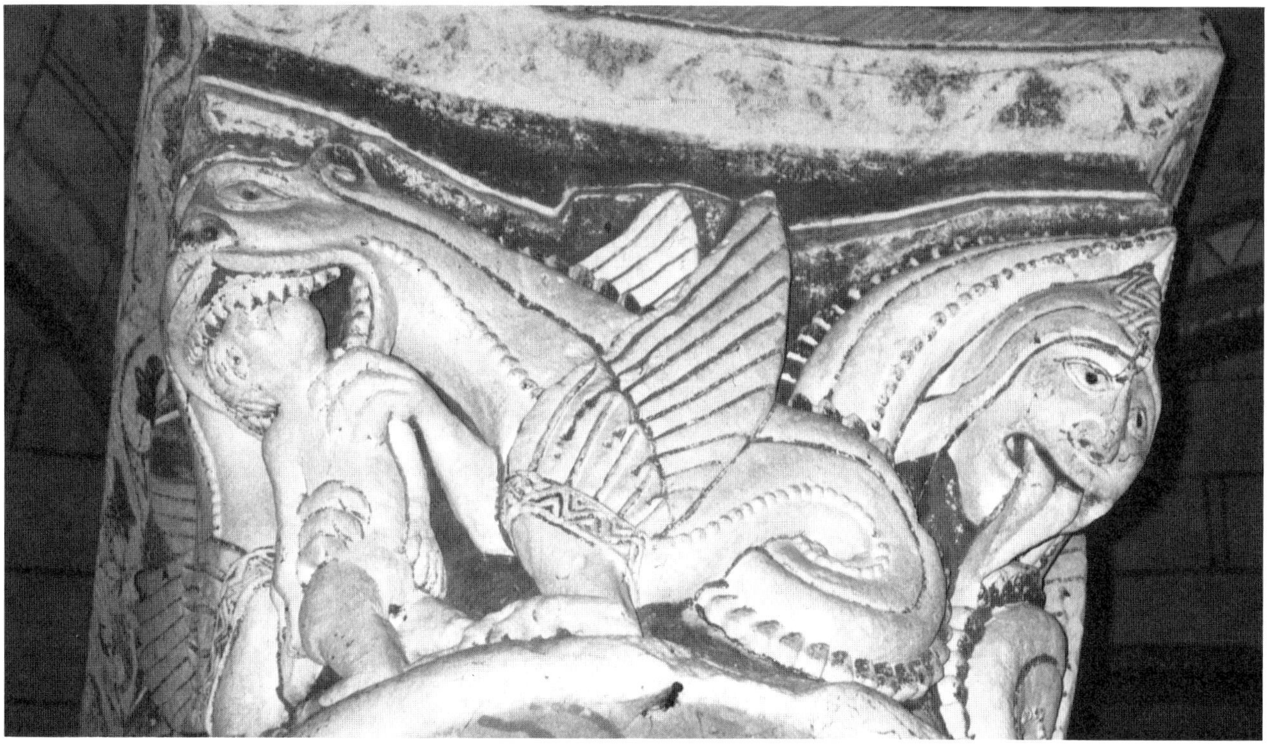

Hell Mouth. Chauvigny (France), Eglise St. Pierre, twelfth century.

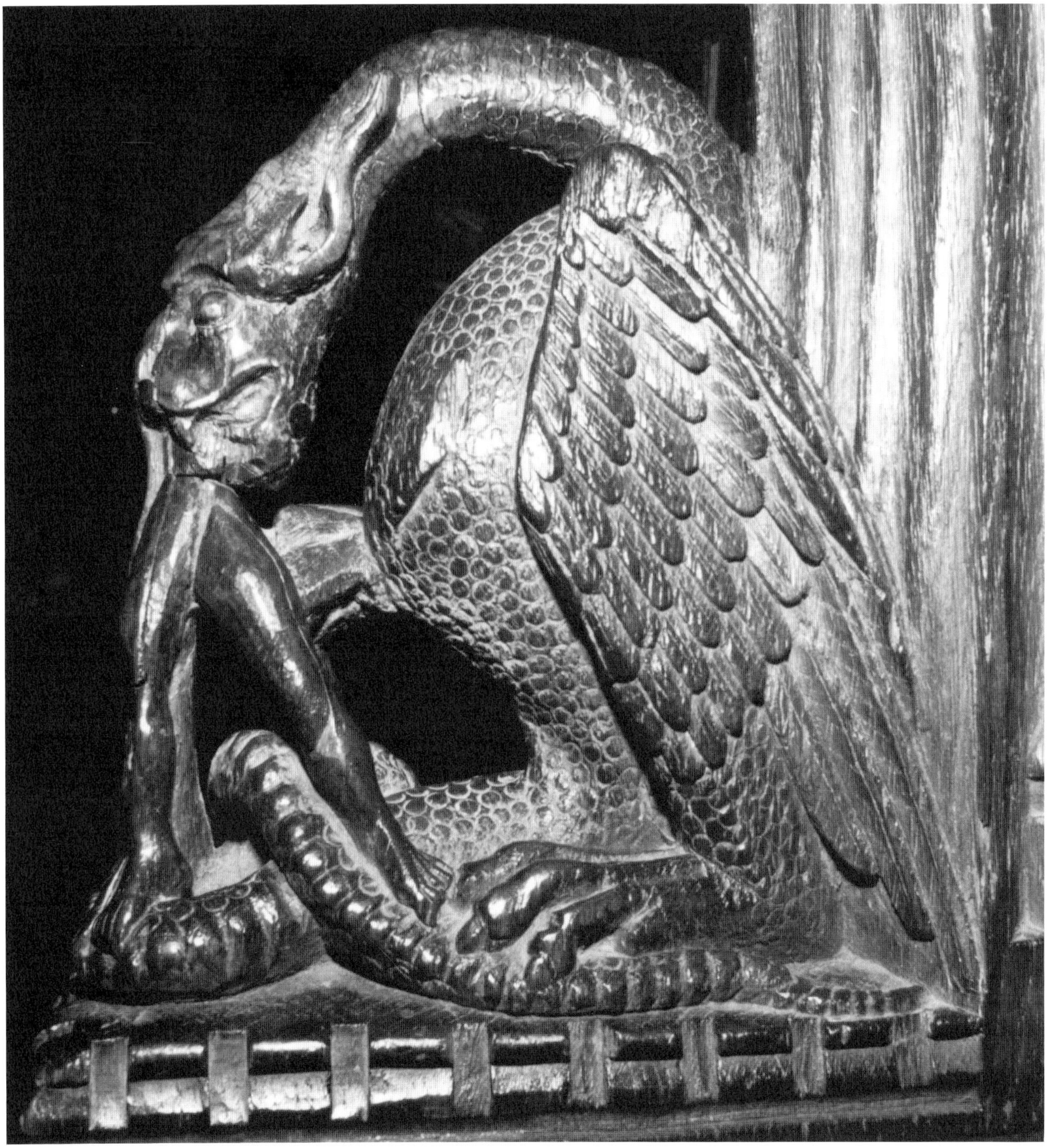

Hell Mouth. Chester (Cheshire), The Cathedral, c.1380.

shown being herded to their fate by the dragons themselves. A Bristol carver tried to underscore this point by having the rare double-headed dragon as the escort.

The audience found it especially amusing when the demons carted the clergy off to the Jaws of Hell. A monstrous demon carries a monk on his back in the fine carving below; in the next carving another demon wheels three monks and a fox toward the Hell Mouth. The fox character is used to symbolize deceit; here, with the monks, he signifies the deceit of the clergy.

No doubt, all these treacherous encounters with the devil and his demons gave rise to the adage that "He who sups with the devil better have a long spoon," so charmingly rendered in the following Windsor carving.

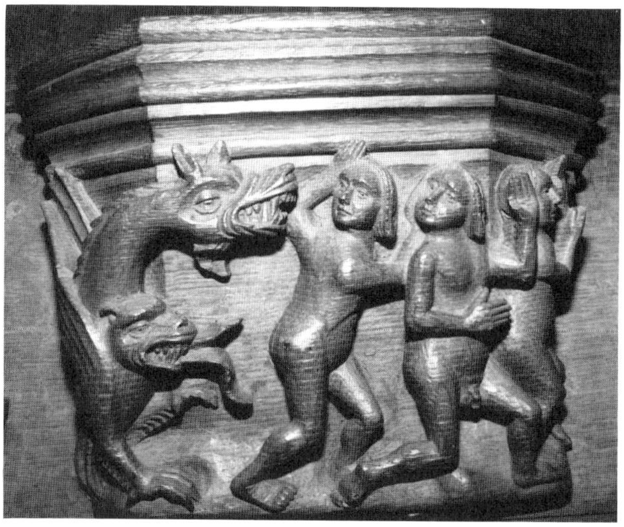

Three damned souls. Bristol (Avon), The Cathedral, 1520.

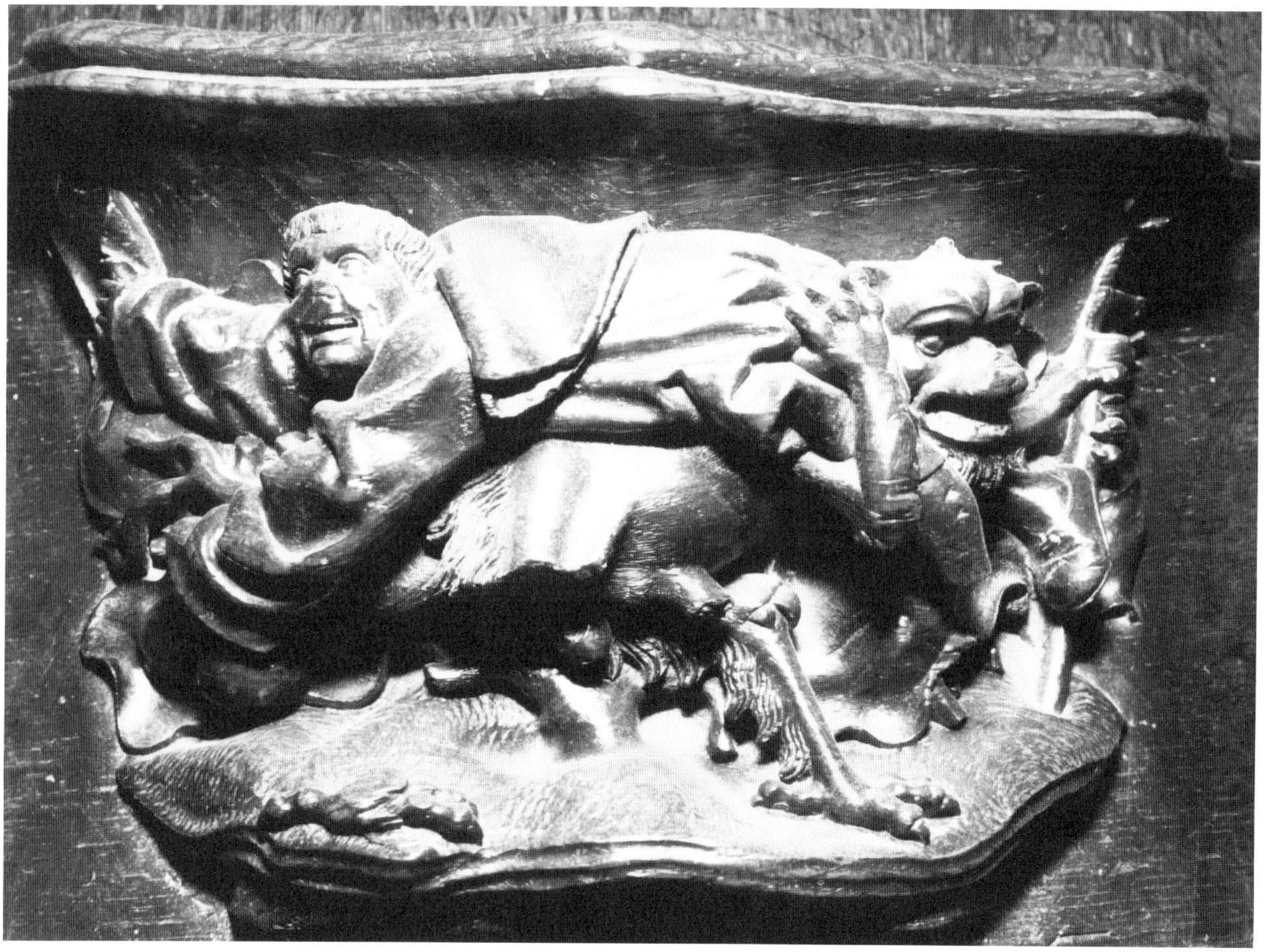

Demon with monk. Westminster (London), The Abbey, sixteenth century.

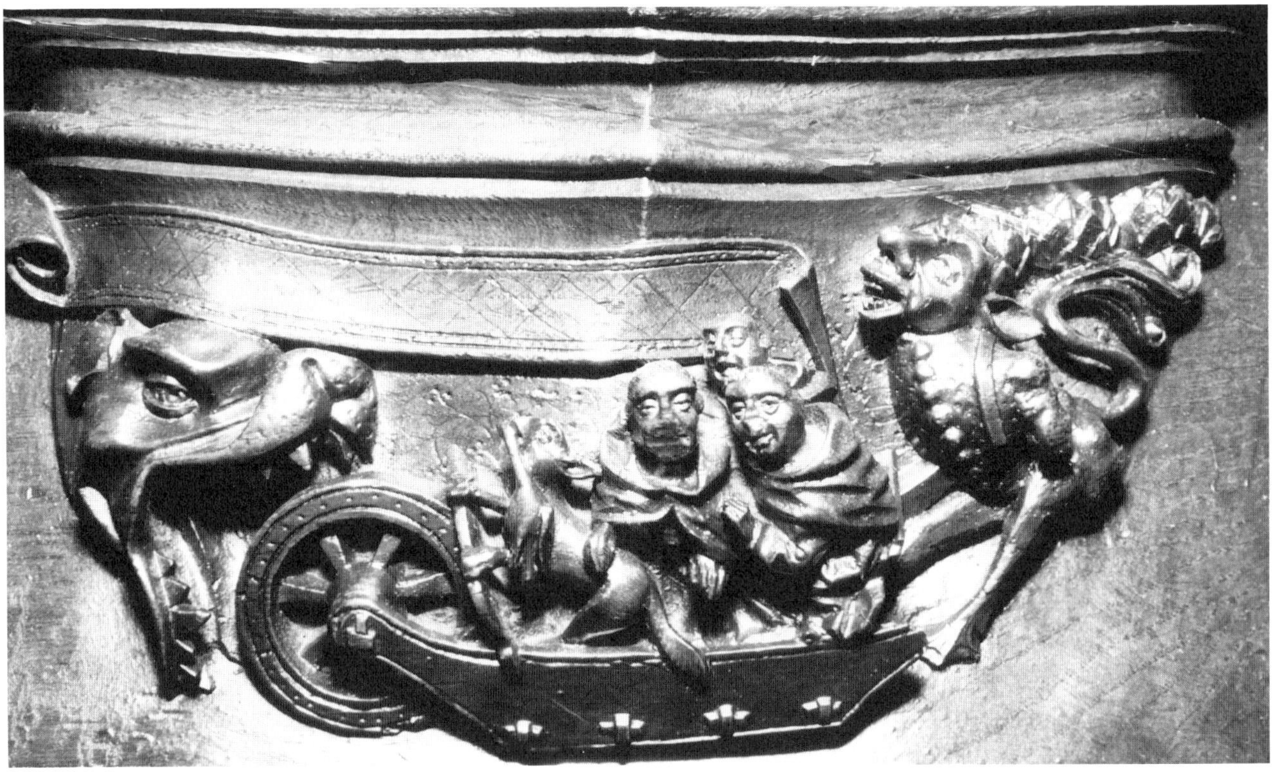

Three monks and a fox. Windsor (Berks), St. George's Chapel, 1477–83.

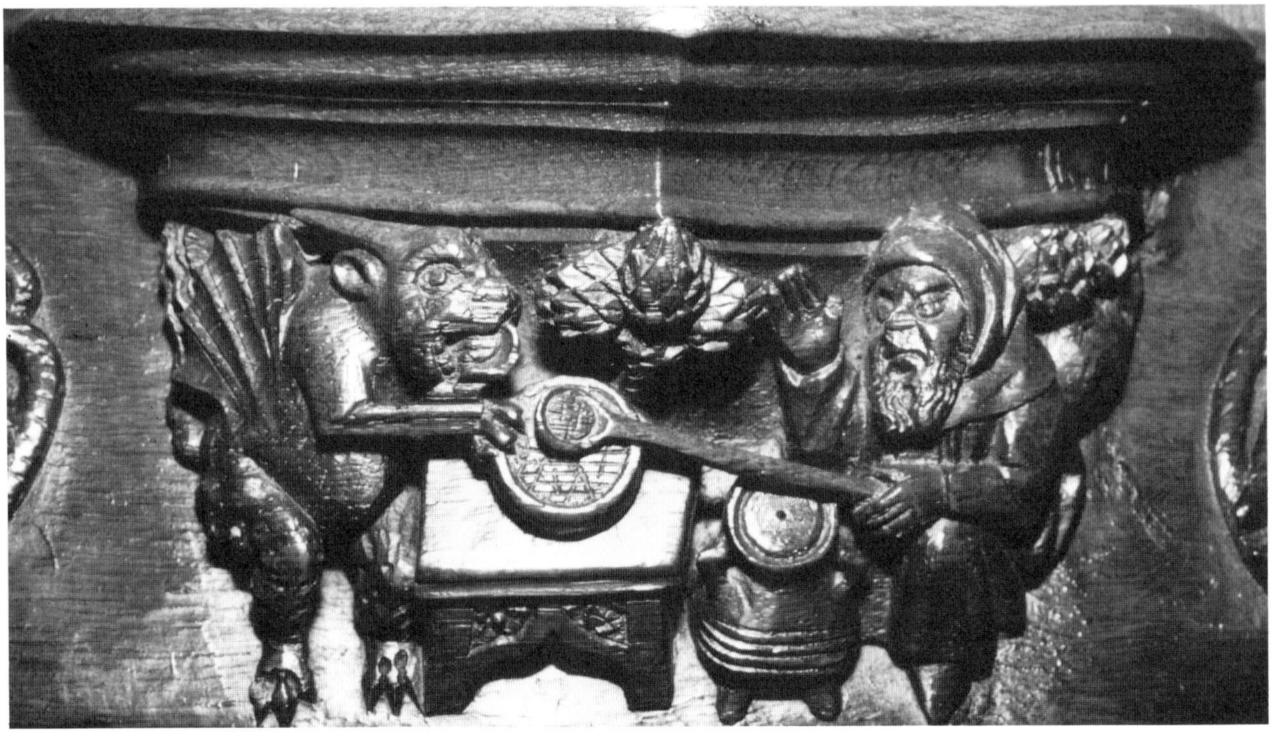

Supping with the Devil. Windsor (Berks), St. George's Chapel, 1477–83.

RESURRECTION

Because these plays, at least theoretically, dealt with salvation and redemption through death, the resurrection was also part of the series. Like the construction of the various Hell Mouths, the resurrection presented technical problems for carvers striving for realism. In the Chester Mystery play, the problem of Christ rising from a sealed tomb is solved by having two angels lift the lid while the soldiers sleep (Anderson 1963). This moment from the resurrection play was reproduced by a Chester Cathedral carver in 1876. His reproduction is said to faithfully replicate a fourteenth-century carving destroyed by a dean who considered the subject matter improper (Remnant 1969).

THE SAINTS

Miracle plays, developing out of mystery plays, also began as church events. Written records of the lives of saints were read aloud in the church on each saint's day from the thirteenth century on. As they moved out into the community, they became more elaborate and, like the mystery plays, lasted several days.

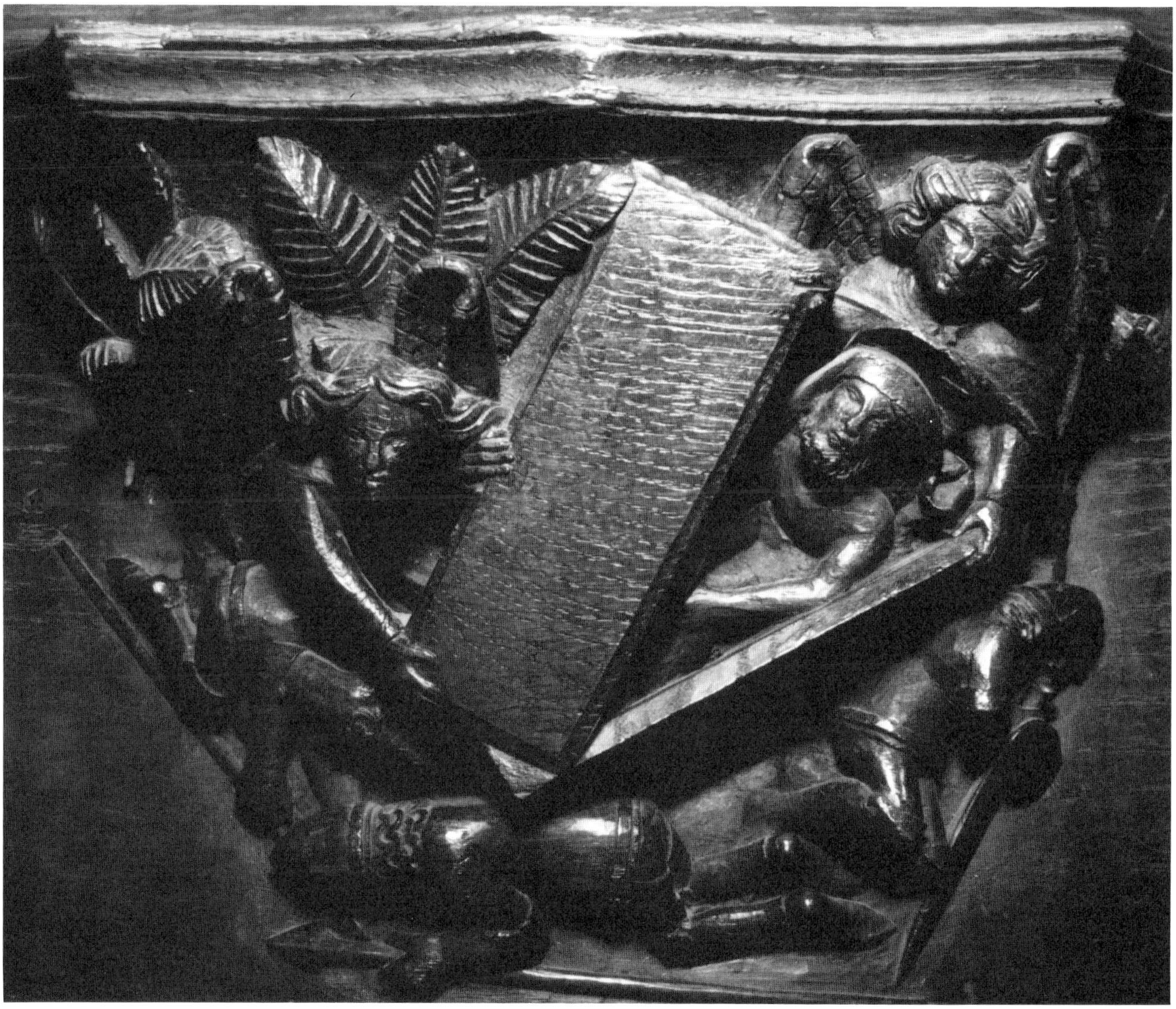

Resurrection. Chester (Cheshire), The Cathedral, 1876.

There are records of plays, for example, lasting three days in Skinners Wells in 1391 and for eight days in the same place in 1409 (Strutt 1810). Although they do not seem to have reached quite the level of complexity as the mystery plays, miracle plays increasingly became concerned with introducing realistic elements. Penn (1933) describes stage sets that include real water for boats and real fire for martyrs' pyres. She also includes the staging of a scene from one of the Mary Miracles where the Virgin serves as midwife:

> The actor would heave and groan, while the Virgin Mary in attendance encouraged him roundly. At the appropriate moment, she would bend down and draw from between the actor's legs a doll wrapped in swaddling clothes
>
> 29

For many saints, the play's realism centered on how they died. St. Thomas, for example, was one of many saints who became the subject of numerous miracle plays after his death and canonization. Like other plays about the saints, the grisly method of the martyrdom was often made more prominent than the saint's miracles. The carving below shows St. Thomas at the moment of his murder. The carver has made the scene more dramatic by exaggerating the size of the sword necessary to fell St. Thomas.

The demise of the mystery and miracle plays was caused by several factors. As they became more elaborate, they became more costly to produce. The Church, while happy with the contributions the guilds made to them from the plays' proceeds, was uneasy about the increasing secularization of the plays. Perhaps the most important factor in phasing out these productions was the growing recognition of the potential for the stage to be used as a political weapon. The religious principles on which the plays were orig-

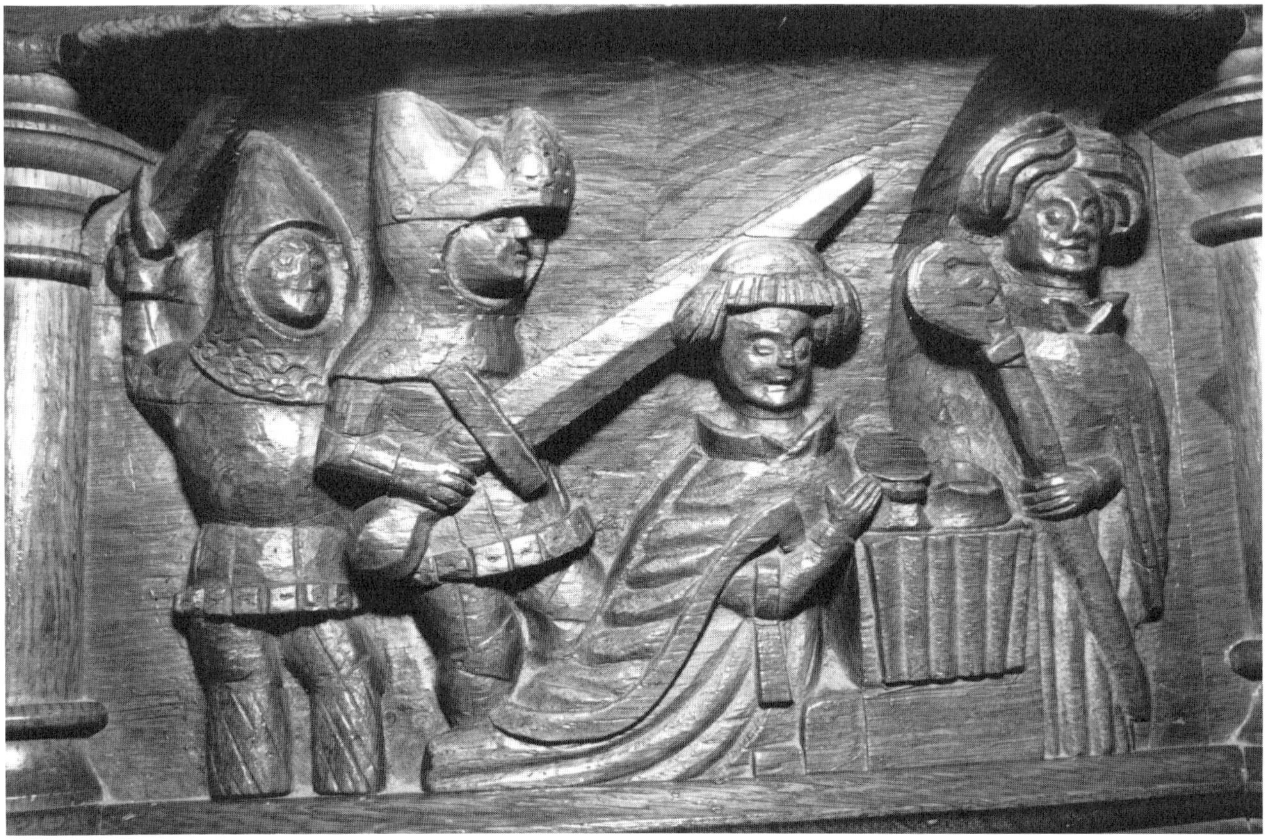

St. Thomas' murder. Fornham (Suffolk), St. Martin, fifteenth century.

inally based—specifically, the notion of "good works,"—were beginning to be challenged in other areas, and it was feared that, with their broad appeal, plays could become vehicles for the spread of dissension. It did not escape the notice of the king and the Church that the stage could be a powerful tool against both of them. As early as 1549, a royal proclamation forbade the performance of interludes because of their tendency to contain material considered supportive of sedition (Wright 1865). Even so, it was not until 1570 that church and state in England jointly agreed to suppress the plays, and not until 1579 that the York plays were outlawed on religious grounds (Lander 1980).

The importance of these dramas to medieval life cannot be overstated. Their contribution in relieving the tedium of daily life was immense, as was their contribution to binding communities together. The influence of early dramas, however, went much further. Emile Mâle, the noted French art historian, is perhaps overly enthusiastic, but nonetheless suggests another contribution made by these plays:

> Their chief merit was that they inspired the greatest painters. To have suggested groupings attitudes, costumes, and even color to Roger van der Weyden, Jean Fouquet, and Hans Memling is to have had no slight effect upon art.
>
> 1949, 111

There is no doubt that the influence of these plays on the craftsmen's art was significant, for their stories were woven into the work of woodcarvers, sculptors, embroiderers, stained glass crafters, and artists in ivory. Perhaps the most significant contribution religious drama made to the life of medieval citizens was to help them take the first step away from Church control. It was the laity, and not the Church that came to control the form of religious drama from the fourteenth century on. And, in so doing, as raucous and uncouth as it may have been, this small separation from the Church prompted medieval men and women to begin to examine life apart from the control of the Church.

Strolling Drama

In addition to the formal staged drama of the Middle Ages, there was a vast network of loosely organized performances. This category included both companies of actors and individual entertainers who performed in the open, or in private residences, without benefit of stage. Traveling from town to town, they depended on their dress, instruments, and antics to entertain. Included in this group were musicians, jesters, tumblers, jugglers, dancers and grimacers, who were present at every fair and festival. They were welcome at monasteries, nunneries, palaces, and, on occasion, churches. No celebration was deemed complete without a complement of these performers, known collectively as minstrels, to enliven the entertainment.

Minstrels as a class are ancient in origin. They were probably based on the Roman character "mimus," whose role it was to make people laugh. The mimus would do this by telling jokes and stories, by dancing and singing, through mimicry, sleight-of-hand, juggling, acting in farces, and dancing on tightropes (Wright 1865). The mimus also would amuse by putting his or her body and face into contorted positions. Any buffoonery that would elicit laughter became their stock-in-trade. Unlike the mystery and miracle plays, there was no moral or lesson to be imparted. Minstrelsy was simply entertainment.

The Anglo-Saxon term for this type of entertainer was *gleeman*, becoming in English *minstrel*, or, in French, *jougleur*[2] during the Middle Ages. During the thirteenth and fourteenth centuries, the term *minstrel* was generally applied to professional secular musicians and *jougleur* to musicians who also sang but, in addition, were talented in other areas such as juggling, tumbling, and training animals (Strutt 1810; Jusserand 1950). Throughout most of the Middle Ages, the terms were interchangeable, although different areas of concentration denoted class differences between minstrels. This difference was most strongly felt in music and is discussed later. First, however, some mention should be made of the type

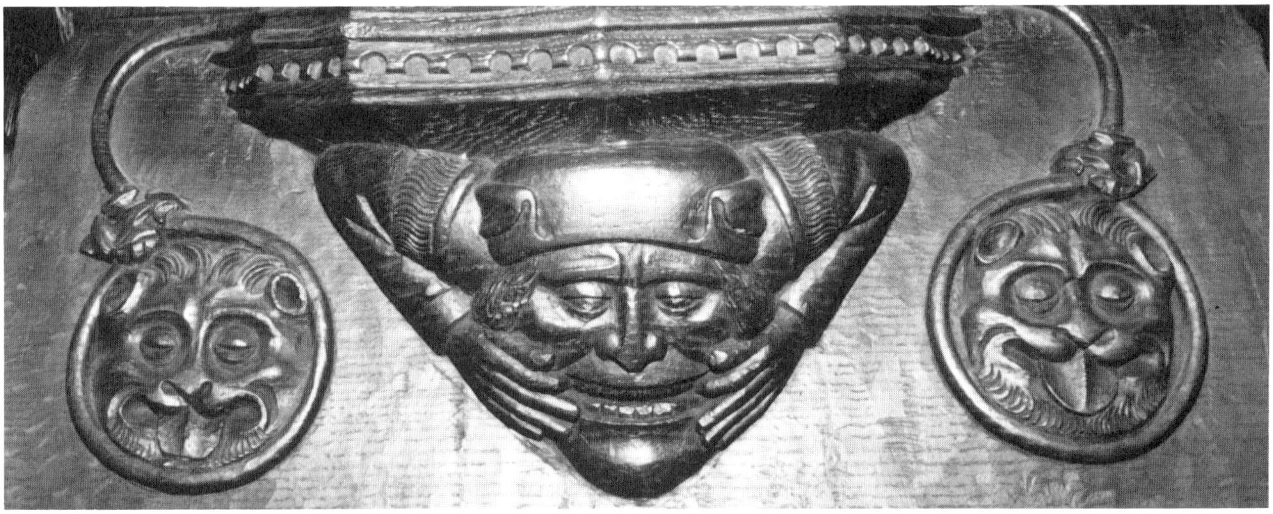

Grimacer. Beverley (Humberside), The Minster, 1520.

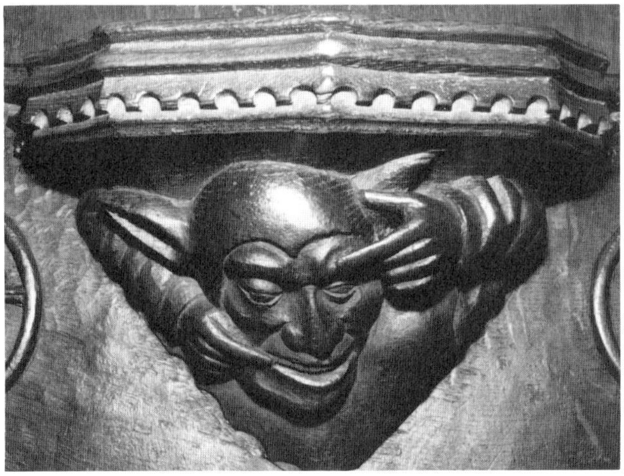

Grimacer. Beverley (Humberside), The Minster, 1520.

of entertainer that was enjoyed by both classes, the *jougleur.*

MOVING MINSTRELS

The passion with which these entertainers were greeted is evident in the large number of misericords devoted to their skills. Not only could the *jougleur* entertain the carver in person, he could re-create that entertainment again in the form of a carving. These entertainers proliferated because they required little in the way of props and little in the way of training. The field was open to anyone willing to use their body as an instrument of amusement.

One of the simplest skills that anyone could acquire was that of grimacing (or "gurning") where the face was twisted into comical or horrible distortions, with individuals competing to see who could make the most grotesque face (White 1974; Smith 1886). The two carvings above are good examples. In the first example, the carver has added a comic element by showing the lion head supporters grimacing, too.

Minstrelsy was a profession open to both men and women, as shown in the following two carvings. The first carving has supporters (the left is damaged) that have been described as either the lady's attendants in the entertainment or other entertainers (Klein 1986).

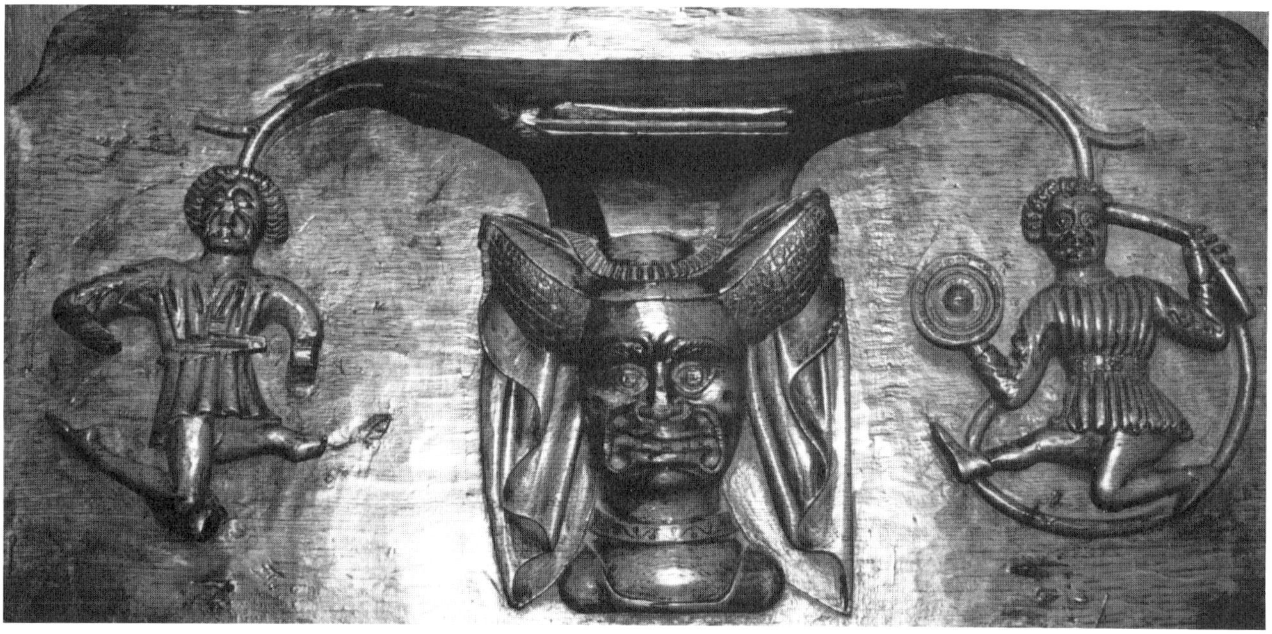
Female grimacer. Ludlow (Salop), St. Laurence, c.1447.

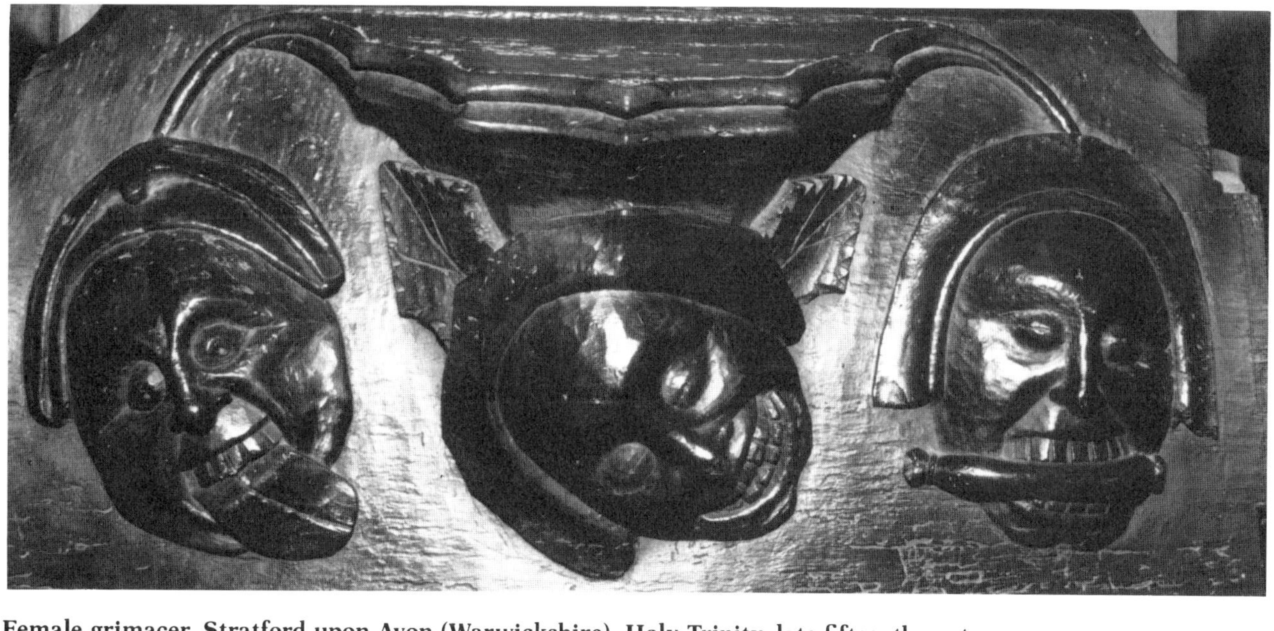
Female grimacer. Stratford-upon-Avon (Warwickshire), Holy Trinity, late fifteenth century.

They wear the traditional short coat of the minstrel. In the second, the carver seems to have taken an exaggerated view of the length of the woman's tongue, no doubt in keeping with the contemporary view of the prominence of a woman's tongue.

Tumbling, another popular activity, required more skill than grimacing. Tumblers could perform individually or in pairs, as in the carving below. This graceful carving shows the tumblers using minimal, but effective, props. They have placed sticks under each others knees to help hold them together as they tumble.

The tumblers in the next carving simply hold on to each other. The carver has used the supporters to portray playful, tumbling animals—lions on the left and griffins on the right.

Contortionists were particularly fascinating, and their skill produced some interesting challenges for the carver. In the Winchester carving the man has drawn his legs over his head; in the Chichester carving, the man is shown pulling one leg up behind him, with the other leg seemingly twisted at the hip to bring it forward.

The skills of the contortionist provided amusement well beyond the late Middle Ages and on occasion even amused the contortionist himself. There is a humorous account of one of the most famous contortionists of all time, Joseph Clark, who lived in the 1600s in England and whose exploits were admiringly re-

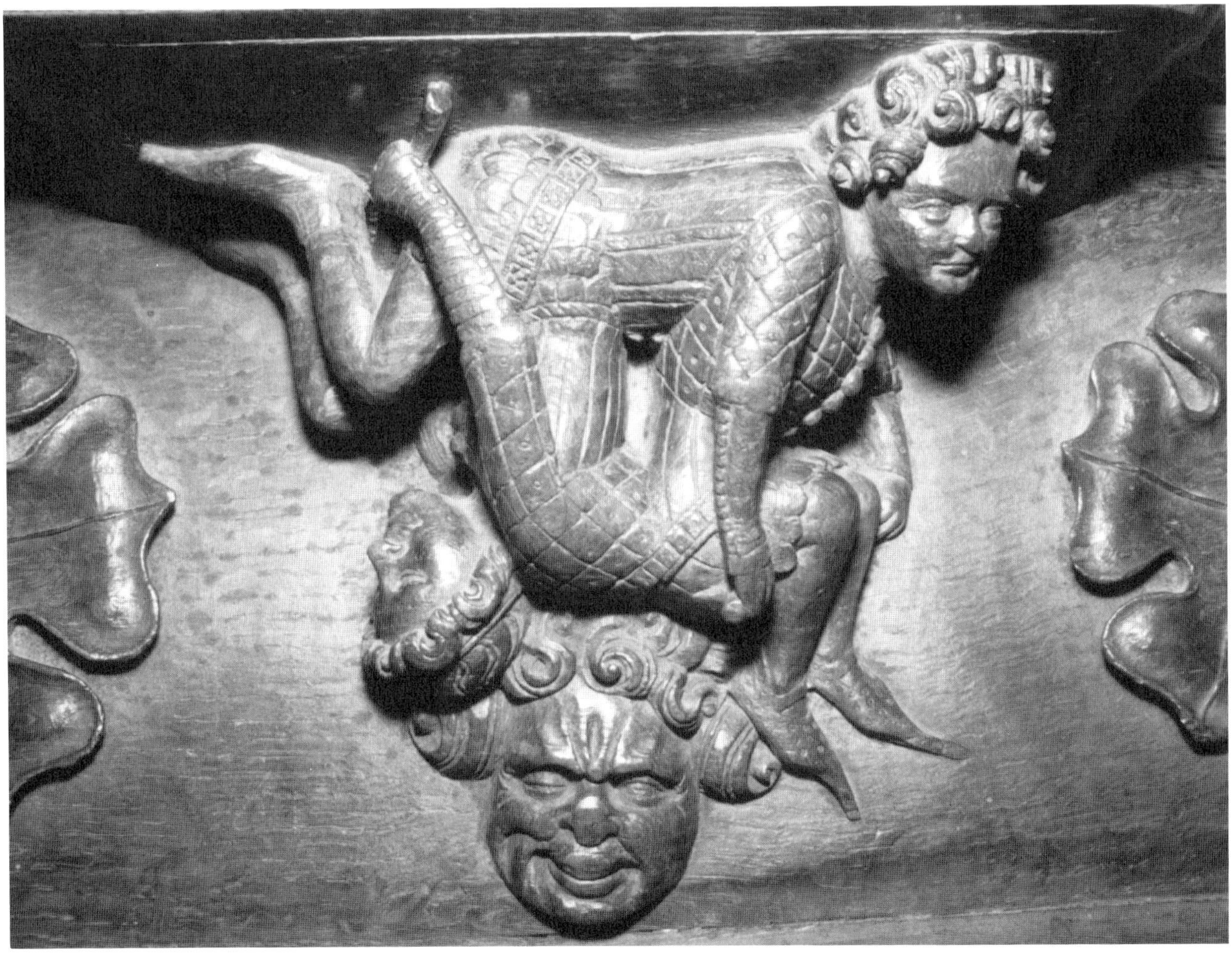

Tumblers. Oxford (Oxon), New College Chapel, late fourteenth century.

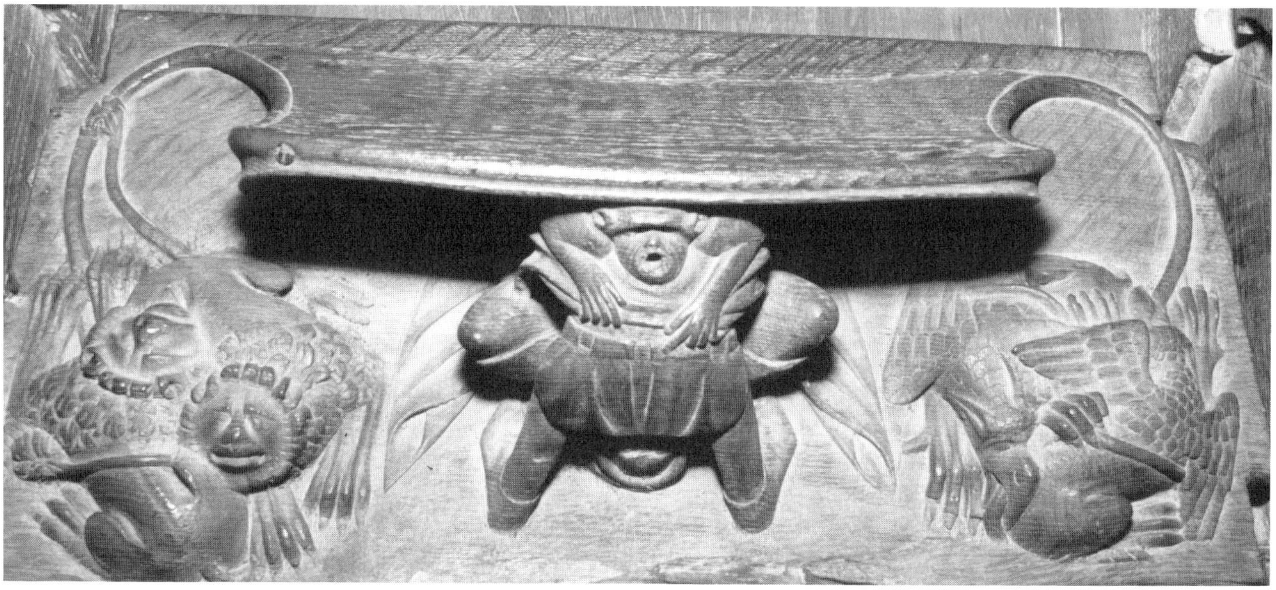

Tumblers. Ely (Cambs), The Cathedral, c.1340.

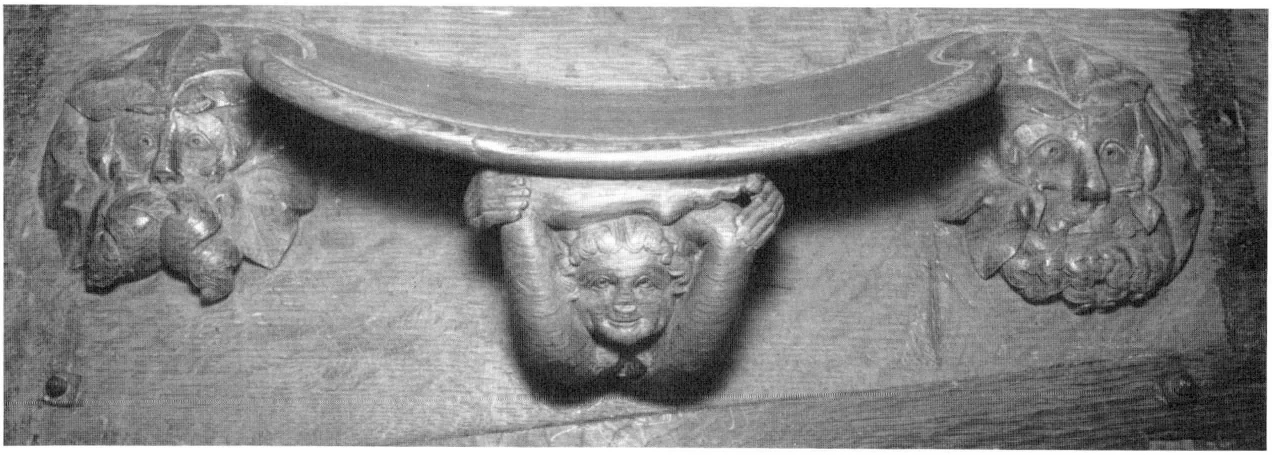

Contortionist. Winchester (Hants), The Cathedral, c.1308.

ported in the *Guardian,* July 8, 1713, as being the "plague" of all the tailors:

> He would send for one of them to take measure of him; but would so contrive it as to have a most immoderate rising in one of his shoulders; when his clothes were brought home and tried upon him, the deformity was removed into the other shoulder; upon which the taylor begged pardon for the mistake, and mended it as fast as he could; but, on another trial, found him as straight-shouldered a man as one would desire to see, but a little unfortunate in a hump-back.
>
> in Strutt 1810, 211

The relationship of the minstrels to the Church was uneven. In some quarters, they were not only tolerated but welcomed by the nuns and monks, on occasion even being allowed to perform in the churches. However, many in the Church denounced these players as lewd and immoral, and constantly tried to discredit them. Interestingly, the more practical ecclesiastics were mindful of how lucrative the profession of minstrelsy was and turned to acting themselves. The monks, however, confined their performances to the churches and to religious topics (Strutt 1810), so it may be

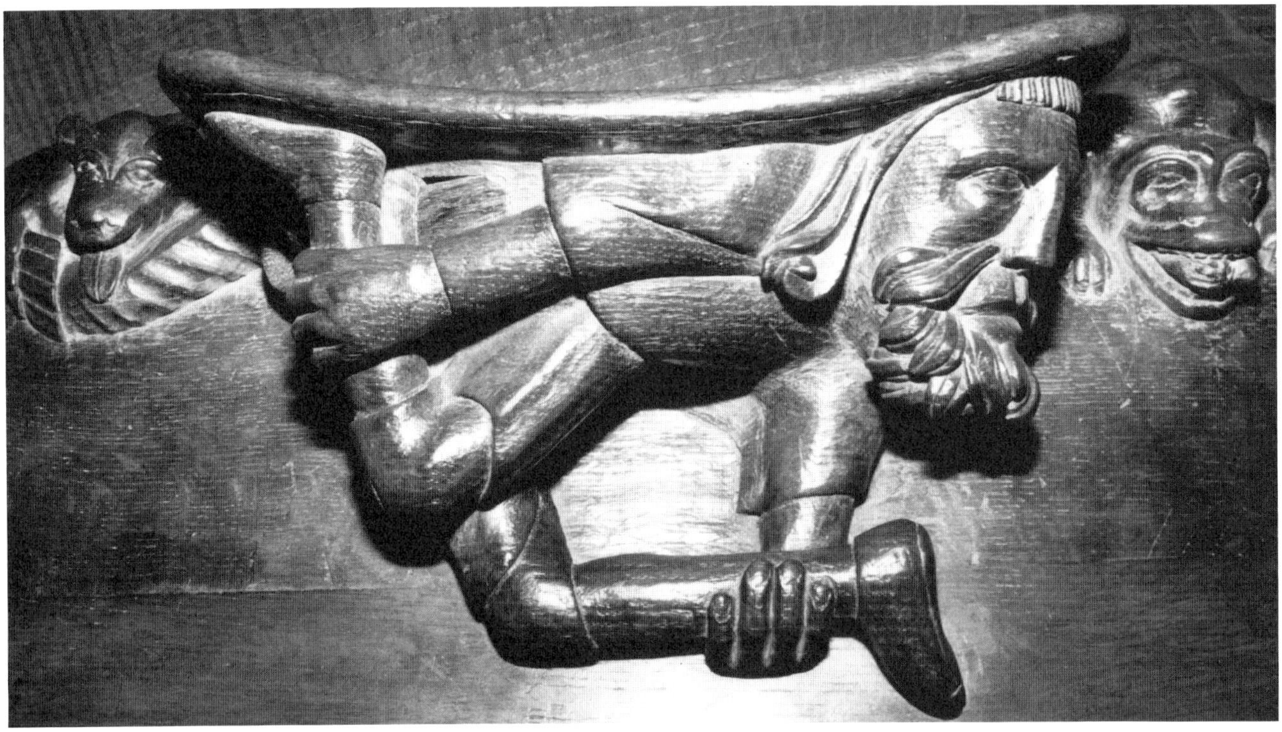

Contortionist. Chichester (W.Sussex), The Cathedral, c.1330.

assumed that their financial gain was far less than that of the strolling minstrels.

MUSICAL MINSTRELS

As mentioned above a class distinction between types of musical minstrels arose during the late Middle Ages that led to antagonism. There was the more professionally competent "house" minstrel who was in the service of the upper classes; and there was the less accomplished minstrel who performed for the people. A major distinction between the two lay in their choice of musical instrument. Professional minstrels were proficient on the more sophisticated stringed instruments, while the common minstrels generally preferred the pipe and tabor. The contrast can be seen in the bench-end carving from Alternon featuring an elegant minstrel playing a stringed instrument and in the Chichester misericord showing a much less formal duet on the harp and pipe.

Because the potential rewards were great, the competition for a position as a house minstrel was keen. The nobility and monarchy were known to be generous in matters of ceremony, and the monarchy, in particular, was lavish in its outlays for state ceremonies. For example, 426 minstrels were on hand for the wedding of the daughter of Edward I (Jusserand 1950). The monarchy and nobility made a practice of having minstrels as members of their permanent staff, necessitating the minstrels' galleries that became an architectural fixture. For a time, these house minstrels were in such demand that some treasuries suffered greatly as a result. Queen Matilda, in the twelfth century, is said to have squandered most of her revenue on poets and minstrels. And she was not alone; minstrels were given gifts other than money, and some even became men of property. They were also given time off in which to pursue their own interests. Thus, it is not surprising that some minstrels came to view themselves as members of the aristocracy. Nor is it surprising that their good fortune would elicit envy from less favored minstrels and from others. William Langland, one of the moral voices of the people, criticized the preferential treatment granted these minstrels in his *Piers Plowman* (1935, 35–39):

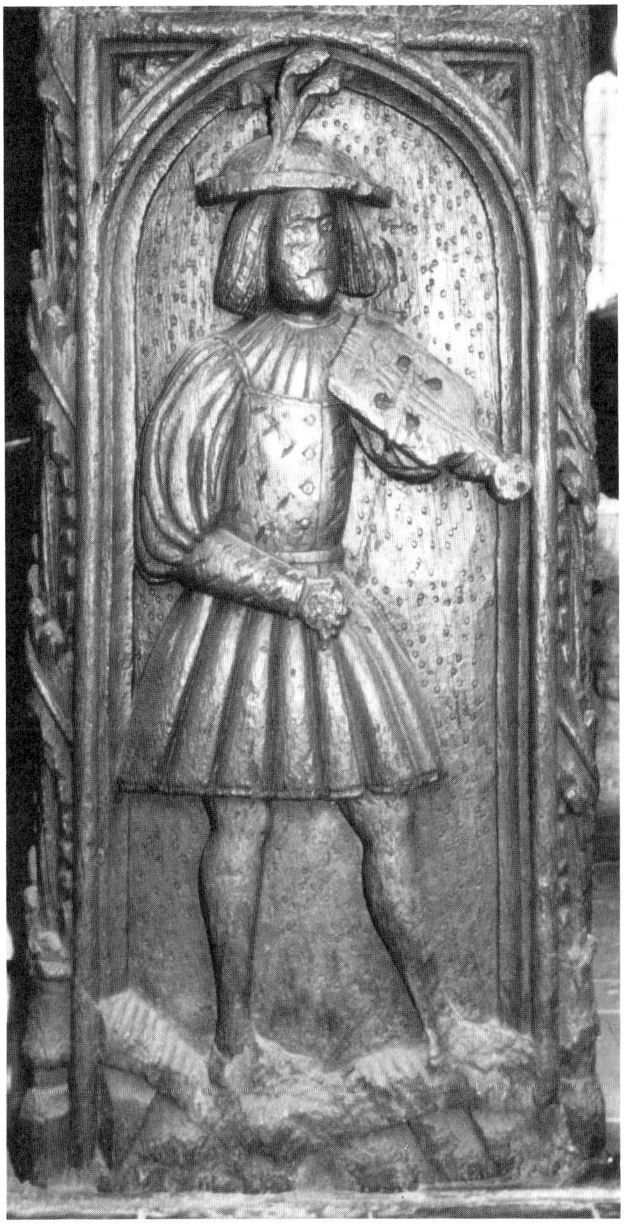

Minstrel. Alternon (Cornwall), St. Nona's, 1510–30.

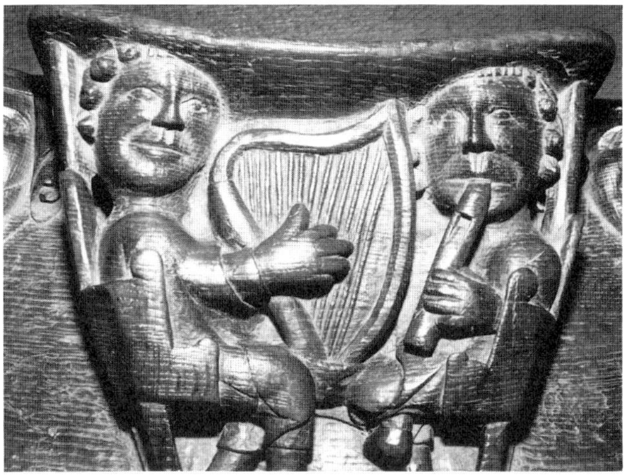

Harpist and piper. Chichester (W.Sussex), The Cathedral, c.1330.

Clerkus and knyghtes welcometh kynges
mynstrales,
And for love of here lordes lithen hem at
festes.
Much more, me thenketh rich men auhte
Have beggars by-fore hem whiche beth
godes mynstrales.

It was inevitable animosity would develop between the two classes of minstrels. Well before the general population began to find these entertainers passé, professional minstrels were being satirized. The professional minstrels had, in the eyes of commoners, become too arrogant as a result of their success, especially their financial success. The humbler musician playing the favored instruments of the people, the tabor and pipe, was much less well treated and very much less well paid (Darwin 1917). In addition, the elegantly clad minstrel playing for an appreciative, wealthy audience had a specially constructed minstrel's gallery in which to perform. The poor taborer, on the other hand, generally played while standing, his tabor attached to his shoulder. He would beat a dance rhythm with one hand while using the other hand to play the pipe. And, for all his exertions, he would generally receive a penny for his pay (Galpin 1965).

Professional minstrels felt themselves to be of such an elevated social status that they could be outspoken in their disdain for the more common minstrels and their instruments. That they considered the pipe and tabor crude at best was made evident in a thirteenth or fourteenth century French poem in which a professional minstrel equated the popularity of these odious instruments with decadence, making the suggestion that this surely represented the coming either of the end of the world or of the Antichrist (Wright 1865). This criticism, along with the general antipathy felt toward the house minstrels, provided the carvers with an impetus to respond. Their response took the form of caricature.

CARVED REVENGE

A number of carvings appeared in which animals or composite figures replaced human minstrels. In the New College carving below, the musicians are centaurs, the one in the center defiantly playing both pipe and tabor.

The use of the centaur is intriguing, for the centaur of antiquity could be either an honorable figure or a savage being (Howey 1923). In medieval mythology, the human half of the animal was said to symbolize Christ (Anderson 1969; 1954); the horse half represented Christ's vengeance on those who betrayed Him (Steer 1973). It is possible the carver is drawing on the latter symbolism to warn: "Beware, not only does the use of the pipe and tabor not proclaim the end of the world, but Christ himself plays these instruments."

To be fair, it was not only the professional minstrels who preferred more "refined" instruments; but, as one anonymous writer noted in writing about the clamor of the tabor:

> God send to that man who first made tabor
> (Which should please none) mischief for his labour;
> When tightly stretch'd, and struck with hearty blow,
> For half a league you'll hear it as you go
> Wildridge 1879, 28[3]

The carvers, however, belonged to that segment of the population that preferred the common pipe and tabor and therefore continued to create unflattering images of professional minstrels. A favorite device was the use of the pig to represent the professional minstrel. The Ripon carving, right, shows a sow playing one of the more "common" instruments, the bagpipes, while her companions dance.

The caricature of the professional minstrel as a comic pig playing such "common" instruments as the pipe and bagpipe is a sharp rejoinder to criticisms made of the instruments used by the ordinary minstrel. The following carving of a sow playing the double pipe while her young pigs suckle, has been described as yet another satire of professional minstrels entertaining the nobility during dinner (Wright 1865). In this carving, however, it is not only the minstrel that is being derided, but the hungry nobility as well, since they are portrayed as hungry piglets.

The animosity between professional minstrels and lesser minstrels was considerable by the fifteenth century. Because being the minstrel of the king or a noble brought monetary reward, minstrels in secure positions were always anxious to protect their treasured position. Others, however, discovered that if they simply dressed in livery and said they were

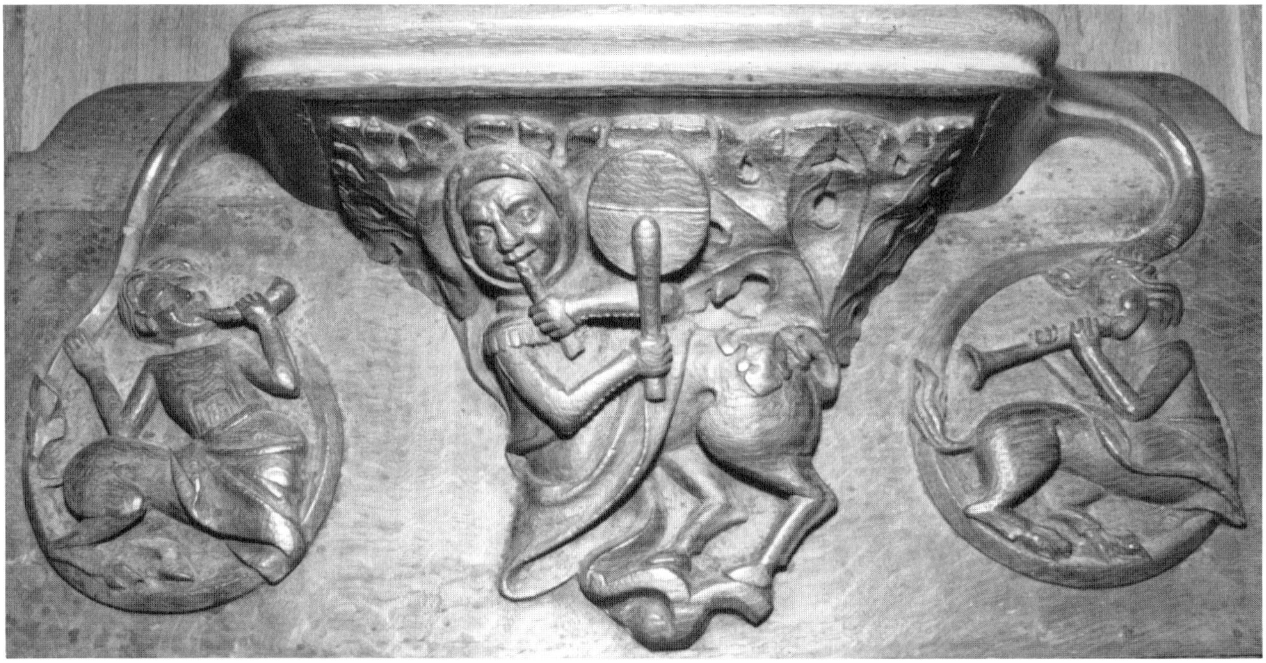

Centaur with pipe and tabor. Oxford (Oxon), New College Chapel, late fourteenth century.

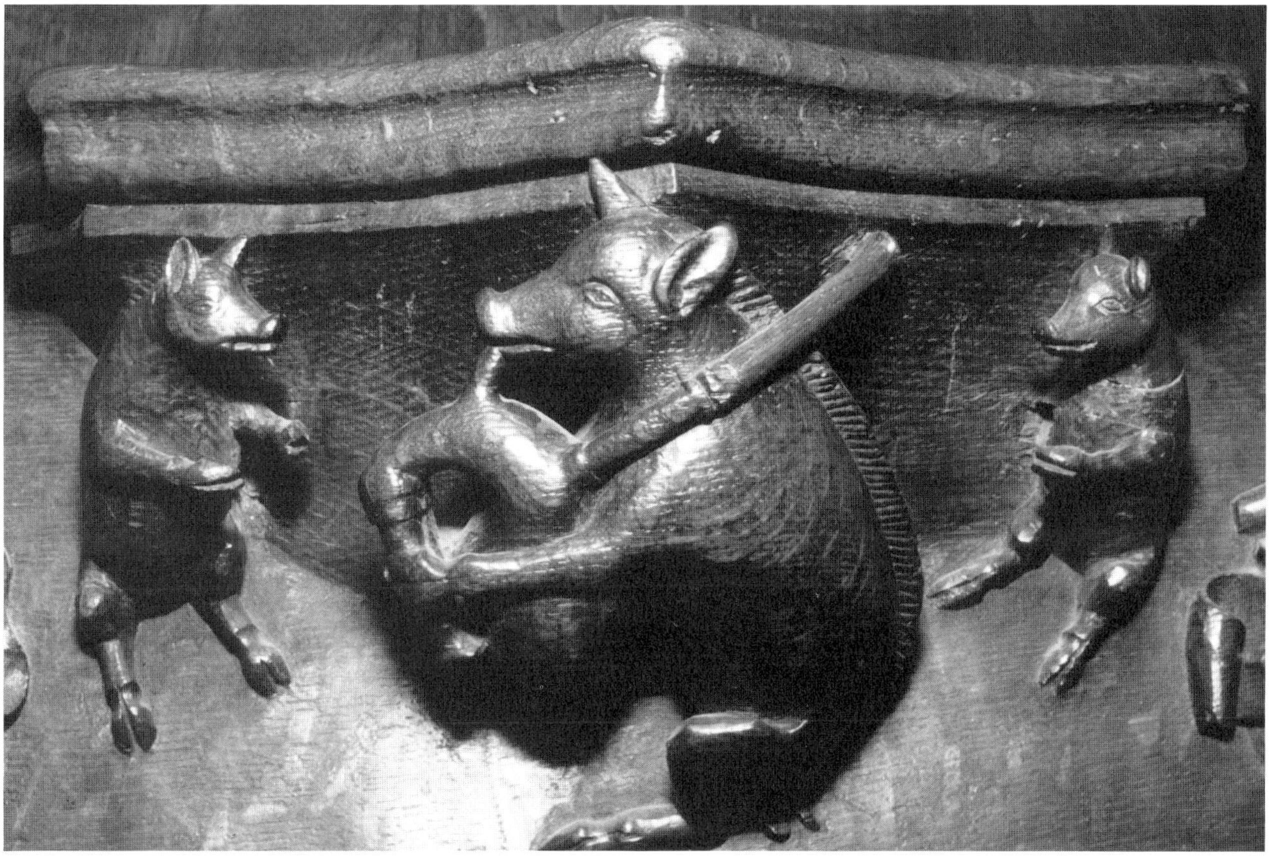

Sow with bagpipes. Ripon (N.Yorks), The Cathedral, 1489–94.

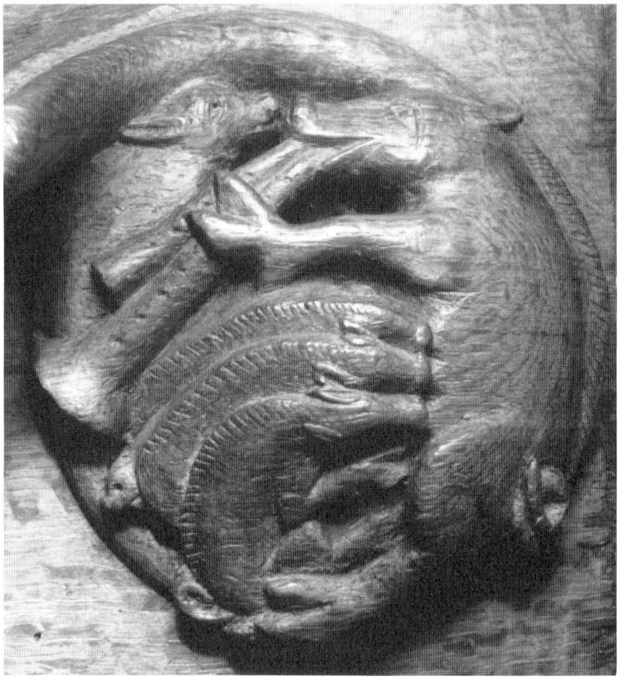

Sow playing double pipe. Winchester (Hants), The Cathedral, c.1308.

the king's minstrel, they could reap many of the benefits bestowed on the king's minstrels. Edward IV's minstrels finally complained about these "uncultured peasants" and asked him to intercede. As a result, Edward granted the minstrels' guild the right to hold inquiries and to fine bogus minstrels (Jusserand 1950).

By the beginning of the sixteenth century, secular strolling actors had become unfashionable and were viewed as vulgar. They were no longer welcome in the wealthy houses, and the profession split into several different segments. Individuals tried to make a living by continuing their acts, but in 1572 laws were passed that classified them as vagabonds (White 1974). By the next century, the term *minstrel* was seldom used, and another segment of their stock-in-trade—performing animals—also receded in popularity.

ANIMAL ENTERTAINERS

Animal entertainment, however, enjoyed a long run. From early times, minstrels provided amusement by incorporating trained animals into their acts. The animals were taught to replicate the actions of humans, with the intention of making human action comic. As early as the tenth century, trained apes, dogs, horses, and bears made the circuit with jougleurs, performing acts normally reserved for humans (Strutt 1810). They were trained to tumble, dance, ride on a horse, walk on a tightrope, and engage in mock battles with each other—all to the immense pleasure of the onlookers. Along with minstrels, they became part of the pageantry of the Middle Ages.

Apes (or monkeys, as the two terms were used interchangeably) on the back of an animal were a common sight. They were trained to ride on all sorts of animals and made to perform this feat publicly. Although these were mostly innocuous activities, minstrels contributed to what became one of the most widely enjoyed pastimes of the Middle Ages—animal-baiting. Minstrels trained bears, bulls, horses, monkeys, and other animals to be baited by dogs (Stow 1633). This was a favorite spectator sport even though, or perhaps because, it was gruesome and cruel. Many members of the nobility kept wild animals for the express purpose of setting them against each other in a bloody battle to the death. William Fitz-Stephen, a twelfth-century monk in the service of Thomas Becket, wrote of winter sports in London:

> In the winter holidays, the youth are entertained in a morning with boars fighting to the last gasp, as likewise with hogs full tusked, intended to be converted into bacon; or game-bulls, and bears of a large bulk, are baited with dogs
>
> 1772, 50

Different beliefs about the beneficial effects of animal-baiting were even constructed, such as the belief that baiting a bull before killing it improved the flavor of the meat (Fitz-Barnard 1983). This belief was formalized in the seventeenth century, when bull-baiting before slaughter became a legal requirement.

Animal-baiting could take place in a formal arena (that is, a "bear garden") or in the open, but it was a central part of civic and royal celebrations. Preceding the event, the animal to be baited was led around town to stir up interest. To enliven the procession, a monkey or ape would ride on the animal's back, surrounded by walking minstrels.

When the potential spectators reached the arena where scaffolding was erected for their viewing ease, they were required to pay a fee to enter the arena, a fee to enter the scaffolding, and a fee for "quiet standing" (Strutt 1810). The animal in question would be chained and staked to the ground, to be set upon by dogs.

In the Beverley scene, right, a bear is being pulled in a basket on the way to the bear-baiting site. On the left supporter, the bear is being muzzled in preparation, while on the right, the trainer is hugging the bear. In the next scene, the bear-baiting has begun as two dogs attack the bear. The bear-warden stands with staff in hand, ready to intervene if necessary.

The practice of including monkeys and horses in the procession is depicted by the Beverley carver (the heads of the trainer and monkey have been lost). The bears, muzzled and chained, are being led by the monkey.

The supporters on this misericord display a certain reversal-of-fortune irony. On the left, a bear chews on a bone, perhaps, fittingly, a dog bone. On the right, an ape holds a dog like a bagpipe and bites its tail to make "music" for the ape's entertainment—a warning to dogs everywhere that those in control today may themselves be chained tomorrow.

These supporters also refer to another popular animal-baiting contest, that between dogs and monkeys. Captain Fitz-Barnard speaks of this practice in London:

> . . . they had a monkey at the Westminster Pit who was a stock performer and put up a great battle with an indifferent dog. The monkey was given a club to assist him, but no monkey, except the very large apes, has any chance with a fighting-dog.
>
> 1983, 188

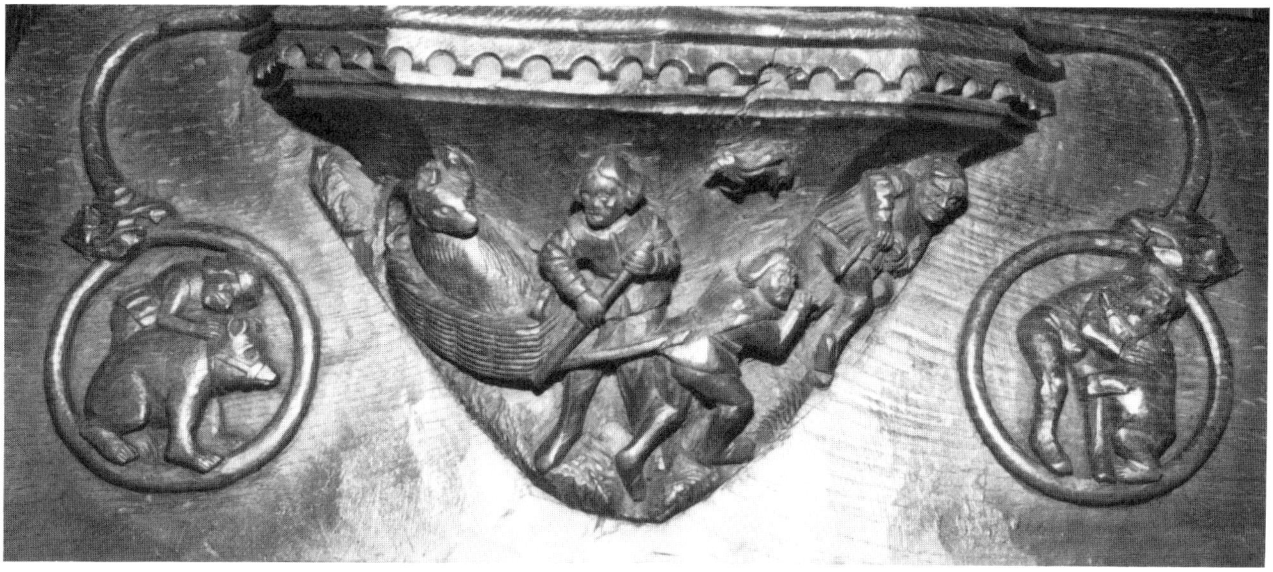

Readying for bear-baiting. Beverley (Humberside), The Minster, 1520.

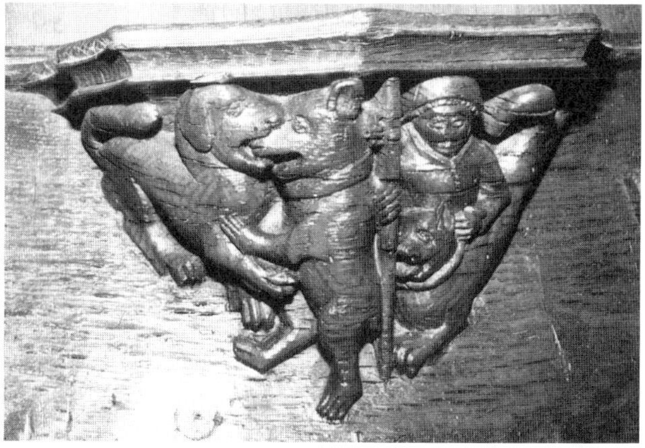

Bear-baiting. Boston (Lincs), St. Botolph, 1390.

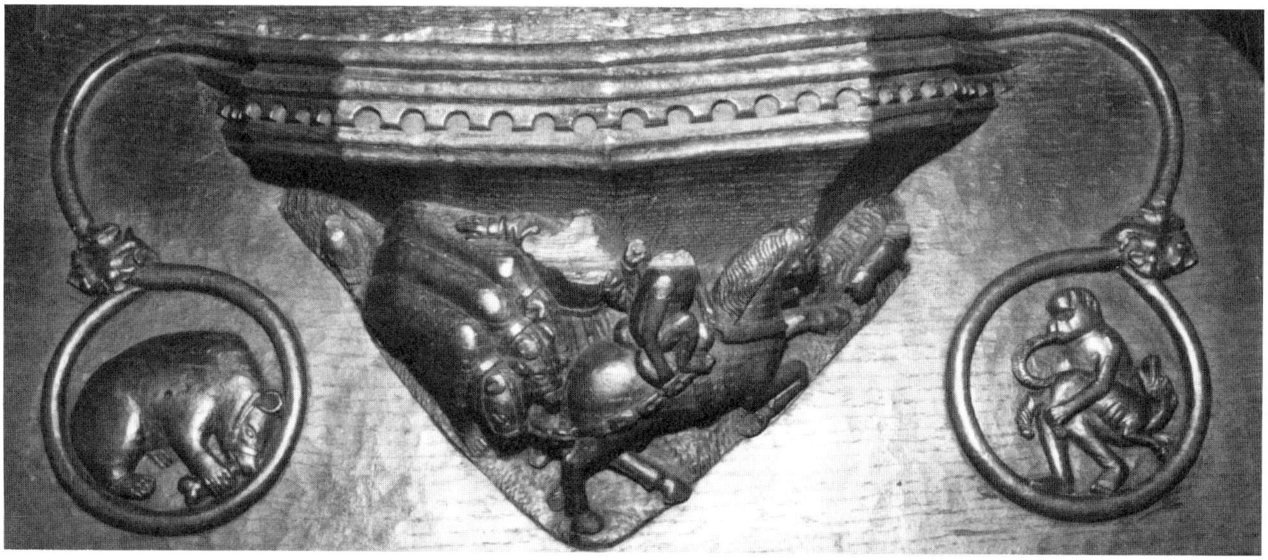

Animal-baiting. Beverley (Humberside), The Minster, 1520.

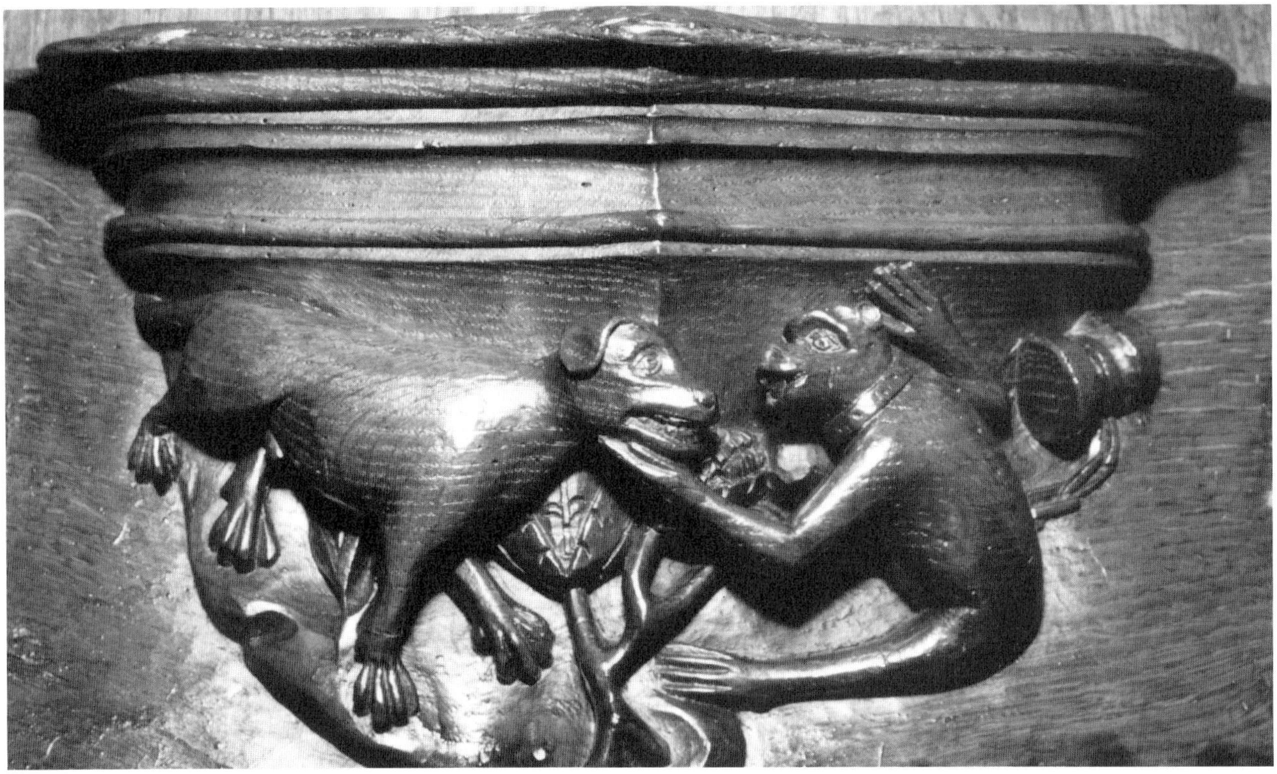

Monkey-baiting. Windsor (Berks), St. George's Chapel, 1477–83.

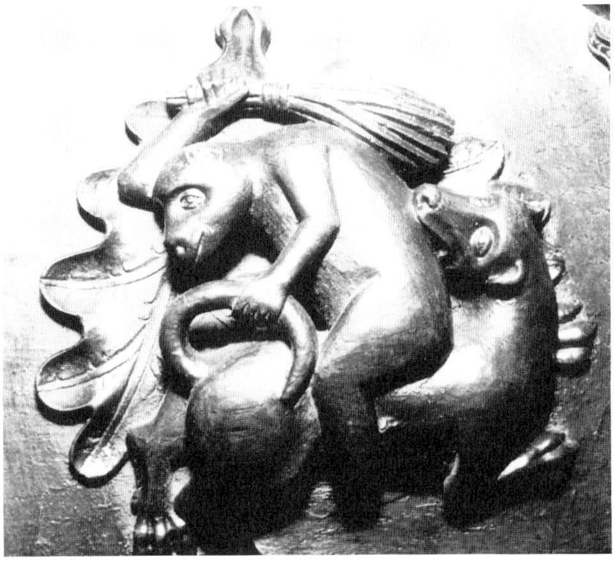

Monkey-baiting. Windsor (Berks), St. George's Chapel, 1477–83.

This contest is the subject of the two Windsor carvings. In the first, the monkey is chained. In the second, both animals are unchained and the monkey has been given what looks to be a switch to aid in the battle against the dog.

Another, highly valued variation was pony-baiting. A Spanish nobleman expressed his pleasure at watching such an event:

> To see the animal kicking amongst the dogs, with the screaming of the ape, beholding the curs hanging from the ears and neck of the pony, is very laughable
>
> Dalrymple 1967, 3:326

The Bristol carving shows the pony as it is being paraded to the arena, a monkey on its back.

The practice of animal-baiting remained in vogue until the seventeenth century, when it came under criticism. Most of the criticism was based on humanitarian grounds, but one seventeenth-century French priest found the growing disfavor of bear-baiting an opportunity to comment on Protestantism:

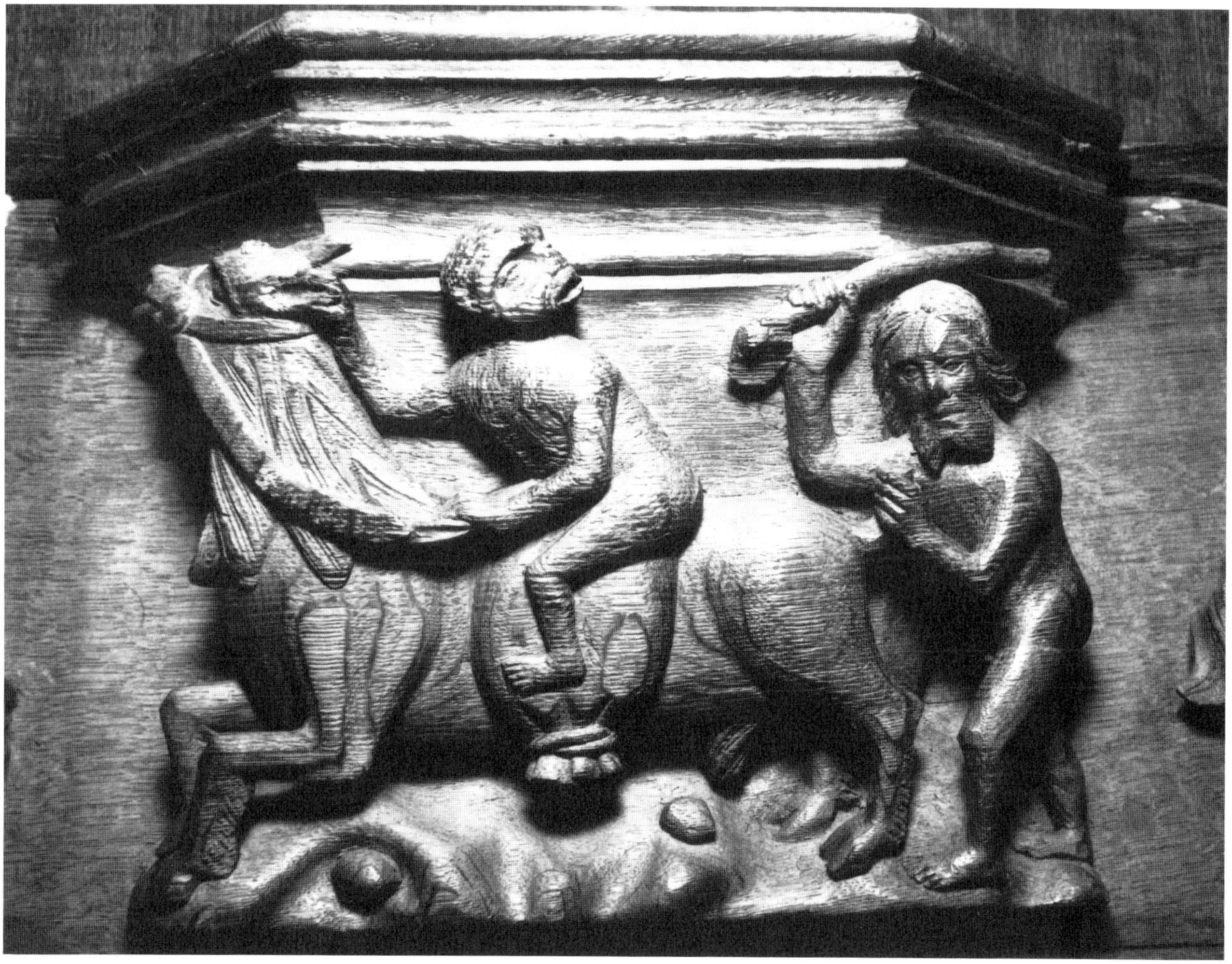

Pony-baiting. Bristol (Avon), The Cathedral, 1520.

> Even Sunday is a day designed for beare-bayting, and even the howse of theyre (Protestants) service is allotted to it, and indeede the tyme is as well spent at the one as at the other
> Brand 1853, 3:403

Animal-baiting was finally outlawed by Parliament in 1835, on the grounds of cruelty (Dalrymple 1967, vol. 3). As an interesting aside, for unknown reasons, bear-baiting was one area in the medieval labor market where women were paid more than men (Griffith 1992).

Institutionalized Mayhem

The late Middle Ages were steeped in pagan imagery in many areas, although outwardly the idea of Christianity had been accepted. Some of the old pagan customs the people had been reluctant to denounce were wisely incorporated by the Church into church ritual; in other cases, the Church simply had to accept that people would be defiant. Youth and lust alone ensured the continuance of some of the pagan celebrations.

Playing the Fool

One of the festivals taken over by the Church had its origins in the Roman festival of the Saturnalia. During the Saturnalia, social rankings were reversed, and slaves became masters. Under the cover of masks, the participants would enact hundreds of different follies; they would also be exempt from any retribution that might normally be expected. For a brief period, the ruled and the rulers exchanged places, allowing the lower classes a measure of controlled defiance (Wright 1845; Strutt 1810). During the medieval period, this defiance was embodied in the annual Feast of Fools, generally held around the first of the year, when lower clergy would dress as fools and conduct a mock service playing the parts of bishop and priests, with many other members of the laity dressing as monks and nuns.

Chambers (1903) suggests that the dress of the fool—which included a hood with animal ears, notably asses' ears—was derivative of primitive festivals in which the actual head of a sacrificial animal was worn by a worshipper at the New Year festival. Over the years, animal sacrifice was excluded, but remnants of the ritual remained in the form of dress. Along with the fool's cap, the fool frequently carried a "marotte" (sometimes called a "death's head")—a doll which was a replica of the fool's head and shoulders, as shown in the Christchurch carving below.

The feast began in France possibly as early as the twelfth century. By the fourteenth century, it was fully established in France and had spread to England (Chambers 1903). All services were conducted with an emphasis on buffoonery and vulgarity. During the "service," there was dancing, dice playing, eating, and people exhibiting themselves in a lewd manner. When the service was over:

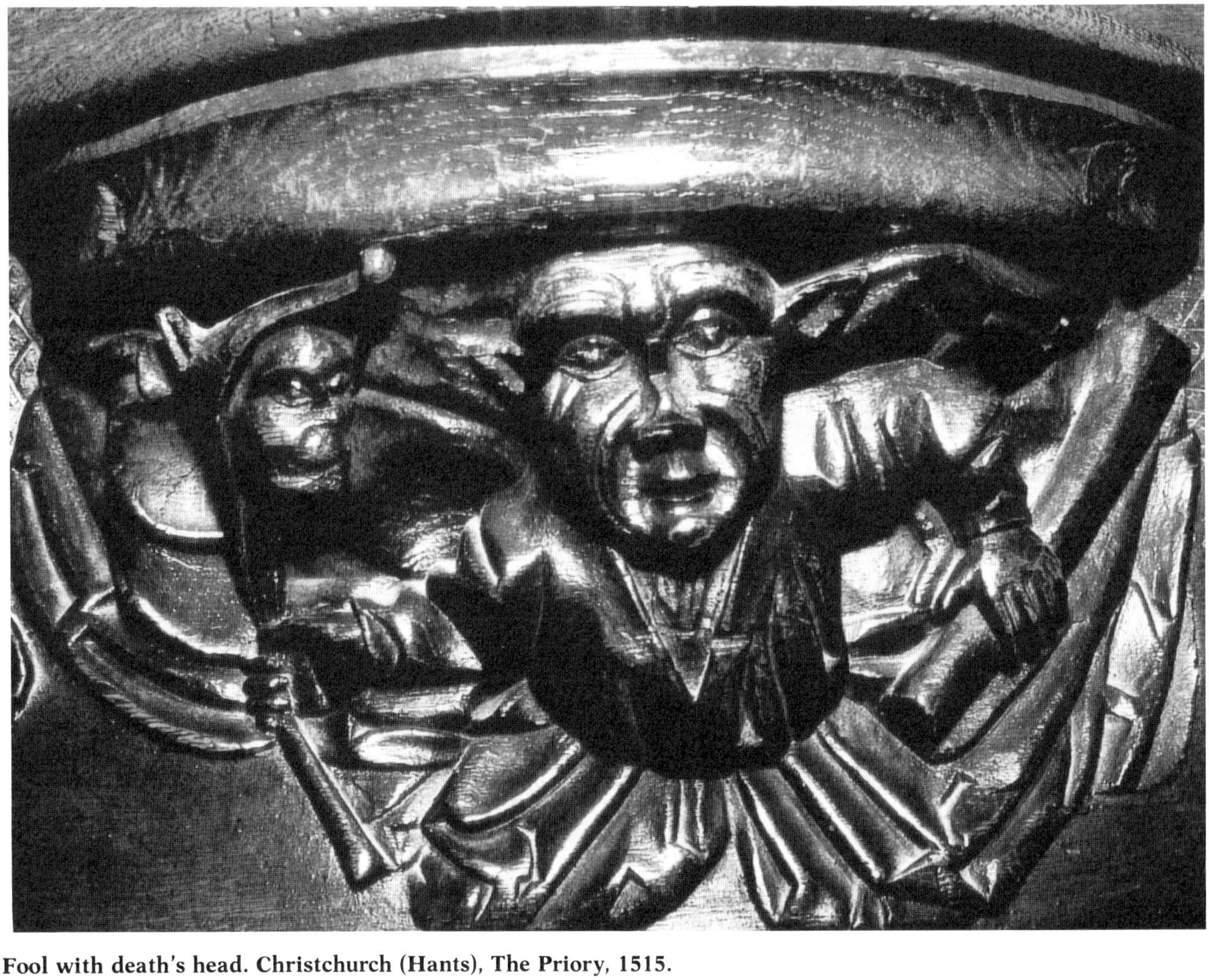

Fool with death's head. Christchurch (Hants), The Priory, 1515.

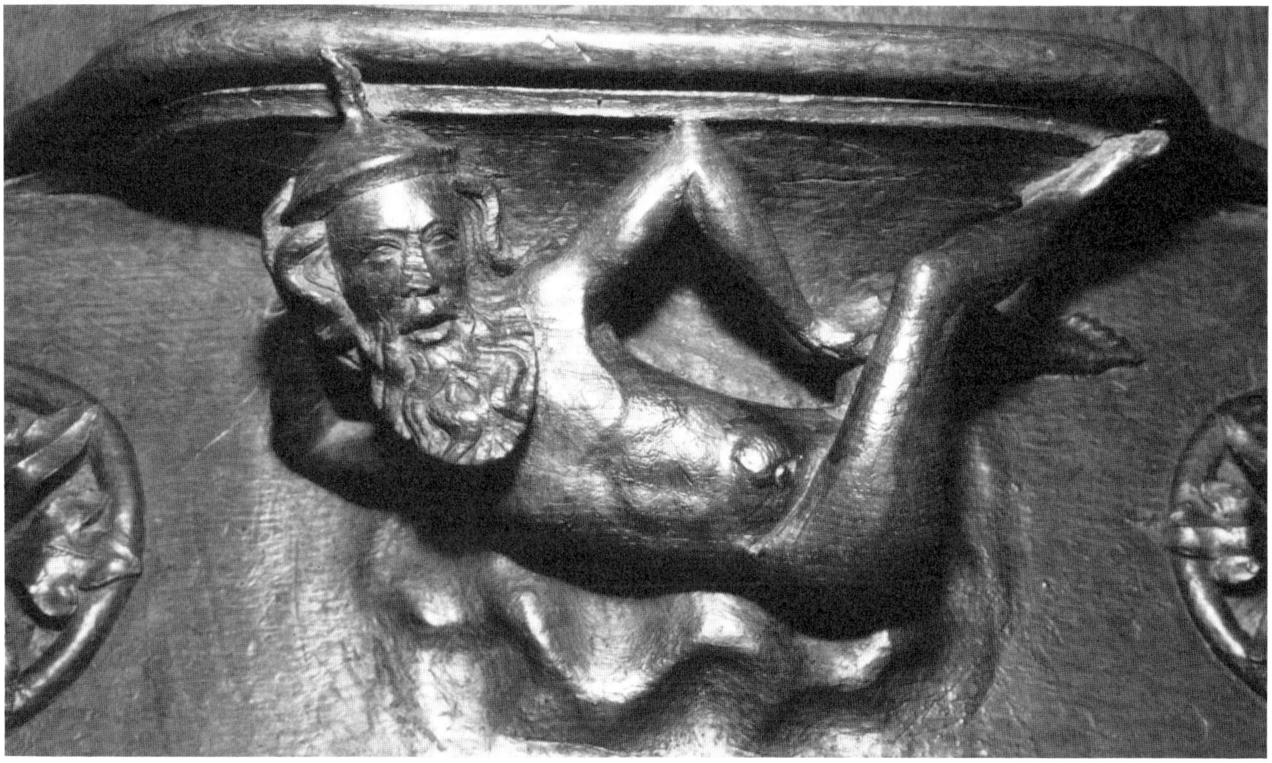

Fool. Hereford (Herefs & Worcs), The Cathedral, c.1380.

> . . . some went so far as to strip themselves naked, and in this condition they were drawn through the streets with tubs full of filth and ordure, which they threw about at the mob. . . . The day was finished with eating and drinking, which merged into all kinds of scandalous disorders, contributing little to the morality of the towns.
>
> Wright 1845, 161

There were some "fool" games in the fourthteenth century, where the person playing the fool would parade naked. This could simply have been an emulation of an idiot, or it may have represented one of the follies of mankind (Billington 1984; Jamieson 1874). The Hereford carving, done in the fourteenth century, represents just such a fool.

This yearly "rebellion," never as tolerated in England as it was in France, finally came under heavy attack by the Church. Prohibited by Bishop Grossteste at Lincoln in 1236 and by Archbishop Courtney in 1390 (Chambers 1945), it was almost suppressed in England in 1391, when the Archbishop of York ordered the Provost of Beverley Minster to abolish the custom. It appears, however, that, although the lower clergy were forbidden to take part in the festival during the fourteenth century, it was still permissible for the laity to do so. Billington (1984), in reading the 1398 Statutes for the better governing of Beverley, found confirmation of the suspension of the "corrupt church custom of regis stultorum" (which applied to the Feast of Fools), but also found a notation that the ancient custom of "les Fulles" (the Fools) would continue. This custom was included in the list of permissible Christmas games for the laity. Billington concludes that, "surviving feasts were secular and, . . . were permitted in preference to the abstention of the entire congregation" (1984, 4).

In England, this secular custom took the form of electing a "Lord of Misrule" during the Feast of Christmas.[4] This "Master of merry disports" was given royal sanction and was invited, along with his merry band, into every noble house as well as the Court (Stow 1633), all for the purpose of entertaining.[5] The custom was also practiced in the community, with many parishes electing their own Lord of Misrule. The actions undertaken were similar to those during the Feast of Fools, as the famous description by the intolerant Puritan, Philip Stubs, shows:

> . . . together with their baudie Pipers, and thundering Drummers . . . they go to church though the minister be at prayer or preaching, dauncing and singing like devils incarnate, with such a confused noise that no man can heare his own voice. . . .
>
> 1595, 107

Stubs goes on to describe what happened when this unruly group left the church and went out into the community demanding money to support their "heathenish devilrie." He berates not only the merrymakers but "another sorte of fantastical fooles (who) bring to these helhounds, the Lord of Misrule and his complices" food and drink (107).

The Lord of Misrule custom passed into disfavor in the sixteenth century, finally being abolished by royal proclamation in 1542 (Wildridge 1879); but by then the figure of the comic fool as a beloved participant in numerous celebrations was well established. The prevalence of fools in the illuminated manuscripts of the period and in the misericord carvings attests to their popularity. Like minstrels, fools frequently enjoyed the patronage of kings and, in rare instances, were liberally rewarded for their antics. King John, for example, granted his fool a landed estate for his services (Thiselton-Dyer 1903).

During this period, fools were garbed in fantastical costumes made of scarves, jewels, rings, and bells. Both their dress and their behavior were intended to amuse. The fool's cap with bells on it derived from these early costumes. In the center of the Beverley carving a group of three fools cavorts. The right supporter shows the noisy pipe and drum so despised by Stubs.

On the bench-end finial from Boston, the caps with bells are clearly shown. The fools here are entertaining by contorting their bodies.

In the fifteenth century, the fool underwent yet another transformation when its character was introduced into the morality plays of the period. In them, the fool personified human folly. This interpretation of the fool became entrenched in England with the publication, in 1509, of Alexander Barclay's translation of Sebastian Brandt's *Ship of Fools* (1874). In this work, 113 different types of fools are described. The book, with its humorous woodcuts of various fools, was widely read throughout the sixteenth century and was used by a number of preachers as a source for sermons.

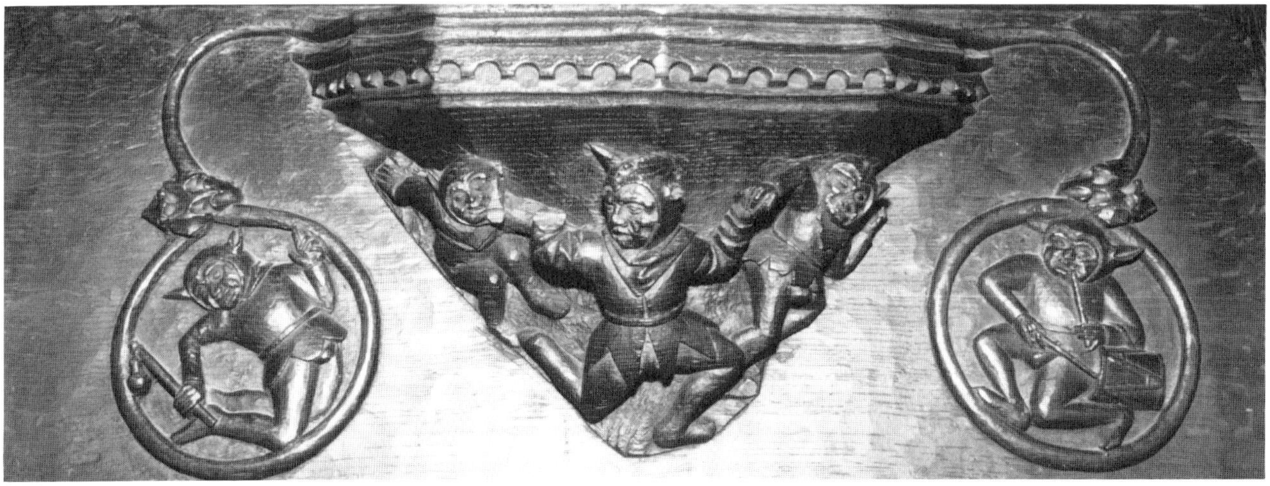

Fools. Beverley (Humberside), The Minster, 1520.

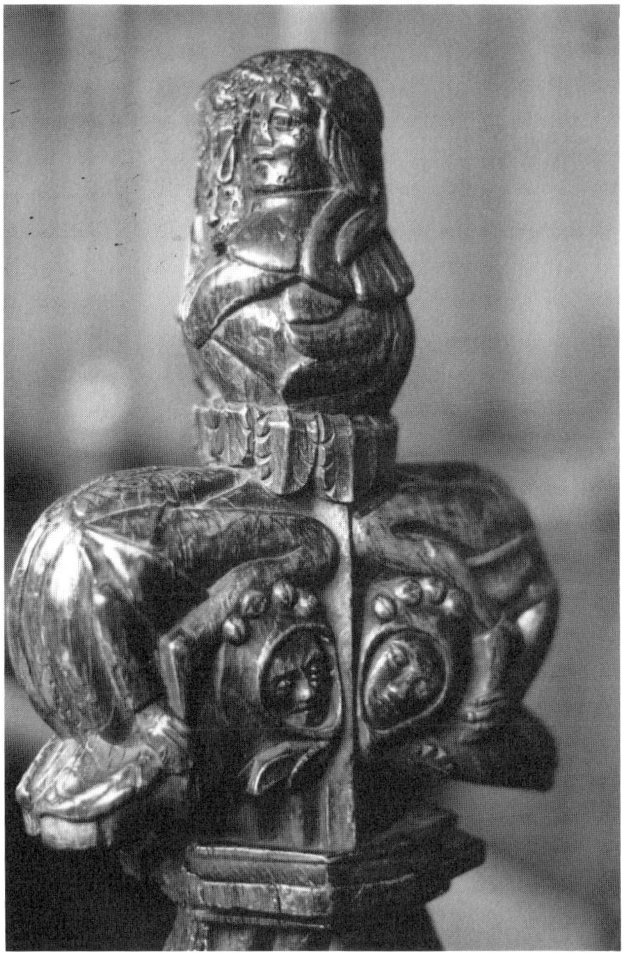

Two fools. Boston (Lincs), St. Botolph, 1390.

DISGUISINGS

Other celebrations were allowed at Christmas time, which included the use of masks. These celebrations represented a reversal of social roles in a way that differed from the festivals' use of the fool. In these customs, individuals were allowed to disguise themselves and behave in ways outside the realm of normal behavior (one important aspect of which was the ability to approach the nobility for donations).

One form of this type of disguise was the Mummer's play, another pre-Christian ritual the Church was unable to suppress. Originally enacted at the winter solstice, the ritual represented the battle between light and dark, with light being triumphant (Whitlock 1979). In order for the gods to favor the community, it was important that the players be disguised and that the ritual be followed precisely. Therefore, from year to year, the same characters were present in each play and the words spoken by each was the same. However, because the words were passed on orally, they became distorted over time until they were virtually meaningless to performers and audience alike. This was of no importance, as long as action and dialogue were believed to remain unchanged (Helm 1991). At the end of the performance, a collection would be taken after the character of Little Johnny Jack gave his speech ending with:

> . . . A jug of Christmas ale, sir, will make our voices ring,
> Money in our pockets is a very good thing.
> So ladies and gentlemen, be at your ease,
> And give us poor Mummers just what you please.
>
> Whitlock 1979, 177

Mummeries, or disguisings, took different forms and participants wearing a disguise would be included in most celebrations. They were not meant to elicit laughter as much as to surprise by the "ridiculous and exaggerated oddity of the visors (masks), and by the singularity and splendour of the dresses" (Strutt 1810, 145). Stow describes a mummery in 1377, for the benefit of young Prince Richard, which included an entourage of forty-eight riders beautifully dressed as knights, one person richly attired as an emperor, another as a pope, followed by twenty-four cardinals and ten others with black masks. As they entered the hall, the mummers saluted the Prince, his mother, and the lords and indicated that they wished to play dice with the Prince. They were, however, mindful of who should win the game:

> shewing by a paire of Dice on the Table, their desire to play with the yong Prince; which they so handled, that the Prince did alwaies winne when he cast at them.
>
> 1633, 78–79

The dice-playing scene is nicely illustrated in the carving below where two men play.

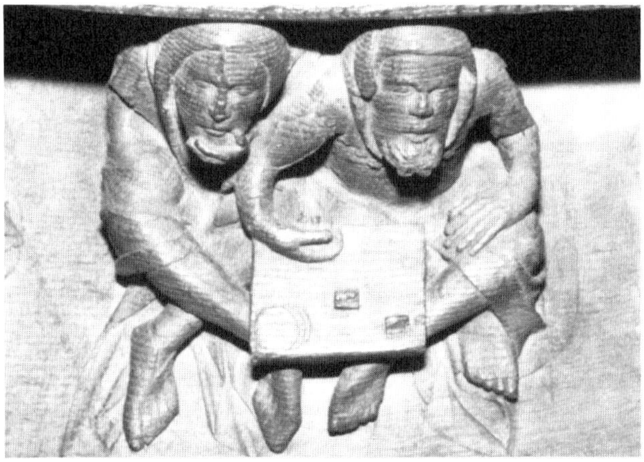

Dice players. Ely (Cambs), The Cathedral, c.1340.

Like stage presentations, the practice of disguising increasingly came to be seen as a potential vehicle for sedition, and laws were passed prohibiting citizens from appearing on the streets wearing masks at Christmas. Such laws were passed in London in 1334 and repeated in 1393 and 1405. In 1417, "mummying" also was classified as a type of disguise and prohibited (Withington 1918). The practice was never fully eradicated, however; to the present day, the old mummer's plays are still enacted in some parts of England.

May Day

In the Middle Ages, two of the spring agricultural rituals surviving from pagan times were Rogationtide and May Day. Both celebrations involve the concept of the death and rebirth of plants from the earth below and, subsequently, human life on the earth above. Rogationtide was taken over by the Church and made a religious celebration; but May Day was harder to wrest from the people and remained more of a pagan celebration. Although the Church did not sanction May Day, it finally gave up trying to suppress the ritual, and so it passed into the realm of institutionalized mayhem.

It is difficult to say whether the celebration of May Day was held onto so tenaciously because of enduring superstitious beliefs or whether the desire for an excuse to participate in licentious merrymaking was stronger. Superstitions aside, May Day was celebrated with all the enthusiasm a youthful, ebullient population could muster. In the words of a twelfth-century wandering scholar:

> Take the pastime that is due
> While we're yet a-Maying;
> I am young and young are you;
> 'Tis the time for playing
>
> Symonds 1931, 139

May Day in the ancient Celtic ritual was called Beltane or Bealtein (Whitlock 1979). It was a ritual of regeneration where bonfires were lit in the fields to cleanse them of any evil spirits that might have gathered there during the winter. After the cleansing, it was safe for livestock to graze in the fields and for new plants to grow. An important feature of later celebrations was the lighting of the Beltane bonfire, believed to be related to the Druids' worship of the sun-god.

May Day celebrations varied from region to region, but all of them involved designating a May King and May Queen, who were the tree spirits. The celebrations were believed to have the power to renew the fields and make them fertile. On May Day, the King and Queen of May were married. In later times, the legend associated Robin Hood and Maid Marian with the King and Queen of May (Whitlock 1979).

The young men and women of the community would retreat to the woods for a night of singing, gathering hawthorn, and lovemaking before returning in the morning to dance around the hawthorn Maypole. Again, the Puritan, Philip Stubs gives his condemning view of the May Day activities:

> And then fal they to banquet and feast, to leape and daunce about it, as the Heathen people did. . . . I have heard it credible reported . . . by men of great gravity, credite, and reputation, that of fourtie, threescore, or a hundred Maids, going to the wood overnight, there have scarcely the third part of them returned home againe undefiled.[6]
>
> 1595, 109

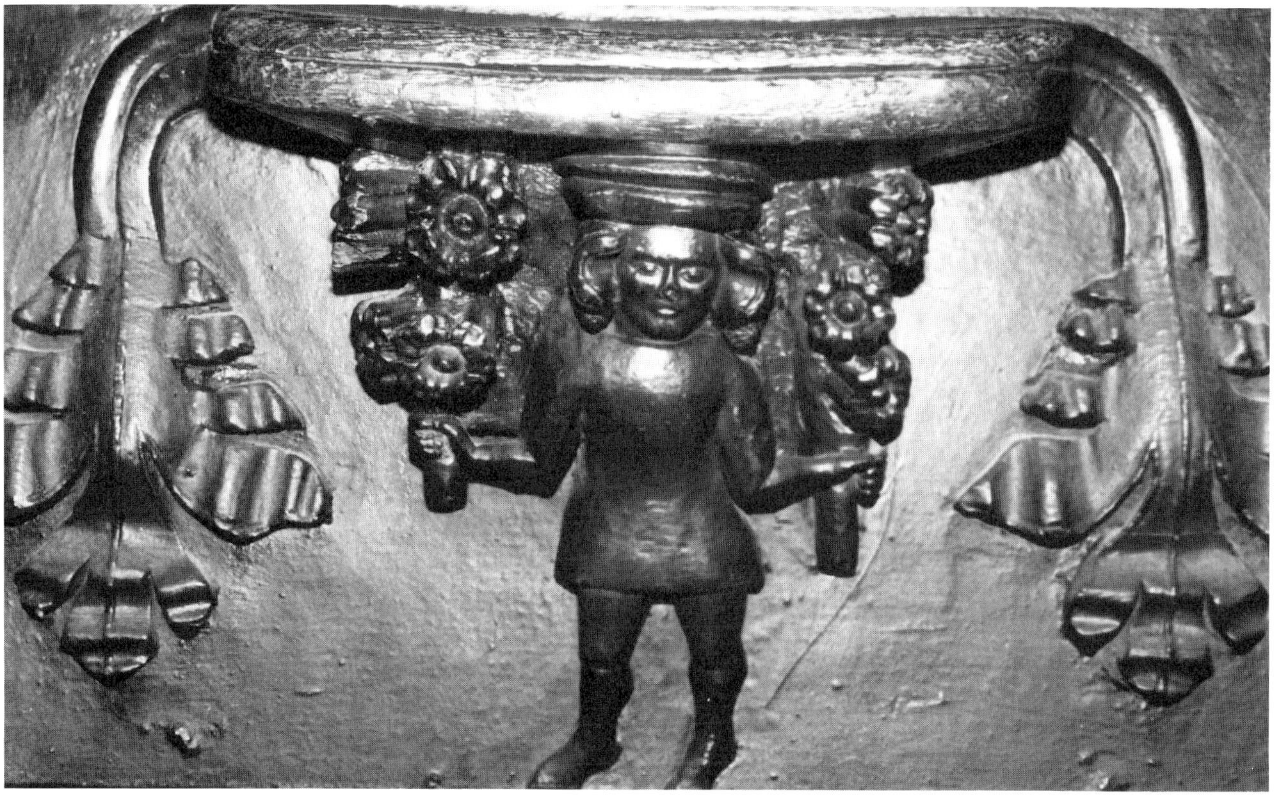

May Day flowers. Great Malvern (Herefs & Worcs), The Priory Church, c.1450–80.

What Philip Stubs abhorred, the people loved; against all criticism, they kept the custom alive. Two carvings depict part of the celebration. The Malvern carving shows a man bringing flowers from the field to add to the Maypole decorations, while the second carving depicts a maiden returning home from the woods, perhaps "defiled" but saucily carrying a bouquet of flowers in her hand.

Predictably, the Church felt that the hawthorn was a bad influence because its scent was said to be sexually arousing (Anderson 1963)—making it all the more desirable to the medieval merrygoer. Despite the Church's criticism, hawthorn continued to play an important role in May Day festivities: it was used for the Maypole, its branches were gathered to decorate the village, and wreaths of hawthorn were worn as personal decoration.

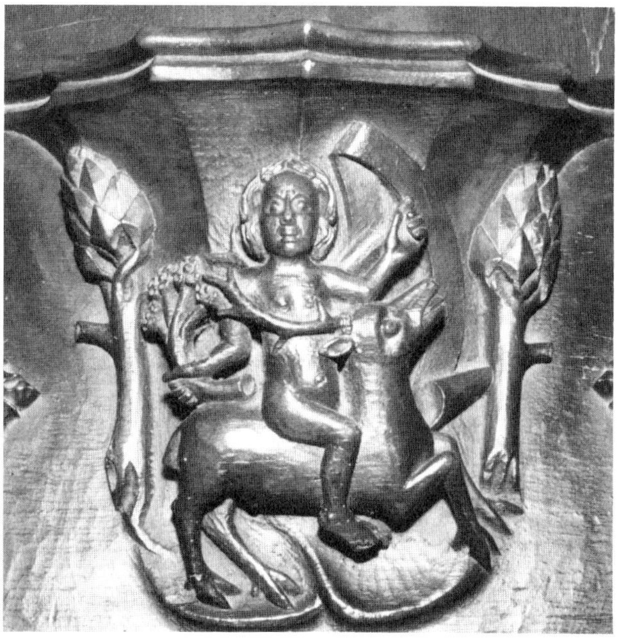

May maiden. Stratford-upon-Avon (Warwickshire), Holy Trinity, late fifteenth century.

Hawthorn had been a symbol of fertility, hope, and marriage since ancient times. In Greek mythology, it was burned at the altar in temples of Hymen, god of marriage, and hawthorn blossoms were made into bridal wreaths. Called "May" in England, the hawthorn was reputed to have numerous powers, including making young women who washed with the dew from the hawthorn, beautiful.

By the sixteenth century, May Day celebrations were becoming tamer, enabling John Stow to provide a more idyllic vision of the happenings:

> . . . on May Day in the morning, every man, except impediment, would walke into the sweet Meddowes and green woods, there to rejoyce their spirits with the beauty and favour of sweet Flowers, and with the harmonie of Birdes, praising God in their kinde.
>
> Stow 1633, 79

This is a celebration that would not have been desired by the medieval May Day celebrants; they much preferred a sensual rejoicing over a spiritual one.

Even with the very real deprivations of the Middle Ages, whenever possible, there was a spirit that simply replaced the feeling of hardship with joy. Plays, festivals, and other celebrations gave medieval people a richness to their lives that ameliorated the dire conditions that filled many days. The medieval period was, among other things, a time when humor and pleasure were quickly seized.

5
Political Wit and Other Rebellions

When the fox preaches, take care of your geese.
English proverb

IT HAS BEEN SAID THAT "CUNNING, TREACHERY AND intrigue" were the vices of the Middle Ages (Wright 1865). The veracity of this statement can hardly be doubted. Individuals in positions of power seem to have spent most of their time plotting to stabilize, expand, or enhance that power, while those in powerless positions calculated how to make their position more tenable. Whether engaging in overt confrontation or in a more subtle battle of wits, the use of cunning was a given in medieval times. In the case of the ordinary citizen, cunning, too, was a necessity; often, it was the only recourse available. Although physical aggression might have been preferred, there were situations where it simply was not a viable option. Given that the rights of the monarchy, nobility, and Church were granted by civil and Church law, there was little ordinary people could do overtly to challenge the unfair treatment received from the establishment.

This did not mean ordinary citizens could not fight back—only that, in most instances, their method of retaliation had to be artful. There were incidents where groups challenged the authorities directly and where overt rebellions occurred; but, most of the time, rebellions were of a quieter, craftier nature. One of the most powerful weapons at hand for the "powerless" was mockery. Misericord carvers, in league with numerous other medieval writers and artists, displayed a creative ability to belittle that made their targets seem ridiculous. Pictorializing the common sentiment in carvings became a major form of collective subversion. The objective was to find a way to tolerate the restrictions of a feudal society when other forms of rebellion were not available. The power to make someone ridiculous through mockery is no small power, especially when done subtly.

Three groups that particularly annoyed the medieval citizenry were the aristocracy, the Church, and the medical profession. Whereas mockery pervaded medieval life, these three groups were targeted for special treatment and were the impetus for some of the most pointed social commentary in the misericords. In what can only be labeled a very sophisticated, sly move on the part of artists and craftsmen, the most potent weapon in their retaliation against the authorities was one small animal—the fox—which triumphed for every person who had ever suffered the oppression meted out by those with power.

THE PEOPLE VS. THE ARISTOCRACY

The allegorical use of animals to make barbed comments on human naure is an old and venerated form of mocking, one the misericord carvers used freely in what became the most popular form of attack on the aristocracy in the late Middle Ages. The exploits of a fox called "Reynard" and, later, his son, Reynardine, provided lessons in cunning and satire; but, most of all, they provided a vehicle for making the ruling class seem ridiculous. Characterized as the most famous medieval "soap opera" (Laird 1986), "Reynard the Fox" stood in for every man as the cleverest rogue of the Middle Ages.

Probably Indo-European in origin (Ellis 1897), the tales of Reynard are most likely the oldest medieval romance. They are traceable back at least to the sixth century when Aesop recorded a fable using the character "Reynard the Fox." In this tale, Reynard sets a trap for the would-be monkey king who falls for it, allowing Reynard to sneer, "You a king, and not understand a trap!" (Fables of Aesop 1926, 121).

It is difficult to determine whether Germany or France should be given more credit for popularizing the tales, but from the twelfth century on, they attained a status of unrivaled acclaim everywhere in western Europe (Anderson 1955). There is evidence of their spread to England by the twelfth century, where an ecclesiastic named Odo de Cirington wrote fables using the names of the characters by which they are still known: Reynard the Fox, Isenberg the Wolf, King Noble the Lion, and so forth (Wright 1865).

In these tales, Reynard has all the characteristics of the fox given in the bestiaries, especially deceit and cunning.[1] As a result, he is constantly devising schemes whereby he outwits stronger animals such as the wolf, bear, and lion. In return, they are always plotting their revenge on Reynard. It is an ongoing contest between an agile mind and brute force. The symbolism has been interpreted in different ways in different versions and by different scholars. In some accounts, Reynard is said to represent the nonaristocratic class; and the lion, bear, wolf, and others, the ruling class (Wright 1865). In a German version, Reynard is said to typify the Church, the wolf the nobility, and the lion the monarchy. In this version, Reynard deceives all these (Phipson 1896). However, the more popular interpretation, at least in England, was that of Reynard as a representative of the oppressed fighting against the more powerful aristocracy. The aristocracy in these tales is always presented as having minimal intelligence even though they have a great deal of power. Reynard, on the other hand, has little formal power but is always able to outwit them because he is intellectually superior. By playing on the greed of "stronger" creatures, the cleverness of Reynard held the medieval world in thrall for centuries.

These tales were so admired that when William Caxton began printing books in England in the fifteenth century, *The History of Reynard the Fox* was one of the first books he chose to print. Caxton, in a cunning move of his own, prefaced his c.1481–82 edition of the book with a message for anyone who might take offense at the tales, " . . . blame not me, but the foxe, for they be his wordes, and not myne"—a position endorsed by the misericord carvers.

Bristol Cathedral contains the largest collection of carved scenes from the Reynard tales, though individual carvings appear elsewhere illustrating various episodes. The Bristol carvings were done about forty years after publication of Caxton's book, giving evidence of their enduring popularity.[2] The flavor of the stories closely resembles that of a serial drama, where each successive episode brings new twists and new solutions.

These stories were so much a part of the grain of medieval life and thought that they deserve more examination than it is possible to give them here. However, some appreciation for their cleverness and charm can be gained through the two excerpted selections presented. They are taken from the Old English metrical version used by Caxton but refined by Ellis in 1897. The verse is illustrated by carvings from Bristol.

EPISODE 1

After many complaints about Reynard's duplicity, King Noble the Lion has finally decreed that Reynard be brought to Court to stand trial. King Noble sends members of his court one by one to bring Reynard in, and one by one they return defeated. Reynard plays on the greed of his would-be captors, successfully outwitting them at every turn.

The first to be given the task of bringing Reynard in is Bruin Bear, who goes with confidence to Reynard's mountain home:

Forth started Bruin on his way,
Rejoicing, light of heart, and gay
As bird in spring, and well assured
That by no Fox could he be lured

18

Reynard welcomes Bruin with words of flattery and friendship, assuring him that he would be happy to start out for Court that day if it weren't for the fact he had "O'erstepped the bounds of temperance" in eating too much. Bruin wants to know what he has eaten, and Reynard tells him it was simple peasant food, like honeycomb, that wouldn't be of interest to better folk like Bruin. Astounded, Bruin assures Reynard that "better folk" like himself would indeed be interested, and promises Reynard:

For my part I
esteem them foremost of all meat,
Fragrant and luscious, soft and sweet,
Past measure: help me to obtain
Good stac thereof, and ye shall gain
My lasting friendship while I live.

22

Reynard tells Bruin if that is so, he can lead him to a place where he might have honey enough for twelve grown bears and more. Bruin, however, assures Reynard that he can eat it all by himself, and they set out for the yard of Lantfert the woodsman. It happened that Reynard knew that Lantfert had felled a large elm tree the day before and had driven wedges in it to hold the massive trunk apart. Reynard shows Bruin the tree and tells him this is where the honey is, but cautions Bruin to be prudent, for he does not want blame to fall on him if his friend eats too much. Bruin, eager to get at the honey, assures Reynard there is no need for worry:

With lumbering leap
The Bear trod toward the oak in haste,
O'erjoyed to think he soon should taste
The longed-for good, his pointed nose
Down thrust he, and his forefeet toes
Set well with the open space;
Forthwith leapt Reynard toward the place
With lightning speed, and deftly twitched,
The oak sprang to, and held the Bear
With iron grip.

25–26

Reynard then sings a taunting song of triumph. Bruin promises Reynard he will be his friend if he will put the wedges back in, but Reynard laughs and leaves him to the approaching Lantfert. When Lantfert spies Bruin, he yells to his neighbors for them to come and participate in the sport of catching a bear:

The Bear to bait, tease, maim, or slay:
Against him now is each man's hand
And, friendless, he the brunt must stand.

29

This episode is illustrated in the carving on the next page. Reynard is shown enjoying the scene of the bear's humiliation.

EPISODE 2

The Court then decides that rather than subduc Reynard with brute force, they will send someone who can match wits with him—Tybert the Cat:

Our will it is that Tybert Cat
Should serve the Summons; Bruin gat
'Tis true, sore handling, far more fit
To match the Fox is Tybert's wit
Than mere brute force.

36

Much the same scene is reenacted with Tybert as occurred with Bruin. Reynard agrees to accompany Tybert to Court the next day, and Tybert thinks he has succeeded in his mission. In settling in, Tybert asks what meat there is to eat; Reynard tells him that there is only honeycomb. Tybert mentions that he much prefers fat rats and, of course, Reynard knows just where to find them. He tells Tybert

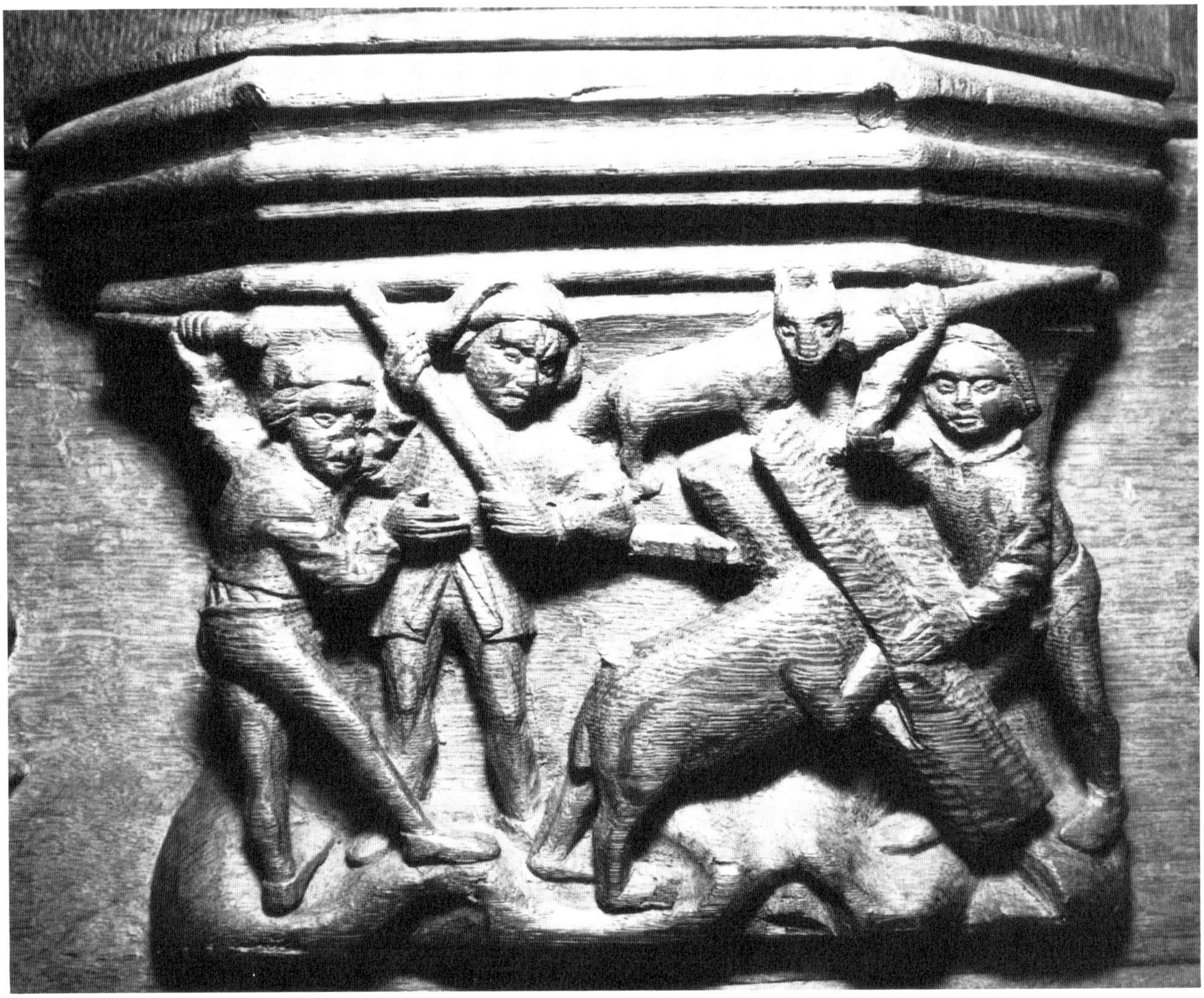

Bruin Bear. Bristol (Avon), The Cathedral, 1520.

of the fat rats he has seen in the priest's barn and they set out to catch them.

What Tybert does not know is that the priest has become so tired of Reynard sneaking into the barn to steal hens that he has set a trap by the hole in the wall where Reynard enters the barn. Aware of the trap, Reynard decides to use it to his advantage. He shows Tybert the hole in the wall while assuring him that many fat mice reside within. Tybert is somewhat reluctant, but greed rules in the end and he plunges through the hole and is caught in the noose.

> In vain attempted he to spring
> From out the hole, the tightening string
> Held fast his neck. False Reynard saw
> His dupe's distress, and heard him wraw
> And shriek with pain, the while, above,
> He laughing stood, and cried: "D'ye love
> Fat mice, dear Tybert? Are they good?"
>
> 42

Tybert's cries awaken the priest's household, and the priest, his aide, Martinet, and wife, Julock all rush out thinking they have finally caught Reynard. Dame Julock lights a torch, and Martinet and the priest grab poles. Tybert manages to elude the blows and leaps onto the priest's leg.

> "Thou shalt die,"
> Roared forth the priest, and drave a blow
> Which missed its aim, or else alow
> The Cat had lain.

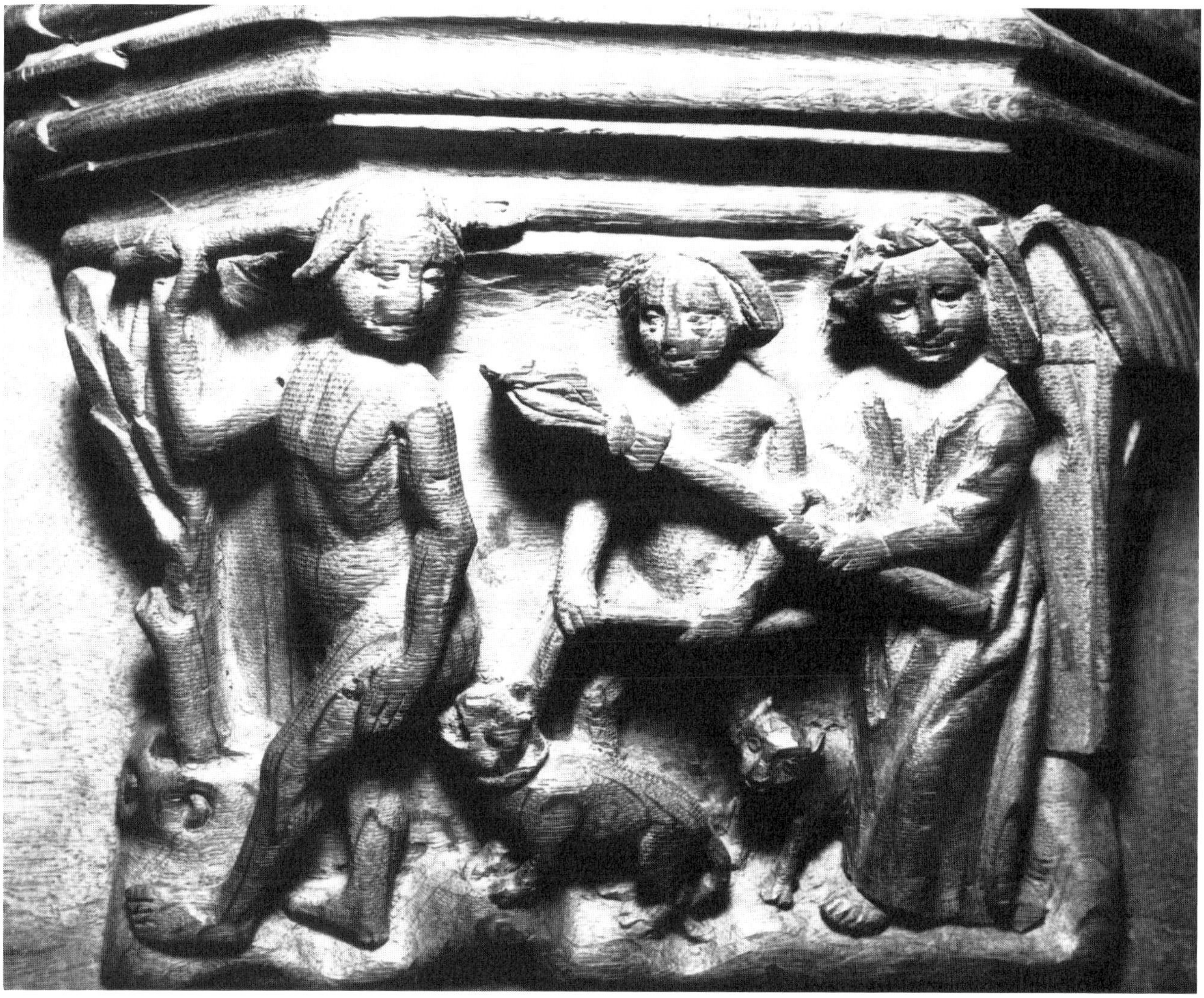

Tybert the Cat. Bristol (Avon), The Cathedral, 1520.

"Nay then my life
Shall dear be bought," above the strife
Shrieked Tybert, as the parson's calf
He seized and wellnigh bit in half.
"Harrowe!" yelled out the priest. "I'm dead."
And fainting, kissed the ground, and bled
In such full tide, that well 'twould seem
His spirit drank dear Lethe's stream.

43

The carving shows the moment either when Tybert is about to bite the priest's leg or immediately after. Reynard is peering safely from between the legs of Martinet and Julock.

Finally, Reynard is convinced that he should go to Court and plead his case. He is tried and condemned to hang. King Noble has charged Bruin Bear, Tybert Cat, and Isegrym Wolf with hanging Reynard, for they have all suffered from his tricks. Reynard is led to the gallows.

In many stories, this would have been the end of Reynard, but Reynard proved harder to kill than St. George and lived to turn the tables on his accusers—but that is an episode for another time. Each of the tales is a moral statement about the corruption of those in power, as well as a demonstration that their own greed makes them vulnerable.

The importance of the Reynard stories in providing ordinary citizens the means to strike back at what was seen as a corrupt ruling class cannot be overstated. Drama and disguisings could be controlled by law, but stories were harder to suppress, as was the outgrowth of artistic renderings. The Reynard

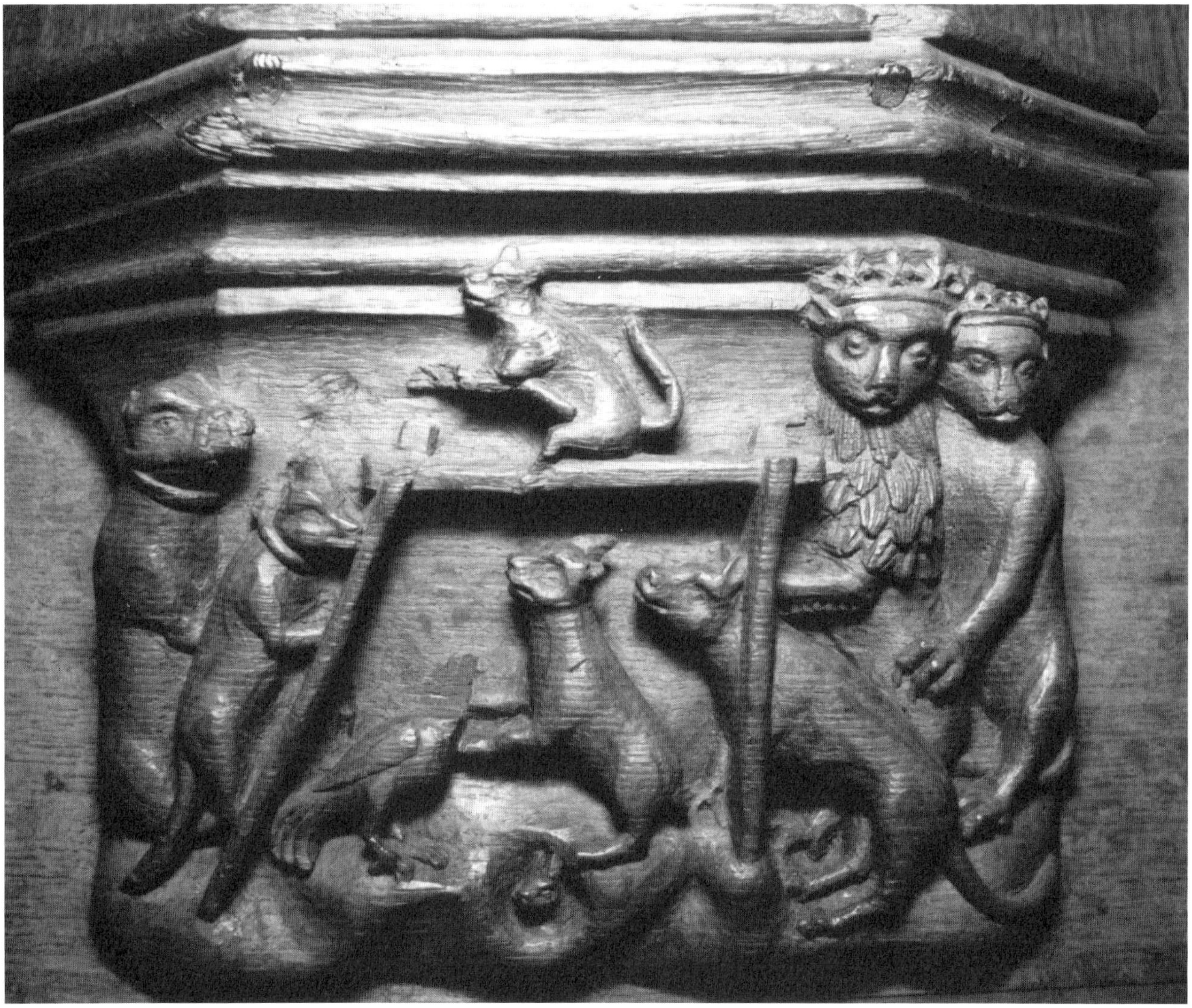

Reynard led to the gallows. Bristol (Avon), The Cathedral, 1520.

tales were represented in every medium—manuscript illustrations, stained glass, stonework, drama, and, of course, woodwork.

The People vs. the Clergy

The utility of the fox figure as a way to belittle was also brought into play for use against another group increasingly seen as a greater enemy of the people—the established clergy. Antipathy toward the Church in the late Middle Ages was widespread, and not just among the peasantry. There is a story of the battle between Pope Boniface VIII (1294–1303) and Philip IV (1268–1314) of France over Philip's attempt to tax the clergy. Philip was so enraged over the Pope's interference that he tried to chastise him publicly by staging the "Procession Renert." In this production, a mummer, covered in the skin of a fox over which he wore a priest's robe, performed a mass, then immediately went out to devour poultry (Day 1872). The monarchy and the Church were frequently at odds over who had supreme power.

The greatest disgust with the clergy, however, emanated from the common people, for they were subject to greater abuses from the clergy. Many saw the clergy, particularly the bishops, abbots and priors as corrupt, lazy, and unfair landlords. They became the butt of numerous jokes. The following medieval story is typical of the common sentiment:

> It is told on very good authority how, in a very well-known town, a certain priest was returning from his leman [mistress] in the dusk, and heard a lamentable voice proceeding from a ruined house; whereupon he drew near and enquired who cried thus in that place. "Who art thou," said the voice, "that enquirest of me?" "A priest," answered he. "What, a priest!" cried that voice in great astonishment, repeating the word twice or thrice. When therefore the priest had enquired wherefore he spoke in such tones of wonder, then said the voice, "They come down so thick among us into Hell, that me thought no priest could be left on earth; wherefore I cried aloud in wonder to hear that one was still alive; for I deemed they were all gone down to Hell!"
>
> Coulton 1928, 3:87

The criticism of the Church was justified. It had been lax in monitoring its own and had overlooked much in its quest for economic gain. The common perception was that, with enough money one could buy any forgiveness or any assurance from the Church—either before death or afterward. The belief that one lingered in purgatory for a period time after death in order to atone for actions taken or not taken during one's lifetime created a ready market for the clergy. If rapid progress through purgatory was desired, the Church could arrange, for a fee, to forgive any transgressions committed before one died and thus speed the journey after death. Or, if desired or if necessary, one could arrange payment before death for a chantry priest to say prayers daily after death for one's soul, on the assumption that the prayers would speed the trip to heaven. These options worked well if one could afford it; but most could not, thus producing a two-tier path to salvation—one that could be bought and one that had to be achieved by working to amass good deeds during one's lifetime.

The shortage of priests even before the Black Death was caused in part by local clergy giving up their posts and going to London to become chantry priests, where they made their living singing requiems for stipends, a much more lucrative enterprise (Page 1909). So prevalent was this practice that in the fourteenth century William Langland commented on it in his celebrated *The Vision of Piers Plowman.*[3] Langland condemned the greed of the clergy when he noted that too many local parsons and parish priests ask

> To haue a lycence and a leue at London to dwelle,
> And syngen here for symonye for siluer is swete.
>
> Langland, 1906, 4

Incidents such as this added to the feeling that the Church had abandoned its obligation to tend to the spiritual needs of the people and was interested only in its own economic gain. In a growing atmosphere of distrust, many people turned to the mendicant friars as their religious intermediaries. The friars—denouncing material wealth, at least ostensibly—roamed the countryside offering prayers, absolutions, and other services normally performed by the church-based clergy. Inevitably, this resulted in feelings of antipathy on the part of the clergy for the friars, not in the least because the activities of the mendicant friars diverted revenue away from the church-based clergy. In addition, these innovative clerics were viewed as subversive because many of them preached the new doctrine of emancipation (Jusserand 1950).

Unlike the church-based clergy, mendicant friars moved among the people, making themselves accessible even though, unlike the local clergy, they actually were not part of the community. Neither were they part of the Church. For both reasons, the friars represented a substantial threat to the Church, which reacted vehemently against them. In 1386, the Council of Salzburg branded them "false prophets" (Jusserand 1950). It has been suggested that the Church reacted not so much from contempt of the friars as from fear (Trevelyan 1904); and, in this, the Church was not alone. The monarchy also was dealt some blows by the power of the friars. When Henry IV usurped the throne in 1399, many friars, angered by the act, roamed the countryside, preaching that Richard II still lived and was the true king. Henry retaliated by having the friars jailed (Jusserand 1950).

Along with the mendicant friars, another group of wandering preachers challenged the control of the Church by preaching egalitarianism. Organized and led by John Wyclif (1328–1384), they were known as his "poor priests." Wyclif challenged the belief that it was necessary for the clergy to act as intermediaries between the people and their God. He taught instead that Christ was the only overlord of man and that the Scriptures were the supreme authority. Wyclif further engendered the wrath of the Church when he suggested that the clergy should own no property. This prompted the Archbishop of Canterbury to sneeringly call Wyclif and his poor priests "lollards," or mumblers of prayers (Hibbert 1992). This derisive label had little impact on Wyclif's popularity, however.

It was during this period—after the meeting of the Council of Salzburg, the growth in influence of the friars, and the increased activity of the poor priests—that Church warnings about false prophets proliferated. The warning was rendered in a common artistic portrayal. Both illuminated-manuscript artists and misericord carvers used the parable of the fox and the geese as a symbol for deceitful clergy. The outcome of this deception, of course, is that the geese are tricked, caught, and eaten; but the question in interpreting these artistic messages is, who were the people being warned against—the established clergy or the mendicant friars and poor priests?

In an interesting continuation of the legend of Reynard, we now find his son, Reynardine, used as a symbol of a false prophet. After Reynard's death, the legend goes, Reynardine and his brother killed the servants who had shown them where to escape with their father's treasure. Fearing capture, Reynardine enlists the help of his cousin, who convinces him that the safest place to hide is in a monastery (Fuchs 1700). In the monastery, Reynardine manages to conduct himself properly until he is placed in the kitchen to serve. There he soon falls prey to temptation and is caught stealing fish. His penance is to fast for two days, whereupon he decides to leave the monastery. As he wanders away and grows hungry, he stops by a pond filled with geese. The geese, seeing his monk's habit, immediately come to him for a blessing, and instead lose their heads. Again, the question must be raised: which type of false prophet does Reynardine represent? From the Church's viewpoint, he is the symbol of the reviled friars and wandering preachers, but is this true from the perspective of the laity?

The scene of the fox tricking the geese was artistically replayed many times, especially in the churches of England (Evans 1896). The carving, right, is a typical example. Although the heads of the geese have been destroyed, the story is still recognizable. The fox is dressed in a clerical robe, grasping a rosary and holding forth in his pulpit before the geese. His friend, the monkey, has already captured one goose which hangs from the stick over his shoulder.

In this and other fox and geese carvings, the fox figure is ambiguous, perhaps deliberately so. There are no key identifying characteristics

Fox in pulpit. Beverley (Humberside), The Minster, 1520.

to indicate whether the fox represents a friar or a monk, making either interpretation plausible. There is little doubt, however, that the carver's meaning was not the one assumed by the monk. A monk looking at the carving would have equated the fox with a false prophet, but a carver or other member of the laity who chanced to see it would have recognized a different scoundrel.

In other carvings, details make clear the carver's intended target; although, if one is looking only cursorily at the carving, it might be missed or misread. These subtleties help explain why it took a while for the clergy to realize that they were the parodied figures.

The St. Mary carving, next, is an example which, on the surface, seems to indicate one thing but which, upon closer examination, indicates quite another. It has been said that the foxes in the carving represent Cistercian friars (Evans 1896) receiving a blessing or instructions from their superior. The fact that each fox has a goose tucked into its cowl is said to illustrate the deceptive nature of friars. This interpretation becomes questionable, however, when the staffs held by the "friars" are recognized as crosiers. Crosiers are the property and symbol not of friars but of bishops, abbots, and abbesses. This addition to the carving allows the interpretation to shift from condemnation of friars to criticism of the established clergy. The carver's message is a warning against the greedy clergy, not the wandering preacher.

Because of the hostility toward the clergy, on one side, and the hostility toward the mendicant friars and other wandering preachers, on the other, it was possible for the fox in the carvings to be interpreted as both a heretical friar who seduces the faithful away from the Church (Robinson 1962; Bond 1910, vol. 1), and as a corrupt prelate (Phipson 1896). These views, of course, coincide with the views of the established clergy, on the one hand, and the laity, on the other. In one of the cleverest acts of medieval rebellion, the sly hand of the devi-

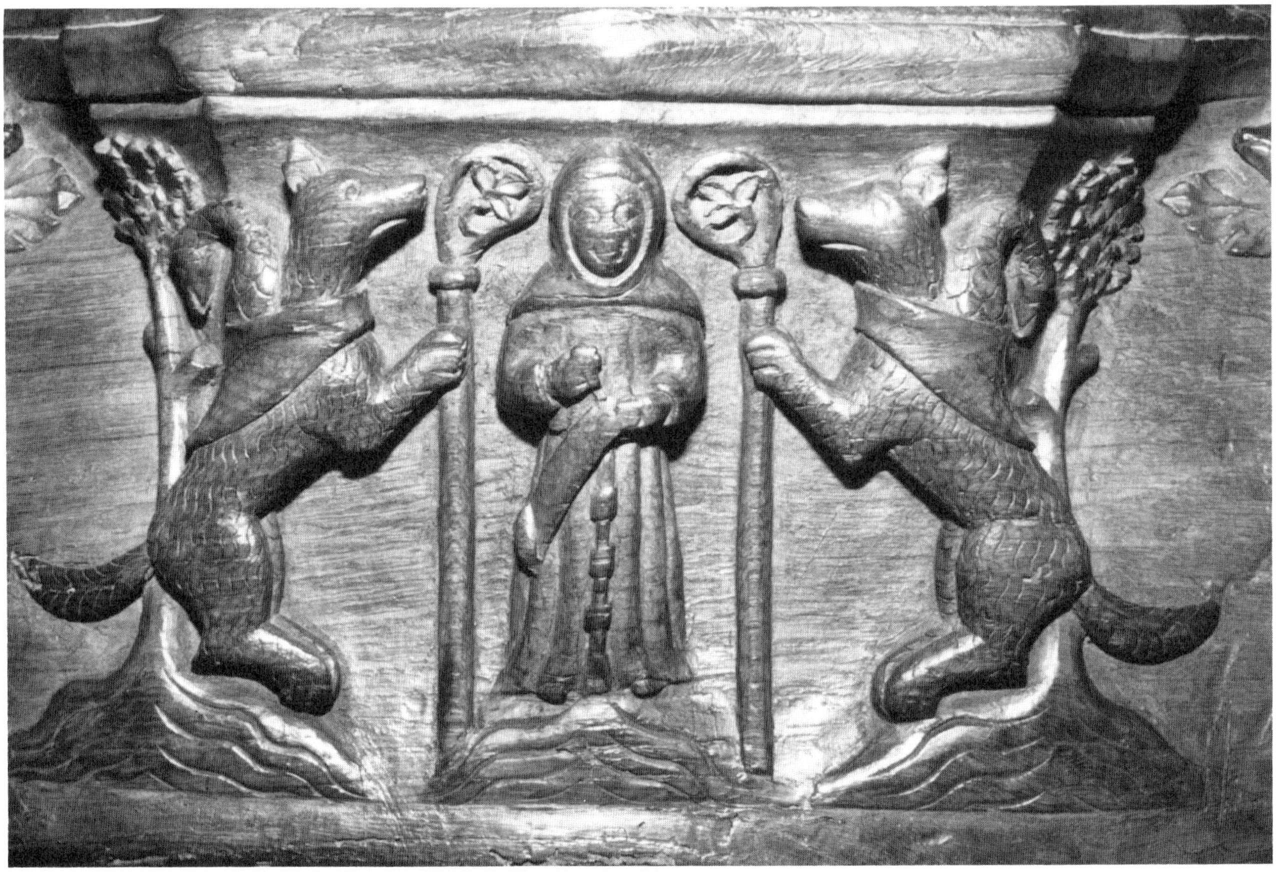

Monk and foxes. Beverley (Humberside), St. Mary, c.1445.

ous misericord carver managed to mock the clergy on the very seats upon which they sat. The monks, on whose stalls the carvings appeared, intended to moralize about the encroaching mendicant friars or Wyclif's "poor priests," but the carver enjoyed recording in wood what the stall-holding monk represented to him. While the Church was busy endorsing carved pictorial warnings about "false prophets," the carver was busy carving warnings about the established clergy.

In the period leading up to the Reformation in England, some fox and geese carvings were damaged or destroyed (Evans 1896), perhaps as the clergy finally realized the true target of the carvers. Their failure to recognize the true aim of the carvings earlier meant that they had participated in their own belittlement, a situation they undoubtedly now found intolerable.

The use of the fox figure to portray deceitful clergymen included another element that was explored by the misericord carvers in a category of carvings aptly labeled by some as "retributive justice" (Phipson 1896). Retributive justice scenes show a reversal of situations—the woman beating her husband or rats hanging the cat, for example. They issue a warning that those taken advantage of today may gain the upper hand tomorrow. Specific to the fox/clergy instance, the Bristol carving is representative. Here, one fox is being hanged by the geese while another fox peeks out from a burrow where perhaps he is contemplating his own future. Note the lower goose who is rendering assistance in hastening the fox's departure by giving his tail a yank.

The association of the fox/clergy with deceitful behavior remained a popular image well beyond the Middle Ages. This view was still present, for example, when an eighteenth-century writer described the idyllic ambiance

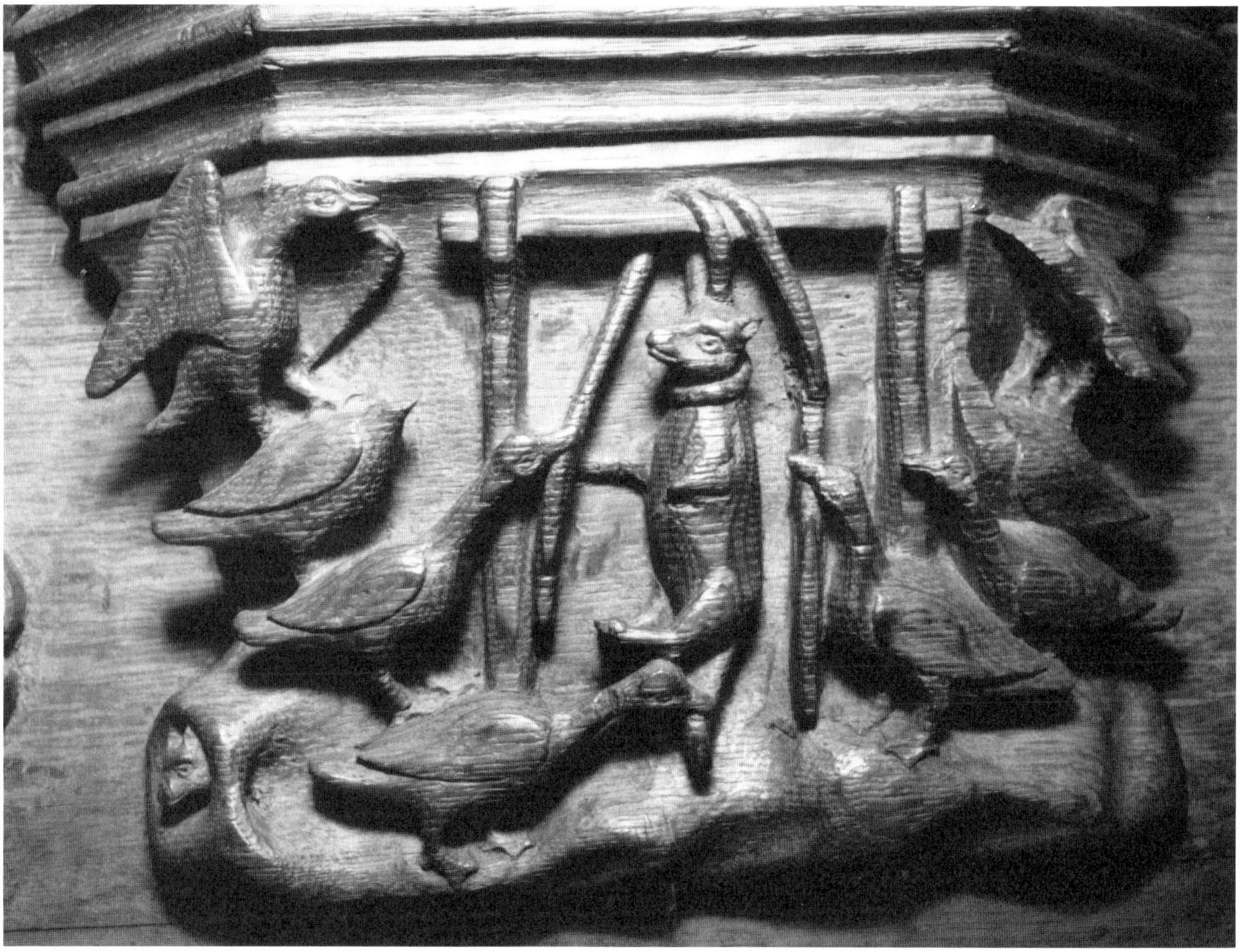

Geese hanging fox. Bristol (Avon), The Cathedral, 1520.

of the Isle of Wight as being due to the fact that, "The Isle of Wight hath no monks, lawyers, or foxes" (Warner 1795).

There also were overt rebellions against the Church in the late Middle Ages, three of which are mentioned here. In the twelfth century, an unusual threat to the Church was mounted by a group known as "wandering scholars." In the thirteenth century, the flagellants made a brief appearance, followed by a group of religious dancers in the fourteenth century. The approach of each group was different, but each directly challenged Church authority.

WANDERING SCHOLARS

Also called "Goliardi" after their fictitious leader, "Golias," these men traveled the countryside indulging themselves. They were students, and because of the nature of education at the time, they did indeed have to wander from place to place to study different topics. They were better known, however, for their dissolute lifestyle and poetry than their scholarship. They differed from most scholars of the period in that they were not primarily from religious orders, but were instead in a curious ranking somewhere between clergy and laity. Clearly, they were not of the laboring class, but neither were they of the regular clergy, although they have been referred to as "vagabond monks" (Bishop 1987). A few may have had some minor connection to the Church; but, by and large, they were a rebellious group that sneered at both laity and clergy, the former for their presumed loutishness and the latter for their known corruption (Symonds 1931). Their primary interest was in making the most of their youth by engaging in carefree exploits and thumbing their collective nose at convention:

> Down the broad way do I go
> Young and unregretting,
> Wrap me in my vices up,
> Virtue all forgetting,
> Greedier for all delight
> Than heaven to enter in
> Since the soul in me is dead,
> Better save the skin.
>
> Rowling 1987

The confusion about their status may have resulted from the scholars' facetious declaration at one point that they would form their own order (Symonds 1931; Wright 1841). And, since orders should have a patron saint, they invented their own—"Golias." Although it is not known where the term came from, it became synonymous with the wandering students, and by extension, with hedonistic living. The always gullible Welshman, Giraldus Cambrensis[4] was not the only person to believe Golias was real; unfortunately, he was one of the few to rush to record his knowledge in print:

> A certain parasite called Golias, who in our time obtained wide notoriety for his gluttony and lechery, and by addition to gulosity [greediness] and debauchery deserved his surname, being of excellent culture but of bad manners
>
> Wright 1863, ix

What is known about their poetry comes from two thirteenth-century manuscripts that have been preserved—one in Germany, the other in England. Written in Latin, the poems were sung by the wandering scholars to entertain themselves, various hosts, and numerous young women. The poems were distinct from those of the troubadours who sang of romantic love played out among members of the upper classes. Unlike the troubadours, the wandering students had no desire to woo and win the patronage of a noble lady. Rather, they focused on less demanding liaisons. For the wandering scholars, life was too brief; therefore, pleasure should be pursued aggressively, and, on occasion, with enticing, polished words:

> List, my girl, with words I woo;
> Lay not wanton hands on you:
> Sit before you, in your face
> Gazing, ah! and seeking grace:
> Fix mine eyes, nor let them rove
> From the mark where shafts of love
> Their flights wing.
> Try, my girl, O try what bliss
> Young men render when they kiss!
>
> Symonds 1931

The success gained from serenading young lasses with such charming words is captured in the Chichester carving, right. The young woman rises to the challenge and leans over after the song is finished to "try what bliss."

Located mostly in northern France, but also in England, wandering scholars were so prevalent during the thirteenth century that they have been described as constituting a "plague" (Columbia Viking Desk Encyc., 1960). They personified the idealized image of men with no obligations other than self-indulgence. Indeed, the verse of the Goliards was intended to speak for the collective. Where the troubadours clearly spoke for themselves, Goliardic verse was written as if emanating from "Golais" speaking for every man (Symonds 1931). One can understand both the appeal and the danger of such a model for the ordinary man.

The threat they posed, however, was not to the ordinary man, no matter how much he might admire them. The real threat was to the Church. It is true that much of the Goliardic poetry extolled the pleasures of "wine, women, and song," but their ongoing, satirical criticism of the Papal Court, and of ecclesiastics in general, was too harsh and too widespread to be ignored.

A carver captured some of the scathing satire the wandering scholars aimed at members of the clergy in the carving, right.

First, the figure of the monk is posed with his robe pulled up to reveal that he is a beast from the waist down. The monk's "real" nature is thus revealed. Second, the monk is shown with two items he is supposed to eschew, the tabor, which is the common instrument of the lower classes, and issuing from his anus, a woman. It is a damning statement of deceit.

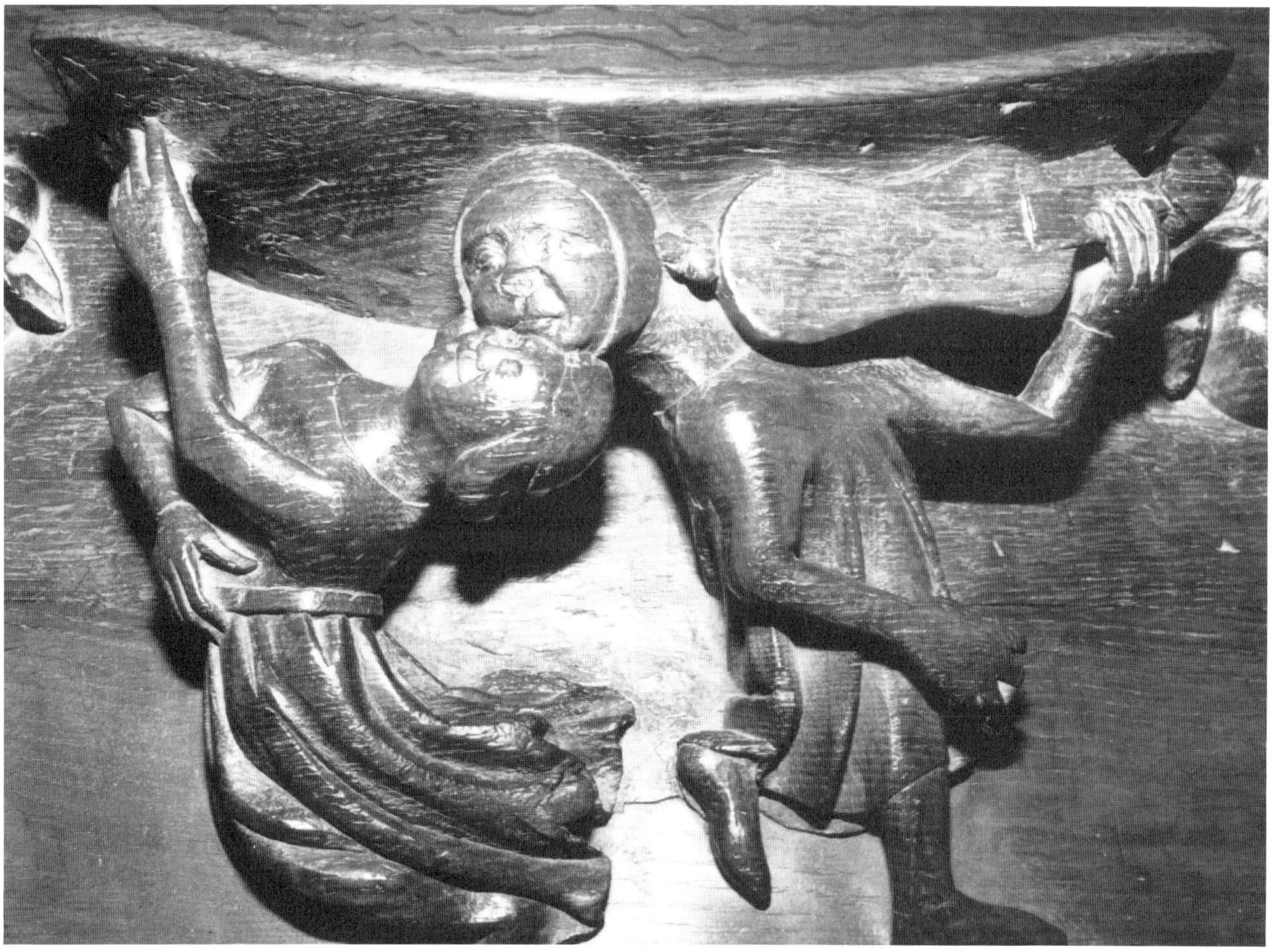

Man and woman kissing. Chichester (W.Sussex), The Cathedral, c. 1330.

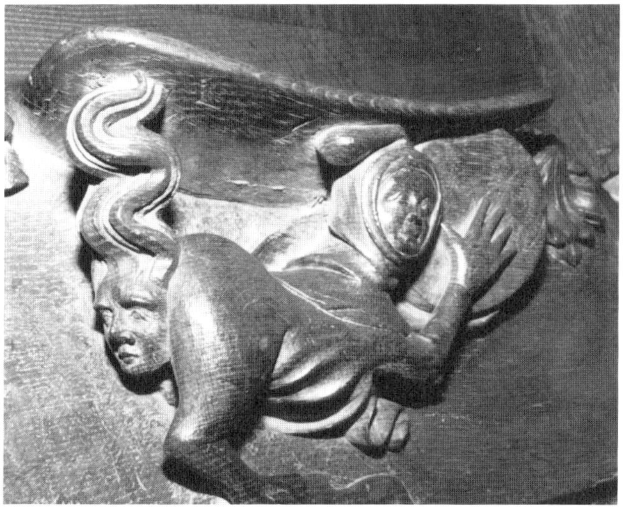

Monk parody. Chichester (W.Sussex), St. Mary's Hospital, c.1290.

The Church had reason to fear the Goliards, on two counts. First, they presented impudent conduct as a model; and, second, they continually levied charges of corruption within the Church. It is not surprising that the Church moved to eradicate them at their height early in the thirteenth century. Whether due to the Church's efforts or not, the wandering scholars did disappear, or perhaps they simply grew old.

THE FLAGELLANTS AND DANCERS

There was an anti-clerical craze marked by the appearance of a group of heretical Christians proclaiming the old Christian punishment of flagellation as the sole foundation for salvation, both for themselves and for the whole of humankind. Within the Church, flagellation had been in use as a form of punishment from early times, but in the thirteenth century, brotherhoods of flagellants were organized in Italy in reaction to several conditions—famine, apocalyptic prophecies, and Franciscan Spirituals. Ignited by fear that the eruption of the plague in the mid-fourteenth century confirmed apocalyptic prophecies, these groups quickly spread throughout Europe. They traveled on foot, whipping themselves in a frenzied manner in public and reading aloud a letter proclaiming flagellation, not ecclesiastical sacraments of penance, as the true way to salvation (Cooper 1870).[5] Anxious to ameliorate what they perceived as the wrath of God, they had little faith in the ability of a corrupt clergy to guide them:

> Organized groups of 200 to 300 . . . marched from city to city, stripped to the waist, scourging themselves with leather whips tipped with iron spikes until they bled. While they cried aloud to Christ and the Virgin for pity, and called upon God to "Spare us!"
>
> Tuchman 1978, 114

As the people flocked to watch and hear the flagellants, their credibility and power grew. They, not the Church, had the ability to save mankind. Such a message—and threat—to the Church had to be addressed, and, in 1349, Clement VI formally condemned flagellation and its followers (Cooper 1870).

In the late fourteenth century, another anticlerical movement developed. After the plague of 1373–74 and other natural disasters, people were further convinced that they must be possessed by devils to be so punished, and a dancing mania took hold in which participants would dance in a frenzied manner to exorcise the demons. Like the flagellants, these dancers traveled from town to town, performing their wild gyrations while reportedly seeing visions. In an attempt to offset what was recognized as a growing challenge to the Church, priests began performing as many public exorcisms as possible. These were to offset the perception that people could rid themselves of the Devil on their own. In addition, the exorcisms were another source of revenue the priests wanted to protect.

An interesting fourteenth-century carving from New College records these events. It has been widely interpreted as a hydra representing the Seven Deadly Sins (Anderson 1954; Steer 1973; Phipson 1896), but this interpretation must be incorrect. Although the central carving might support such a conclusion, the supporters promote a different analysis.

In Christian mythology, the Hydra represented unmitigated evil. Numerous representations show St. Michael engaged in fierce

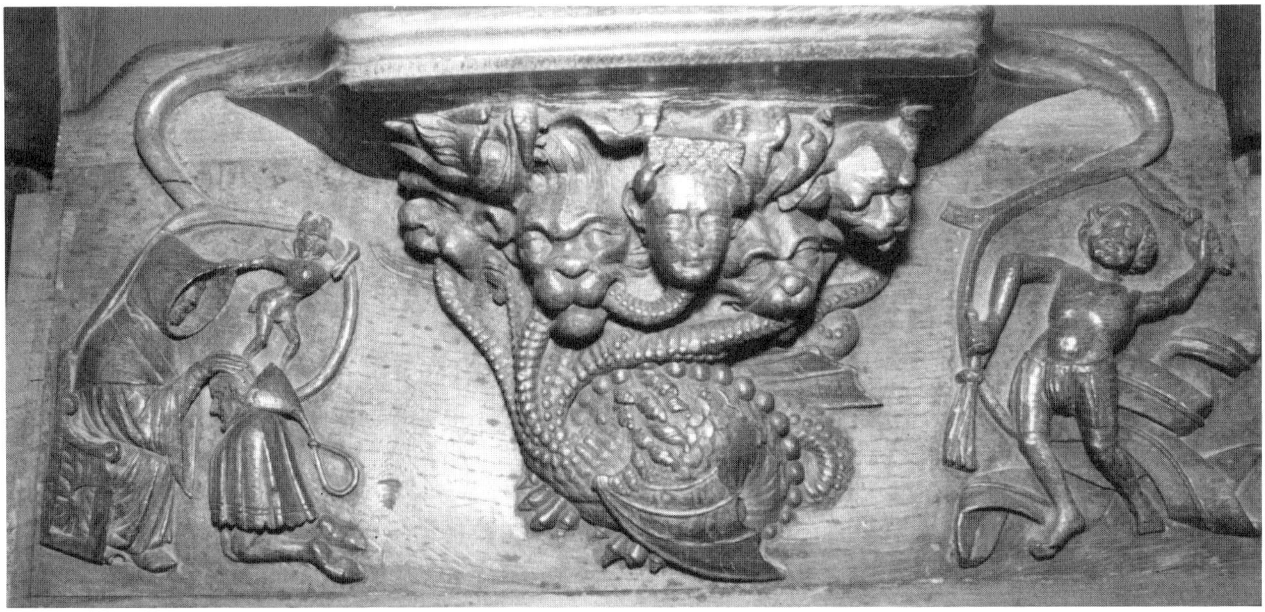

Seven-headed hydra. Oxford (Oxon), New College Chapel, late fourteenth century.

battle with the monstrous multi-headed Hydra. The level of evil associated with the Hydra is far greater than that associated with the deadly sins. For that reason alone, it is reasonable to challenge the labeling of the carving. But there is additional, stronger, evidence for a different meaning to be found in the scenes on the supporters. The supporter on the right shows a flagellant, stripped to the waist, scourging himself in an attempt to save mankind. The priest in the left supporter is shown doing the same through the use of exorcism. Both flagellant and priest confront the unmitigated evil of the plague as represented by the Hydra in the center carving. The carver has shown two major responses to that threat—that of the people and that of the Church. Interpretation is left open as to which is the more effective, but when one notices that the exorcised demon is playfully pulling on the priest's hood, there is a sly suggestion: Is the priest being hoodwinked?

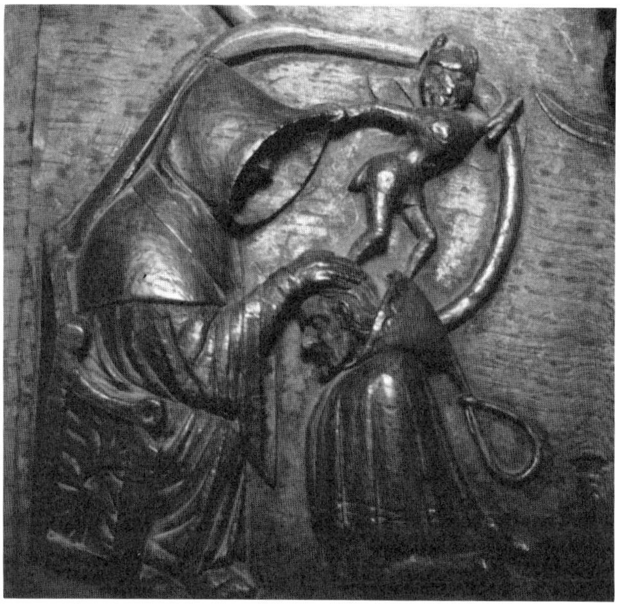

Exorcism. Oxford (Oxon), New College Chapel, late fourteenth century.

A final comment on exorcism: however serious the battle against the Devil was perceived to be, the carvers maintained a sense of humor. In the next two carvings an unusual method of exorcising the Devil is proffered.

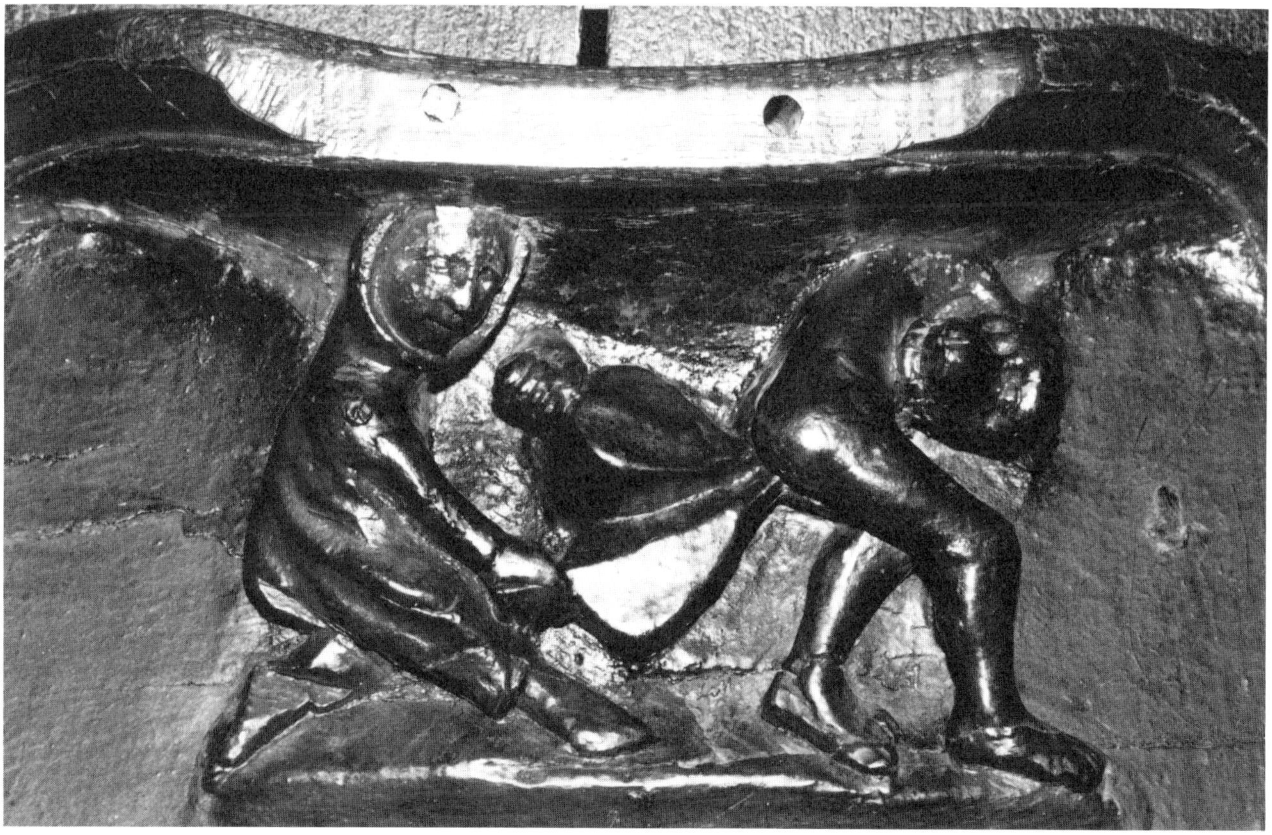

Blowing Devil away. Great Malvern (Herefs & Worcs), The Priory Church, c.1350–80.

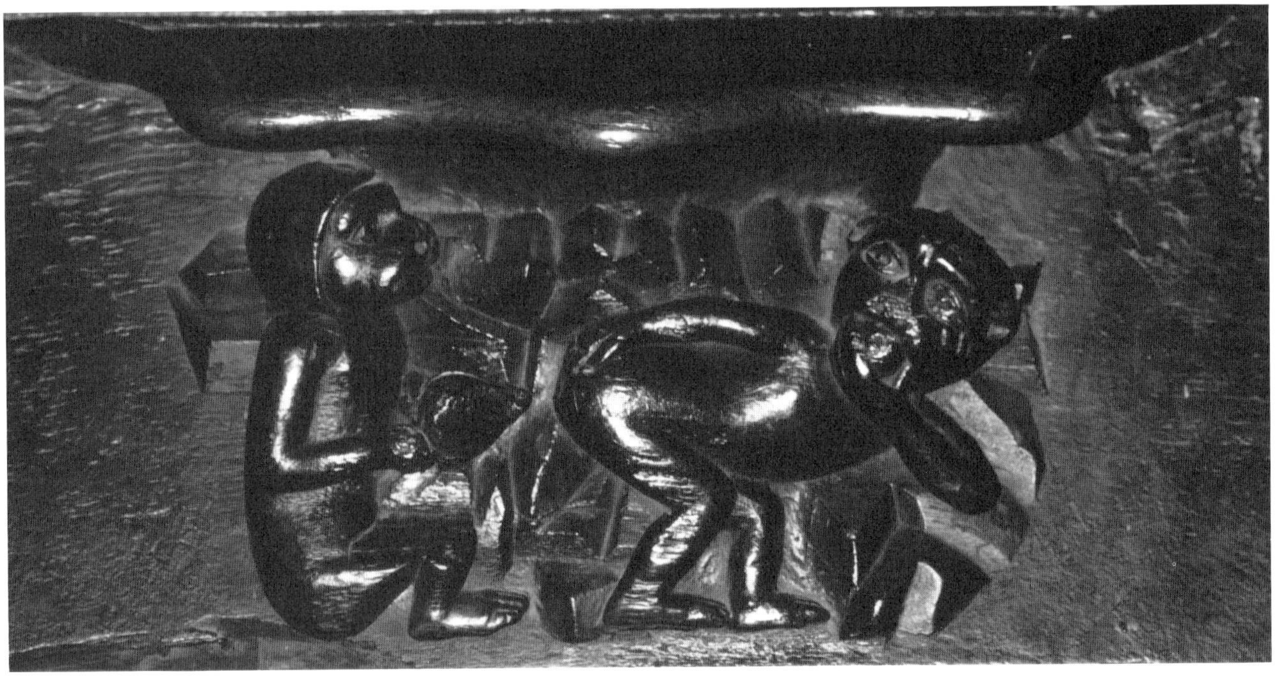

Blowing Devil away. Villefranche-de-Rouergue (France), Notre Dame, fifteenth century.

Here, the bellows are employed to blow the Devil out of one's system.

Where this idea came from is not known, but it was recognized throughout Europe. In the second carving from Villefranche, another satiric twist is added, replacing humans with apes. The ape on the left seems to be waiting to see if his efforts have had any effect, while the ape on the right seems to be saying, "Ohhhh!"

The general disdain for the aristocracy and the Church was matched by an equal distrust of another group with some authority—medical practitioners.

The People vs. the Medical Profession

The practice of medicine in the late Middle Ages was similar to earlier medical practices—and just as generally distrusted. The majority of the population relied on folk remedies, tinged with sorcery, which had the weight of tradition behind them. Although the Church tried to restrict the practice of sorcery, its use in curing ailments had a long and venerated history not easy to eradicate. As early as 79 A.D., Pliny decried the difficulty of eliminating the use of magic in healing. He denounced it as the "most deceptive of all known arts," but because it was practiced like a religion, incorporating astrology and promising good health, "The senses of men being thus enthralled by a three-fold bond . . . it holds sway throughout a great part of the world, and rules the king of kings" (*Natural History of Pliny* 1856, 5:421).

Not only did peasants incline away from doctors, doctors, in turn, preferred to treat a wealthier clientele. Medicine as a practice in the Middle Ages was almost totally confined to the upper classes, but this did not necessarily mean that the upper classes always trusted physicians.

Early practitioners of medicine were sometimes put to the test by the aristocracy. Rowling (1987, 178) relates a story about a monk healer who performed healings using urine analysis. The Duke of Bavaria, deciding to test the monk to make sure his urine analyses were not a bit of fakery, substituted a flask of urine from a pregnant woman. The monk examined the urine and turned to the Duke saying, "God is about to perform a miracle. Within 30 days, the Duke will give birth to a child." The monk was promptly made the ducal physician. The problem with treating the aristocracy was that, if they were not pleased with the outcome, they could, and often did, punish the practitioner. There is the tale of King John of Bohemia who asked a doctor to cure his cataract. When the doctor's efforts proved unsuccessful, King John had him sewn into a sack and thrown in the river (Bishop 1987).

Although medical advances were made during the Middle Ages, the most enduring diagnostic tool remained urine analysis. It was based, as were so many things, on a theory of Pliny's that the color of the urine indicates different conditions in the body. It is hard to believe from his description that there are any healthy colors of urine:

> When the urine is red, it is a bad sign; but when it is swarthy, it is the worst sign of all. So, too, when it is thick and full of bubbles, . . . and when a white sediment forms, it is a symptom of pains in the region of the viscera or in the joints. A green-coloured urine is indicative of disease of the viscera, a pale urine of biliousness, and a red urine of some distemper of the blood . . . A thin, white, urine also is in a diseased state; but when it is thick and possessed of an offensive smell, it is significant of approaching death. . . .
>
> *Natural History of Pliny* 1856, 5:301

Servants hurrying along carrying urine flasks to the doctor was a common sight on medieval streets (Rowling 1987). So common was urine analysis that the urine flask became the universal symbol of doctors. In a typical scene from the times, a carving shows a wife supporting her sick husband in bed as the doctor examines two urine flasks. It was said that if the doctor dropped a flask, that meant the patient had no hope of recovery. Here, the doctor deliberates.

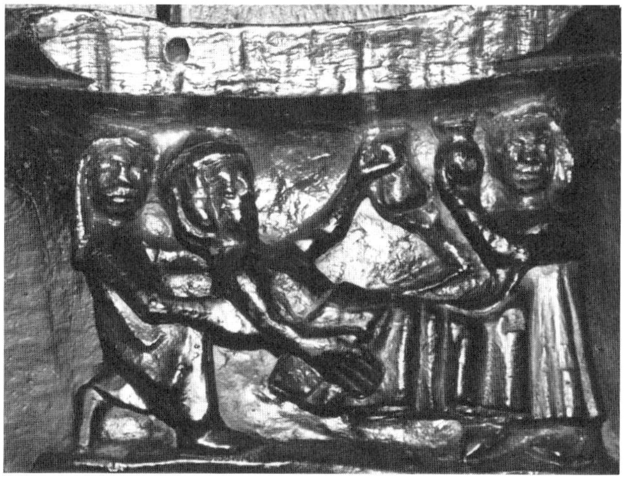

Doctor examining urine flasks. Great Malvern (Herefs & Worcs), The Priory Church, c.1350–80.

For most families, medical treatment was managed by the woman of the house as part of the sexual division of labor. In most households, it was part of a wife's training; spells, herbal mixtures, and complex healing rituals were all learned and put to use. Even though doctors frequently relied on similar remedies, greater faith was placed in the healing power of the women. There is the well-known story of a fifteenth-century wife in England, Margaret Paston, whose husband contacted her for medical advice when he fell ill on a trip to London. Because her letters have been kept, we know that her immediate response was to tell him to avoid contact with a doctor; then she proceeded to tell him how to treat himself.

Suspicion of doctors' motives was pervasive, as was a general fear that they lacked competence. Unlike the upper classes, the majority of the population had no physical recourse in the event of malpractice. In addition, like the clergy, most doctors were viewed with skepticism relative to how much they really wanted to render aid. The more common belief was that they simply wanted to increase their income.

This communal view of the medical profession found expression again through the use of mockery. And, again, the main character in the running satire on doctors was the sly fox, Reynardine. A tale in the legend of Reynardine forms the basis for the people's attack on medicine. In the tale, Reynardine has been caught stealing fowl and has retreated to his home, wondering what to do. His sympathetic friend, Fairlimb the Ape, suggests that Reynardine go into medicine, assuring him that it would be an easy way to get rich. When Reynardine wonders how he can be trained, Fairlimb scoffs:

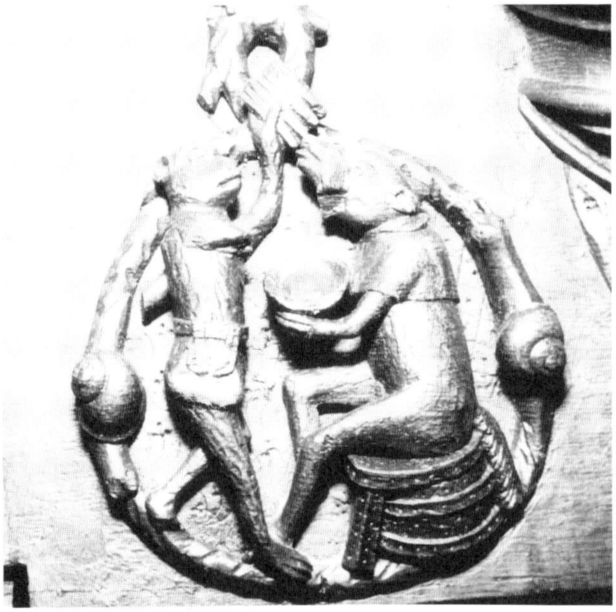

Dying Reynard's hair. Windsor (Berks), St. George's Chapel, 1477–83.

"Brass! A bold front and a few hard words—Greek is the best—such as mu xi tau rho pi phi psi chi, which, when put in lieu of a string of words, would make some folks stare. . . . If you can but hit on a draught—a pint of ink is as good as aught else—call it by a big name, puff it well, say it will be sure to cure all the ills that flesh is heir to, and pay a few beasts to tell lies, that they took the stuff and got well in a trice—which you can soon do—you will make a mass of wealth, and can live like a prince

Day 1872, 189

The ape offers to help Reynardine with a disguise, so he can call himself a leech from Spain, with Fairlimb as his assistant. Part of the disguise involves dyeing Reynardine's hair black. This is the subject of the Windsor carving showing Reynardine seated holding a bowl of dye while Fairlimb combs it through his hair.

To equip Reynardine with the tools of his trade, Fairlimb offers to outfit him with items he and some associates have stolen from a sleeping peddler. A unique illustration of this part of the legend comes from Bristol in the form of a twentieth-century needlework cushion replicating the sixteenth-century misericord underneath.[6]

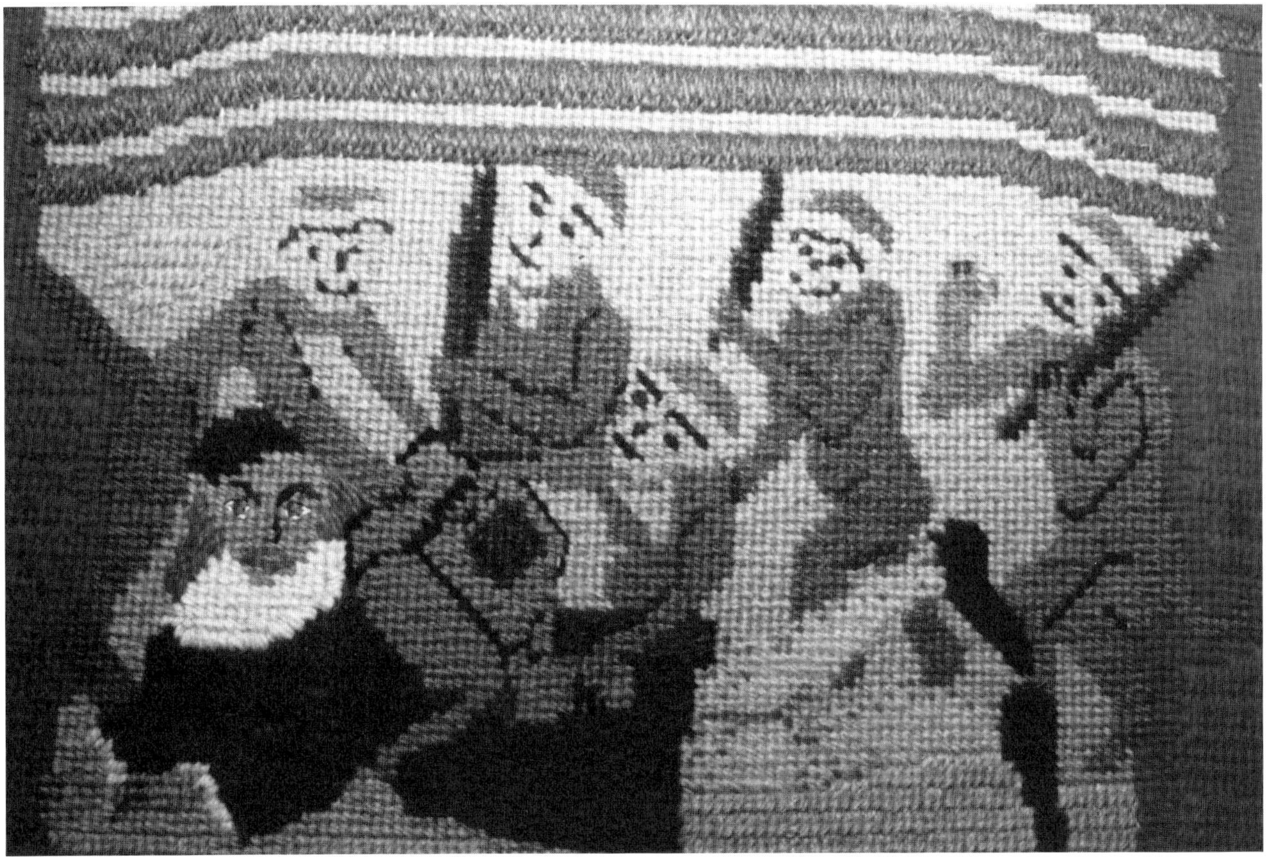

Apes robbing peddler. Bristol (Avon), The Cathedral, 1520.

In the Boston carving below, Fairlimb presents Reynardine with the necessary items, including the all-important urine flask. They are now ready to start practicing medicine.

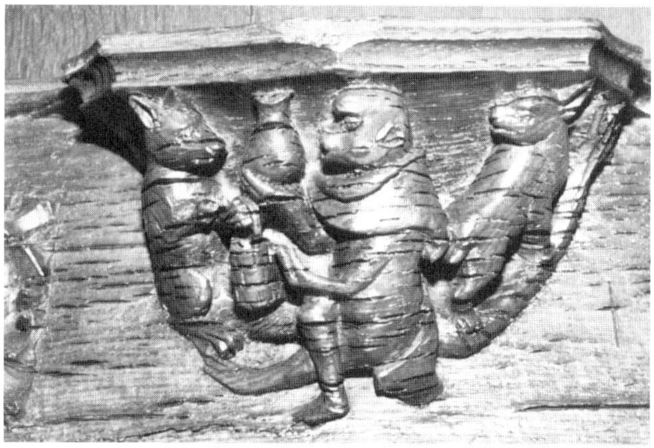

Fairlimb and Reynardine. Boston (Lincs), St. Botolph, 1390.

Finally, Reynardine and his assistant, Fairlimb, examine a patient. Fairlimb is looking into the dog's mouth while Reynardine examines the urine.

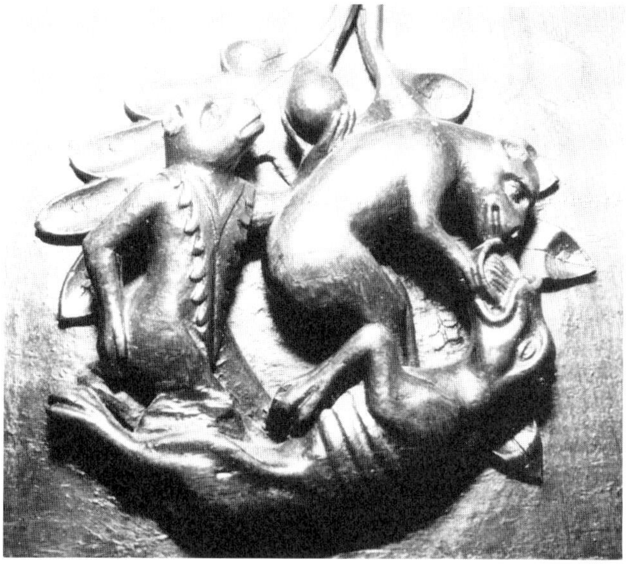

Fairlimb and Reynardine. Windsor (Berks), St. George's Chapel, 1477–83.

Predictably, in the end, Reynardine betrays even his friend, Fairlimb, and finally is brought before a court and sentenced to die. He was not quite as cunning as his father, and so die he did—and this, most would say, was a fitting end to a bogus doctor. These stories articulated in humorous form what organized medicine was thought to be about.

There was some legal recourse against bogus physicians, but this was instigated primarily by the medical profession in an attempt to protect the doctors' domain. Their target was a group of wandering healers, sometimes called quacks or charlatans, who roamed the countryside hawking remedies and cures. Some were legitimate healers, but many were entrepreneurs who saw, as Fairlimb did, the economic possibilities of doctoring. Because of their nomadic lifestyle, in the country they were able to elude legal oversight by moving quickly from place to place, but they were less successful in the towns, where the law was more vigilant in bringing these "false" physicians to punishment. For example, there is a record of a wandering herbalist in London who was charged with illegally practicing medicine when he proposed that a woman wear a particular parchment around her neck to cure her ailment. His punishment was the same as that for many offenses: to be paraded around town riding backward on his horse, without a saddle and with:

> parchment and a whetstone round his neck, unseemly pottery hanging round his neck and down his back, in token that he had lied
>
> Jusserand 1950, 98

The charlatan in the Bristol carving is riding without the clattering pottery and other indications of his offense, but nonetheless is being paraded in public. A colleague watches his progress.

The use of herbal remedies and "magic" was not questioned, only who was qualified to apply these types of cures. As we have seen, to most people, this honor was reserved for the women of a family. Later, for example, in the sixteenth century, the position of these "wise women" changed, when many of them were charged with witchcraft. But, until that time, either they or the local "leech" were considered the appropriate medical healers to consult. The collective feeling about doctors remained similar to that of Pliny centuries earlier: "For what profession has there been

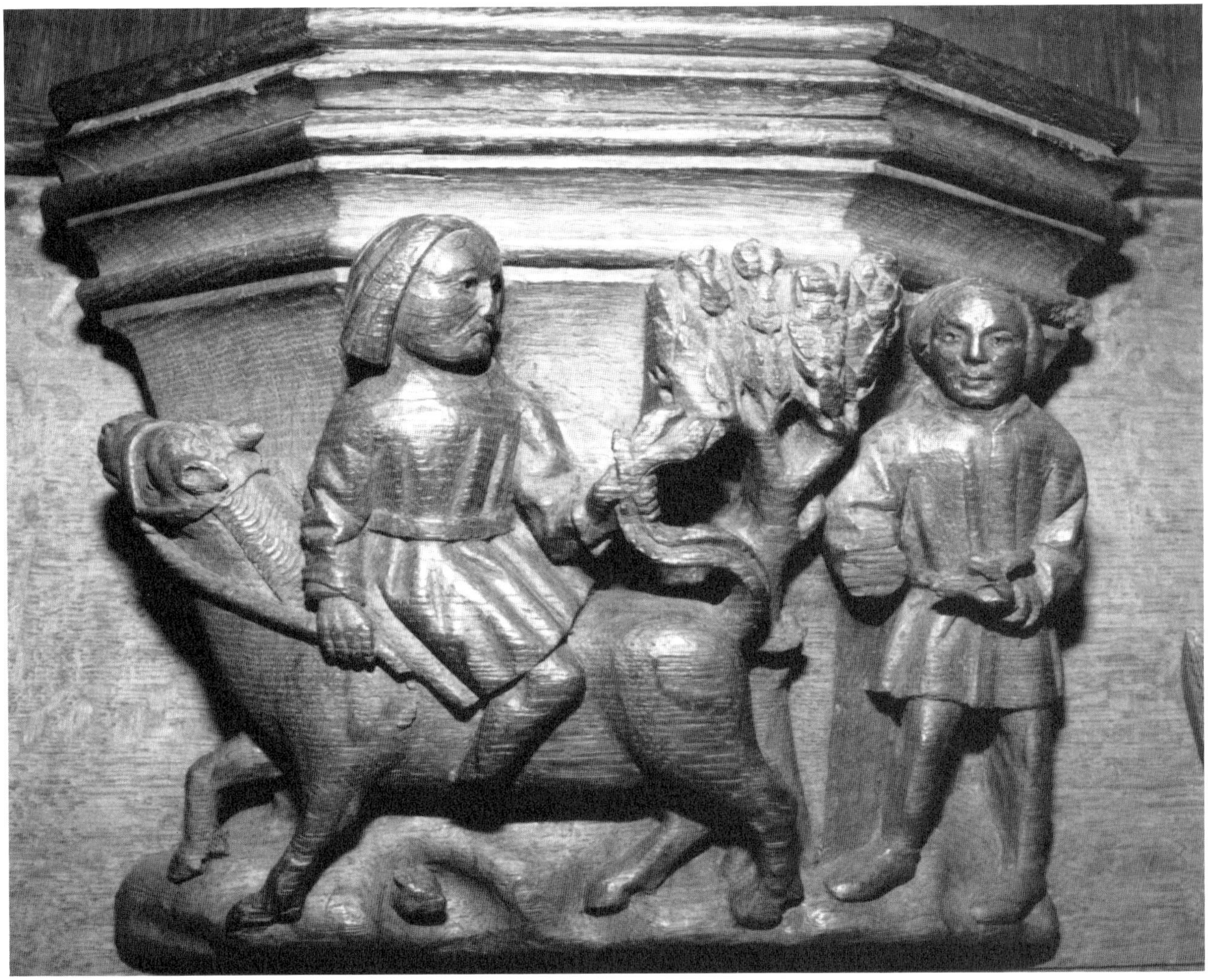

Charlatan riding backward on horse. Bristol (Avon), The Cathedral, 1520.

more fruitful in poisonings or from which there have emanated more frauds upon wills?" (*Natural History of Pliny* 1856, 5:378).

The antipathy felt for the medical establishment was a combination of many things, but a major one was fear of knowledge that differed from the knowledge embedded in traditional lore. With the availability in the fourteenth and fifteenth centuries of a large number of books on healing and magic written in the vernacular, traditional knowledge was further entrenched. Now literature was being circulated that showed people how to heal themselves. Books of charms and divinations once available only to the clergy were now being printed and distributed to the laity (Kieckhefer 1990). This exacerbated the schism between the people and the newly emerging university-trained doctor. The two areas of knowledge, magic and medicine, frequently overlapped; what was at issue was who appropriately "owned" the knowledge.

With the advent of university-based medical schools in the twelfth century, the medical profession moved to restrict not only medical knowledge but the practice of medicine to a designated group—those with degrees or training from universities. It was also during this period that medicine became a secular science, with laws being passed prohibiting the clergy from practicing medicine. Women were excluded from the formal practice of medicine, not by law initially, but by the admission policies of the universities. In

England, unlike Italy, no woman was ever admitted to the medical schools at Cambridge or Oxford during the Middle Ages (Hughes 1943).

As science and superstition diverged, popular methods of healing that relied on potions, incantations, herbs, and rituals retained their place in the daily life of most people. But the pending scientific revolution would make folk medicine, and its practitioners, obsolete—at least until the twentieth century. Before that time, however, the carvers continued to comment on life's inequities in their own inimitable fashion, proving once again that humor can be the best weapon.

6

Deadly Reminders—The Battle for the Soul

> Thus still repentance is deferred
> From one day to another;
> Until the day of Death is come,
> And Judgment is the other.
> *The Considerations of Drexelius upon Eternity,* 1632

It was previously noted that the misericords are thought surprising because they appear in holy places but seldom have religious subjects. This perception is colored by the contemporary manner in which we interpret reality—that is, rationally. There is no disputing that the carvings *appear* to be almost totally without religious content; but, if they are examined the way a medieval person would have examined them, as having "layers of meaning," they yield to a different interpretation. It is true that there are very few Scriptural scenes in the carvings, but there are many that would be considered religious if we understand that they are couched in an allegorical framework of moral lessons.

Medieval Christianity attempted to bring a new way of understanding the world, and of the place of humans within it; but the attempt met with a strong reluctance on the part of the laity to completely let go of the old pagan explanations and superstitions. Where possible, the Church found its way round this reluctance by incorporating pagan views, by substituting new names and meanings. An example of this tactic was the Celtic belief in different, coexistent worlds. According to the Celts, there is both a visible and an invisible world. They believed that certain individuals can make contact with, or exist in, both worlds. Supernatural beings included not only the likes of fairies and pixies, but also sacred plants, bodies of water, and other sacred elements. People existed in a tangible world but were always subject to the influences of intangible worlds above and below. Christianity adapted this belief to its purposes, simply renaming the different levels heaven, earth, and hell (Coulton 1923, vol. 1). It was characteristic of medieval thought that movement was vertical, the best being the highest and the worst the lowest (Bakhtin 1968).

The accommodation of both belief systems, pagan and Christian, in the Middle Ages was achieved through allegory. The art of saying one thing to mean another was one of the most popular literary forms in the Middle Ages, and many books were written in the allegorical format (Evans 1966). Religious information produced on the Scriptures in the Middle Ages also used allegory in the belief that this popular form of expression would be more easily understood and accepted. St. Augustine taught that lessons from the Scriptures stated figuratively were much more effective than statements made literally. It was an exercise in looking beyond the given word to the underlying meaning. Much of the literature and art of the Middle Ages was meant to lead one beyond the obvious—generally, to an appreciation of the spiritual world—or from the visible to the invisible world (Robinson 1962). This was done in two major ways during the Middle Ages: through the allegorical vehicle of the bestiaries, in which animals were assigned good and bad characteristics; and through "moralities," plays that used abstract characters to represent the vices and virtues of humans. The bestiaries were used primarily to warn of the omnipotent influence of beings from the world below, in the form of the Devil and his cohort, although they also contained lessons about the goodness of certain traits and actions. The moralities were used to point out the importance of amassing enough good deeds during one's lifetime to ensure a quick passage from purgatory to heaven after death. In the first instance, danger is perceived to come from external forces in the form of demons; in the second, danger comes from within the person in the form of incorrect behavior or thought.

Danger from Without—Fighting the Demons

Bestiaries

Stories from the bestiaries were better known than those from the Scriptures. They were much older stories that had been in the public realm for centuries. The Bible, on the other hand, was not translated into English until the fourteenth century; nor was it widely distributed until the fifteenth century. In this sense, it can be said, at least for the ordinary person, that bestiaries were far more important to medieval Christianity than was the Bible.

Bestiaries were the most respected source of knowledge about birds, reptiles, fish, and other animals for their time. The earliest known bestiaries date from the tenth century, but their immediate source, the *Physiologus* (*The Naturalist*), is from a much earlier period, probably the second century A.D. (Clark and McMunn 1989). The author of the *Physiologus* is unknown, but it is thought to be Egyptian in origin (James 1928; Robin 1932). There were different versions containing between 20 and 50 chapters, each devoted to the lore of a different bird, reptile, fish, animal, plant, or even stone. The presumed Egyptian origin is based on the highly developed worship of animals in the Egyptian religion. Not only were myriad animals worshipped in their own right, but the Egyptians also had a number of deities in which humans and animals were united in one body.

At a later point, Christian writers applied morals to the text of the *Physiologus*. While the early versions of the *Physiologus* were translated into several languages, including Old English, the bestiaries derive from the Latin version, most being compiled in the twelfth and thirteenth centuries, although the vernacular versions were still popular in the fifteenth century. Each version was idiosyncratic and included the text in Latin, as well as illustrations in the margins (Clark and McMunn 1989). They were translated into dialect and enjoyed a wide circulation among the lay population, becoming some of the most popular books of the late Middle Ages (Payne 1990; James 1928; Evans 1896). With their moral tales, bestiaries were a normal part of the monastery library and were used for both religious instruction and sermons.

Sermons and preaching occurred infrequently in the medieval church, perhaps, on average, once or twice a year (Owst 1926). When they did occur, sermons contained many exampla designed to capture the attention of the audience. Preachers would use material from several different sources—the miracle plays, for example (Wright 1865)—or contemporary tales and poetry. The ordinary citizen soon became bored (as did many preachers), so, by necessity, preachers became "distributors of news and popular knowledge, writers in prose and verse, jesters, and story-tellers" (Owst 1926, xi).

Preaching became more popular with the rise of the mendicant orders, especially the Franciscans and Dominicans, who were not attached to particular churches but instead traveled around England stopping to preach wherever they went. They made extensive use of bestiaries as sources for their sermons (Payne 1990), as did other ecclesiastics. As early as the twelfth century, Honorius d'Autun produced a collection of sermons for use on festival days in "rude" verse that relied heavily on the symbolism used in the bestiaries (Clarke 1920). Popular as this practice was, the Church was not amused and finally, in 1585, the Council of Bordeaux disallowed the use of fables in sermons, on the grounds that, they tended to "move their hearers to laughter, instead of drawing tears of contrition from their eyes, as they ought to do" (Evans 1896, 184).

These beasts—some real, many fabulous—were found in abundance in Church decoration, in the margins of illuminated manuscripts, on maps, and on heraldic devices. In heraldry, as in religion, each animal was thought to represent certain characteristics. The allegorical meanings attached to the beasts were commonly understood and appreciated, although often there was a misfiring between the verbal description and the artistic renderings that resulted in even more fabulous beasts being constructed (Barber and Riches 1971). Mythical animals described in

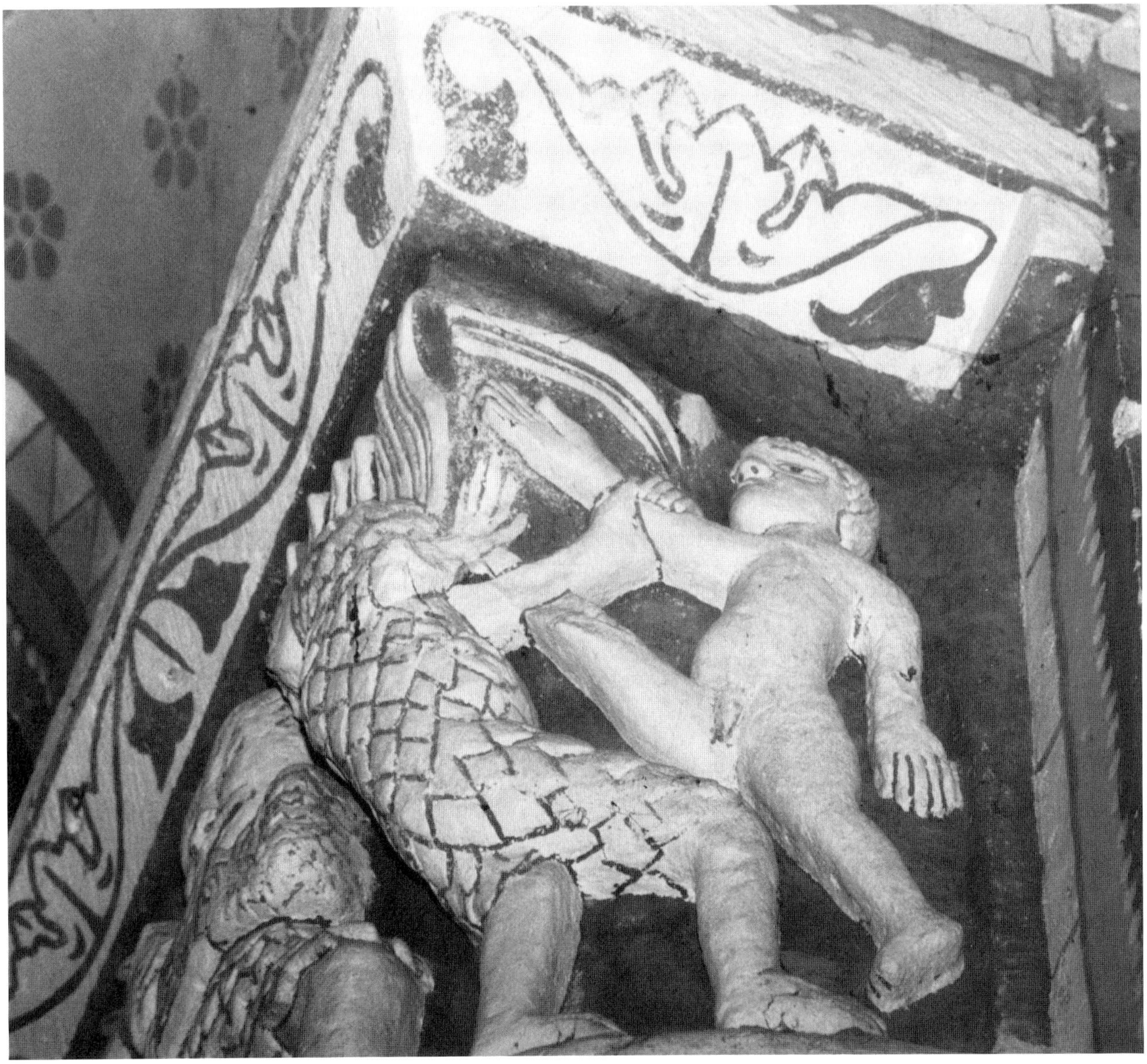

Man fighting demon. Chauvigny (France), Eglise St. Pierre, twelfth century.

the bestiaries, such as griffins and dragons, were not only perceived as real by the ordinary citizen, but also by the clergy, monarchy, and nobility. It was not unusual to have various learned men and travelers verify their existence in their writings—or even embellish the animals' characteristics. The tales of fabulous beasts themselves bestowed an aura of authenticity that made the unbelievable seem true.

Therefore, it was entirely believable when men like Giraldus Cambrensis, a twelfth-century ecclesiastic writing a description of Ireland and Wales, mentioned a number of composite beasts—half-man, half-ox, half-dog, and half-monkey, for example. Indeed, Giraldus believed that these composite beasts derived from sexual unions between humans and animals, and he "documented" numerous such couplings. His disgust with such unions sounds suspiciously overdone, as he records these events in great detail. He expresses his outrage over the reported sexual misuse of the king's goat by the woman charged with its care:

> O foul and disgraceful deed! How dreadfully has reason given rein to sensuality! . . . But though brutes are destined by nature for the service of men, they were created for use, not abuse.
>
> 1863, 86

Giraldus also warns that such alliances may be addictive, on both sides, and cites the story of a lion given to Louis VII's son. The lion "was in the habit of having bestial intercourse with a silly girl, whose name was Joan" (86).

The bestiaries, like belief systems, adapted to their times. The fifteenth-century versions, for example, combined bestiary lore with other, more timely materials, including greater attention paid to scientific observation (Clark and McMunn 1989). Thoughout most of the Middle Ages, however, the message they imparted was one of evil forces pitted against good intentions. Indeed, there was a vision of a battle taking place over the soul, and this battle had gone on for centuries. A Romanesque carver captured some of the drama of resisting the Devil in the capital carving.

Demonic Beasts

One outgrowth of a body of knowledge steeped in moral lessons was the immense importance given to the Devil and his demons. In order to strive for what was good, it was necessary to have what was bad as the backdrop. The Devil was blamed for all sorts of questionable acts, and his presence was assumed to be ubiquitous. One's soul was never safe for very long. This might have been the intended message in the carving below where a demon is shown grasping a man's mouth, perhaps trying to reach in and steal his soul.

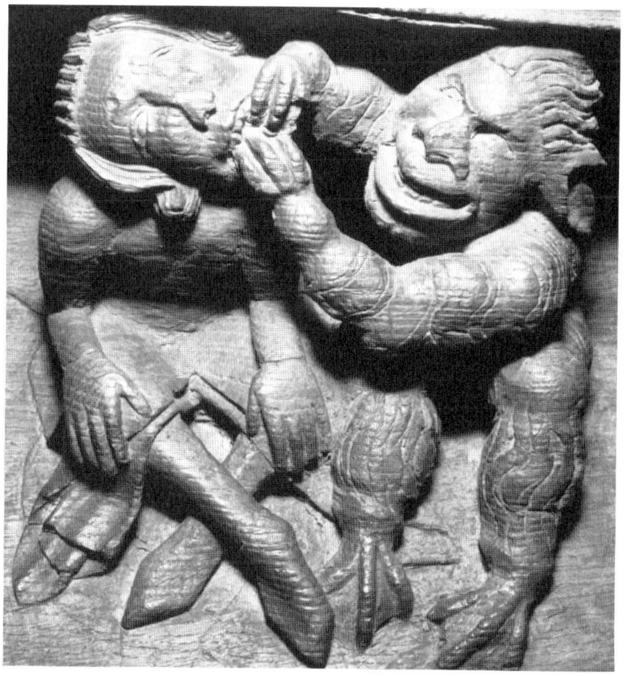

Demon with man. Ely (Cambs), The Cathedral, c.1340.

Most medieval preaching stressed the need to beware of the Devil's wickedness rather than veneration of Christ's goodness. The evidence of the Devil's existence was everywhere—hence, the need to know the signs of his presence. This accounts, in part, for the large number of representations of the Devil and other demons in medieval art. The old pagan gods now took on the form of the Christian concept of the Devil (Whitlock 1979).

With so many symbols of the Devil at hand, the medieval mind was crowded with potential forms. As always, however, the possibility has to be considered that there was less fear than fascination associated with the various forms of the Devil. To the ordinary person, stories of the existence of fabulous beasts probably were more compelling than the attached moral allegory. This was true for many members of the clergy as well, for the lower clergy were drawn from the lower ranks of the people. Christian moralizing was an attempt by the Church to use the old accepted myths, but altered in interpretation so that the focus was shifted toward Christian thinking. Whether the Church was successful is debatable.

Less questionable is the evidence that threatening beasts continued to occupy a prominent place at the heart of medieval life. The prevalence of bestiary representations among the misericords is further evidence of the widespread awareness of the bestiaries and of their moral tales. The carvers were particularly fond of carving these allegorical creatures, and in many cases, seemed to vie with each other to produce the most outlandish beasts. As will be readily seen, the Devil took many disguises. Although almost every animal found in the bestiaries is represented in the misericords, only a sampling of those animals is included in the commentary here.

DRAGONS

The importance of dragons to the legend of St. George has already been recounted. In the bestiaries, dragons were symbolic of the Devil and were believed to have emerged from the deserts of Ethiopia or India, rising up out of the heat like the Devil rising from hell. This may be one reason why the Jaws of Hell or Hell Mouths, are always represented by a dragon's open mouth. In the misericords, they were the most prevalent symbol of Satan (Grössinger 1989).

To illustrate how powerful the dragon as Devil could be, bestiaries frequently recount the allegory of the dragon waylaying the elephant, which, in the bestiaries, is virtuous and mighty. The message was: If the virtuous elephant can be waylaid, so too can you. The lesson to absorb was that the Devil always lies in wait on the path to heaven and will have many tricks with which to deceive the unsuspecting (Payne 1990).

It is interesting to contrast some of the original writings on natural history before Christian moralizations were added. Pliny describes the battle between elephants and dragons as perpetual, one in which both of these giants of the animal world can suffer mortal wounds:

> . . . the dragon, which is perpetually at war with the elephant, and is itself of so enormous a size, as easily to envelope the elephants with its folds, and encircle them in its coils. The contest is equally fatal to both; the elephant vanquished falls to the earth, and by its weight, crushes the dragon which is entwined around it.
>
> *Natural History of Pliny* 1855, 2:259

One thing dragons were said to fear was the Peridexion tree of India, which provided food and shelter for doves (Payne 1990). Doves at different times represented the Holy Ghost, Jesus, and various saints, prophets, and martyrs. In the Middle Ages, the Peridexion tree often represented the Tree of Life, or God. The doves were protected from the dragon as long as they did not leave the tree, symbolizing that souls are safe in the shadow of the Almighty, as explained in a thirteenth-century bestiary written by a Norman cleric:

> The doves fear the dragon,
> and contrariwise the dragon fears
> to approach the tree and its shadow
>
> Guillaume 1936, 82

This standoff is portrayed in the Ripon carving where two doves are shown on leaves of the Peridexion tree, safe from the dragon between them.

The carvers were as fascinated with representing the dragon as they were the mermaid. Since no one had ever seen a dragon, although many claimed to have done so, the carvers were free to chisel at will. And, similar to the mermaid depictions, although these creatures were to be feared, carvings of the dragon frequently take on a mesmerizing beauty.

A rare carving showing the dragon with four rather than two legs is found at Norwich. The

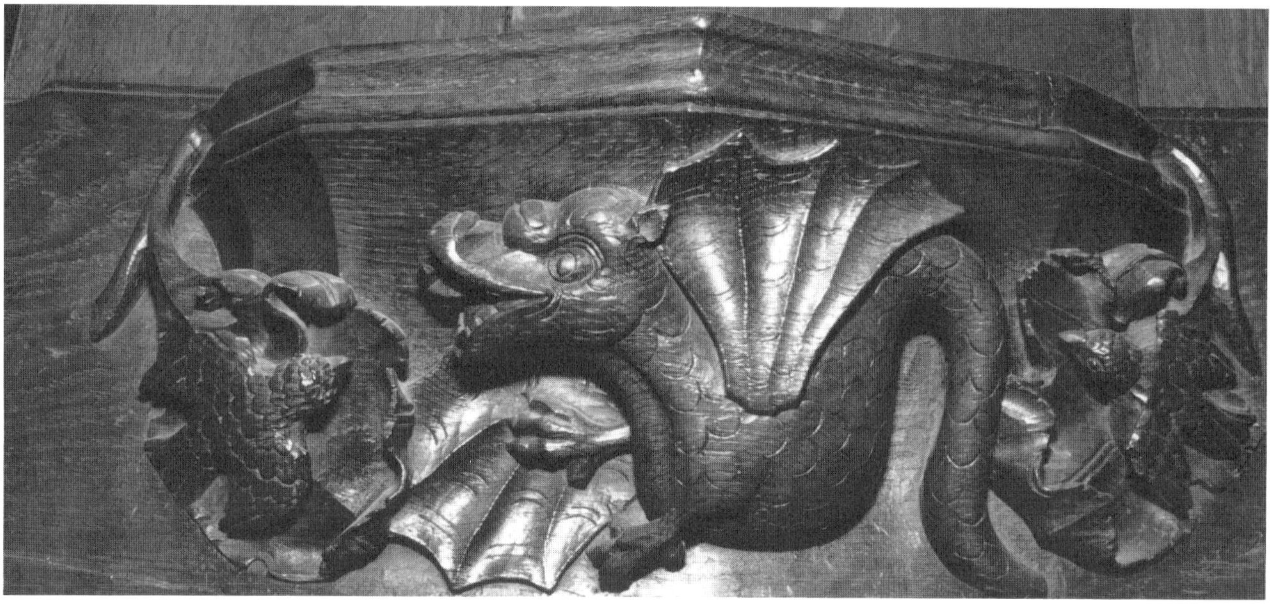

Dragon and doves. Ripon (N.Yorks), The Cathedral, 1489–94.

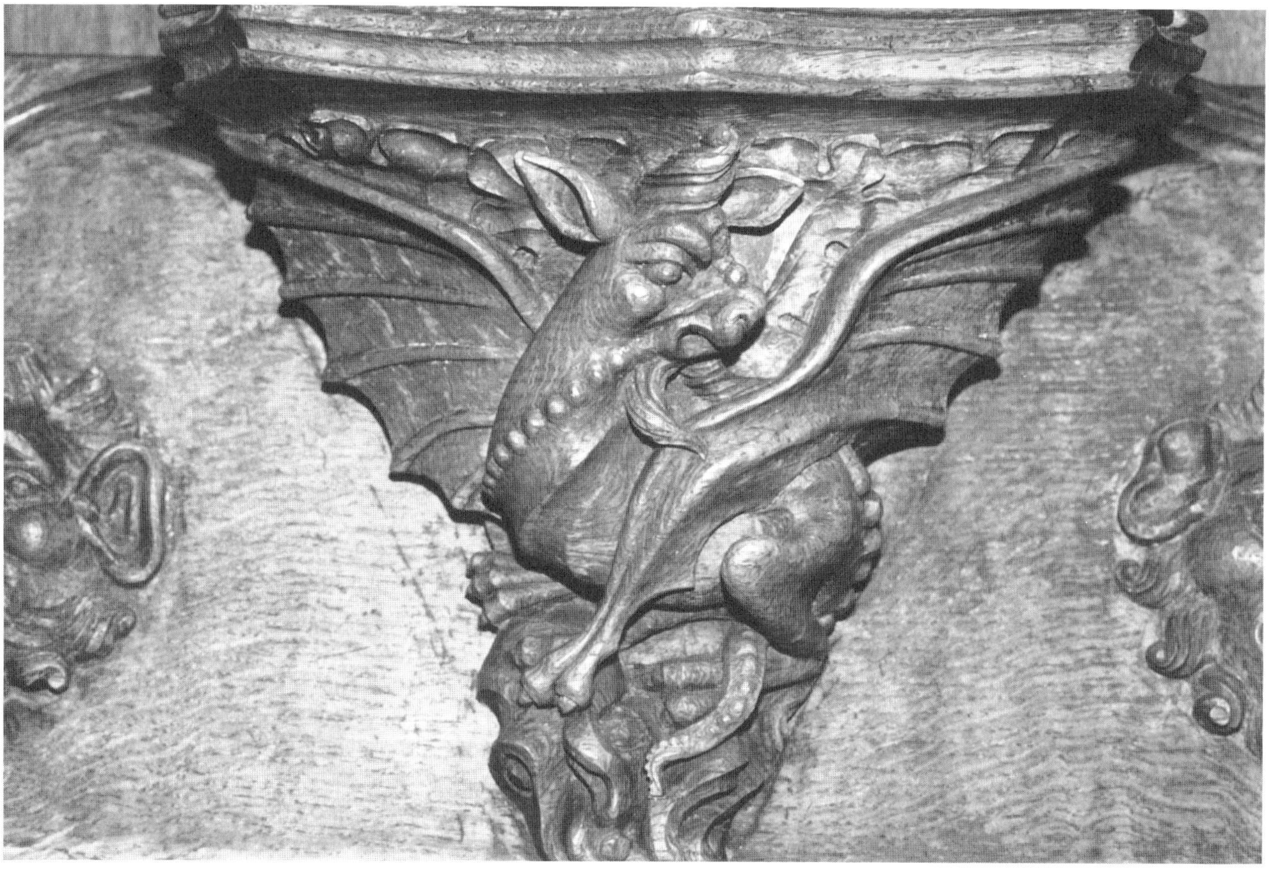

Dragon. Norwich (Norfolk), The Cathedral, 1420.

front leg is the extension of the wing and looks somewhat misplaced.

The bestiaries often portrayed the dragon attacking the elephant; more often, the misericords show the dragon doing battle with the lion. Opinions differ as to what this battle

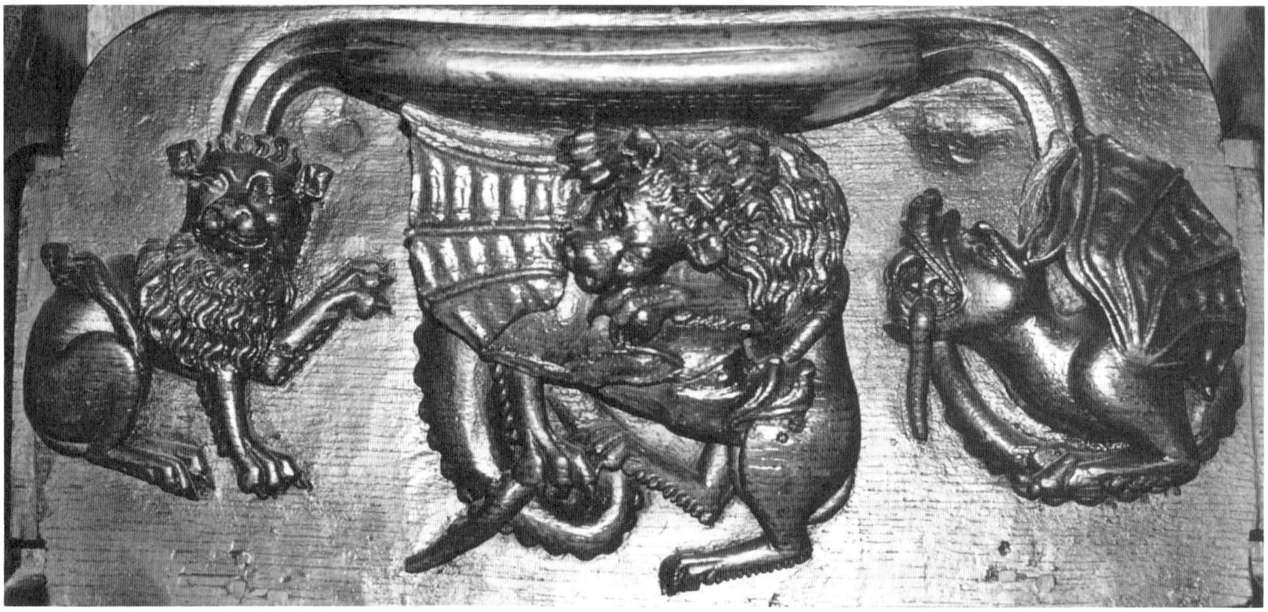

Dragon and lion. Worcester (Herefs & Worcs), The Cathedral, late fourteenth century.

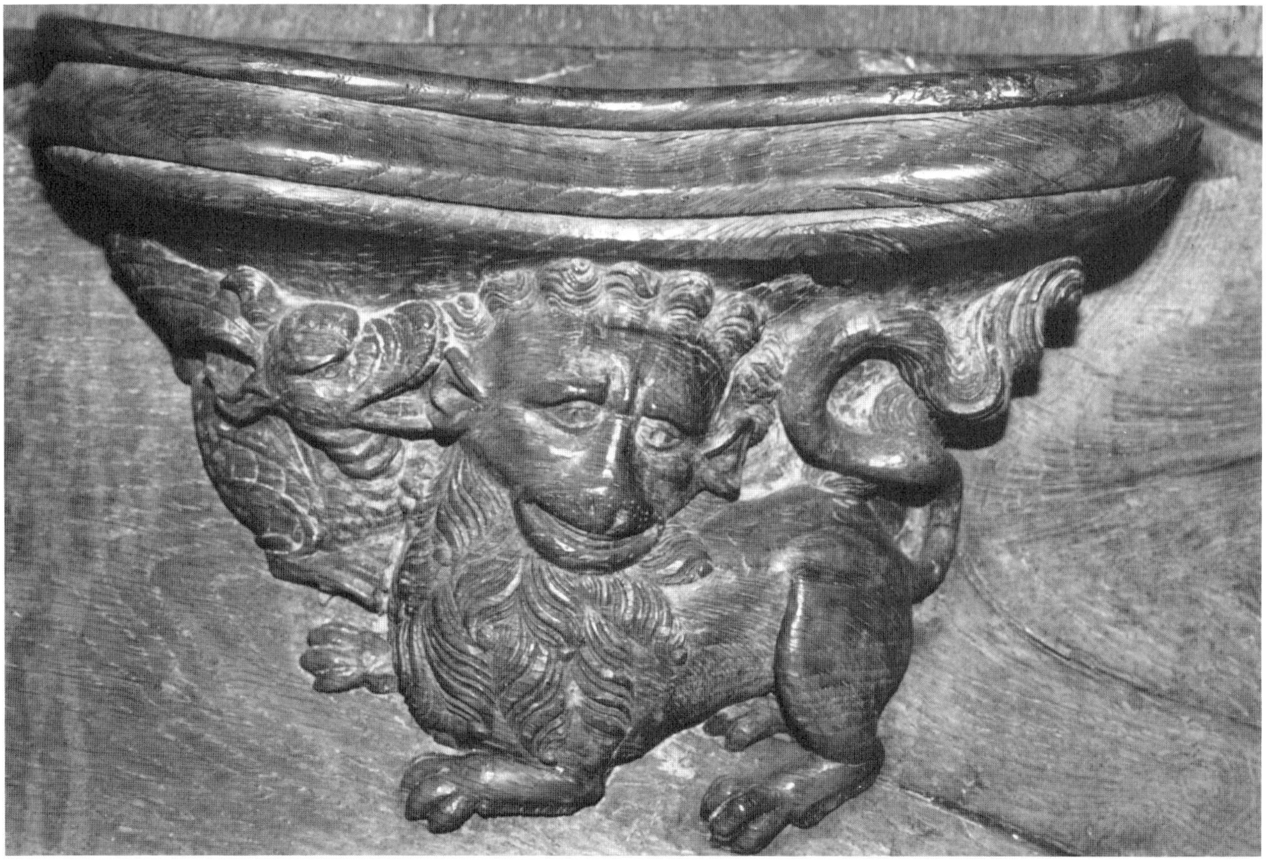

Temptation. Norwich (Norfolk), The Cathedral, 1480.

symbolized. Anderson (1969) suggests that when the lion fought with the dragon, it was the battle between good and evil. Clarke (1920), drawing on the teachings of St. Augustine and Honorius d'Autun, finds the lion and the dragon together to be the strongest possible representation of the Devil and evil. The passage in the Bible, "the young lion and the dragon shalt thou trample under feet" (Psalms 91:13) is taken to mean that Christ will triumph over the forces of evil.

Whether the lion represents Christ or the Antichrist in the battle with the dragon, the battle is lively. The intensity is depicted well in the carving from Worcester. The supporters show the lion on the left pointing to the battle as if in victory, while the dragon on the right is left with only his tail to battle (or is it tail-in-cheek?).

In other instances where the lion is the symbol of good, the dragon can be as cunning as the Devil he represents. Shown here, the dragon is enticing the good lion by whispering sweet temptations in his ear. The lion's face has an expression of agonized debate as he tries to resist the dragon's seductive message. It is a sympathetic rendering of everyone's struggle with the Devil's temptations.

TIGERS

Another tale charmingly illustrated in the bestiaries is the allegory of the tiger—namely, the female tiger. The defining characteristic of tigers was their speed. It was told that when a hunter wanted to steal a tiger cub, he knew he would not be able to outpace the mother tiger in her pursuit to retrieve the cub; so the hunter resorted to a trick. He would throw down a glass ball in which the mother tiger could see her reflection. Because the curve of the ball distorted the image, making it smaller, the mother would think it was her cub and stop to fondle the ball.

The reason a hunter might want to steal a tiger cub has been lost. The moral remains but is somewhat disjointed; it warns that the Devil distracts people from saving their souls by tempting them with worldly extravagances such as fine clothes, fine food, beautiful

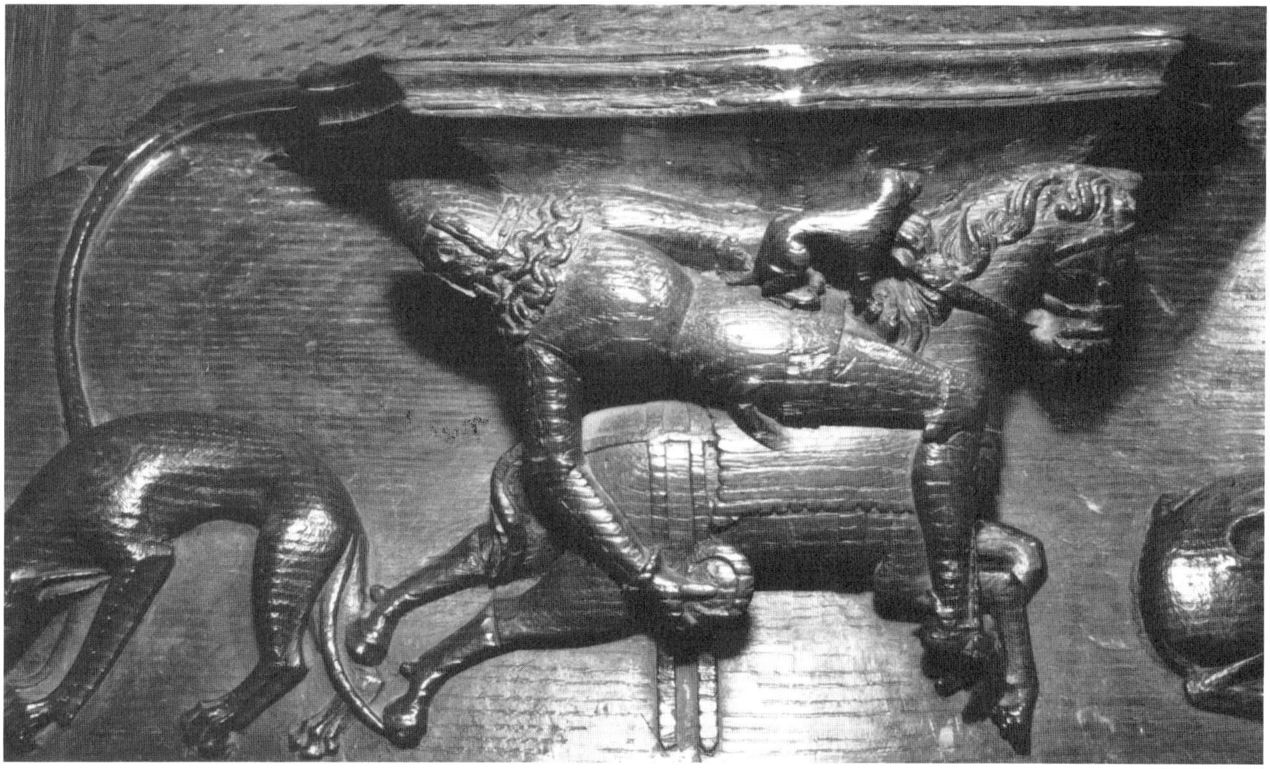

Knight stealing tiger cub. Chester (Cheshire), The Cathedral, c.1380.

women, and other sinful temptations (Payne 1990); in this case, a glass ball in which to admire one's reflection. This also diverts one from his or her chosen path (of rescuing the cub).

Though rare in misericord carvings, the Chester carver has caught this story perfectly. A knight who has just stolen a tiger cub, shown resting on his lap, leans back to drop the glass ball in front of the mother tiger.

HEDGEHOGS

Another animal equated with the Devil was the hedgehog who, in stealing fruits from the field, was likened to the Devil who was always attempting to steal a person's spiritual fruits. As Guillaume le Clerc warns in his rhyming *Bestiary:*

> As soon as the devil learns,
> That the cares of the world take thee
> He hastes to drag thee fully in,
> He wastes thy spiritual fruits,
> He shakes thy vine and thine apple tree;
> Thus he wars on thee all round.
>
> 1936, 39

This image was fostered by the belief that hedgehogs would climb the vines of the grape or the branches of an apple tree and shake the fruit to the ground. The hedgehog would then roll on the fruit so it would stick to its spines and carry it off to feed its young. Although the belief that the hedgehog would impale fruit on its spines to carry to its burrow is ancient, it has no basis in fact. Nor does the old belief that hedgehogs sucked the milk from sleeping cows (Whitlock 1979).

A particularly apt example of this moral tale is contained in a carving at New College, Oxford. In this carving, the hedgehog has been greedy indeed, for he has already gathered apples on his spines and is now attacking a grapevine. He will not be successful in this attempt, however, for a female centaur stands ready to dispatch both the vine and the hedgehog with her ax.

In Greek mythology there are centaurs who were savage beings typifying the uncontrollable forces of nature. There also were accomplished, kind centaurs who were tutors to the gods (Howey 1923). Indeed, the centaur was the only fabulous beast of antiquity to be given positive traits (Bulfinch 1942). In the Middle Ages, the figure of the centaur continued to be used in both negative and positive ways. In the misericord carving, the female centaur is used to indicate that even good people need to guard their "spiritual fruit."

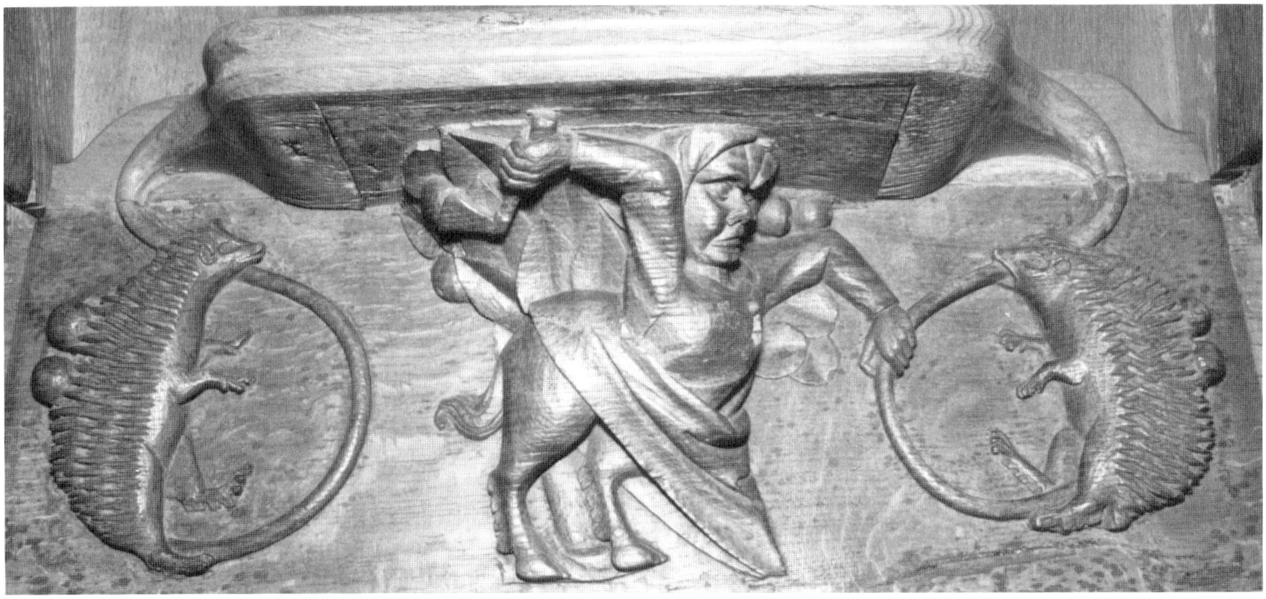

Female centaur with hedgehogs. Oxford (Oxon), New College Chapel, late fourteenth century.

FOXES

In the bestiaries, the devious fox is considered another symbol of the Devil. One bestiary illustration of the fox's untrustworthiness is the story of the hungry fox. In the story, the fox is unsuccessful in his hunt for food and devises a scheme to fool the elusive birds. First, he rolls in some red-colored mud to simulate blood, then he "plays dead." The unsuspecting birds, believing the fox to be dead, finally are brave enough to come down from the trees and land on his chest where they begin to peck at him. Suddenly the fox comes to life, grabs the birds, and eats them.

This tale was realistically re-created by the carver at Chester at the point just before the birds become aware of having been duped. The fox lies on the ground, surrounded by an aura of innocence while a bird has landed on his front leg and another on his hind leg. The moral is somewhat confusing, probably suffering in the translation; but, in essence, it is a warning to those who love the corrupt things in the world or who obey the lusts of the flesh; for they will be lured to their own destruction (Evans 1896). More to the point, it is another warning about the Devil's ability to deceive.

WOLVES

Yet another animal equated with the Devil was the wolf. Unlike the fox, the wolf was not considered amusing. It was thought to be vicious and to have a voracious appetite, whether for food or for sex. The wolf would prowl in the darkness, searching for human souls. So powerful were its eyes that if a per-

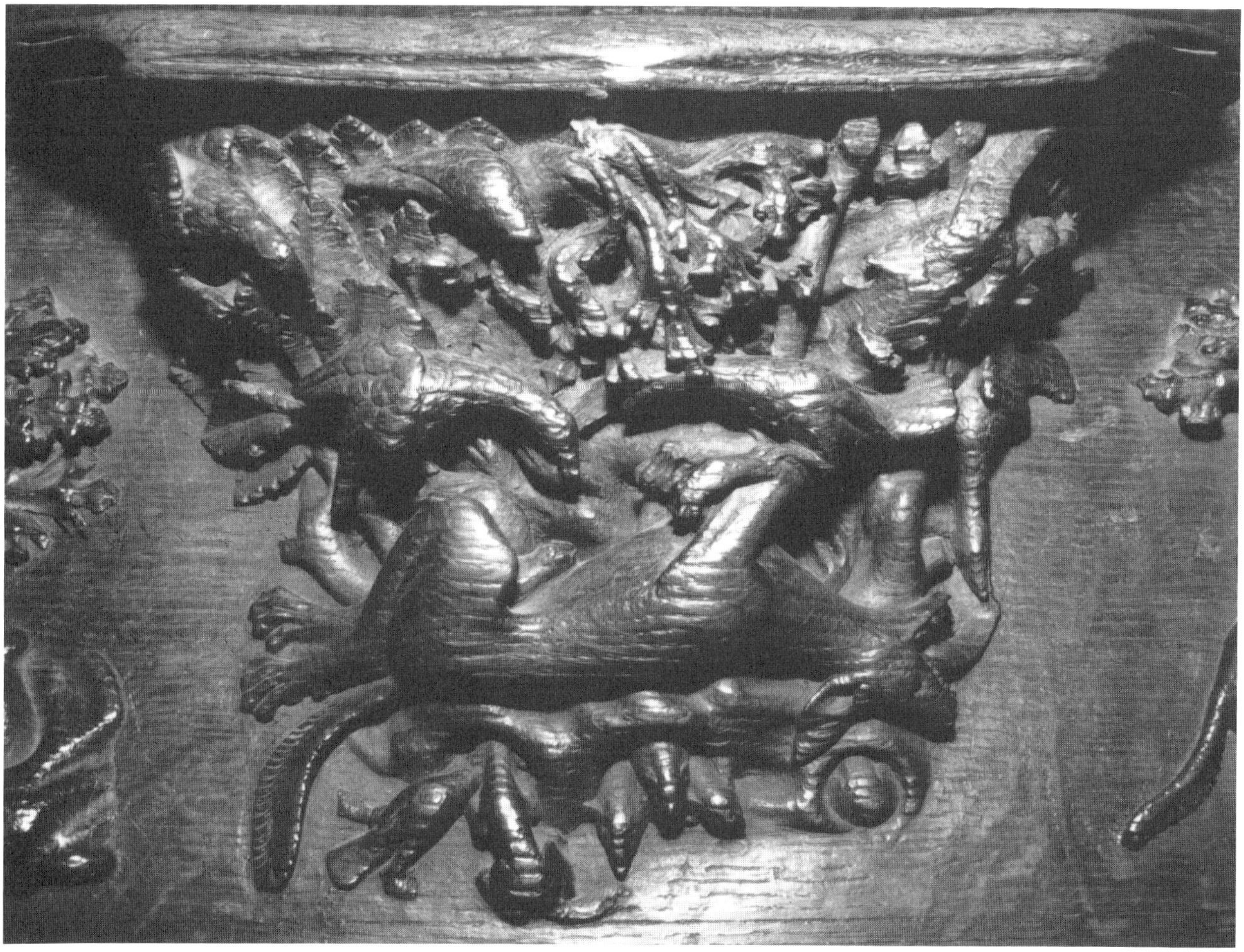

Fox playing dead. Chester (Cheshire), The Cathedral, c.1380.

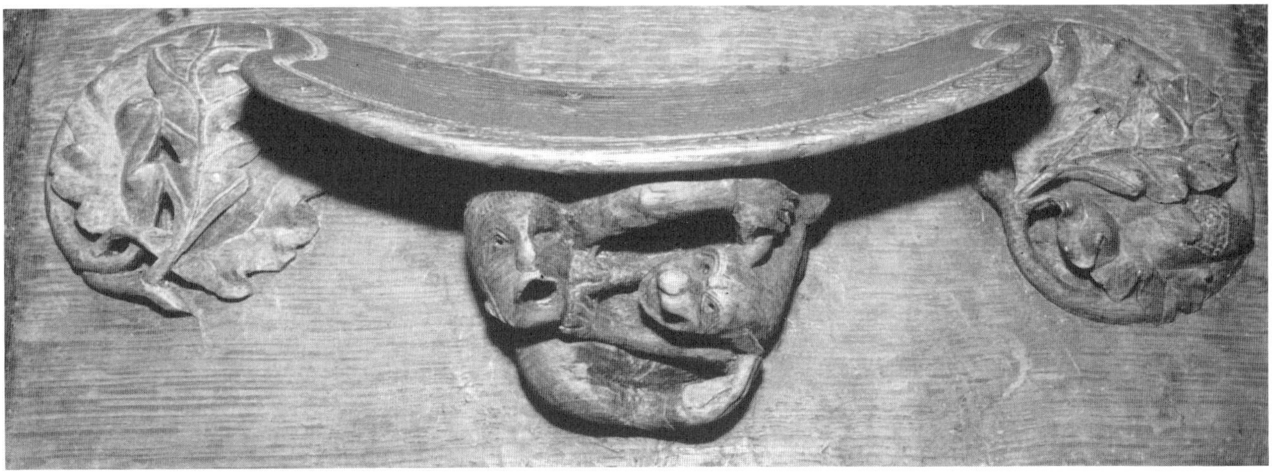

Man and wolf. Winchester (Hants), The Cathedral, c.1308.

son was seen by it, that person would be struck dumb. Once spotted by a wolf, a person's only defense was to immediately strip off all clothing, pick up two rocks, and start banging them together. The wolf was afraid of stones. This symbolized man throwing off his sinful ways and turning to Christ and the saints for help in fighting off the Devil (Payne 1990).

This is rarely portrayed in the misericords. Perhaps the only example is the Winchester carving depicting the point at which the man has been seen and struck dumb (Laird 1986). His mouth is open in a silent scream, for the wolf has pounced before he can remove his clothing or reach for the protective stones.

HYENAS

Finally, in the list of symbolic devils, none was more despised than the hyena. It was considered virtually without positive characteristics. It was said that the hyena could imitate the human voice and thereby lure humans to be devoured. It could also paralyze any animal by walking around it three times. Both Aristotle and Pliny discounted the story that the hyena possessed both male and female genders, but the bestiary writers revived this myth and attached a Christian moral to it. Once again, the attitude of the Church toward women is made clear. The story states that the two genders possessed by the hyena symbolized the children of Israel. At first, the Israelites, acting as men, were loyal to the teachings of God; but later, acting like women, they abandoned Him for the worship of false idols. Guillaume decried:

> Far too many there are in the world
> Who are neither male nor female,
> In a word, in practice they are twins,
> Double-minded and weak and lying. . . .
> No man can serve two masters.
>
> 1936, 48

Predictably, this lesson was less captivating to the medieval carver than the more repellent characteristic of the hyena: its practice of digging up and devouring dead bodies. This characteristic was said to symbolize vice fattening on corruption (Evans 1896) and is the subject of the Carlisle carving, right. The hyena apparently has retrieved the body from the grave and is commencing to devour it.

Remnants of the pervasive fear of the enveloping presence of the Devil still exist in England. The village of Veryan, in Cornwall, has four round houses situated at each end of the village as protection. It was believed that the Devil hid in the corners of a house; but, if the house were round, he would have no place to hide. The crosses on top of the houses are extra protection.

Devil houses. Veryan (Cornwall), nineteenth century.

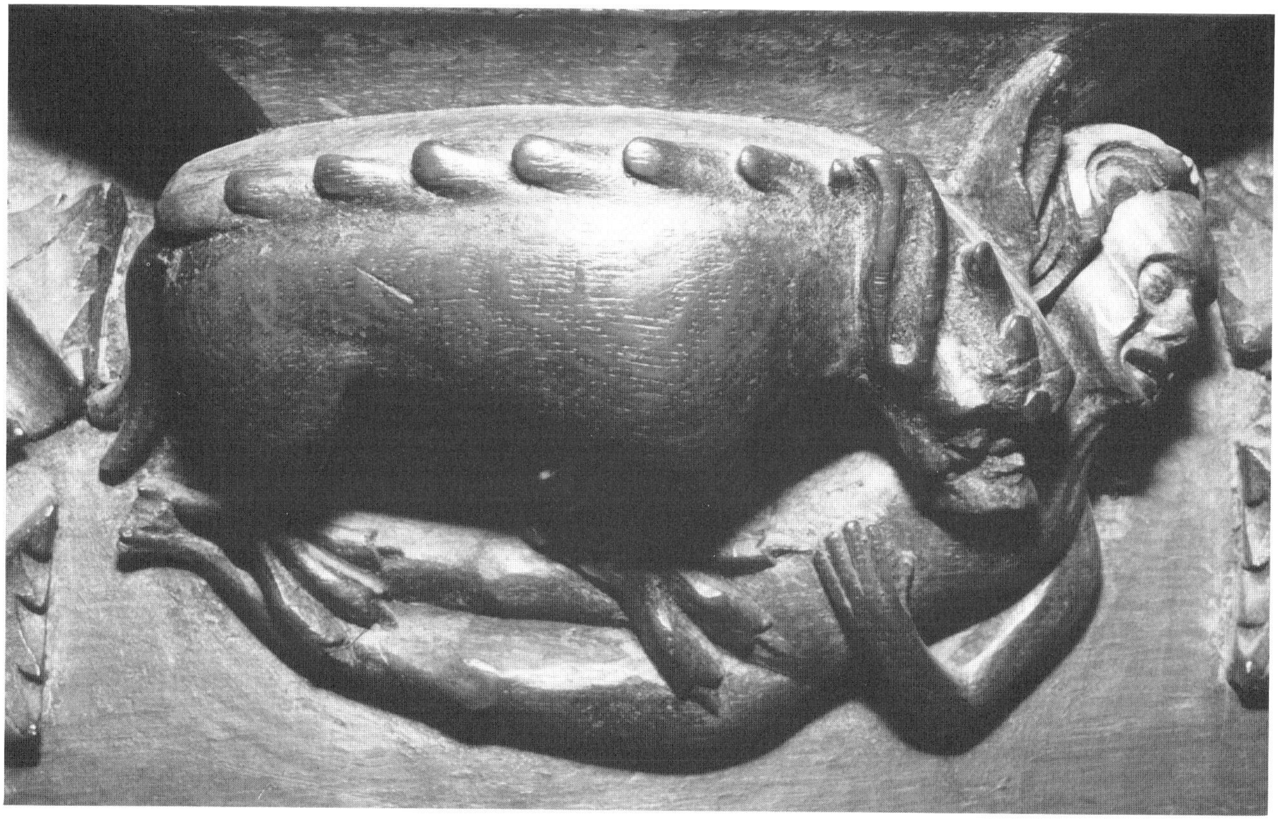

Hyena with corpse. Carlisle (Cumbria), The Cathedral, 1399–1413.

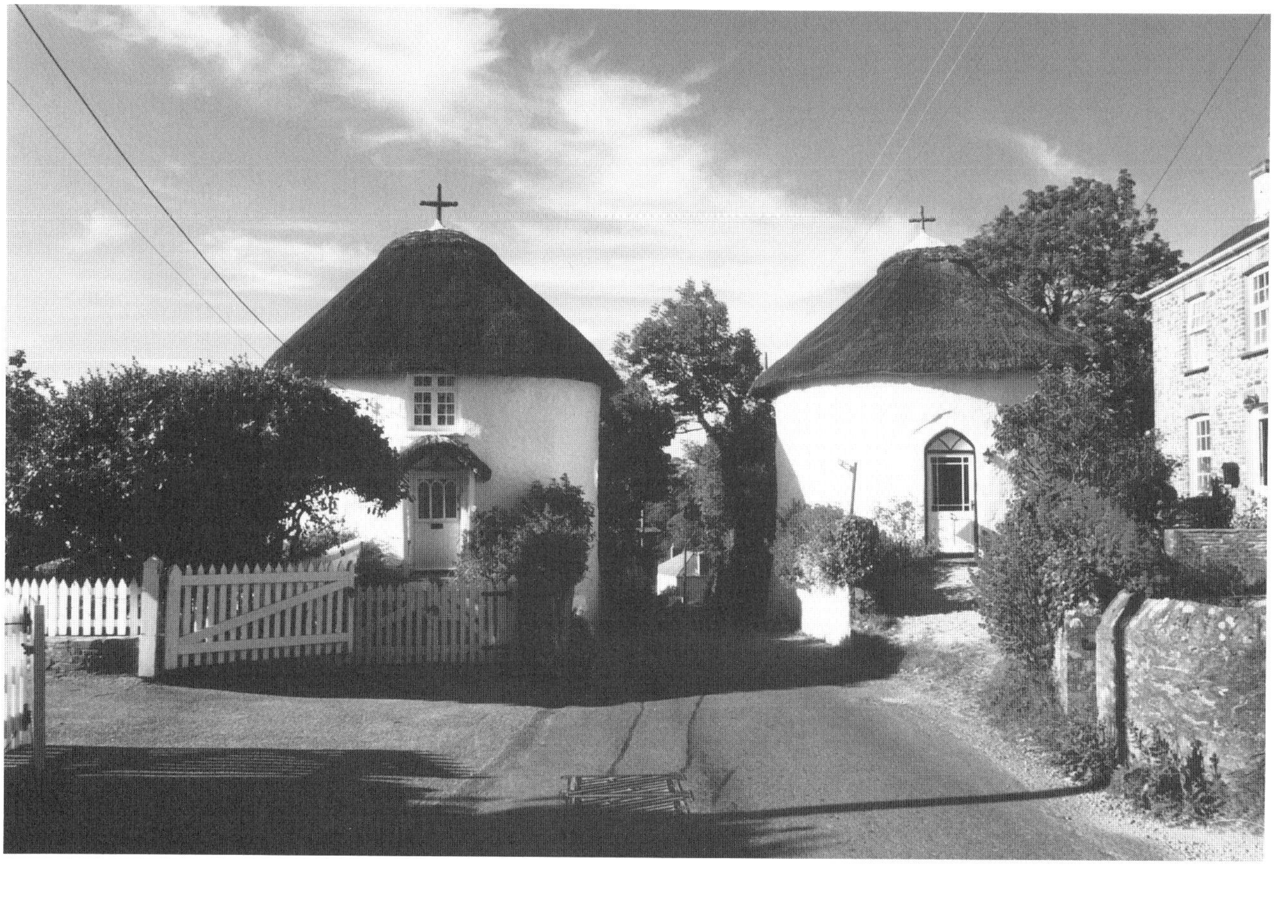

Kindly Beasts

There were many other animals in the bestiaries with positive characteristics offering lessons in correct thought and behavior as an antidote to the Devil's influence. While the carvers may have preferred the challenge of carving demonic beasts, they also recorded many of the kindly beasts—only a few of which are presented here.

UNICORNS

Like many fabulous beasts, the unicorn was said to be associated with the sacrifice of Christ. Its major attributes of fleetness and ferocity made it the victor in most battles with other beasts—and all but impossible for human hunters to catch. The ancients believed the unicorn was so fierce that it could be killed but never taken.

Aside from the Christian allegory, the horn of the unicorn was said to possess a number of characteristics that made capture desirable. It was thought by some to be an aphrodisiac (Pritchard n.d.). Others thought the horn was an antidote for poison (Robin 1932), and yet others believed it possessed such purifying qualities that simply dipping it in a body of water would instantly purify the water (Barber and Riches 1971).

The legend was born that there were only two ways to catch a unicorn. One was to challenge it to attack and then hide behind a tree. The unicorn in its attack would embed its horn in the tree and be helpless, depicted in the carving below.

In the other, more prevalent myth about catching a unicorn, the medieval theme of sexual contact followed by death is again played out. In this version, it was believed that the way to snare a unicorn was to have a virgin (in some accounts, a naked virgin) sit in the woods. Eventually, the unicorn would find the

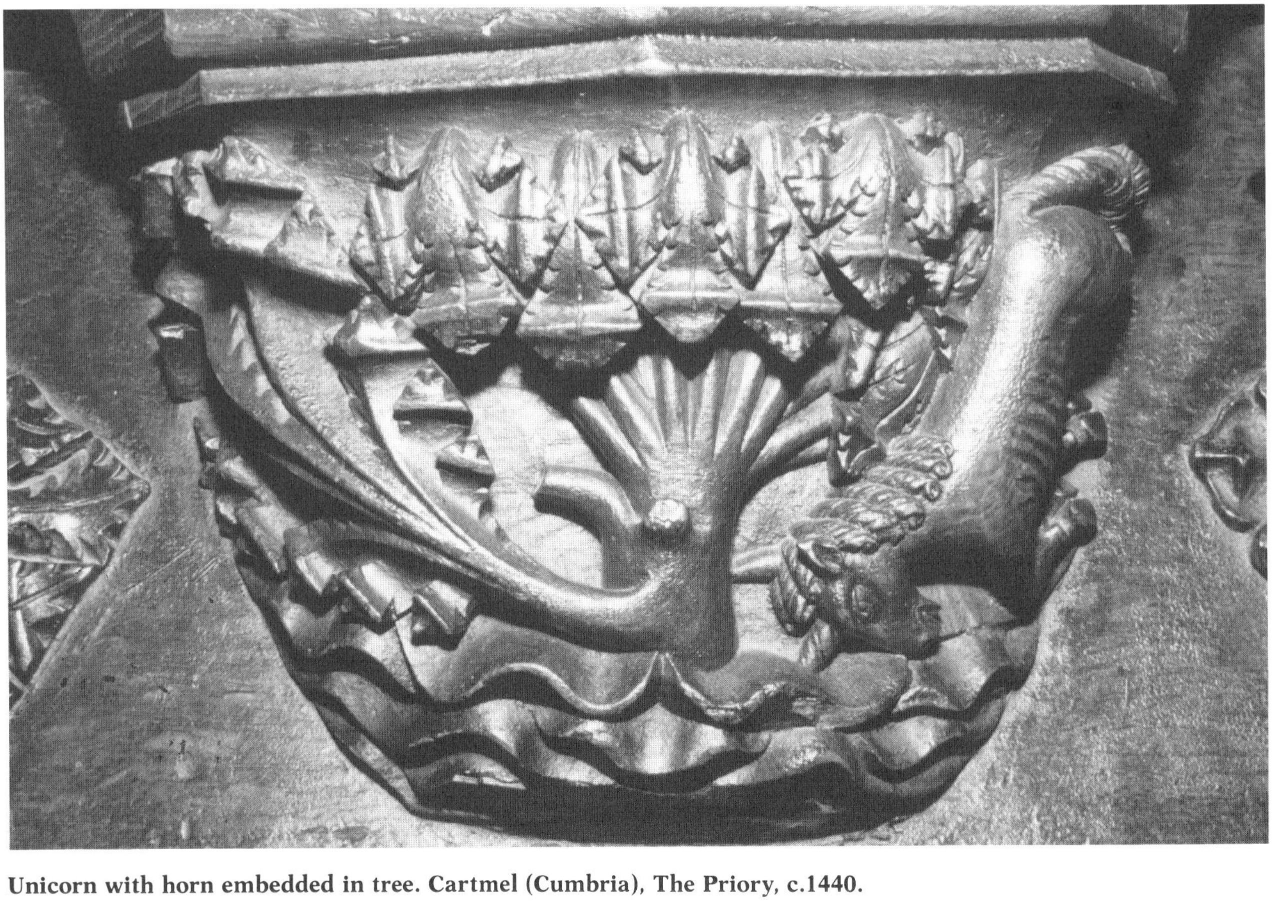

Unicorn with horn embedded in tree. Cartmel (Cumbria), The Priory, c.1440.

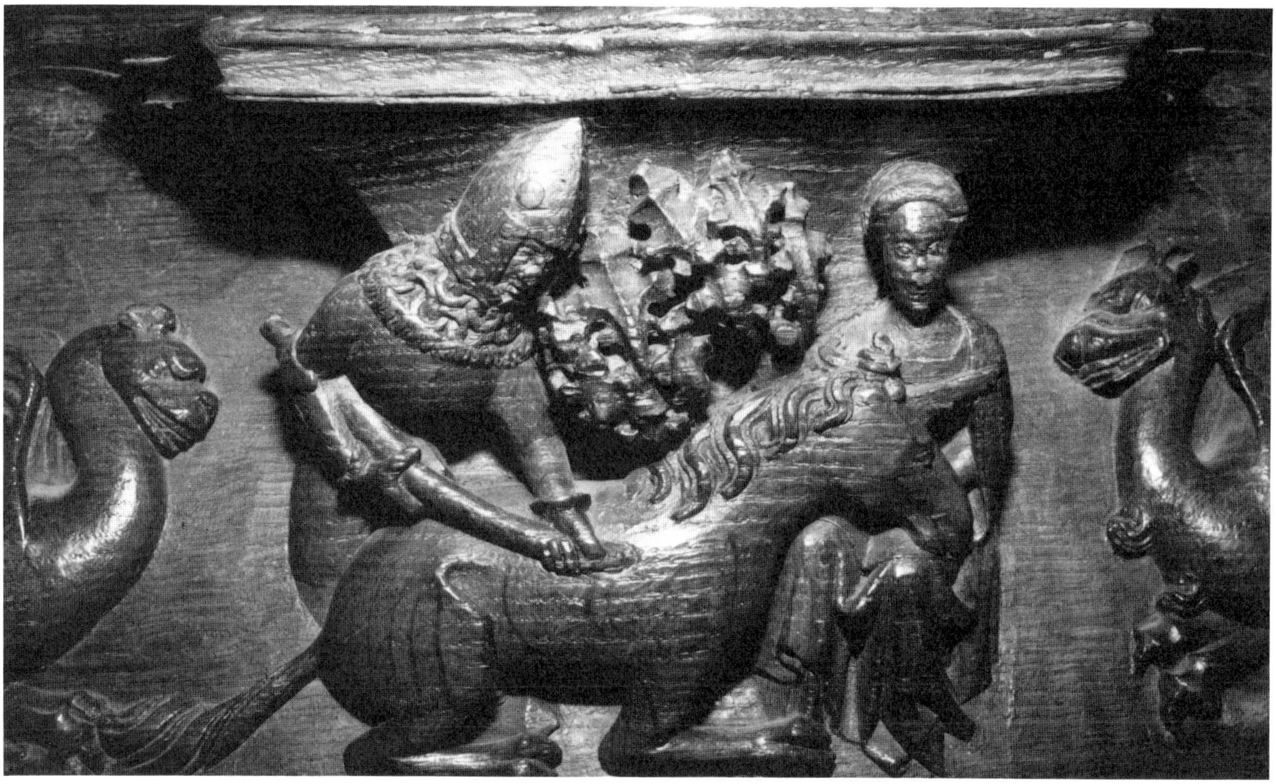

Capture of a unicorn. Chester (Cheshire), The Cathedral, c.1380.

virgin, sport with her, and finally place its head in her lap and be lulled to sleep. One bestiary version has a virgin sitting in a forest with one breast bared. The unicorn kisses the bared breast and falls asleep (Wright 1845). One account of the myth, however, warns that if the woman is not really a virgin, the unicorn will kill her (Johnsgard and Johnsgard 1982). Unicorns had strict standards.

In all the virgin-and-unicorn variations, hunters lie in wait to slay the sleeping unicorn. Again, Guillaume provides us with details on how a young virgin lures a unicorn into the trap:

> . . . they make her sit and wait
> At its lair, for to capture the beast . . .
> With the girl it sports so much,
> That in her lap it falls asleep.
> Those who are spying at once rush out:
> There they take and bind it.
>
> 1936, 44

This process was Christianized, and the unicorn came to represent Christ and His incarnation. The virgin in the story represents Mary receiving Christ in her womb, while the unicorn represents Christ in his human form. The hunters represent the Jews who seized Christ (Payne 1990). The lesson to be taken from the story is that of appreciating the sacrifice of Christ.

In the Chester carving, the unicorn has fallen asleep on the virgin's lap and the hunter is shown attacking the unicorn with his spear.

PEACOCKS

Other bestiary animals were used to warn of harmful behavior. The peacock, for instance, warns against the dangers of pride, considered by some the most serious of the Seven Deadly Sins and the root of the other six (Skeat 1906).

The peacock was used to symbolize many different things from ancient times on, its enduring fascination no doubt aided by the bird's unique plumage. Peacocks were sacred birds in both Greece and Rome. After Christianity came to Rome, the peacock became a popular Christian symbol for everlasting life. Its flesh was said to be incorruptible (Smith

1886; Hare 1952; Anderson 1969) and its plumage an emblem of the glories of heaven (Evans 1896). In the bestiaries, however, Christian moralists warn against the sin of pride, using the peacock's outspread tail to symbolize vanity.

In one rendering, the peacock was said to be quite vain but was ashamed of its ugly black feet. This reaction was likened to a man who, while living a luxurious life and being proud of his accoutrements, is suddenly confronted with his sins. The man, afraid of being condemned for his sins, and the peacock, glimpsing his ugly feet, would each cry out (Smith 1886). This story accounts for the raucous cry of the peacock. Another from the *Physiologus* tells how the peacock strolling along, happy in the glory of its beautiful plumage, turns a somersault and glances around proudly. However, when he looks down at his feet, which are not in keeping with his otherwise impressive appearance, he screams (Payne 1990). The prominence of the peacock's feet in the Wells carving refers to these stories.

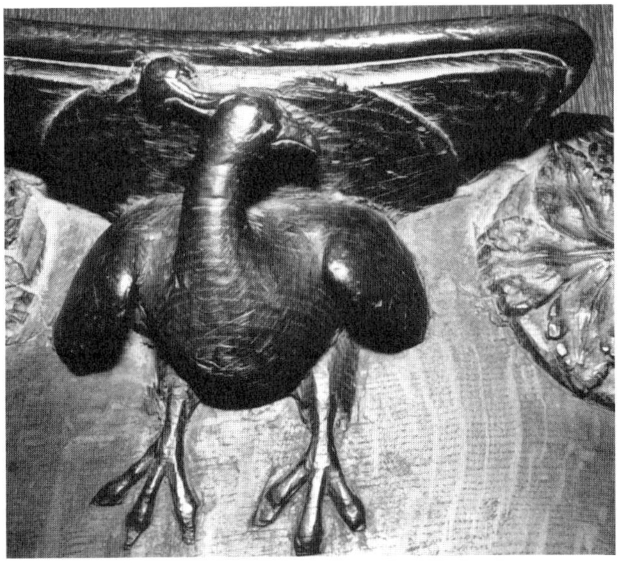

Peacock. Wells (Somerset), The Cathedral, c.1330–40.

In an anonymous verse, attributed to John Skelton, the peacock recognizes the poor quality of his voice but discounts that as being of any importance in light of the beauty of his tail feathers:

Than sayd the pecocke
All ye well wot
I syng not musycall;
For my brest [voice] is decayd,
Yet I have, he sayd
Fethers angellicall.

Collier 1843, 2:51

The bestiary artists and other illuminators, along with the misericord carvers, all seemed to agree and generally tended to focus on trying to show the peacock's beauty. One of the most interesting examples is the carving from New College, Oxford. It is reminiscent of an old Devon saying, "All's well that ends well, as the peacock said when he looked at his tail" (Hare 1952).

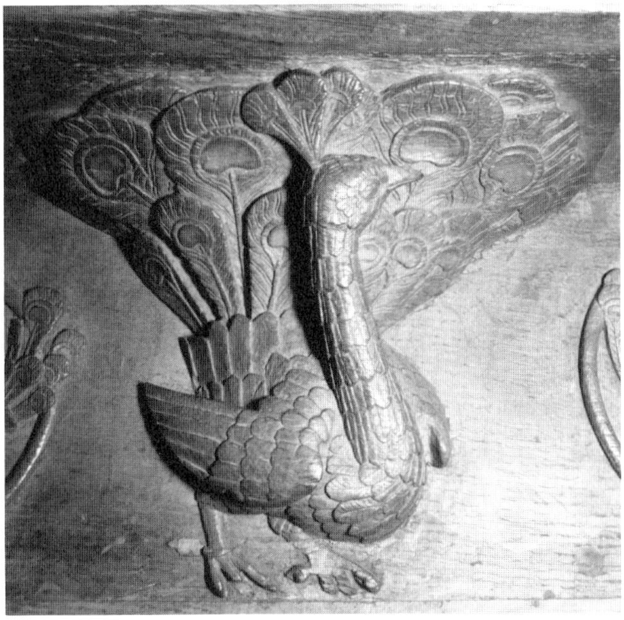

Peacock. Oxford (Oxon), New College Chapel, late fourteenth century.

One of the most convoluted moralizations about the peacock's tail to come out of the bestiaries has to do with the issue of foresight. The reasoning went thus: a man who lacks prudence is like a peacock who has lost its tail because the tail symbolizes foresight. The tail symbolizes foresight because it is behind that which is to come, and foresight is the wisdom of taking into account that which is to come (Evans 1896). One can see how easy it was to become confused on the road to salvation.

PELICANS

One of the most frequently carved scenes of redemption is the allegory of the pelican and its piety. The story has several versions, but in medieval times came to represent the passion of Christ. According to the story, the parents of the young pelicans became angry with them as they grew older and became disobedient. In anger, the parents killed their offspring but were immediately overcome with remorse. They mourned for three days until the distraught mother (or father, in some versions) pecked at her breast until it bled. The blood brought the young pelicans back to life. This represented the redemption of mankind through the Blood of Christ. Christ became known as the "Pelican of Piety" by early Christians because he gave his blood for sinners (Hare 1952).

The idea of self-sacrifice and parental devotion in this style first appeared in the *Physiologus*, but an ancient Greek translation of the Old Testament, the Septuagint, also records this symbol of self-sacrifice, giving it entree into the Christian world (Robin 1932). This legend was made poetic in another verse attributed to John Skelton:

> Than sayd the pellycane,
> When my byrds be slayne,
> With my bloude I them revyve,
> Scrypturc doth record,
> The same did our Lord,
> And rose from deth to lyve.
> Collier 1843, 11

As in many superstitions and legends, there is a factual basis for the myth—in this case, in the natural habits of the pelican. To feed her young, the mother pelican lowers her head to cast up partially digested food. The inside of her bill is pink, which could resemble blood (Hare 1952).

The Cartmel carving, right, is one of the loveliest and most skillfully done. The mother spreads her wings in a protective gesture while underneath the young birds are revived. The nest is made of twigs. Pelicans in the bestiary drawings and in the misericords were not carved naturalistically but were understood to be pelicans by the scene which, in the misericords, never varies.

The moral lessons to be garnered from the bestiaries all, in some manner, point out the

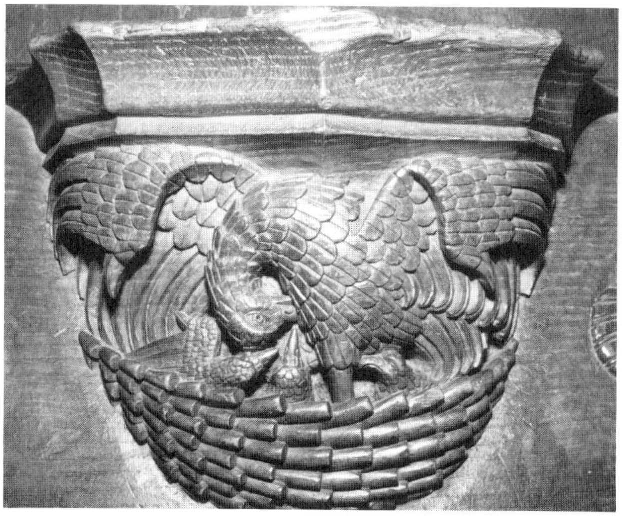

Pelican and piety. Cartmel (Cumbria), The Priory, c.1440.

pitfalls to the Christian on the way to salvation. The belief in good and bad influences was strong and was reinforced by the great theological and philosophical thinkers of the time. For example, Thomas Aquinas (1225–1274), in his attempt to meld Greek philosophy with religious thought, firmly held that not only are angels a real presence, but so are demons. He believed that demons are not only real, but that they do enormous harm (Durant and Durant 1950).

Certain activities were to be avoided, and "good works" were vigorously encouraged, not necessarily to avoid an eternity in hell, but to shorten the length of time one must spend in purgatory. In the Middle Ages, it was assumed that few people actually were transported to hell, for there were too many avenues of penance for one to die without having one's sins forgiven. But it was equally assumed that, to cleanse the soul, a period of time in purgatory was required. The point of good works was to build a reserve for Judgment Day so that when one rose from the dead to be evaluated, acceptance into heaven would be rapid. The Sherborne carving shows this process beginning as

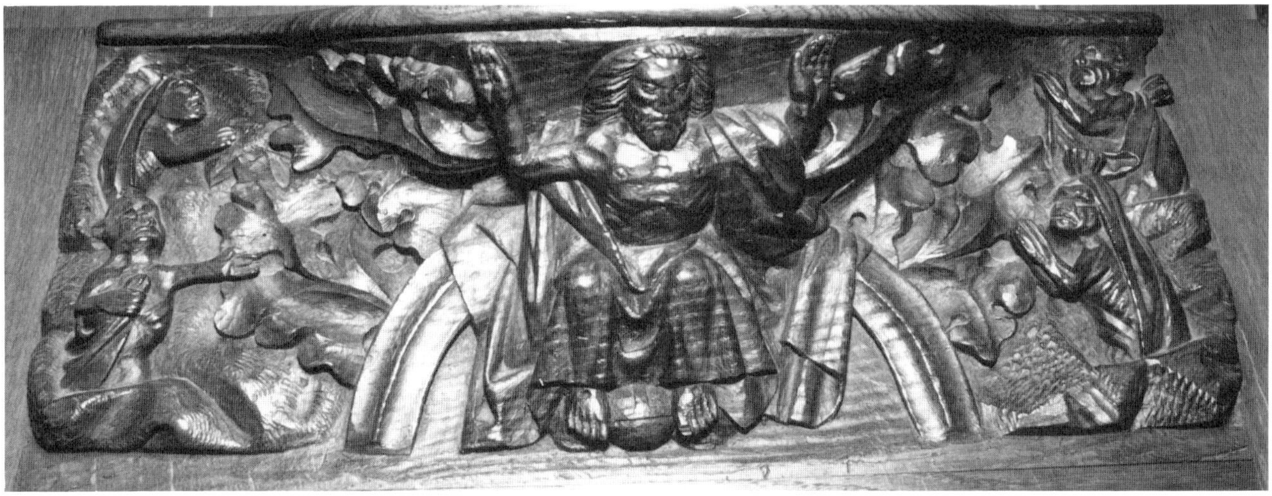

Last Judgment. Sherborne (Dorset), The Abbey, 1436.

the dead rise from their graves while Christ sits displaying the wounds on his hands and feet from his sacrifice.

The belief in a day of judgment and a requirement for previous good works meant that individuals were dependent on the Church in the most fundamental way. If one did not contribute enough good works, generally in the form of donations to the Church, to offset sinful behavior, that person could remain in purgatory indefinitely. It is understandable that, in the face of such restrictions, the people would find ways to subvert the official requirements—the cult of the Virgin was one such response before the doctrine of good works was challenged directly.

Danger from Within—Fighting the Impulses

The Moralities

By the fifteenth century, interest had developed in what constituted moral behavior or the lack of it, and a number of plays emerged under the general classification of "moralities." The authors of these plays as they were passed down, are unknown, but they appeared at a time when the several bouts with the Black Death left individuals familiar with the finite nature of human life and the seemingly serendipitous nature of who would be stricken. Not that people were unconcerned with death before (indeed, Christianity based everything on the period after death), but the moralities heralded a subtle shift in what one should be concerned about. The bestiaries warned against the pervasive and duplicitous nature of the Devil and the need to avoid being ensnared. In the moralities, the emphasis shifts from the danger without to the danger within. They warn that a person must be cautious to take the high moral ground so that when death comes, that individual will have sufficient good works to tip the scales in his or her favor.

The moralities also use allegory, but in a different manner from the bestiaries. Rather than assign good or bad characteristics to different animals, the moralities took the abstract characteristics of "good" and "bad" and made them the main characters in the plays—prudence, charity, faith, lust, pride, and so forth. These personified characteristics were meant to extol virtue and condemn vice for the salvation of mankind. One of the most influential of these plays, *Everyman,* is a paean to the virtue of "good works." In the poem, the author warns "everyman" that, in the end, it is only one's good works that will count:

> Save his good dedes there doth he take.
> But beware/ for if they be small
> Before God, he hath no help at all . . .
>
> 1906, 52

Different plays focused on different characteristics. In *Mankind,* for example, the main characters included Mercy, Mischief, Now-a-Days, and Nought, with Titivillus in the character of the Devil (Farmer 1907). Another, *The Castle of Perseverance* (1948), uses similar allegorical themes with the abstract characters of the Good and Bad Angel, the World, the Flesh and the Devil, the Seven Virtues, and Death. The Coventry Play is unique among English cycles in its personification of the heavenly virtues: Truth, Mercy, Justice, and Peace (Pollard 1890). All, however, are concerned with trying to ensure the salvation of one's soul by building up credits before death strikes one down. Now, not only is the Devil lying in wait around every corner, but time is running out for building a good character reference.

Of special importance during this period of looking for danger from within were the concepts of the Seven Deadly Sins and the Dance of Death.

The Seven Deadly Sins

The concept of the Seven Deadly Sins came from ancient Greek writings of unknown authorship and date, but they greatly influenced the early Christians, Jews and Muslims. These writings stressed that all things emanate from God and return to God. All things flow from God to man through a set of angelic ranks. When death occurs, there is a reverse process by which all creatures are led back to God through nine orders of celestial hierarchy (Durant and Durant 1950). These works influenced theologians such as Thomas Aquinas, who wrote his classic work verifying of the existence of angels and demons. His work, along with others, brought renewed interest in the deadly sins during the Middle Ages. He taught that the sins were deadly not just because they were morally offensive, but because they led to other sins. Traditionally, the Seven Deadly Sins comprise pride, covetousness, lust, envy, gluttony, anger, and sloth.

An adjunct of the belief in hierarchies that one passed through before redemption was reinforced by another early belief, that at certain times, particular people could "die" for a brief period and their soul could transverse the realms of purgatory, hell, and heaven before coming back to life. These journeys presumably allowed the individual to view firsthand the consequences of sin and the rewards of devoutness before returning to the body where, if the lesson had been learned, the person had a chance to correct his or her ways and to act as a witness for the worlds beyond. One popular version of this idea was retold and widely circulated from the twelfth to the fifteenth century in a tale constructed by a monk named Marcus in Regensburg, Germany. In his *The Visions of Tondal* (1990),[1] an Irish knight's soul briefly leaves his body to travel with his guardian angel through hell, purgatory, and heaven before returning to his body intent on mending his sinful ways. This story was written as if it were an account of a real journey and, as such, was retold by other theologians, storytellers, and producers of sermons in Europe and Great Britain, generally without attribution to Marcus. The tale was written in both Latin and the vernacular in several languages and was so well distributed that 243 manuscripts of the tale remain today (Wieck 1990).

These tales focused on the punishments meted out for specific sins and the rewards given for particular virtues. Interestingly, in Tondal's vision, the sin of lust was assigned to "unchaste priests and nuns," and their fate is especially gruesome as they are turned over to a terrifying creature:

> This beast had two feet and two wings, a very long neck, and an iron beak and iron claws. From its jaws it breathed fire and flame and stood upon a large pond, all frozen. There it would devour all the souls it could reach.
>
> Marcus 1990, 49

But this was not the end of suffering, for:

> When it had eaten all the souls, and they had been reduced to nothing in its belly, the beast would defecate, dropping them onto the ice where their torments were renewed.
>
> 49

This action is the topic of the Windsor carving below showing one demon evacuating a man and another demon grabbing him as he emerges.

The Windsor carver also produced an interesting reversal of this process, perhaps at the behest of the choir stall owner, in which a monk is shown treating the demon with the same disdain. The carver may have been conveying an alternative message, however, implying that monks' bodies themselves were inhabited by demons.

As popular as Marcus's tale was, there was

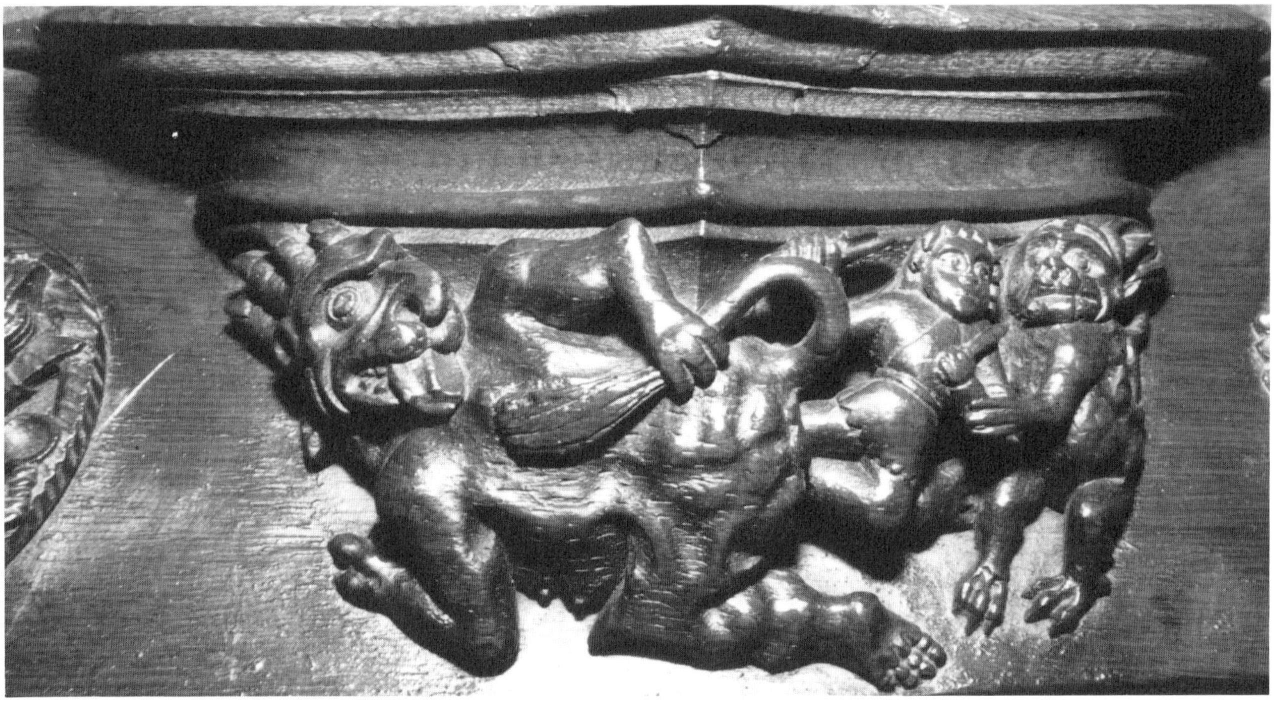

Demon evacuating man. Windsor (Berks), St. George's Chapel, 1477–83.

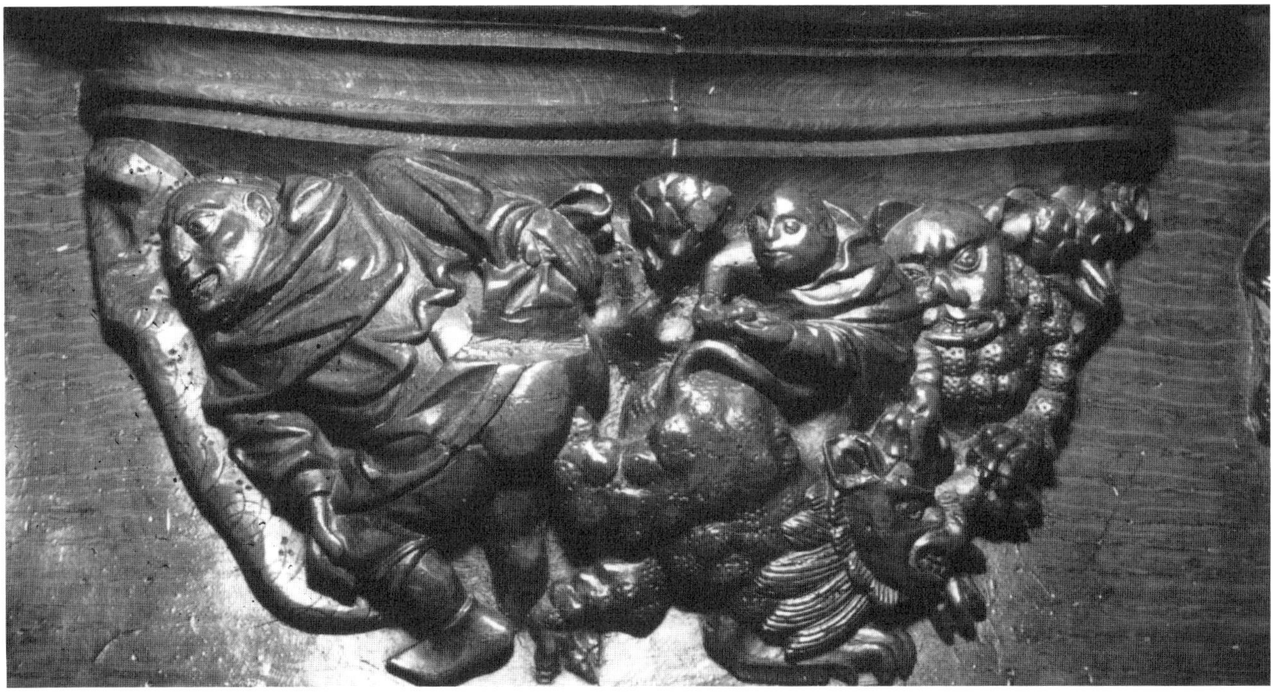

Monk evacuating demon. Windsor (Berks), St. George's Chapel, 1477–83.

an even more widely read and revered work treating the subject of passing through various levels of atonement before finally being redeemed. Dante (1265–1321), one of the most important figures of the Middle Ages, immortalized this journey in his *Comedy* (much later called *Divine Comedy*). Writing about 150 years after Marcus, his description, written in verse and in the vernacular, gave his version of the Catholic otherworld—hell, purgatory, and heaven. Dante, however, formed his verse around his view of the political structure in which he lived, a structure that had caused him to be exiled from Florence. The verses in the books of the *Divine Comedy* are on one level, used as revenge on those who had slighted him, producing biting social commentary. On another level, they were another confirmation that heaven was an attainable goal for every individual (MacAllister 1954). Part Two of the *Comedy,* "Purgatorio," invokes the concept of the Seven Deadly Sins by making these the seven levels of penance through which one had to ascend before being accepted into the last level of purgatory, Earthly Paradise.

At each level of purgatory, the deadly sin associated with it must be purged by doing the appropriate penance before passing on to the next circle; that is, for example, the proud must bear heavy stones to make them more humble. When each atonement is performed, a guardian angel of the complementary virtue recites a benediction and receives the soul of the now purified sinner—the angel of humility, for instance, receives the sinner guilty of pride (Schimmel 1992). In all these types of journeys, angels were given great importance, for it was they who acted as guides and ensured a successful passage through the horrors to arrive eventually at paradise. In an unusual carving from Lincoln, a feathered angel

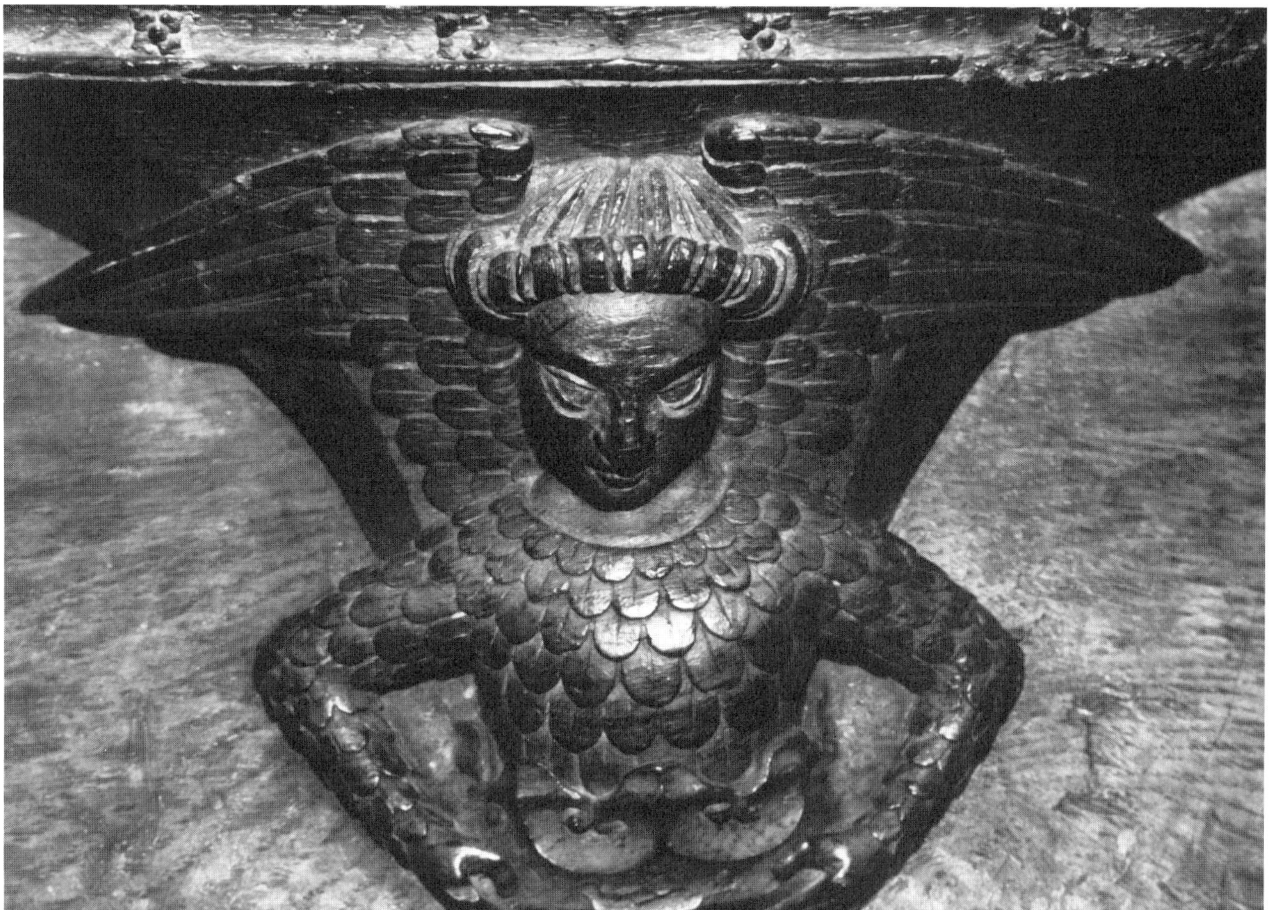

Angel with crown. Lincoln (Lincs), The Minster, 1370.

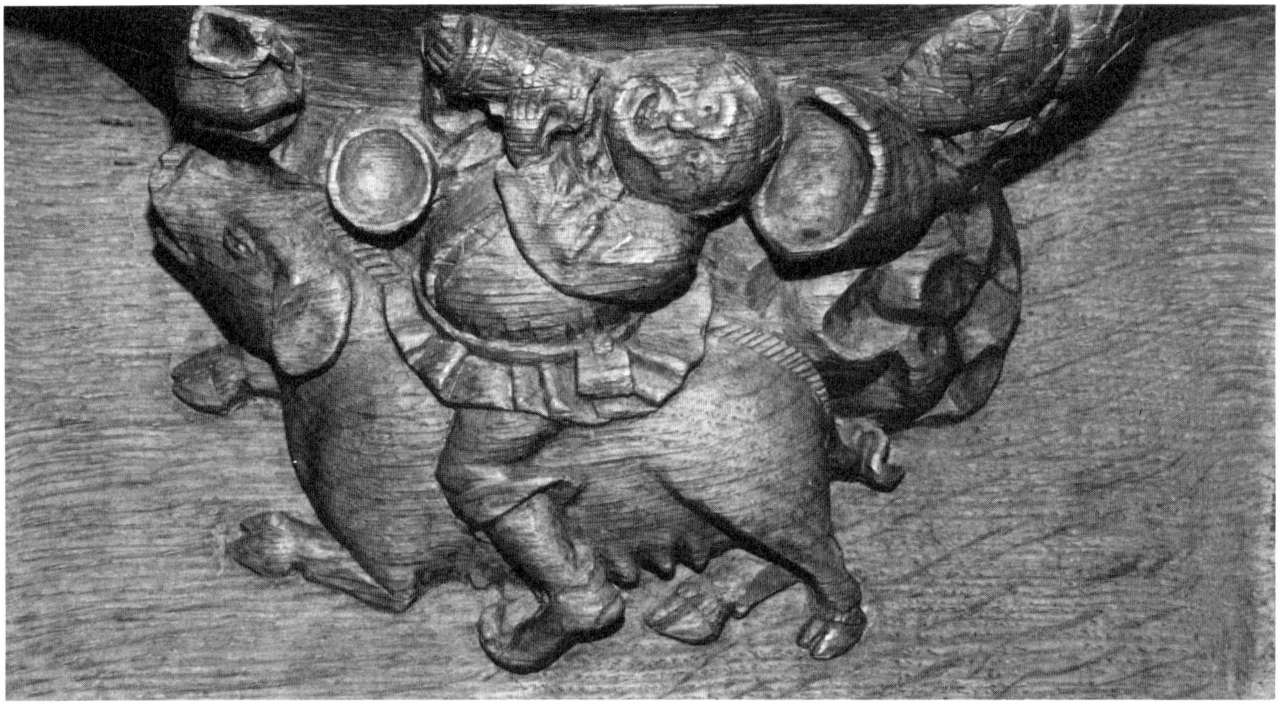

Gluttony. Norwich (Norfolk), The Cathedral, 1480.

awaits, crown in hand, to welcome the traveler to the last level.[2]

The Church, being particularly interested in bringing the concepts of personal virtue and personal vice before the people, took special care to make sure these concepts were understood. In York, for example, Archbishop Thoresby, in 1357, took the unusual step of ordering that certain instructions be given regularly by his parish priests to parishioners. The topics included the Seven Corporal Acts of Mercy, the Ten Commandments, and the Seven Deadly Sins. To ensure that the message was fully understood, Archbishop Thoresby stipulated that these instructions were to be given in English rather than the usual Latin or French (Purvis 1951).

Apparently, the message about the seven sins was received by the people, albeit perhaps not as seriously as the Church would have hoped. Perhaps because it was a common failing, the deadly sin most often encountered in the carvings is that of gluttony, in the form of drunkenness. This, of course, offered a great opportunity for comedic interpretation.

Norwich, which possesses more carvings of the deadly sins than any other church (Anderson 1969), has a particularly fitting carving of drunkenness. The rider in this scene sits on a sow, clutching his tankard in both hands, and looks to be in danger of falling off. We can tell by his enlarged stomach that he is prone to overindulgence.

Spenser, writing in the sixteenth century, gives a description of the glutton that seems to have been written for the Norwich carving:

> And by his side rode loathsome Gluttony,
> Deformed creature, on a filthy swine,
> His belly was up-blowne with luxury . . .
>
> . . . And in his hand did beare a bouzing can,
> Of which he supt so oft, that on his seat
> His drunken corse he scarce upholden can;
> In shape and life, more like a monster than a man.
>
> 1611, Canto IIII, v.21–22

Two supporters from Windsor are more whimsical. The first shows the drunken man dancing, the second has a demon helpfully pushing the man's head toward the tankard.

The subject of the treachery of drink is age-

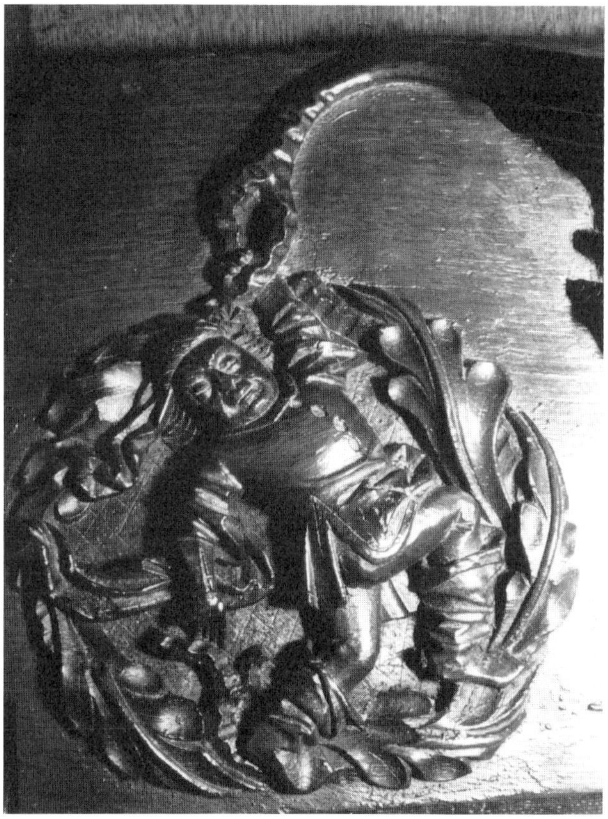

Drunk dancing. Windsor (Berks), St. George's Chapel, 1477–83.

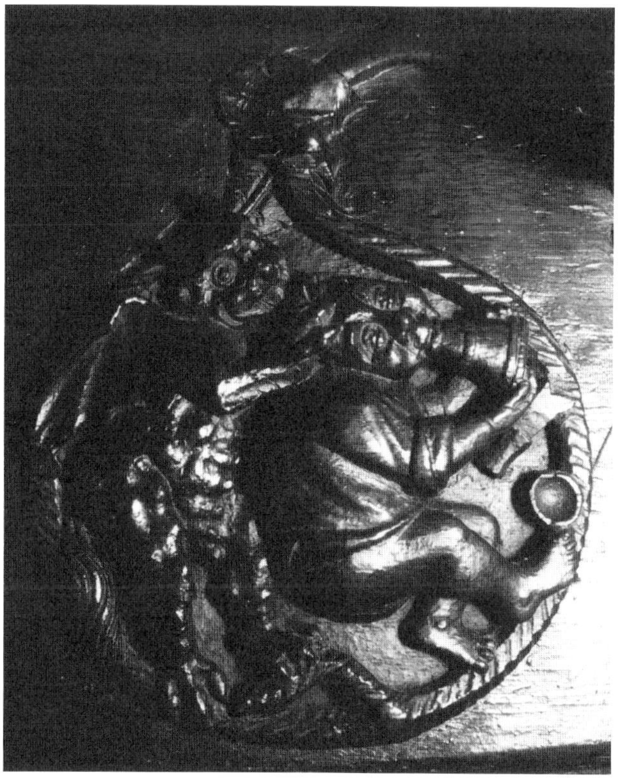

Drunk with demon. Windsor (Berks), St. George's Chapel, 1477–83.

less, as are the humorous anecdotes surrounding drunkenness. One of the most amusing is the episode from a seventeenth-century parody on some of Ovid's epistles. The tale is told of an Englishman who is imprisoned in Paris for murder but escapes by wooing the Keeper's daughter. She accompanies him to Calais, assuming that she will continue on to England with him. He takes advantage of her, however, and steals away as she lies "snoaring." This is her letter to him:

Had I not drank that Brandy over night,
I cou'd have wak'd, and so have stopt your Flight.
Curst be the Wind which was so kind to you;
Curst be the Boat, and curst be all its Crew;
Curst may I be for trusting what you said;
Curst may all Lovers be that snore in Bed.

Radcliffe 1680, 32

Lust was another vice of interest and one could pay for favors as in the Westminster carving. Here the woman of choice is holding

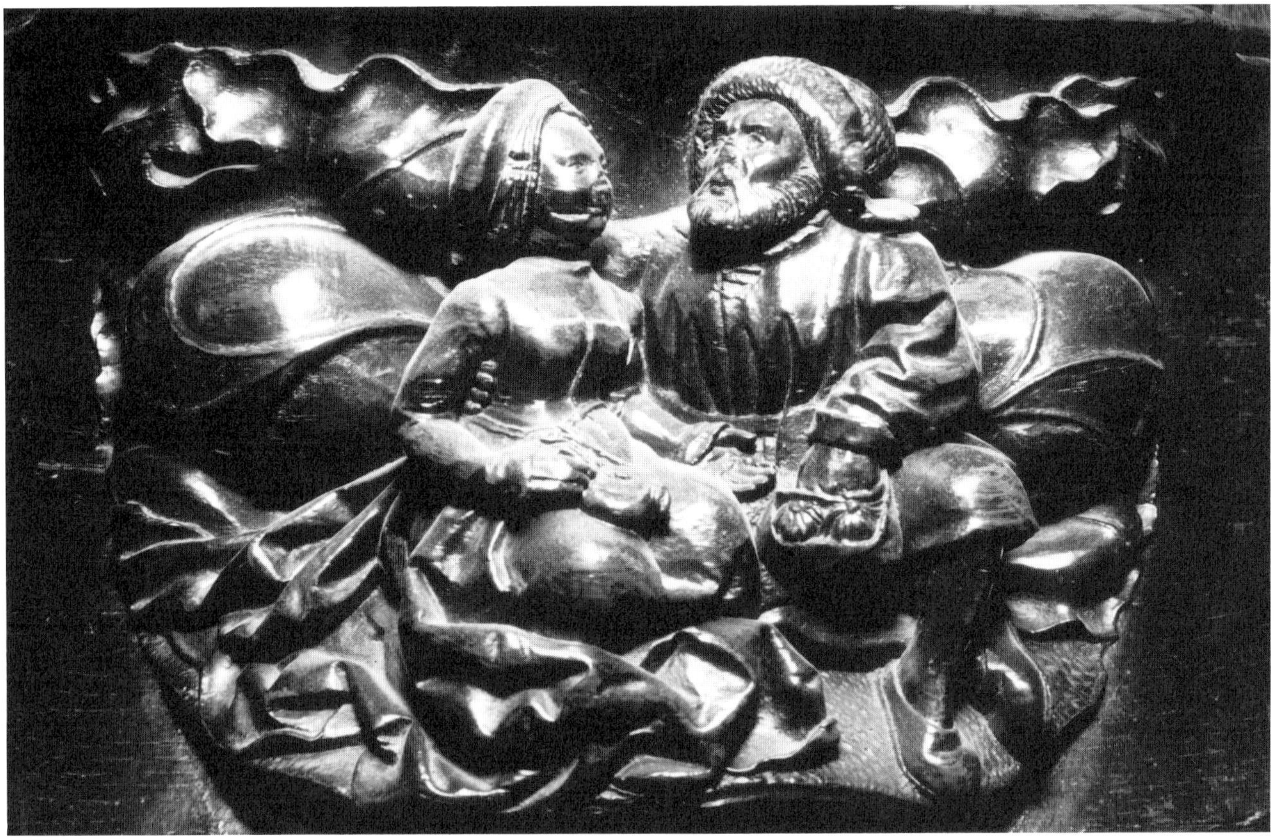

Paying for favors. Westminster (London), The Abbey, sixteenth century.

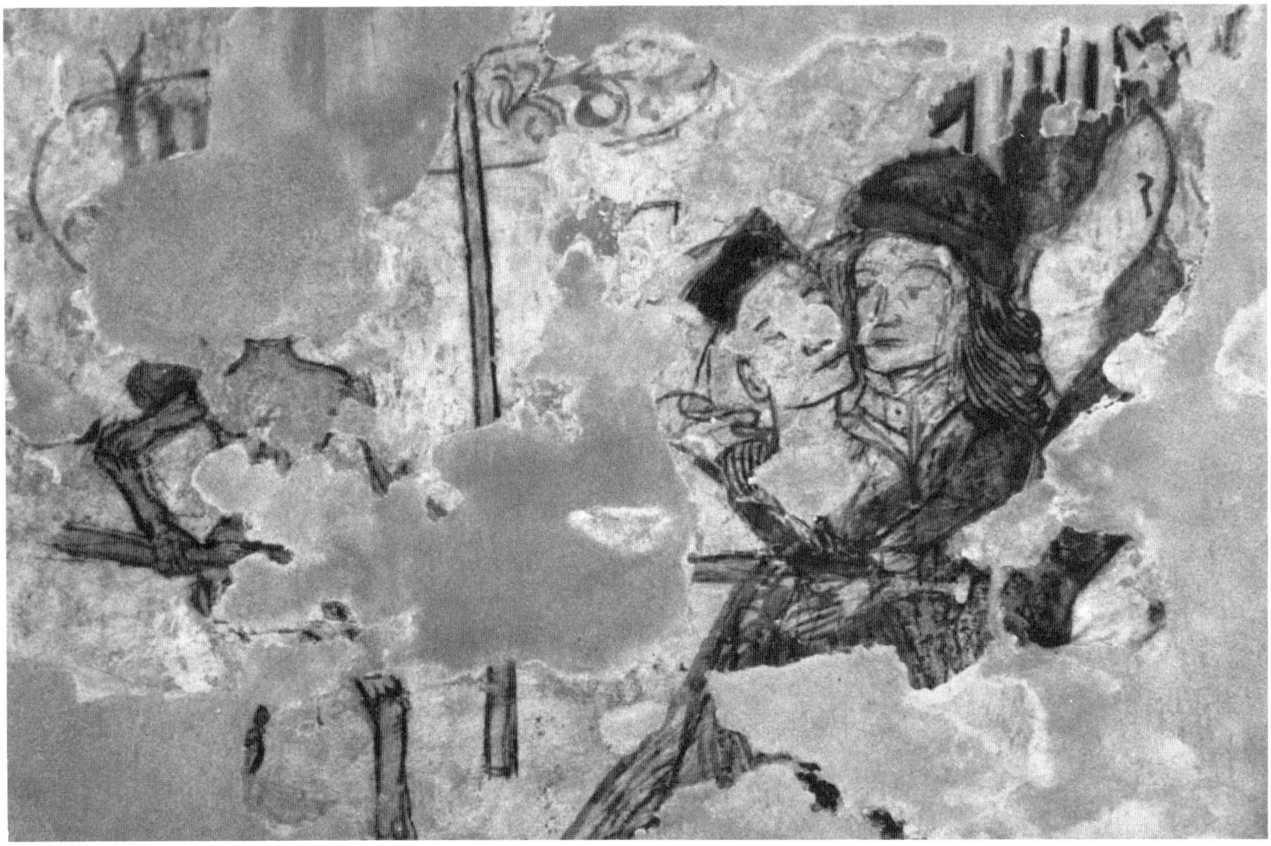

Lust. Branscombe (Devon), Parish Church of St. Winifred, fifteenth century.

out her hand as her client digs into his purse for the exchange premium.[3]

More commonly, however, were the natural urges aided and abetted by the Devil. In the only remaining mural of the deadly sins at Branscombe, a portion of a demon can be seen with a long stick prodding a willing couple to carry on.

The fight against temptation and the Devil's tricks continued unabated throughout one's life. Sometimes the fight was settled in the Devil's favor, sometimes in the individual's. Some had greater temptations than others; some enjoyed their sins more than others. There were many experiences in medieval life that were not equally shared, but in one area it was an incontrovertible fact that experience would be universal—death. Death would, indeed, come to everyone, and death, like the Devil, came to be perceived as a corporal being. As *Everyman* reminds us in the charge God gives to Death:

> Go thou to Everyman,
> And show him in my name
> A pilgrimage he must on him take,
> Which he in no wise may escape;
> And that he bring with him a sure reckoning
> Without delay or any tarrying.
>
> 1906, 8

Dance of Death

The "Danse Macabre" that appeared in France in the fourteenth century may or may not have preceded its appearance in the morality plays; too few fragments of the plays are left to ascertain which came first. Its origins may have been from as early as the thirteenth century, however, for there is a record of a wedding celebration at Jedburgh in 1285, in which a Dance of Death masque was held (Clark 1950). The earliest known pictorial example is from a fresco at the Cemetery of the Innocents, in Paris (destroyed in 1669), in which the entire hierarchy of society is presented in a stately dance. Each living person is paired with a dead person who is escorting him or her to the grave. The dead person represents the image of what the living person will soon become. It is a fate that awaits everyone, rich as well as poor. In the carving below, a wealthy man sits surrounded by his material wealth as death takes him by the arm.

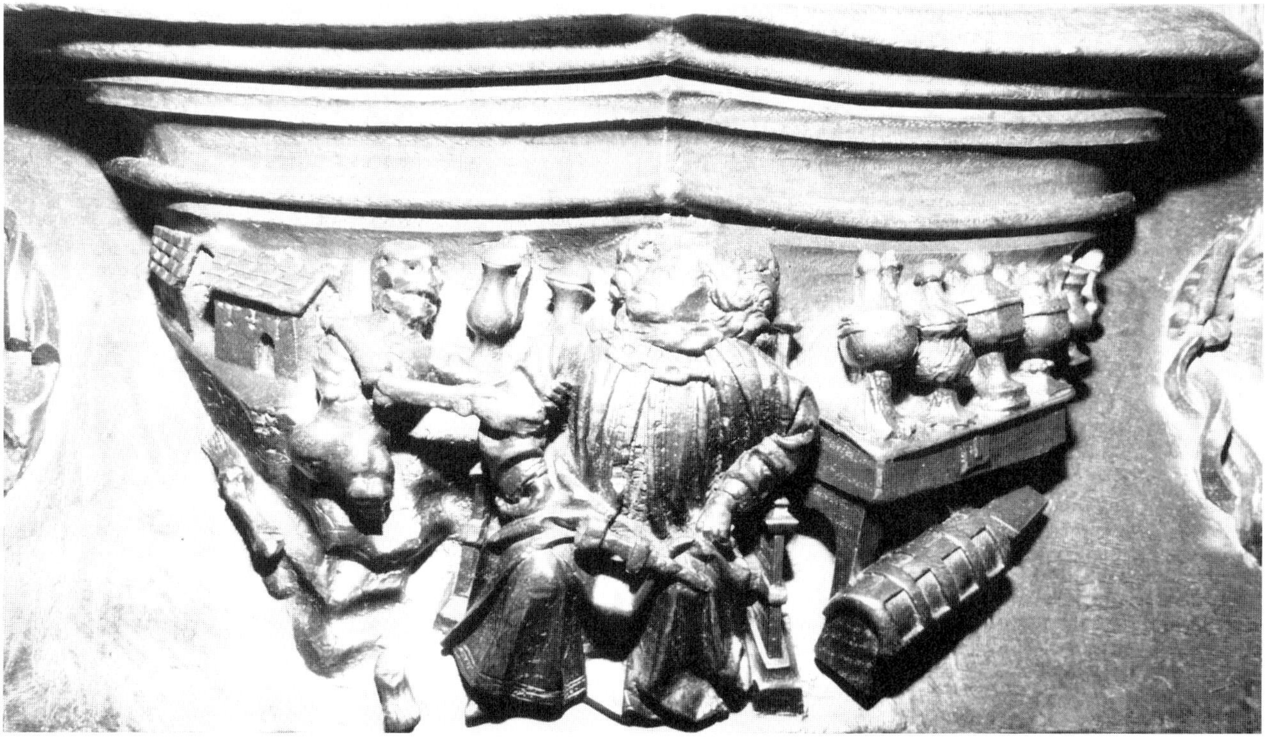

Death comes to the rich man. Windsor (Berks), St. George's Chapel, 1477–83.

The Dance of Death has often been associated with the legend of the Three Living and the Three Dead, which appeared first in a thirteenth-century French poem and later in the thirteenth century in an English manuscript, the Psalter of Robert de Lisle (Rouse 1968).[4] In this legend, three kings are paired with three dead men, always shown as skeletons. The message is "As I am, so thou shalt be. Therefore repent, before it is too late" (Clark 1950, 95). In the Dance of Death, however, there is no warning and no opportunity for repentance. The moment of death is at hand and it comes in the same manner to everyone. The cartoon for the mural at La Ferté Loupiére illustrates this "death as the great equalizer" aspect, showing individuals from all segments of society being tapped for their dance with death.

The Dance of Death readily lent itself to dramatic presentation, and there are records of performances given enacting this admonition. In Candebec, in 1393, actors each holding a symbol of social rank would dance and then disappear as if dead (Mâle 1949). In 1424, the Danse Macabre was danced publicly before the Duke of Bedford in the Cemetery of the Innocents (Wright 1865). In 1485, a Parisian printer, Guyot Marchant, published the first edition of the Dance of Death using wood carvings to illustrate the conversations between the living and the dead (Mâle 1949). The dialogue in the woodcuts was copied from the frescoes in the Cemetery of the Innocents, which was the basis for all subsequent works.

The zenith of popularity for the Dance of Death series came in 1538, when an acclaimed set of drawings on the theme was published in Lyon by Melchior and Gaspar Trechsel. The book had forty-one woodcuts, was printed in several languages, and appeared in twelve editions up to 1573 (Wildridge 1887).[5] After the sixteenth century, the topic faded away.

Whereas death had been promoted as a state of sleep in earlier times, the concept of death took on a new coloration in the Gothic period. It was now a more aggressive actor who snatched you away:

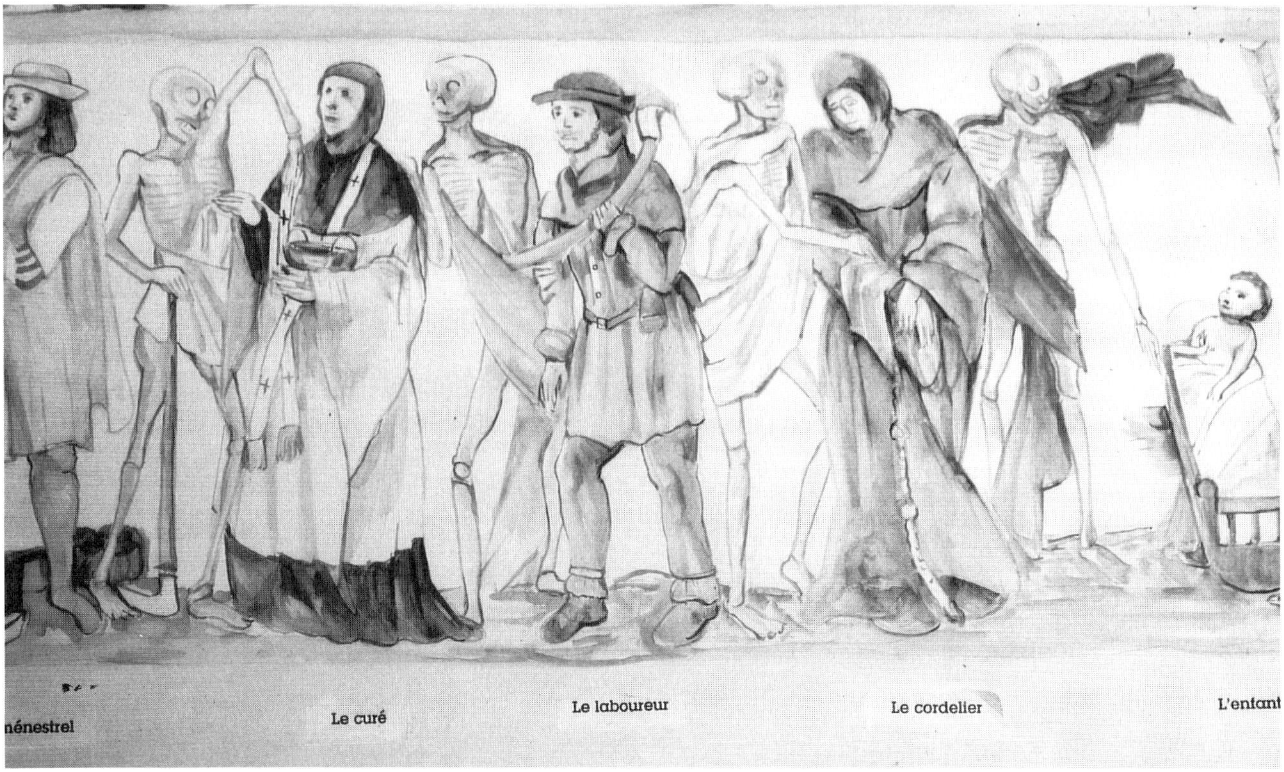

Dance of Death. La Ferté Loupiére (France), Parish Church, late fifteenth–early sixteenth century.

Tho' Death with drowsie Eyes does wink
at Health,
And lets you live a little while
by stealth;
Yet he'll awake, and vext at past
delay,
Snatch you with sad surprising
haste away
Wildridge 1887, 8

The verses attached to the pictures were harsh, humorous, and political. Whereas part of the idea was to emphasize the universal nature of death—death as the great equalizer—part of the new aggressive view of death also allowed social retribution:

> To the pastor "who devoured the living and the dead" the poet declares with ferocious joy that he will henceforth be devoured by worms. . . . He pokes fun at the bourgeois who will have to give up his revenues, at the physician who cannot heal himself. . . .
>
> Mâle 1949, 148

In other cases, the point is satire in which different segments of society show some reluctance at joining their double in the dance. As the laborer from Windsor might have responded when he was asked to dance:

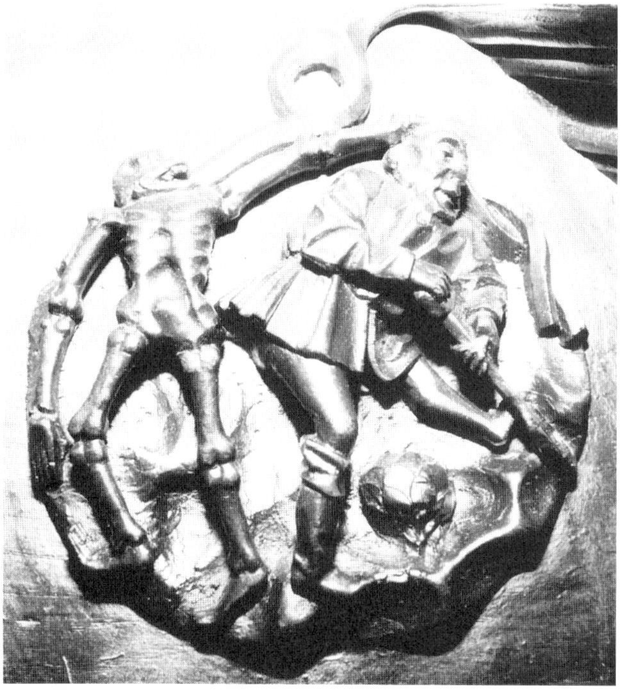

Often have I death besought;
Now he comes, I want him not,
Let it rain or let it blow,
Rather I'll the vineyard hoe
Mâle 1949, 149

The scenes from the Cemetery of the Innocents in Paris were the inspiration for a cycle in the Pardon churchyard, near old St. Paul's, in London. John Lydgate had returned from a trip to France in 1440 and translated the verses explaining the scenes (Anderson 1935; Clark 1950). Only fragments of the various scenes are left in England. Windsor has the only misericord with its central carving and two supporters showing scenes from the Dance of Death series. A few other carvings serve as reminders that death awaits, however. One at Ely shows this awareness, for example. Here, a woman is making her confession in the central carving while the scull on the left supporter serves as the reminder of death to come.

One is also reminded of the fate that can befall sinners after dying, when they reach purgatory. Dante has a grisly description of Cerberus, the three-headed dog of hell, as he contemplates the punishment of Judas:

> In every mouth he worked a broken sinner
> between his rake-like teeth. Thus he kept
> three
> in eternal pain at his eternal dinner. . . .
>
> "That soul that suffers most," explained my
> Guide,
> is Judas Iscariot, he who kicks his legs
> on the fiery chin and has his head inside.
>
> 1954, 284–85

This scene was portrayed by the carvers, but they substituted a dragon for Cerberus, which was the usual symbol in the misericords for

Death comes to the laborer. Windsor (Berks), St. George's Chapel, 1477–83.

the Jaws of Hell. In the Carlisle carving, however, the supporters are dogs, perhaps in reference to Cerberus. In the Bible, a dog was always referred to as a contemptible character (Clarke 1920). Either way, the warning is clear.

It was a tricky balancing act for medieval citizens to conduct their lives in a manner that would ensure their immortality while at the same time allowing them a measure of enjoyment in their mortal life. Perhaps they were saved from agonizing unduly over their situation by their acceptance of the world as a complex place. They assumed the presence of contradiction everywhere and simply created solutions to handle it—through ritual, faith, or humor.

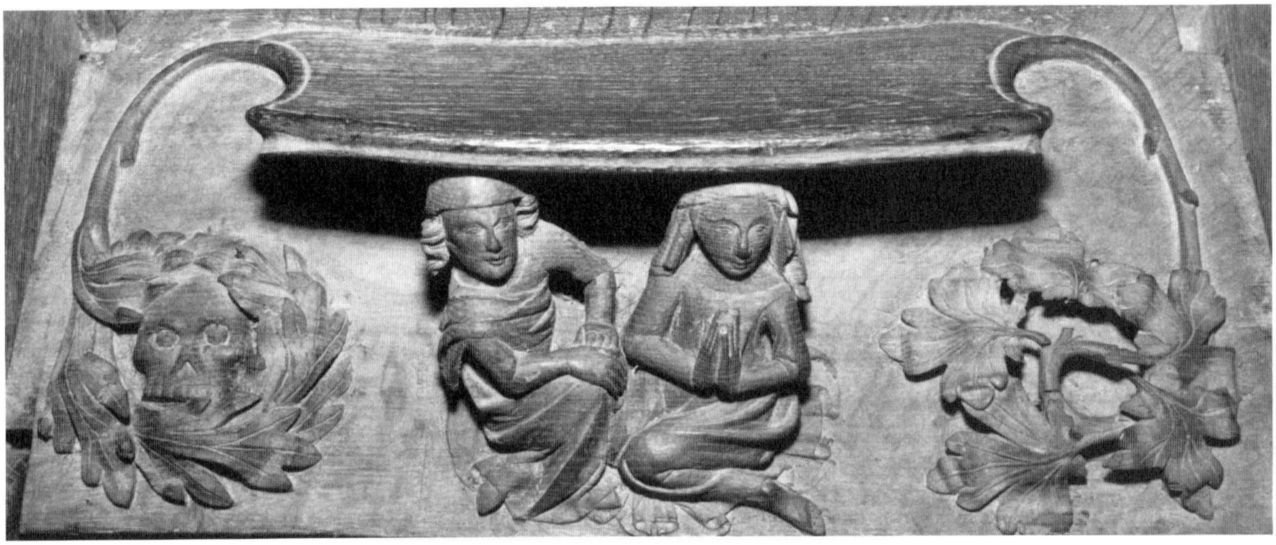

Woman confessing. Ely (Cambs), The Cathedral, c.1340.

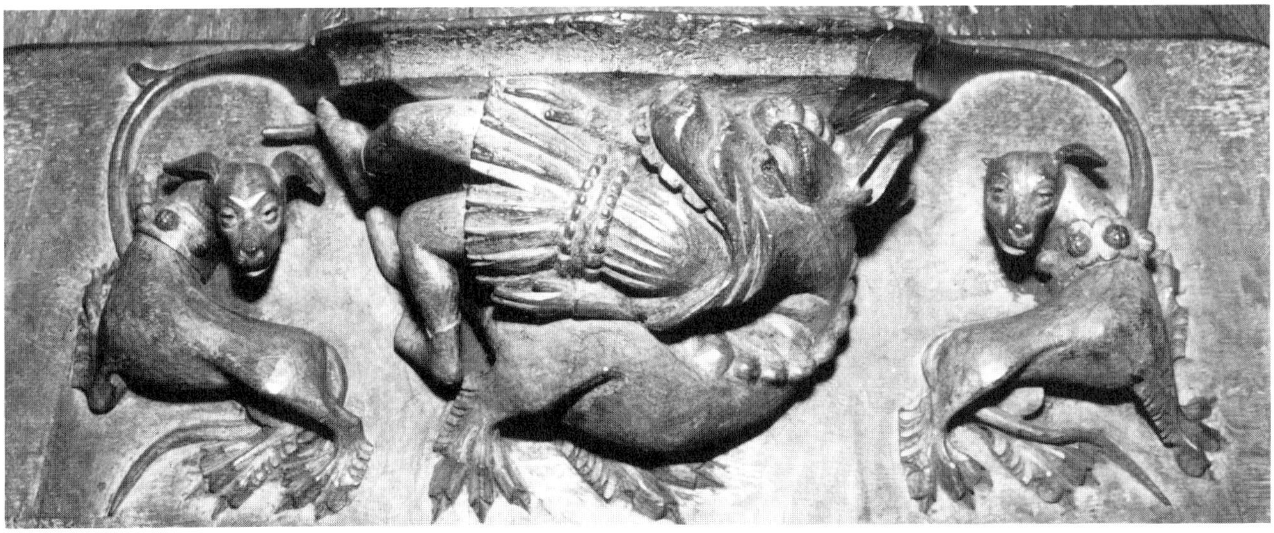

Judas in Jaws of Hell. Carlisle (Cumbria), The Cathedral, 1399–1413.

7
Conclusion

> The faculty for myth is innate in the human race. . . . It is the protest of romance against the commonplace of life.
> W. Somerset Maugham, *The Moon and Sixpence*, 1919

THAT THERE IS SOME TYPE OF MYTHICAL MAGIC associated with every age is indisputable. For those of us who have been both exhilarated and humbled by the display of human potential in the Gothic masterpieces, the magic of that period lives on. But it is a magic that is tempered by the knowledge that what was known and believed by the medieval person can be appreciated but never experienced by modern people, for the Gothic period did end. As it ended, the inventiveness that was such a mark of the Gothic misericord carver also ceased. The Renaissance—and, later, misericord carvings—could perhaps be called lovely or interesting, but they would never be called magical. In many cases, they became much more technically well done, but they suffer from the stamp of uniformity.

Winchester Cathedral, for example, has two carvings that were done recently to replace missing seats. The carver has taken as her topic two of the better-known stories from the bestiaries, the pelican and her piety (an allegory for the Passion of Christ) and the lion breathing life into her dead cubs (an allegory for the Resurrection).

The figures have been carved more realistically than most of those in the Gothic carvings, and the beautiful craftsmanship cannot be denied. They have a beauty of their own; but for the Gothic purist, they seem incomplete. Missing is the feeling of unexpectedness that surrounds the Gothic carvings where one can imagine the carver smiling as he devised each unique presentation.

Many have said that it was the Renaissance that destroyed the Gothic world. This is true, but the Renaissance was simply the outcome of other events. More accurate is the view that many of the changes occurring between the fourteenth and sixteenth centuries both created the Renaissance and made the Gothic view of the world obsolete.

The historical events and changes in thinking that ultimately closed the Gothic era were numerous, but changes occurring in the fourteenth century were especially significant. At that time there was a rapid expansion throughout Europe in the population and a growing discontent among the population over inequities. In England, some men achieved freedom from serfdom by royal edict, and some as a result of the Black Death. The craftsmen who did not succumb to the plague were much more sought after, allowing them to make unprecedented demands for more control over their work and their wages.

The Church also was dealt a blow by the

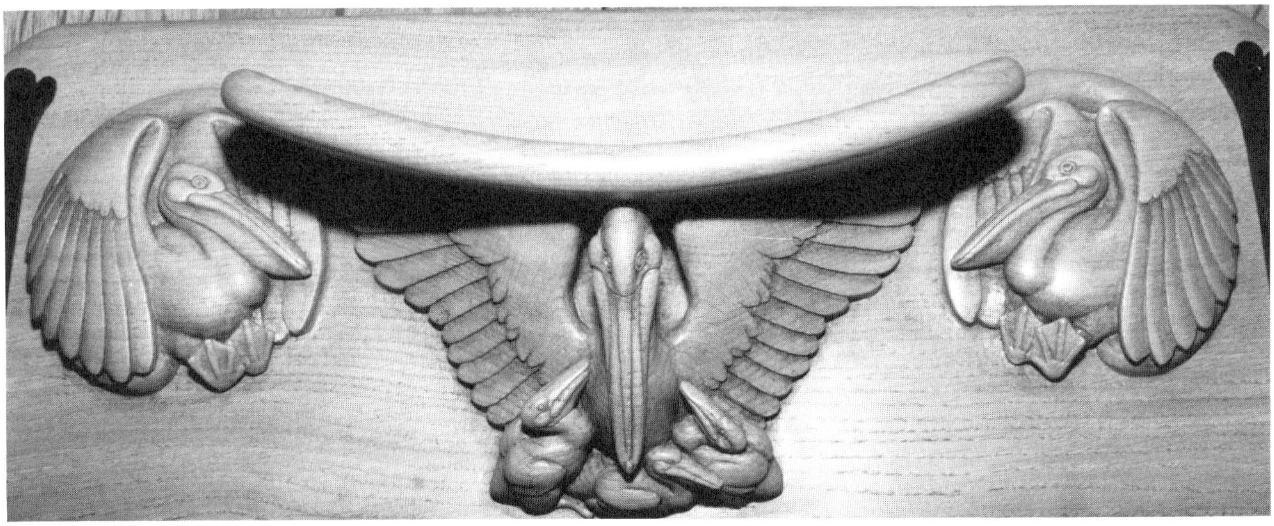

Pelican and piety. Winchester (Hants), The Cathedral, twentieth century.

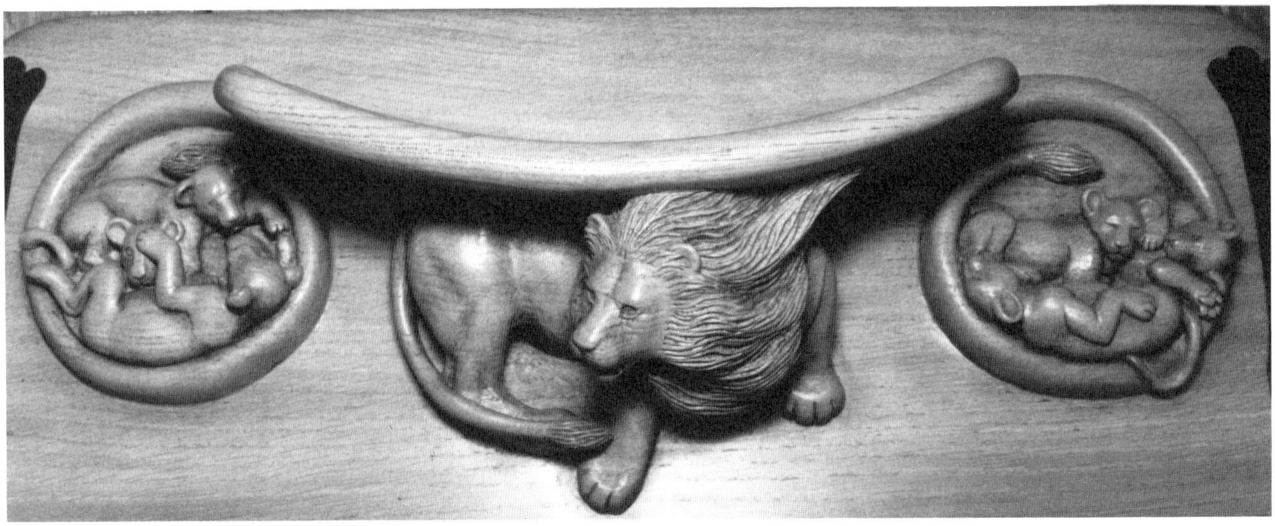

The Resurrection. Winchester (Hants), The Cathedral, twentieth century.

plague. Not only did the plague reduce the number of actual and potential clergy, but it reduced as well the number of lay members available to do the heavy labor of the monasteries. At the same time as its membership fell, the Church was being criticized by a resentful laity who believed that the Church was more interested in economic gain and political power than in serving the people. Add to that the notion proffered by Wyclif and others, that individuals need not receive sacraments or do "good deeds" to gain a place in heaven, and basic religious tenets were further eroded. Wyclif asserted that faith alone could ensure an afterlife, thus giving individuals greater control over their own salvation.

The idea that one could commune directly with God without a papal intermediary, and that one could, and should, read the Bible directly, depended on public access to the Bible. The advent of printing was to be the major event of the fifteenth century. Indeed, it was perhaps the most significant event contributing to the end of the Gothic age.

Shortly after the Gutenberg Bible was printed at Mainz in 1455, other presses were set up in Europe: Italy, 1465; Switzerland, 1467; France, 1470; Austria and the Netherlands, 1473; and Spain, 1474. The English presses came two years later, initiated by William Caxton in 1476, at Westminster, and followed by presses at Oxford in 1478 and St. Albans in 1479. Although the English production of printed books and Bibles appeared later than did the presses in Europe, unlike their Continental counterparts, the English presses were producing books in their native language rather than Latin. Moreover, though not true for Oxford and St. Albans, these were produced for general readers rather than scholars. For this reason, it has correctly been said that the most important literary figure of the fifteenth century was not an author but a printer (Sampson 1970).

As the Bible reached more people, the nature of the relationship between laity and clergy changed, and the need for the Church to teach the laity through the use of church artwork decreased. The people could refer directly to the Bible for their lessons. The Church's function as a repository of all knowledge declined and the need for carvings, paintings, stained glass windows, and so forth, as tools for teaching, was reduced. The Church would always remain an important institution in the lives of the citizenry, but its unquestioned authority was itself in question.

The challenge to church authority that be gan in the fourteenth century reached a pivotal point in the sixteenth century. In 1517, Martin Luther affixed the theses of his doctrine to the church door at Wittenberg, stressing the same tenets voiced by John Wyclif earlier—that humans would be saved by faith alone, not by good works or sacraments. In Geneva, in 1536, John Calvin began preaching against Catholicism. The erosion of church power accelerated, taking with it the medieval belief that there was only one point of entry into heaven.

Not only did this change the way one thought about religion, but also the way one thought about religious buildings. As Harvey (1947) points out, after 1550, religion ceased to be as much a part of everyday life and instead became more a "matter of Sundays." One major consequence of this shift was that everyday life ceased to be incorporated into the fabric of the Church. Included in that loss were the humorous carvings, grotesques, and remnants of pagan celebrations. Religious institutions became more singular in function.

New houses of worship were constructed or old houses altered to accommodate new ideas. The dissolution of the monasteries in England, completed by 1540, changed the monasteries into either cathedrals or collegiate churches; but the vast amounts of money and labor that had gone into the construction and adornment of Gothic churches prior to that time was now curtailed. After the break with Rome, royalty and the nobility paid more attention to their own establishments than to churches.

The sixteenth century brought other changes in the way a medieval person thought. Just as religious beliefs began to alter, other taken-for-granted beliefs about the world inhabited were challenged. There was a rapid increase in travel and greater exposure to the world beyond as a result of sea routes being opened by explorers such as Christopher Columbus and Vasco da Gama. Kenrad von Gesner, of Germany, published his *History of Animals* in 1551 and thus founded modern zoology (Robin 1932). These and other events brought a more scientific exploration of the "known" world, with serious consequences for a world based in large measure on myth and superstition. For example, when travelers and scientific investigators failed to corroborate the existence of such beasts as unicorns and dragons, the replication of fabulous beasts in woodcarving and other art forms began to seem outdated and even questionable. The outlook became more scientific and less spontaneous as proof preempted belief. The primacy of the subjective over the objective world had been reversed.

For the English woodcarvers, the rapid spread of printing had a disruptive effect on the traditional way of creating their art. The printing press made standardized pattern books possible, thus less innovation was required in both the conception and execution of woodcarvings. This process was accelerated as Henry VIII brought increasing numbers of foreign craftsmen into England. These new craftsmen not only brought new ideas but also new pattern books, especially the German and Flemish (Howard and Crossley 1927). These new forms placed greater emphasis on uniformity, so that the resulting products were more identifiable as the work of a "school" rather than of an individual.

In addition, a distinction came to be made during the Renaissance between craft and fine art, with fine art being regarded as superior (Lucie-Smith 1981). Craft items could be produced in mass fashion, with different woodcarvers producing the same carving; but fine arts such as paintings and sculptures were one of a kind, produced by individual artists. The appreciation for crafts and craftsmen was ebbing.

There is a final significant factor in the fading of Gothic craftsmanship—the growing attention given to time. Clocks were introduced into Europe by the late thirteenth century and were placed in churches both to mark the time of the daily offices and to serve as the community timepiece. The introduction of public clocks, however, also made it possible to time activities, which eventually contributed to a change in perception about how work should be done. Crafts began to be costed out on the basis of the length of time it took to produce them, as opposed to a total figure for an entire job (Lucie-Smith 1981). Attention to the concept of "time is money" further eroded the creative process that had produced so much individualized woodcarving.

The fading of the Gothic period was inevitable, and one accepts that philosophically. What is harder to accept is that there is so little woodwork left to enjoy from that time. We can only speculate on the richness that was, and treasure the English misericords all the more for what they represent: unique records of ordinary life during an extraordinary period.

Notes

Chapter 2. Necessary Enticements

1. The ploy of substituting another in the marital bed on the wedding night is used in a number of stories. One of the more amusing is about the Queen of Spain in the fourteenth century, who is said to have substituted her cousin for herself on her wedding night. The cousin refused to remove herself from the bed the next morning, thus enraging the Queen, who promptly tied the cousin down and set fire to the bed (Penn 1933).

Nonvirginal ladies without a willing handmaiden to participate in such a ruse were not without recourse. A thirteenth-century doctor had several recommendations, among them was the advice to expectant brides that on the day before their marriage they should very carefully place a leech on the labia and allow a trickle of blood to flow that would form a crust. When the sexual union occurred, the crust would be broken causing more blood to flow and thus deceive the husband into thinking his wife was a virgin (O'Faolain and Martines 1973).

Chapter 3. Men and Challenges

1. This is gone into more fully in Chapter 6. That the life of the individual was inextricably joined with the Church, and vice versa, is evidenced in the estimate that in England in the late Middle Ages, there was a church for every forty to fifty households (Bishop 1987).

2. Bestiaries and the battle for the soul are more fully discussed in Chapter 6.

3. I am indebted to Mr. Fred Perry, Steward, Cartmel Priory, for drawing my attention to the "Alexander" misericord. The interpretation is my own, however.

4. The wild man has been called by several other names, including "woodwose" and "wodehouse." He is sometimes thought to be associated with the Green Man, the Green Knight in *Sir Gwain and the Green Knight*, and with the figure of the satyr, but he is a separate being.

Chapter 4. Mayhem and Merriment

1. The term *pageant* was at first applied only to the movable platform on which the actors performed but very quickly came to refer to the play itself.

2. Thomas Wright explains that the term *mimus* went through numerous translations before finally becoming known by the French term *jougleur*. Many translators have used *jongleur*, which, Wright says, is a mistranslation: "I may remark that, in medieval manuscripts, it is almost impossible to distinguish between the "u" and the "n," and that modern writers have misread this last word as jongleur, and thus introduced into the language a word which never existed, and which ought to be abandoned" (1865, 107).

3. The pipe and tabor can be traced back to the thirteenth century and remained popular instruments through the nineteenth century, to accompany Morris Dancers. They were also known as the "whittle and dub" in the Cotswolds (Wortley 1967).

4. There was a much milder, and therefore longer-lasting, custom of reversing social positions in England during the same period. This was the election of a boy from the choir to be "Boy Bishop." He, with his appointed fellows, would take over the church service and then go out into the community collecting money. This ritual generally had the support of the Church and was considered more traditional and less rowdy (Chambers 1903). The practice was outlawed by Henry VIII, brought back by his daughter Mary, and then finally died out (Strutt 1810).

5. Billington (1984) related a popular medieval joke about the association of fools with royalty. It was said that the state of the king and the fool were the only ones to which one had to be born and could not attain otherwise.

6. Philip Stubs's zealous position was, in the end, his undoing. He was unwise enough to speak out on the marriage negotiations between Queen Elizabeth I and the Duc de Alencon. He issued a pamphlet in which he not only raised the issue of her being past the childbearing age, but the impropriety of a sexual union with a "syphilitic French Catholic." It is difficult to know which of these characteristics Stubs found the more offensive. Queen Elizabeth promptly had him arrested and had his right hand chopped off for his impudence (Coote 1993).

Chapter 5. Political Wit

1. Bestiaries are books based on earlier writings on the natural world, but which have assigned good and

bad characteristics to some of the animals, birds and reptiles contained in the earlier works. Bestiaries and their impact are discussed more fully in Chapter 6.

2. Indeed, the use of the Reynard stories as political parables continues into the twentieth century. Wladyslaw Starewiz, a Polish filmmaker, released his "Tales of the Fox" in Paris in 1941, a reprint of which was shown in Berkeley, California, in 1994.

3. It is assumed that Langland—or, as some have argued, William Langley—wrote the work from a line in the poem which reads: "I have lived *long* in the *land;* Long *Will* men call me" (1935, 161).

4. Giraldus Cambrensis was born in Wales in the mid-twelfth century. Although he served under various English kings, beginning with Henry II, he never realized his dream of becoming Bishop of St. David's. He became famous primarily for the unbelievable anecdotes he reported in his writings as real. His documentation of half-animal/half-human creatures in Ireland, for example, made later scholars wince.

5. Women flagellants also participated, but their penance was performed in the privacy of their home, while the men took to the streets.

6. The ladies of Bristol Cathedral have uniquely replicated the scenes from the misericords on the lovely needlework pillows.

Chapter 6. Deadly Reminders

1. I am indebted to Linda Ogden for first bringing this legend to my attention.

2. As an interesting historical note, when St. Thomas was being criticized after his death, particularly for his vigorous insistence on the existence of angels, Dante came to his defense in *Comedy*, by choosing St. Thomas as his guide to the highest level (Durant and Durant 1950).

3. This carving is based on a print by Dürer, c.1495 (Laird 1986).

4. Now in the British Manuscript Library, known as the Arundel Psalter.

5. There is disagreement as to whether these drawings are actually by Holbein, but they have generally been described as "Holbein's Dance of Death."

References

Agate, John. 1980. *Benches and Stalls in Suffolk Churches.* Suffolk: Suffolk Historic Churches Trust.

Allen, Percy S. 1914. *The Age of Erasmus: Lectures Delivered in the Universities of Oxford and London.* Oxford: Clarendon Press.

Anderson, Mary D. 1935. *The Medieval Carver.* Cambridge: Cambridge University Press.

———. 1954. *Misericords: Medieval Life in English Woodcarving.* London: Penguin Books.

———. 1955. *The Imagery of British Churches.* London: John Murray.

———. 1963. *Drama and Imagery in English Medieval Churches.* Cambridge: Cambridge University Press.

———. 1969. The Iconography of British Misericords. In *A Catalogue of Misericords in Great Britain* by G. L. Remnant. Oxford: Clarendon Press.

Andreas Capellanus. 1941. *The Art of Courtly Love.* Translation and introduction by John Jay Parry. New York: Columbia University Press.

Aristotle. 1862. *History of Animals.* Translated by Richard Creswell. London: Henry G. Bohn.

Armstrong, Edward A. 1973. *Saint Francis: Nature Mystic.* Berkeley: University of California Press.

Bakhtin, Mikhail. 1968. *Rabelais and His World.* Translated by Helene Iswolsky. Cambridge: Massachusetts Institute of Technology Press.

Barber, Richard and Juliet Barker. 1989. *Tournaments: Jousts, Chivalry and Pageants in the Middle Ages.* Woodbridge: Boydell Press.

Barber, Richard and Anne Riches. 1971. *A Dictionary of Fabulous Beasts.* London: Macmillan.

Barclay, Alexander, adapter and translator. 1874. *Ship of Fools* by Sebastian Brandt, 1494. 2 vols. Adapted and translated by Alexander Barclay, 1509. Introduction by Thomas A. Jamieson. Reprint, Edinburgh: William Peterson.

Barnes, Timothy D. 1971. *Tertullian: A Historical and Literary Study.* Oxford: Clarendon Press.

Barnes, Trevor. 1991. Nelson's Column: A Modern Grinling Gibbons. *The Illustrated London News,* 279:8 (Summer).

Bates, Katherine L. 1893. *The English Religious Drama.* New York: Macmillan.

Beckwith, John. 1985. *Early Medieval Art.* 1969. Reprint, London: Thames & Hudson.

Bell, Susan G. 1989. "Medieval Women Book Owners: Arbiters of Lay Piety and Ambassadors of Culture." In *Sisters and Workers in the Middle Ages.* Edited by Judith M. Bennett, Elizabeth A. Clark, Jean F. O'Barr, B. Anne Vilen, and Sarah Westphal-Wihl. Chicago: University of Chicago Press.

Bellingham, David. 1990. *An Introduction to Celtic Mythology.* Secaucus, NJ: Chartwell Books.

Bennett, Brian T.N. 1979. *The Choir Stalls of Chester Cathedral.* Chester: S. G. Mason.

Bernart De Ventadorn. 1962. *The Songs of Bernart De Ventadorn.* Edited and translated by Stephen G. Nichols and John A. Galm. University of North Carolina, Studies in the Romance Languages & Literature, No. 39. Chapel Hill: University of North Carolina Press.

Bernheimer, Richard. 1952. *Wild Men in the Middle Ages: A Study in Art, Sentiment, and Demonology.* Cambridge, Mass.: Harvard University Press.

Bevan, Bryan. 1990. *King Richard II.* London: Rubicon Press.

———. 1992. *Edward III: Monarch of Chivalry.* London: Rubicon Press.

Billington, Sandra. 1984. *A Social History of the Fool.* Sussex: Harvester Press.

Bishop, Morris. 1987. *The Middle Ages.* 1969. Reprint, Boston: Houghton Mifflin.

Bokenham, Osbern. 1938. *Legends of Hooly Wummen.* Edited by Mary S. Serjeantson from MS Arundel 327. London: Early English Text Society.

Bond, Francis. 1910. *Wood Carvings in English Churches.* 2 vols. London: Oxford University Press.

Bradshaw, Henry. 1887. *The Life of Saint Werburge of Chester.* Re-edited by Carl Horstmann. London: Early English Text Society.

Brand, John 1853. *Observations on the Popular Antiquities of Great Britain.* 3rd ed. Vol. 2. Arranged, revised, and greatly enlarged by Henry Ellis. London: Henry G. Bohn.

Briggs, Asa. 1983. *A Social History of England.* London: Weidenfeld & Nicolson.

Briggs, Katherine M. 1976. *A Dictionary of Fairies, Hobgoblins, Brownies, Bogies and Other Supernatural Creatures.* London: Allan Lane.

Bulfinch, Thomas. 1942. *The Age of Fable or the Beauties of Mythology.* New York: Heritage Press.

Butler, Lionel and Chris Given-Wilson. 1979. *Medieval Monasteries of Great Britain.* London: Michael Joseph.

Caesarius of Heisterbach. 1929. *The Dialogue on Miracles.* Vol. 1. Translated by H. Von E. Scott and C. C. Swinton Bland. London: George Routledge & Sons.

Camille, Michael. 1992. *Image on the Edge: The Margins of Medieval Art.* London: Reaktion Books.

Carew, Richard. 1723. *The Survey of Cornwall.* London: Samuel Chapman, Daniel Browne, and James Woodman.

The Castle of Perseverance. 1948. From the Macro Play, *Castel of Perseverance.* 1425. Adapted by Iwa Langentels. London: S.P.C.K. for The Religious Drama Society.

Cervantes Saavedra, Miguel de. 1958. *The Ingenious Gentleman Don Quixote de la Mancha.* Translated, based on first editions of 1605 and 1615, with variant readings, variorum notes, and introduction by Samuel Putnam. New York: Viking Press.

Chambers, Edmund K. 1903. *The Mediaeval Stage.* Vol. 1. Oxford: Clarendon Press.

———. 1945. *English Literature at the Close of the Middle Ages.* Oxford: Clarendon Press.

Chaucer, Geoffrey. 1966. *The Canterbury Tales.* Translation and introduction by Nevill Coghill. Baltimore: Penguin Books.

Chesterton, Gilbert K. 1959. Introduction. In *The Song of Roland.* Translated by Charles K. Scott Moncrieff. Ann Arbor: University of Michigan Press.

Chrétien de Troyes. 1987. Eric and Enide. Chap. 1 in *Arthurian Romances.* Translated by Douglas D. R. Owen. London: J. M. Dent & Sons.

Ciardi, John. 1954. Chapter Footnotes. In *The Inferno* by Dante Alighieri. New York: Mentor Books.

Clark, James M. 1950. *The Dance of Death in the Middle Ages and the Renaissance.* Glasgow: Jackson, Son & Co.

Clark, Willene B. and Meredith T. McMunn, editors. 1989. *Beasts and Birds of the Middle Ages: The Bestiary and Its Legacy.* Philadelphia: University of Pennsylvania Press.

Clarke, Kate M. 1920. *The Misericords of Exeter Cathedral.* Exeter: James G. Commin.

Coghill, Nevill. 1966. Introduction. In *The Canterbury Tales* by Geoffrey Chaucer. Baltimore: Penguin Books.

Colchester, Linzee S. 1978. *Wells Cathedral.* Watford: Woodmansterne Publications, Ltd.

Collier, J. Payne, editor. 1843. *The Harmony of Birds in Early English Poetry, Ballads, and Popular Literature of the Middle Ages.* Vol. 7. London: T. Richards for the Percy Society.

Cooper, William M. 1870. *Flagellation and the Flagellants.* London: J. C. Hotten.

Coote, Stephen. 1993. *A Play of Passion: The Life of Sir Walter Raleigh.* London: Macmillan.

Corry, Percy N. 1965. *The Quire and Misericords of St. Mary's Parish Church, Nantwich, Cheshire.* Warrington: Garside & Mackie, The Guardian Press.

Coulton, George G. 1923. *St. Bernard, His Predecessors and Successors, 1000–1200 A.D.* Vol. 1 of *Five Centuries of Religion.* Cambridge: Cambridge University Press

———. 1928. *Men and Manners.* Vol. 3, 2nd ed. *Life in the Middle Ages.* Selected, translated, and annotated by George G. Coulton. Cambridge: Cambridge University Press.

———. 1930. *Monks, Friars and Nuns.* Vol. 4, 2nd ed. *Life in the Middle Ages.* Selected, translated, and annotated by George G. Coulton. Cambridge: Cambridge University Press.

———. 1960. *Medieval Village, Manor and Monastery.* 1925.Reprint, New York: Harper Torchbooks.

Dalrymple, Brian W. 1967. Bearbaiting. *Encyclopedia Britannica,* 3:325–26. Chicago: William Denton.

Dante Alighieri. 1954. *The Inferno.* Translation and footnotes by John Ciardi. New York: Mentor Books.

Darwin, Sir Francis. 1917. *Rustic Sounds and Other Studies in Literature and Natural History.* London: John Murray.

Day, Samuel P. 1872. *The Rare Romance of Reynard the Fox, The Crafty Courtier: Together with the Shifts of His Son Reynardine.* London: Cassell, Petter & Galpin.

de Gamez, Gutierre Diaz. 1928. *The Unconquered Knight: A Chronicle of the Deeds of Don Pero Niño, Count of Buelna.* Translated and selected from *El Vitorial* by Joan Evans. London: George Routledge & Sons.

Dodgson, Campbell. 1905. Alexander's Journey to the Sky: A Woodcut by Schaufelein. *Burlington Magazine,* 6:395–97.

Druce, George C. 1915. Some Abnormal and Composite Human Forms in English Church Architecture. *The Archeological Journal,* 72:135–86.

Durant, Will and Ariel Durant. 1950. The Age of Faith. Vol. 4 in *The Story of Civilization.* New York: Simon & Schuster.

Edminson, Vera L. n.d. *Ancient Misericords in the Priory Church, Great Malvern.* St. Albans: Campfield Press.

Ellis, Frederick S. 1897. *The History of Reynard the Fox, His Friends and His Enemies, His Crimes, Hairbreadth Escapes and Final Triumph.* London: David Nutt.

Evans, Edward P. 1896. *Animal Symbolism in Ecclesiastical Architecture.* London: William Heinemann.

Evans, Joan. 1966. The Final Heritage: The End of the Middle Ages. In *The Flowering of the Middle Ages.* Edited by Joan Evans. London: Thames & Hudson.

Everyman: A Morality Play. 1906. 2nd ed. Reprinted in modern English from the 1st edition by A. L. Gowans. London: Gowans & Gray.

Fables of Aesop. 1926. London: John Lane.

Farmer, John S. 1907. *Early English Dramatists*. London: Early English Drama Society.

The Female Advocate. 1686. London: Printed by H. C. for John Taylor.

Fitz-Barnard, Lawrence. 1983. *Fighting Sports*. Hindhead, Surrey: Triplegate.

Fitzstephen, William. 1772. *Fitz-Stephen's Description of the City of London*. Translated by Samuel Pegge. London: B. White.

Fuchs, K. Reinicki. 1700. *The History of Reynard the Fox and Reynardine his Son*. London: n.p.

Galpin, Francis W. 1965. *Old English Instruments of Music*. 4th ed. Supplemental notes by Thurston Dart. London: Methuen & Co.

Gies, Frances. 1984. *The Knight in History*. New York: Harper & Row.

Gies, Frances and Joseph Gies. 1978. *Women in the Middle Ages*. New York: Crowell.

Gilgamesh. 1984. Translated by John Gardner and John Maier. New York: Knopf.

Gillingham, John. 1992. The Early Middle Ages 1066–1290. Vol.2, Part 1 of *The Oxford History of Britain*. Edited by Kenneth O. Morgan. Oxford: Oxford University Press.

Giraldus Cambrensis. 1863. *The Historical Works of Giraldus Cambrensis*. Edited and revised by Thomas Wright. Translated by T. Forester and Sir R. C. Hoare. London: H. G. Bohn.

Glasscoe, Marion and Michael Swanton. 1978. *Medieval Woodwork in Exeter Cathedral*. Newton Abbot, Devon: Wotton.

Griffith, Ralph A. 1992. The Late Middle Ages: 1290–1485. Vol. 2, part 2 of *The Oxford History of Britain*. Edited by Kenneth O. Morgan. Oxford: Oxford University Press.

Grössinger, Christa. 1989. *Ripon Cathedral Misericords*. Ripon: The Dean and Chapter, Ripon Cathedral.

Grundy, Thirlie. 1991. *The Misericords of Carlisle Cathedral*. Carlisle: Colophon Press.

Guillaume le Clerc. 1936. *The Bestiary of Guillaume Le Clerc*. 1210–11 MSS translated by George Claridge Druce. Ashford, Kent: Headley Brothers.

Hare, Charles E. 1952. *Bird Lore*. London: Country Life.

Harris, Mary D. 1898. *Life in an Old English Town*. London: Swan Sonnenschein & Co.

Harthan, John. 1978. *Books of Hours and Their Owners*. London: Thames & Hudson.

Harvey, John. 1947. *Gothic England: A Survey of National Culture, 1300–1550*. London: B.T. Batsford.

———. 1984. *English Medieval Architects: A Biographical Dictionary Down to 1550*. Contributions by Arthur Oswald. Gloucester: Alan Sutton.

Hatcher, John. 1977. *Plague, Population and the English Economy*. London: Macmillan.

Hayman, Richard. 1989. *Church Misericords and Bench Ends*. Aylesbury, Bucks: Shire Publications.

Helm, Alex. 1981. *The English Mummer's Play*. Woodbridge: D. S. Brewer.

Herolt, Johannes. 1928. *Miracles of the Blessed Virgin Mary*. Translated by C. C. Swinton Bland. Introduction by Eileen Power. London: George Routledge & Sons.

Hibbert, Christopher. 1992. *The Story of England*. London: Phaidon Press.

Hindley, Geoffrey. 1979. *England in the Age of Caxton*. London: Granada Publishing.

The History of Reynard the Fox. Circa 1481–82. Translated by William Caxton. Westminster: n.p. (now in the British Museum).

Hogarth, Peter with Val Clery. 1979. *Dragons*. London: Allan Lane.

Houwen, Luuk. 1996. Sex, Songs and Sirens: A New Score for an Old Song. *The Profane Arts of the Middle Ages*, 5(1):103–21.

Howard, Frank E. and Frederick H. Crossley. 1927. *English Church Woodwork: A Study in Craftsmanship During the Mediaeval Period A.D. 1250–1550*. New York: Scribner's.

Howey, M. Oldfield. 1923. *The Horse in Magic and Myth*. London: William Rider & Son.

Hughes, Muriel J. 1943. *Women Healers in Medieval Life and Literature*. New York: Kings Crown Press.

Hurd-Mead, Kate Campbell. 1938. *A History of Women in Medicine: From the Earliest Times to the Beginning of the Nineteenth Century*. Haddon, Conn.: Haddon Press.

Jacobus de Voragine. 1948. *The Golden Legend of Jacobus de Voragine*. 2 vols. Translated and adapted by Granger Ryan and Helmut Ripperger. London: Longmans, Green.

James, Montague R. 1928. *The Bestiary*. London: The Roxburgh Club.

———. 1985. *St. George's Chapel, Windsor: The Woodwork of the Choir*. 1933. Reprint, Slough: Chiltern Printers.

Jamieson, Thomas H. 1874. Introduction. In *Ship of Fools* by Sebastian Brandt. 1494. 2 vols. Adapted and translated by Alexander Barclay. 1509. Reprint, Edinburgh: William Peterson.

Janson, Horst W. 1971. *History of Art*. Englewood Cliffs, N.J.: Prentice-Hall.

Jervis, Simon. 1976. *Woodwork of Winchester Cathedral*. Winchester: The Friends of Winchester Cathedral.

Jewitt, Llewellynn. 1875. Art Under the Seats: A Few Words Upon "Miseres." *The Art Journal*. 14:53–56; 85–88; 145–48.

Johnsgard, Paul and Karin Johnsgard. 1982. *Dragons and Unicorns*. New York: St. Martin's Press.

Johnson, Paul. 1973. *The Life and Times of Edward III*. London: Weidenfeld & Nicolson.

Jusserand, Jean J. 1950. *English Wayfaring Life in the Middle Ages*. 4th ed. Translated by Lucy Toulmin Smith. London: Ernest Benn.

Kieckhefer, Richard. 1990. *Magic in the Middle Ages*. Cambridge: Cambridge University Press.

Klein, Peter. 1986. *The Misericords & Choir Stalls of Ludlow Parish Church*. Birmingham: The Studio Press for Ludlow Parochial Church Council.

Kostoff, Spiro. 1985. *A History of Architecture: Settings & Rituals*. New York: Oxford University Press.

Krása, Josef. 1983. Introduction and Commentary on the

Plates. In *The Travels of Sir John Mandeville.* New York: George Brazillar.

Kraus, Dorothy and Henry Kraus. 1976. *The Hidden World of Misericords.* London: Michael Joseph.

Laird, Marshall. 1986. *English Misericords.* London: John Murray.

Lamb, Harold. 1946. *Alexander of Macedon: The Journey to World's End.* London: Robert Hale.

Lander, Jack R. 1980. *Government and Community: England 1450–1509.* London: Edward Arnold.

Langland, William. 1906. *The Vision of William Concerning Piers the Plowman.* c. 1377. Ninth edition Edited by Walter W. Skeat. Oxford: Clarendon Press.

Langland, William. 1935. *The Vision of Piers Plowman.* Translated by Henry W. Wells, Introduction by Nevill Coghill. London: Sheed & Ward.

Laslett, Peter. 1966. The Study of Social Structure from Listings of Inhabitants. In *An Introduction to English Historical Demography: From the Sixteenth to the Nineteenth Century.* Edited by E. A. Wrigley. London: Weidenfeld & Nicolson.

The Lawes Resolution of Women's Rights. 1632. London: n.p.

Lucie-Smith, Edward. 1981. *The Story of Craft: The Craftsman's Role in Society.* Oxford: Phaidon Press.

MacAllister, Archibald T. 1954. Introduction. In *The Inferno* by Dante Aligheri. Translated by John Ciardi. New York: Mentor Books.

Mâle, Emile. 1949. *Religious Art From the Twelfth to the Eighteenth Century.* London: Routledge & Kegan Paul.

Marcus. 1990. *The Visions of Tondal.* Translated by Madeleine McDermott and Roger S. Wieck. From the Library of Margaret of York. Malibu, Cal.: J. Paul Getty Museum.

Martindale, Andrew. 1966. The Rise of the Artist. In *The Flowering of the Middle Ages.* Edited by Joan Evans. London: Thames & Hudson.

Moore, Bruce. 1992. Wild Men in the Misericords of St. Mary's Church, Beverley. *Yorkshire Archaeological Journal.* 64:135–43.

The Natural History of Pliny. 6 vols. Translated by John Bostock and H.T. Riley. London: Henry G. Bohn, vols. 1–3, 1855; vol. 5 vols. 4–5, 1856.

Nichols, Stephen G. 1962. Introduction. In *The Songs of Bernart De Ventadorn.* Edited and translated by Stephen G. Nichols and John A. Galm. University of North Carolina, Studies in the Romance Languages & Literature, No. 39. Chapel Hill: University of North Carolina Press.

O'Faolain, Julia and Lauro Martines, editors. 1973. *Not in God's Image.* London: Maurice Temple Smith.

Ottley, William Young. 1826. *A Collection of Fac-Similies of Scarce and Curious Prints, by the Early Masters of the Italian, German, and Flemish Schools; Illustrative of The History of Engraving.* London: Published for the Proprietor.

Ovid [Publius Ovidius Naso]. 1959. *The Art of Love.* Translated by J. Lewis May. London: Bestseller Library.

Owst, Gerald R. 1926. *Preaching in Medieval England: An Introduction to Sermon Manuscripts of the Period, c.1350–1450.* Cambridge: Cambridge University Press.

Page, William, editor. 1909. *The Victoria History of the Counties of England: A History of London.* Vol. 1. London: Constable & Co.

Parry, John Jay. 1941. Introduction. In *The Art of Courtly Love* by Andreas Capellanus. Translated by John Jay Parry. New York: Columbia University Press.

Payne, Ann. 1990. *Medieval Beasts.* London: The British Library.

Penn, Dorothy. 1933. *The Staging of the "Miracles de Nostre Dame par Personages" of Ms. Cangé.* New York: The Institute of French Studies, Columbia University.

Phipson, Emma. 1896. *Choir Stalls and Their Carvings: Examples of Misericords from English Cathedrals and Churches.* London: B. T. Batsford.

Plot, Robert. 1677. *The Natural History of Oxford-Shire, Being an Essay toward the Natural History of England.* Oxford: The Theater.

Pollard, Alfred W., editor. 1890. *English Miracle Plays, Moralities and Interludes.* Oxford: Clarendon Press.

Power, Eileen. 1928. Introduction. In *Miracles of the Blessed Virgin Mary* by Johannes Herlot. Translated by C. C. Swinton Bland. London: George Routledge & Sons.

Prior, Edward S. and Arthur Gardner. 1912. *An Account of Medieval Figure-Sculpture in England.* Cambridge: Cambridge University Press.

Pritchard, R. E. n.d. *The Choir and Misericords of St. Mary's, Nantwich.* Nantwich: Johnsons of Nantwich.

Purvis, John S., editor. 1951. *The York Cycle of Mystery Plays.* London: S.P.C.K.

———. 1924. *The Lost Choir Stalls of Bridlington Priory.* n.p.

Radcliffe, Lexander. 1680. *Ovid Travestie, A Burlesque Upon Several of Ovid's Epistle's.* London: Judge's Head for Jacob Tonson.

Remnant, George L. 1969. *A Catalogue of Misericords in Great Britain.* Oxford: Clarendon Press.

Robin, P. Ansell. 1932. *Animal Lore in English Literature.* London: John Murray.

Robinson, Durant W., Jr. 1962. *A Preface to Chaucer: Studies in Medieval Perspectives.* Princeton, N.J.: Princeton University Press.

Rouse, E. Clive. 1968. *Discovering Wall Painting.* Tring, Herts: Shire Publications.

Rowling, Marjorie. 1987. *Everyday Life in Medieval Times.* New York: Dorset Press.

Ryan, Granger and Helmut Ripperger. 1948. Introduction. In *The Golden Legend of Jacobus de Voragine* by Jacobus de Voragine. Translated and adapted by Granger Ryan and Helmut Ripperger. London: Longmans, Green.

Sampson, George. 1970. *The Concise Cambridge History of English Literature.* Cambridge: Cambridge University Press.

Saunders, O. Elfrida. 1932. *A History of English Art in the Middle Ages.* Oxford: Clarendon Press.

Schimmel, Solomon. 1992. *The Seven Deadly Sins: Jewish, Christian, and Classical Reflections on Human Nature.* New York: The Free Press.

Seward, Desmond. 1983. *Richard III: England's Black Legend.* London: Country Life Books.

Shakespeare, William. 1982. *The Taming of the Shrew.* Edited by H. J. Oliver. Oxford: Clarendon Press.

Skeat, Walter W., editor. 1906. Chapter Notes. In *The Vision of William Concerning Piers the Plowman.* c. 1377. 9th ed. Oxford: Clarendon Press.

Smith, Lucy Toulmin. 1886. *A Common-place Book of the Fifteenth Century.* London: Trübner & Co.

———, editor. 1924. *English Gilds: The Original Ordinances of More Than One Hundred Early English Gilds.* 1870. From original MSS of the 14th & 15th C. Reprint, London: Oxford University Press for Early English Text Society.

———, editor. 1963. *York Plays.* 1880. Reprint, New York: Russell & Russell.

Snape, H. C., editor. 1978. *The Parish Church of Saint Mary All Saints, Whalley, Lancashire, England.* 6th ed. n.p.

Spenser, Edmund. 1611. *The Faerie Queen.* London: Printed by H.L. for Matthew Lownes.

Sprenger, Jakob and Heinrich Kramer. 1928. *Maleus Maleficarium.* Edited and translated by Montague Summers. London: Hogarth Press.

Steer, Francis W. 1973. *Misericords at New College, Oxford.* London: Phillimore & Co.

Stow, John. 1633. *The Survey of London.* London: Elizabeth Purslow.

Stranks, C. J. 1987. *A Walk Round Durham Cathedral.* Durham: Douglas (Printers), Ltd.

Strutt, Joseph. 1810. *Sports and Pastimes of the People of England.* 2nd ed. London: T. Bensley.

Stubs, Philip. 1595. *The Anatomie of Abuses.* 4th ed. London: Richard Iohnes.

Symonds, John A. 1931. *Wine, Women and Song.* London: Chatto & Windus.

Taylor, Duncan. 1959. *Chaucer's England.* New York: Roy Publishers.

Temple, Robert. 1991. *He Who Saw Everything: A Verse Translation of the Epic of Gilgamesh.* London: Rider.

Thiselton-Dyer, Thomas F. 1903. *Royalty in all Ages.* London: John C. Nimmo, Ltd.

———. 1906. *Folk-Lore of Women.* Chicago: A. C. McClury.

Thomson, John A. F. 1983. *The Transformation of Medieval England: 1370–1529.* London: Longman Group UK.

Thrupp, Sylvia L. 1948. *The Merchant Class of Medieval London (1300–1500).* Chicago: University of Chicago Press.

Tracy, Charles. 1987. *English Gothic Choir-Stalls, 1200–1400.* Woodbridge, Suffolk: Boydell Press.

———. 1990. *English Gothic Choir-Stalls, 1400–1540.* Woodbridge, Suffolk: Boydell Press.

Trevelyan, George M. 1904. *England in the Age of Wycliffe.* London: Longmans, Green & Co.

Tuchman, Barbara W. 1978. *A Distant Mirror: The Calamitous 14th Century.* New York: Knopf.

Verey, David and David Welander. 1979. *Gloucester Cathedral.* Gloucester: Alan Sutton.

Warner, Marina. 1976. *Alone of All Her Sex.* London: Weidenfeld & Nicolson.

Warner, Richard. 1795. *Collections for the History of Hampshire and the Bishopric of Winchester.* Vol. 3. London: n.p.

White, Mary F. 1974. *Fifteenth Century Misericords in the Collegiate Church of Holy Trinity, Stratford-upon-Avon.* Stratford-upon-Avon: Philip Bennett.

Whitlock, Ralph. 1979. *In Search of Lost Gods: A Guide to British Folklore.* Oxford: Phaidon Press.

Wieck, Roger S. 1990. The Visions of Tondal and the Visionary Tradition in the Middle Ages. In *The Visions of Tondal* by Marcus. Translated by Madeleine McDermott and Roger S. Wieck. From the library of Margaret of York. Malibu, Cal.: J. Paul Getty Museum.

Wildridge, T. Tindall. 1879. *The Misereres of Beverley Minster.* Whitefriargate, Hull: J. Plaxton.

———. 1887. *The Dance of Death in Painting and in Print.* London: George Redway.

Withington, Robert. 1918. *English Pageantry: An Historical Outline.* Vol. 1. Cambridge, Mass.: Harvard University Press.

Wortley, Russell. 1967. *How to Play the English Pipe and Tabor.* London: English Folk Drama and Song Society.

Wright, Thomas. 1841. *The Latin Poems Commonly Attributed to Walter Mapes.* London: John Bowyer Nichols & Son for the Camden Society.

———, editor. 1845. *The Archaeological Album; or, Museum of National Antiquities.* London: Chapman & Hall.

———. 1865. *A History of Caricature and Grotesque In Literature and Art.* London: Virtue Brothers.

———, editor. 1868. *The Book of the Knight of La Tour Landry.* Translated with introduction and notes by Thomas Wright. London: Trubner & Co. for Early English Text Society.

Wrigley, Edward A. 1966. Family Reconstitution. In *An Introduction to English Historical Demography: From the Sixteenth to the Nineteenth Century.* London: Weidenfeld & Nicolson.

Wynne, John H. 1779. *Riley's Emblems, Natural, Historical, Fabulous, Moral, and Divine: For the Improvement and Pastime of Youth: Serving to Display the Beauties and Morals of Ancient Fabulists.* London: G. Riley.

Zarnecki, George. 1966. The Contribution of the Orders. In *The Flowering of the Middle Ages.* Edited by Joan Evans. London: Thames & Hudson.

Index